Curriculum Edition

Maths
The Basic Skills

June Haighton   **Deborah Holder**

Bridget Phillips   **Veronica Thomas**

Nelson Thornes

Text © J Haighton, D Holder, B Phillips, V Thomas 2004
Original illustrations © Nelson Thornes Ltd 2004

The right of J Haighton, D Holder, B Phillips and V Thomas to be identified as
authors of this work has been asserted by them in accordance with the Copyright,
Designs and Patents Act 1988.

All rights reserved. No part of this publication may be reproduced or transmitted in
any form or by any means, electronic or mechanical, including photocopy, recording
or any information storage and retrieval system, without permission in writing from
the publisher or under licence from the Copyright Licensing Agency Limited, of
Saffron House, 6-10 Kirby Street, London EC1N 8TS.

Any person who commits any unauthorised act in relation to this publication may be
liable to criminal prosecution and civil claims for damages.

Published in 2004 by:
Nelson Thornes Ltd
Delta Place
27 Bath Road
CHELTENHAM
GL53 7TH
United Kingdom

10 11 12 13 / 15 14 13 12 11 10 9 8

A catalogue record for this book is available from the British Library

978 0 7487 7700 6
Illustrations and page make-up by Mathematical Composition Setters Ltd, Salisbury, Wiltshire

Printed in China

Contents

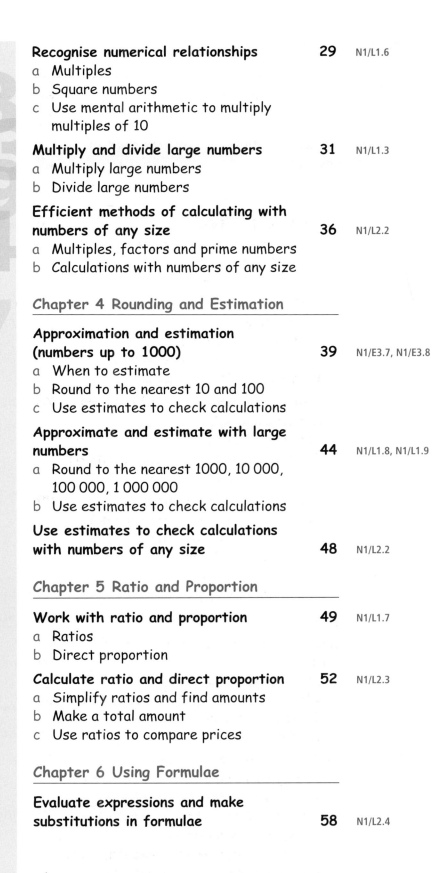

Chapter 7 Mixed Operations and Calculator Practice

Chapter 8 Fractions

2 Measures, Shape and Space

3 Handling Data

Introduction

About this book

This book is divided into the three main sections of the Adult Numeracy Core Curriculum:

- **Number**
- **Measures, shape and space**
- **Handling data**

The level of the work ranges from Entry level 3 (E3) through Level 1 (L1) to Level 2 (L2). Entry levels 1 and 2 are covered in separate Worksheet Packs.

The curriculum elements covered in each topic are given in the contents list and at the beginning of each topic. Some topics include more than one level of work. These topics begin with work at the lowest level (usually E3) and progress to the higher levels. The icons shown here indicate where the level of difficulty   **L1**   **L2** of the work increases.

How to use this book

This depends on what you are aiming for, but in all cases it is recommended that you work through the levels you need, starting with E3. If you already have some knowledge of a topic, you may be able to miss out some parts, but always look through the work to make sure.

Is your main aim to improve your understanding of a particular mathematical topic?
If so, look for the topic in the Contents list and work through from E3 to the level you need.

Are you preparing for a qualification at Entry level 3?
If so, work through all the topics labelled E3.
You will probably have to do some assignments as well. These vary from one awarding body to another. Ask your tutor for advice.

Is your main aim to prepare for the Adult Numeracy Test at Level 1?
If so, work through all the topics labelled E3 or L1.
The Level 1 Adult Numeracy Test is a set of multi-choice questions.
Practice papers can be found on the awarding bodies' websites.

Is your main aim to prepare for the Adult Numeracy Test at Level 2?
If so, work through all of the topics in this book. (You may be able to miss out some parts if you already have some knowledge of the topics.)
The Level 2 Adult Numeracy Test is a set of multi-choice questions.
Practice papers can be found on the awarding bodies' websites.

Number

1 Number Value

Numbers up to 1000

a Place value

There are three hundred and sixty-five days in a year.

The number 365 has

		H T U
3	Hundreds	3 0 0
6	Tens	6 0
5	Units	5
		3 6 5

3 Hundreds, 6 Tens and 5 Units

The 3, 6 and 5 are called digits.

Practice

1 Write the following numbers in figures.
Example: Six hundred and seventy
Use columns like this on squared paper.

H	T	U
6	7	0

- **a)** One hundred and sixty-five
- **b)** Fifty-three
- **c)** Two hundred and twelve
- **d)** Four hundred and three
- **e)** Nine hundred and ninety
- **f)** Sixty-eight
- **g)** Eight hundred and twenty
- **h)** Seven
- **i)** Two hundred and seventeen
- **j)** Nine hundred and two

2 Write the following numbers in words. Then write the value of each digit.
Example: 245 is **two hundred and forty-five**
245 has **2 hundreds, 4 tens, 5 units**.

	H T U		H T U		H T U		H T U		H T U
a)	2 3 6	**b)**	1 0 5	**c)**	6 1 7	**d)**	8 2	**e)**	7 5 0
f)	5 0 0	**g)**	1 2 3	**h)**	9 0	**i)**	9 3 8	**j)**	3 4 4

3 Copy this table.

Planet	Number of days to go round the sun	Planet	Approximate number of years to go round the sun
Earth		Pluto	
Mercury		Jupiter	
Mars		Neptune	
Venus		Saturn	
		Uranus	

Read the information below.
Write the coloured numbers as figures in your table.

> It takes the **Earth** three hundred and sixty-five days to go round the sun.
>
> It takes **Mercury** just eighty-eight days, **Mars** six hundred and eighty-seven days and **Venus** nearly two hundred and twenty-five days.
>
> The other planets take a lot longer.
>
> **Pluto** takes nearly two hundred and forty-eight years and **Jupiter** nearly twelve years.
>
> **Neptune** takes nearly one hundred and sixty-five years, **Saturn** nearly thirty years and **Uranus** eighty-four years.

4 List the planets in order according to how long they take to go round the sun.
Start with the planet that takes the **least** time.

Activity

Pick 3 **different** digits. (Choose from 0, 1, 2, 3, 4, 5, 6, 7, 8, 9.)
See how many different numbers you can make from them.
Put the numbers you have made in order, starting with the **smallest**.
Try this again but with 2 digits the same and the other one different.
What happens if all of the digits are the same?
Write a rule for making the **largest** possible number with 3 digits.
Write a rule for making the **smallest** possible number with 3 digits.

b Count in 10s

If you add or subtract 10, the Tens digit changes. The Units digit doesn't change.

Adding:	9 +	19 +	119 +	Subtracting:	18 −	58 −	158 −
	10	10	10		10	10	10
	19	29	129		8	48	148

The Hundreds digit may change.
It changes if adding 10 takes you up into the hundred above.

91 +	99 +	191 +	399 +
10	10	10	10
101	109	201	409

It changes if subtracting 10 takes you down into the hundred below.

106 −	103 −	206 −	503 −
10	10	10	10
96	93	196	493

Practice

1   Copy each list. Fill in the missing numbers by adding 10.

a)

11	21	31		51	61	71	81		101	111		131	141

b)

441	451		471	481	491		511	521		541	551	561	

c)

383	393		413	423	433		453	463	473		493	503	

2   Copy each list. Fill in the missing numbers by subtracting 10.

a)

195	185	175		155	145	135		115	105	95		75	65

b)

596	586		566	556		536	526	516		496	486	476	

c)

139	129		109		89	79	69	59		39	29	19	

c Count in 100s

If you add or subtract 100, the Hundreds digit changes. The Tens and Units digits don't change.

Adding:	234 +	Subtracting:	586 −
	100		100
	334		486

Practice

1 Copy each list. Fill in the missing numbers by adding 100.

a)

| 25 | 125 | | 325 | 425 | | 625 | | 825 | |

b)

| 63 | | 263 | | 463 | 563 | | 763 | | 963 |

2 Copy each list. Fill in the missing numbers by subtracting 100.

a)

| 982 | 882 | | 682 | | 482 | 382 | | 182 | 82 |

b)

| 907 | | 707 | | 507 | 407 | | 207 | 107 | |

d Odd and even numbers

An **even** number is any number that **you can divide exactly by 2.**
All the answers in the 2 times table are even numbers.
If you count up in 2s, all the numbers you get are even numbers.
All the other counting numbers are **odd** – they **cannot be divided exactly by 2.**

Practice

1 a) Copy and complete the following table.

$1 \times 2 =$		$6 \times 2 =$		$11 \times 2 =$		$16 \times 2 =$	
$2 \times 2 =$		$7 \times 2 =$		$12 \times 2 =$		$17 \times 2 =$	
$3 \times 2 =$		$8 \times 2 =$		$13 \times 2 =$		$18 \times 2 =$	
$4 \times 2 =$		$9 \times 2 =$		$14 \times 2 =$		$19 \times 2 =$	
$5 \times 2 =$		$10 \times 2 =$		$15 \times 2 =$		$20 \times 2 =$	

b) Complete the first sentence in the box.

> ▶ All **even numbers** end in _, _, _, _ or _.
>
> ▶ All **odd numbers** end in **1, 3, 5, 7 or 9.**

2 List the numbers below that are **even.**

| 8 | 80 | 23 | 180 | 17 | 280 | 15 | 172 | 501 | 754 |
| 466 | 123 | 99 | 300 | 256 | 312 | 89 | 202 | 11 | 125 |

3 List the numbers below that are **odd.**

| 3 | 209 | 148 | 77 | 774 | 20 | 99 | 403 | 127 | 501 |
| 700 | 162 | 713 | 680 | 1000 | 14 | 19 | 471 | 345 | 176 |

4 Say whether each statement is *True*, *False* or *Maybe True*.
Give reasons for each answer.

a) If the houses in a street are numbered so **all the even numbers are on one side** and **all the odd numbers are on the other side**, numbers 32 and 180 will be on the **same** side of the street.

b) If there are 435 people working at a factory, there could be an equal number of men and women.

c) If 500 boxes need packing, the work can be shared equally between two people.

d) If a car park with 1000 spaces is on 2 levels, there are an equal number of spaces on each level.

Large numbers

a Place value

In 1851 the population of London was about two million, six hundred and eighty-five thousand.

pop 2 685 000

The number 2 685 000 has

2	**Millions**	2 000 000
6	**Hund**red **Thou**sands	600 000
8	**Ten Thou**sands	80 000
5	**Thou**sands	5 000
0	Hundreds	000
0	Tens	00
0	Units	0
		2 685 000

To read large numbers split the digits into groups of three (starting at the end).

Example	7 302 064 is:

7   302   064
seven million,   three hundred and two thousand   and sixty-four

and

3 020 500 is three million, twenty thousand, five hundred.

	Thousands					
M	**H**	**T**	**U**	**H**	**T**	**U**
7	3	0	2	0	6	4
3	0	2	0	5	0	0

Practice

1 Copy the headings onto squared paper.
Write these numbers as figures in the correct columns.

	Thousands					
M	**H**	**T**	**U**	**H**	**T**	**U**

a) Two thousand   b) Thirty-two thousand

c) One hundred and sixty-five thousand, two hundred

d) One hundred and nine thousand, eight hundred and seventy

e) Four million, two hundred thousand

f) Ninety thousand, seven hundred and fifty

g) Eight thousand and twenty-five

h) One hundred and nineteen thousand

i) Six million, two hundred and ninety-nine thousand

j) Nine million, three hundred and six

2 Write each number in words.

		Thousands								Thousands					
	M	**H**	**T**	**U**	**H**	**T**	**U**		**M**	**H**	**T**	**U**	**H**	**T**	**U**
a)			4	5	0	0	0	**b)**		3	7	5	0	0	0
c)	6	7	0	0	0	0	0	**d)**		2	0	5	0	0	0
e)			7	0	7	5	0	**f)**	1	2	0	0	0	0	0
g)			5	0	6	5	**h)**			2	0	3	0	6
i)			4	0	3	5	2	**j)**	9	6	7	0	0	8	0
k)	5	0	9	0	4	0	0	**l)**	3	5	0	3	2	4	1

3 List the numbers in question 2 in order of size, starting with the **smallest**.

4 a) Copy the table.

  b) Read the information below.
  Write the coloured numbers as
  figures in your table.

Year	Estimated population of London
1100	
1300	
1500	
1600	
1801	
1851	
1939	
2000	

In **1100** the population of London was about twenty-five thousand.
By the year **2000** it was about seven million, six hundred and forty thousand.
Between these two dates the population both increased and decreased.
By **1300** the population could have been as large as one hundred thousand.
Due to the black death it fell to about fifty thousand by **1500**.
Research shows that by **1600** the population had reached two hundred thousand.
The first census in **1801** recorded a population of one million, one hundred and seventeen thousand.
The population doubled by **1851** reaching two million, six hundred and eighty-five thousand.
At the beginning of the Second World War in **1939** London's population reached eight million, seven hundred thousand.

c) Use your table to answer the following questions.
  i)   Between which years did the population fall?
  ii) In which year was the population the highest?

b Greater than > and less than <

Symbols can be used to show that one number is greater (larger) than or less (smaller) than another.

> means **greater than**   < means **less than**

5 is greater than 4.   This can be written as $5 > 4$.
100 is greater than 50.   This can be written as $100 > 50$.
6 is less than 9.   This can be written as $6 < 9$.
25 is less than 50.   This can be written as $25 < 50$.

▶ **The larger number always goes at the open end of the symbol.**

Practice

1 Rewrite each of these using < or >.
  a) 1 is less than 3   **b)** 7 is greater than 5   **c)** 9 is greater than 4   **d)** 0 is less than 1

2 Copy these. Write < or > between each pair of numbers.
  a) 2   8   **b)** 6   1   **c)** 18   13
  d) 19   23   **e)** 99   101   **f)** 170   159

3 Rewrite each of these using < or >.
  a) 269 is less than 270   **b)** 15 000 is greater than 2 500
  c) 9 900 is greater than 7 500   **d)** 50 000 is less than 75 000
  e) 9 is less than 900   **f)** 10 500 is greater than 10 499
  g) 99 900 is less than 100 000   **h)** 4 010 000 is greater than 4 009 999

Positive and negative numbers in practical contexts   N1/L1.2

Positive numbers are **greater than** 0.
Negative numbers are **less than** 0.

Negative numbers are sometimes used to describe
temperature.
For example, –2°C is 2 degrees **colder** than 0°C.
Note that, –6°C is **colder** than –2°C.

Negative numbers are also used to describe overdrawn
bank accounts.
For example, a balance of –£25 means that £25 is **owed** to
the bank.

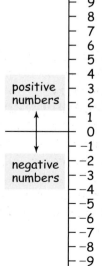

Practice

1 In each part, put the temperatures in order.
   Start with the **coldest**.

   a) −5°C   8°C   4°C   0°C   −2°C   1°C
   b) 10°C   −8°C   −10°C   9°C   −7°C   6°C
   c) 0°C   12°C   −15°C   20°C   −18°C   −10°C

2 A supermarket chain needs to store food at the following temperatures to meet health and safety regulations:

Chilled food	Between 0°C and 8°C
Frozen vegetables	−18°C or less
Ice cream	−20°C or less

   The temperatures below were recorded at different supermarkets.
   Write down the temperatures that do not meet health and safety regulations.

   a) Chilled food   5°C   9°C   7°C   −1°C   3°C   2°C
   b) Frozen vegetables   −20°C   −16°C   −19°C   −17°C   −21°C   −14°C
   c) Ice cream   −18°C   −21°C   −19°C   −23°C   −17°C   −24°C

3 Four bank accounts have these balances:

Account name	M Patel	J Robinson	R Dale	C Yeung
Balance (£)	255	−365	−50	75

   a) Which account has the most money in it?
   b) Which account is the most overdrawn?

4 An account holder has arranged an overdraft of £200 with his bank. If he owes any more than this he has to pay a fee. When the balance of the account is zero the account holder writes two cheques, one for £125 and one for £100.
   Will he have to pay a fee?

Compare numbers of any size

N1/L2.1

A **billion** is one thousand million.   In figures **1 billion = 1 000 000 000**
The distance from the earth to the sun is about 150 billion metres (150 000 000 000 m).

Four billion, five hundred and thirty million
is written like this:

	Millions			Thousands					
B	H	T	U	H	T	U	H	T	U
4	5	3	0	0	0	0	0	0	0

Very large numbers can be written neatly using decimals.

Examples

1 500 000 (one million, five hundred thousand) is **1.5 million**.
3 450 000 000 (three billion, four hundred and fifty million) is **3.45 billion**.
(Put the decimal point after the whole millions or billions.)

Practice

1 Copy the headings from the previous page. Write these numbers in full.

   a) 2.5 million   **b)** 2.56 million   **c)** 1.7 billion
   d) 1.85 billion   **e)** 30 million   **f)** 300 million
   g) 1.3 billion   **h)** 0.5 billion   **i)** 0.25 million

2 Write these numbers in millions or billions, using decimals where necessary.

   a) 2 500 000   **b)** 5 600 000   **c)** 4 750 000
   d) 3 800 000 000   **e)** 2 950 000 000   **f)** 1 050 000 000
   g) 20 000 000   **h)** 600 000 000   **i)** 34 500 000

3 The table gives the biggest lottery wins during the first
four years it was played.
Write each amount in full and put them in order of size,
starting with the **largest**.

Year	Largest win
1994	£17.9 million
1995	£22.6 million
1996	£14 million
1997	£14.1 million

4 A company's turnover (the amount of business it does) and profit (the amount of money it
makes) are often large numbers.
A **negative profit** means the company made a **loss**.

Use the table to answer the questions.
  a) Which company had
     i)   the greatest turnover
     ii) the smallest turnover
     iii) the greatest profit?
  b) **i)**   Which companies made a loss?
     ii) Which company made the
          greatest loss?

Company	Turnover £	Profit £
A	2.6 billion	1.5 million
B	12 billion	45.6 million
C	20 million	−99 000
D	45 million	60 000
E	8 billion	−1.5 million
F	1.2 billion	125 000
G	0.9 billion	−25 000

Number

2 Addition and Subtraction

Three-digit numbers   N1/E3.2, N1/E3.3

a Add in columns

Line up the numbers in columns to add Units to Units, Tens to Tens, etc.

Example	$332 + 265$

```
H T U
3 3 2 +
2 6 5
─────
5 9 7
```

▶ **Words for adding:**
   total, altogether, sum, plus

Add the Units, then the Tens, then the Hundreds.

If the Units total is 10 or more, carry 10 to the Tens column as 1 Ten to be added to the other Tens.

Example	$336 + 45$

```
H T U
3 3 6 +
  4 5
─────
3 8 1
  1
```

$6 + 5 = 11$
so 1 Ten is carried over to the Tens column.
Then $3 + 4 + 1$ makes a total of 8 in the Tens column.

▶ **It doesn't matter where you put the number you carry – some people write it at the top and some at the bottom. Take care to add it to the correct column.**

If the total of the Tens column is 10 or more, carry 10 Tens to the Hundreds column as 1 Hundred.

Example	$765 + 165$

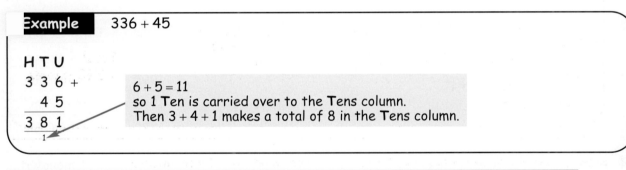

```
H T U
7 6 5 +
1 6 5
─────
9 3 0
1 1
```

$5 + 5 = 10$ so 1 Ten is carried over to the Tens column
Then $6 + 6 + 1$ makes a total of 13 in the Tens column.
3 Tens go in the Tens column and 1 Hundred (10 Tens) is carried over to the Hundreds column and added to the 7 and 1.

Practice

1 Copy and complete these.

a) 234 +
        145
        ___

b) 530 +
        249
        ___

c) 403 +
         93
        ___

d) 188 +
        301
        ___

e) 415 +
        365
        ___

f) 528 +
        144
        ___

g) 269 +
        125
        ___

h) 458 +
        329
        ___

i) 160 +
        340
        ___

j) 193 +
        125
        ___

k) 675 +
        271
        ___

l) 194 +
        111
        ___

m) 199 +
        201
        ___

n) 834 +
         97
        ___

o) 363 +
        258
        ___

p) 255 +
        355
        ___

You can add more than 2 numbers – line them all up in columns.

Example   476 men, 195 women and 72 children attend a football match. How many people is this altogether?

        4 7 6 +
        1 9 5
          7 2
        _____
        7 4 3
        2   1

In the Tens column:
7 + 9 + 7 + 1 = 24
Put 4 in the Tens column
Carry the 2
Add 4 + 1 + 2 in the
Hundreds column

In the Units column:
6 + 5 + 2 = 13
Put 3 here
Carry 1 ten

Total
= **743** people

---

2 Line up the Hundreds, Tens and Units in columns, then add the numbers.

a) 890 + 76 + 23   **b)** 99 + 109 + 264   **c)** 189 + 7 + 45

3 An insurance company has 258 full-time employees and 83 part-time employees. How many employees do they have altogether?

4 A secretary photocopies a letter for every child in a school. There are 208 boys and 232 girls. How many photocopies are needed?

5 A lorry travels 162 miles from Dover to Peterborough, then 188 miles from Peterborough to Liverpool. How far does the lorry travel altogether?

6 In a stocktake, shop staff count 42 boxes of disks on display and 440 in the stock room. How many boxes of disks are there altogether?

7 A customer buys a computer for £699, a scanner for £89 and a dust cover for £7. How much does the customer pay altogether?

8 A holiday company charges £279 for a flight and accommodation, plus a £9 booking fee and £38 for insurance. What is the total cost of the holiday?

9 A swimming pool sells 45 adult tickets, 162 child tickets and 8 infant tickets in an afternoon. How many tickets is this altogether?

▶ **Now use a calculator to check your answers.**

b Add in your head

Examples

$63 + 24$	Add the **Tens** and **Units** separately in your head. $6 + 2 = $**8**, $3 + 4 = $**7** giving **87**

$253 + 145$ Add the Hundreds, **Tens** and **Units** separately.
$2 + 1 = $**3**, $5 + 4 = $**9**, $3 + 5 = $**8**, giving **398**.

▶ **Try different methods.**

$71 + 27$ Count on in tens, then add the units:

71   81   91   **98**
$+ 10$ $+ 10$ $+ 7$

$(27 = 10 + 10 + 7)$

$234 + 45$ 234 244 254 264 274 **279**
$+ 10$ $+ 10$ $+ 10$ $+ 10$ $+ 5$

$(45 = 10 + 10 + 10 + 10 + 5)$

$156 + 45$ Break up the number to be added. Here break 45 into 40, 4 and 1:
$156 + 40 = 196$ $+ 4 = 200$ $+ 1 = $**201**

$199 + 76$ Round to a near number (here 200) then adjust the answer:
$200 + 76 = 276$ then subtract $1 = $**275**

Practice

Experiment with these.

1 a) $35 + 22$ b) $41 + 16$ c) $32 + 37$ d) $29 + 14$
   e) $57 + 15$ f) $38 + 25$ g) $49 + 36$ h) $19 + 79$

2 a) $216 + 25$ b) $159 + 22$ c) $199 + 199$ d) $154 + 233$
   e) $145 + 63$ f) $129 + 56$ g) $250 + 156$ h) $123 + 123$
   i) $206 + 156$ j) $149 + 152$ k) $312 + 256$ l) $209 + 329$
   m) $515 + 59$ n) $267 + 104$ o) $311 + 190$ p) $297 + 196$

c Subtract in columns

Line up the numbers so Units are subtracted from Units, Tens from Tens, etc.

| Example | 365 – 45 |

```
H T U
3 6 5 –
  4 5
3 2 0
```

▶ **Words for subtracting:**
   take away, difference, minus

Subtract the Units, then the Tens and then the Hundreds.

Sometimes changes are needed to make subtracting possible.

Method 1

| Example | 382 – 165 |

```
H T U
   7 1
3 8 2 –
1 6 5
2 1 7
```

Look at the Units – you cannot subtract 5 from 2.
So take one 10 from the Tens column and put it with the 2 to make
12 Units. This leaves 7 Tens.
(The 382 was changed into 3 Hundreds, 7 Tens and 12 Units.)

| Example | 512 – 291 |

```
H T U
4 1
5 1 2 –
2 9 1
2 2 1
```

Start with the Units.
Now look at the Tens – you cannot subtract 9 from 1
So take a Hundred and put it in the Tens column as 10 Tens.
You can now subtract the 9 Tens from 11 Tens.
(The 512 was changed into 4 Hundreds, 11 Tens and 2 Units.)

| Example | 306 – 159 |

```
H T U
2 9 1
3 0 6 –
1 5 9
1 4 7
```

Start with the Units. You cannot subtract 9 from 6.

You cannot take a Ten because there aren't any!
Take a Hundred. Put it in the Tens column as 10 Tens.
Now take a Ten and put it with the 6 to make 16 Units.
This leaves 9 Tens.
(The 306 was changed into 2 Hundreds, 9 Tens and 16 Units.)

▶ **Some people use a different method called 'paying back'.**
  If the 'paying back' method below looks more familiar, use it instead.

Method 2 (Paying Back)

Example   382 – 165

```
H T U
    1
3 8 2 –
  7
1 6 5
2 1 7
```

Start with the **Units**. You cannot subtract 5 from 2.

Make it 12 and 'pay this back' by adding 1 to the **Tens** column of the number you are subtracting.
(This increases both numbers by 10, the difference stays the same.)

Example   512 – 291

```
H T U
  1
5 1 2 –
3
2 9 1
2 2 1
```

Start with the **Units**. Then the **Tens** – you cannot subtract 9 from 1. Make it 11 and 'pay this back' by adding 1 to the **Hundreds** column of the number you are subtracting.

Example   306 – 159

```
H T U
  1 1
3 0 6 –
2   6
1 5 9
1 4 7
```

Start with the **Units**. You cannot subtract 9 from 6.

Make it into 16 and 'pay this back' by adding 1 to the **Tens** column of the number you are subtracting, making it 6.
You cannot subtract 6 from 0. Make it 10 and 'pay this back' by adding 1 to the **Hundreds** column of the number you are subtracting.

Whichever way you subtract, you can check your answer by adding.

For example if   403 –   then   226 +
                  177   177
                  226   403

▶ **Adding takes you back to the number you started with**. Adding is called the **inverse** of subtracting.

Practice

1   Copy and complete these, then check the answers.

a) 465 –
    254
    ____

b) 927 –
    606
    ____

c) 763 –
    563
    ____

d) 670 –
    155
    ____

▶ **Not all of these sums need changes.**

e) 832 –
    523
    ____

f) 276 –
     49
    ____

g) 300 –
    230
    ____

h) 201 –
    170
    ____

i) 518 –
    365

j) 330 –
    131

k) 523 –
    344

l) 721 –
    654

m) 500 –
    255

n) 206 –
    137

o) 901 –
    602

p) 700 –
    199

q) 404 –
     75

r) 600 –
    301

> ▶ When subtracting remember to put the larger number at the top.

2 Line up the **H**undreds, **T**ens and **U**nits in columns, then subtract.

  a) 465 – 78　　　**b)** 503 – 406　　　**c)** 783 – 85

3 175 envelopes are used from a box of 500.
How many are left in the box?

4 A television costing £399 is reduced by £75 in a sale.
What is the sale price?

£399 reduced by £75

5 A company employs 412 men and 285 women.
How many more men than women does it employ?

6 A travel company charges £329 for a holiday in April and £435 for the same holiday in July. What is the difference in price?

7 The journey from London to Edinburgh is 413 miles. I have already driven 250 miles of this journey. How far have I left to go?

d Subtract in your head

Examples		▶ Try different methods.

Start with the smaller number.

53 – 29　　Count on to the next ten, then count on in tens:

     29 + 1 = 30　+ 20 = 50　+ 3 = 53　　　　　Answer **24**

230 – 175　175 + 5 = 180　+ 10 = 190　+ 10 = 200　+ 30 = 230　　Answer **55**

71 – 19　　Subtract a near number, then adjust:
       71 – 20 = 51　　+ 1 = **52**

234 – 45　　234 – 44 = 190　　– 1 = **189**

199 – 172　Break the number up:　199 – 100 = 99　　– 70 = 29　　– 2 = **27**

Practice

Experiment with these:

1. a) 42 – 19   b) 54 – 38   c) 75 – 47   d) 81 – 25
   e) 56 – 37   f) 89 – 47   g) 90 – 53   h) 63 – 29

2. a) 200 – 51   b) 249 – 50   c) 183 – 34   d) 832 – 210
   e) 600 – 199   f) 350 – 145   g) 460 – 254   h) 321 – 122
   i) 459 – 133   j) 650 – 160   k) 679 – 522   l) 880 – 181
   m) 301 – 102   n) 479 – 180   o) 900 – 191   p) 786 – 492

Add and subtract large numbers   N1/L1.3

With large numbers take even more care to line up the digits in columns.
Leave a space between the thousands and hundreds.

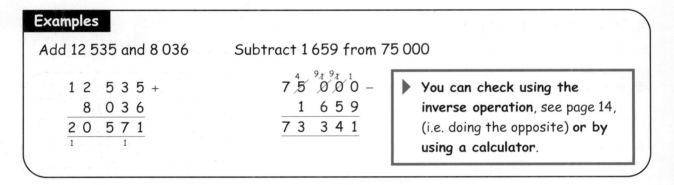

Examples

Add 12 535 and 8 036   Subtract 1 659 from 75 000

```
  1 2  5 3 5 +              7 5  0 0 0 –
     8  0 3 6                  1  6 5 9
  2 0  5 7 1                7 3  3 4 1
    1      1
```

▶ You can check using the **inverse operation**, see page 14, (i.e. doing the opposite) or by using a calculator.

Practice

1. Write the numbers in columns before adding or subtracting them.
   Check each answer.

   a) 50 360 + 1 999   b) 2 652 + 36 853   c) 945 + 27 650
   d) 136 500 + 23 999   e) 3 565 000 + 175 000   f) 6 500 000 + 27 500
   g) 325 156 – 13 067   h) 250 000 – 37 525   i) 1 675 000 – 149 500
   j) 902 856 – 7 580   k) 500 000 – 136 750   l) 301 000 – 4 650

2. It is 11 934 miles from London to Melbourne by air.
   How many miles will you travel if you fly there and back?

3. A couple earn £28 000 and £19 762. What is their joint income?

4. A live concert is also shown on the television. There are 12 000 people at the concert and 1 320 000 people watch it on television. How many people watch the concert altogether?

5 The diagram shows the mileage of a car at the start and end of a journey. How far has the car travelled?

Start   End

48576   50310

6 In its first year of trading a company has a turnover of £78 600. In the second year its turnover is £1 265 000. By how much has the turnover increased?

7 A charity is trying to raise £1 000 000. It raises £45 650 from charity shop sales and £19 500 from donations.

   a) Altogether how much money has the charity raised so far?
   b) How much more does the charity need to raise?

8 In an election 659 208 people voted for Party A, 330 629 for Party B and 78 344 for Party C.

   a) How many people voted altogether?
   b) How many more people voted for Party A than either of the other parties?

Add and subtract numbers of any size
N1/L2.2

You may have to work with positive and negative numbers or very large numbers.

Example   The table gives the temperature at midnight in some European cities. How much warmer is it in London than in Berlin?

The difference in temperature is

$$\begin{array}{r} 7.2 - \\ 1.8 \\ \hline 5.4 \end{array}$$

City	Temperature (°C)
Berlin	−7.2
Brussels	−2.5
Dublin	2.3
London	−1.8
Paris	3.1

┌ 0
├ −1.8 (London)
│ difference in temperature
└ −7.2 (Berlin)

London is 5.4°C warmer than Berlin.

Example   In June 2002 two national lottery prizes were not claimed. One prize was £700 000 and the other was £1.04 million. What was the total?

Work in millions   or   write the numbers in full.

$$\begin{array}{r} 0.7 + \\ 1.04 \\ \hline \textbf{£1.74} \text{ million} \end{array}$$

$$\begin{array}{r} 700\ 000 + \\ 1\ 040\ 000 \\ \hline 1\ 740\ 000 \end{array} = \textbf{£1.74 million}$$

Example   In its first year of trading a company makes a profit of £50 000. In its second year the company makes a profit of −£25 000 (i.e. a loss of £25 000). By how much has the profit fallen in the second year?

The answer is **£75 000**.
(£50 000 down to 0 and then a further £25 000 down to −£25 000)

Practice

1   Use the city temperatures given in the Example on page 17.
    Find the difference in temperature between
    a) London and Paris   **b)** Berlin and Brussels
    c) Dublin and Brussels   **d)** London and Brussels.

2   Calculate the following. You may need to write some numbers in full first.
    a) 3 million + 0.5 million   **b)** 6.5 million – 3.9 million
    c) £1.2 million – £86 500   **d)** £15 billion – £8.5 billion
    e) £2 billion + £250 million   **f)** £3.2 billion – £790 million

3   In one national lottery game the prize for 6 balls was £2.35 million and the prize for
    5 balls and the bonus ball was £160 000.
    What is the difference between these prizes?

4   The table below shows the profits made by a company's outlets.

| Outlet | Profit for year (£ millions) | | | | |
	2000	2001	2002	2003	Total
A	0.5	1.2	1.3	1.7	
B	0.9	0.1	–0.7	–1.1	
C	2.6	2.4	2.8	2.9	
D	–2.5	–1.7	–0.7	0.5	
Total	1.5	2	2.7	4	

Remember
positive means **profit**
negative means **loss**.

a) Calculate the total profit for each outlet.
    Check your answer by adding the totals for each year together. The result should agree
    with your total for the four outlets.
b) Use the table to answer the following questions.
    i) What is the difference between Outlet A's profits in 2002 and 2003?
    ii) By how much did Outlet B's profits fall between 2001 and 2002?
    iii) By how much did Outlet D's profits increase between 2002 and 2003?
    iv) What is the difference between Outlet A and Outlet B's total profit for the
        4 years?
    v) What is the difference between Outlet C and Outlet D's total profit for the
        4 years?
    vi) What is the difference between Outlet B and Outlet D's total profit for the
        4 years? Explain your answer.

Number

3 Multiplication and Division

Recall multiplication facts

N1/E3.5

Use multiplication facts that you know to help you work out others.

Example 3×9

Do you know the answer?
Does it help if you turn it round? 9×3
or you may know that $3 \times 10 = 30$
Take off one 3 $3 \times 9 = 30 - 3 = \mathbf{27}$

▶ Words for multiplying:
  times, product, lots of

Example 6×6

Do you know the answer?
If not, you may know that $5 \times 6 = 6 \times 5 = 30$
Add an extra 6 $6 \times 6 = 30 + 6 = \mathbf{36}$

Practice

1 Answer the following.
   Use the tables you know to help you with any that you don't know.

   a) 3×5 b) 8×10 c) 7×2 d) 4×4
   e) 5×5 f) 6×3 g) 4×9 h) 6×7
   i) 9×9 j) 4×8 k) 6×8 l) 7×9
   m) 8×8 n) 4×7 o) 7×7 p) 9×6

All the tables up to 10×10 are on this multiplication grid.

×	1	2	3	4	5	6	7	8	9	10
1	1	2	3	4	5	6	7	8	9	10
2	2	4	6	8	10	12	14	16	18	20
3	3	6	9	12	15	18	21	24	27	30
4	4	8	12	16	20	24	28	32	36	40
5	5	10	15	20	25	30	35	40	45	50
6	6	12	18	24	30	36	42	48	54	60
7	7	14	21	28	35	42	49	56	63	70
8	8	16	24	32	40	48	56	64	72	80
9	9	18	27	36	45	54	63	72	81	90
10	10	20	30	40	50	60	70	80	90	100

Look at the arrows.

They show that
$$3 \times 5 = 15$$

Use the grid to check all your answers to question 1.

The numbers in this row are called **multiples of 8**.

The numbers in this column are the **multiples of 3**.

2 a) i) What digits do the multiples of 2 end in?
   ii) Which of the following do you think are multiples of 2?
        23   30   50   75   86   99   162   204   318

   b) i) What digits do the multiples of 5 end in?
   ii) Which of the following do you think are multiples of 5?
        65   79   80   100   115   123   125   203

   c) What do you notice if you add the digits in each of the multiples of 3?
       (e.g. 3, 6, 9, $1 + 2 = 3$, $1 + 5 = 6$, $1 + 8 = 9$.)

   d) What do you notice about the multiples of 9?

Hint:
Look down column 3 in the grid.

You can use your tables to help you multiply larger numbers.

When you multiply by 10, the numbers move one column to the left.
This is because each column is worth 10 times more than the last.

H T U   H T U
   $3 \times 10 =$ 3 0
$1 2 \times 10 =$ 1 2 0

When a whole number moves left, it leaves a space in the units column.
Fill this with a 0.

Example   Calculate 4×30

Multiplying 4×30 is the same as multiplying $4 \times 3 \times 10$
                                                          $4 \times 3 = 12 \times 10 =$ **120**

3 Multiply these. Use the number grid to help you if necessary.

a) 3×20 b) 4×50 c) 6×60 d) 5×70

e) 3×90 f) 4×70 g) 6×90 h) 8×90

i) 8×80 j) 9×70 k) 8×60 l) 9×90

Multiplication methods

Example 21×3

You can break up the 21 into $20 + 1$, then multiply each of these by 3
There is more than one way to write this out.
Like this:

$$
\begin{array}{c|c|c}
\times & 20 & 1 \\
\hline
3 & 60 & 3
\end{array} = \mathbf{63}
$$

$3 \times 20 = 60$ and $3 \times 1 = 3$
Add the 60 and the $3 = 63$

Note: $3 \times 2 = 6$
so $3 \times 20 = 60$ (10 times as big)

or like this:

$$
\begin{array}{r}
2\ 1\ \times \\
3 \\
\hline
\mathbf{6\ 3}
\end{array}
$$

$3 \times 1 = 3$ (or $1 \times 3 = 3$)
Put 3 in the **Units** column
$3 \times 2 = 6$ (or $2 \times 3 = 6$)
Put 6 in the **Tens** column

Example 45×7

$$
\begin{array}{c|c|c}
\times & 40 & 5 \\
\hline
7 & 280 & 35
\end{array} = \mathbf{315}
$$

$7 \times 40 = 280$ and $7 \times 5 = 35$
Add the 280 and the $35 = 315$

or

$$
\begin{array}{r}
4\ 5\ \times \\
7 \\
\hline
\mathbf{3\ 1\ 5} \\
\scriptstyle 3
\end{array}
$$

$7 \times 5 = 35$ (or $5 \times 7 = 35$)
Put 5 in the **Units** column
Carry the 3
$7 \times 4 = 28$ (or $4 \times 7 = 28$)
Add the 3 making 31

It doesn't matter which method you use. Using boxes shows how the calculation works. The other way does it all at once. Use the method that is more familiar, or try both methods and see which one you prefer.

Practice

1   Multiply these. Use the multiplication grid to help you if necessary.

   a) 24×2 **b)** 31×3 **c)** 44×2 **d)** 42×3
   e) 35×3 **f)** 43×4 **g)** 65×4 **h)** 75×6
   i) 39×6 **j)** 56×8 **k)** 76×4 **l)** 89×6
   m) 88×7 **n)** 49×9 **o)** 97×5 **p)** 93×9

2   There are 12 curtain rings in each pack. How many are there in 5 packs?

3   There are 25 paper plates in each pack. How many are there in 3 packs?

4   How many minutes does a 3 hour video tape last? (1 hour = 60 minutes)

5   A care-worker earns £7 an hour. How much does the care-worker earn for a 37 hour week?

6   A hotel has 7 floors. Each floor has 23 bedrooms.
   How many bedrooms does the hotel have altogether?

7   An office assistant makes 9 photocopies of a 42 page report.
   How many pages is this altogether?

8   A commuter travels 85 miles each day to get to work and back.
   Altogether how many miles does the commuter travel in 5 days?

9   The instructions on a packet of rice say, 'Allow 75 grams per person.'
   How many grams do you need for 8 people?

▶ **Now use a calculator to check your answers.**

Division
N1/E3.6

a Different ways

You can think of division in different ways:

● the opposite of multiplication

● how many times a number goes into another

● how many times you can take one number away from another.

▶ **Words for dividing:**
share, goes into

> **Example** $12 \div 4$
>
> **'How many 4s are there in 12?'**
>
> $3 \times 4 = 12$ so $12 \div 4 = 3$ or   4 into 12 goes **3 times**
>
> If 12 disks are shared equally between 4 people, they each get **3**.
>
> You can use times tables or the multiplication grid to calculate this.
>
> To use a multiplication grid for $12 \div 4$
> go down from the 4 until you reach 12,
> then go across to find the answer **3**.
>
> **Look at the multiplication grid on p. 20.**
>
> You can also think of $12 \div 4$ as how many times can 4 be taken away from 12.
> $12 - 4 = 8$ (once) $8 - 4 = 4$ (twice) $4 - 4 = 0$ (**three** times)

> **Example** $13 \div 4$
>
> **'How many 4s are there in 13?'**
>
> $3 \times 4 = 12$ (not quite enough) and $4 \times 4 = 16$ (too much).
> The closest you can get is **3 with one left over**.
>
> **You can write this as 3 r 1.**
>
> So $13 \div 4 = $ **3 remainder 1**.
>
> Sometimes the remainder can be broken down further.
> For example, a bill of £13 shared between 4 people is £3 each and £1 left over.
> The £1 can be broken down into 25p each.
> However it is not always possible to do this. For example, if you are sharing a box of
> 13 disks you cannot divide the remaining disk.

Practice

1 Calculate these. (Some have remainders.)

a) $25 \div 5$ b) $50 \div 10$ c) $24 \div 6$ d) $28 \div 4$
e) $32 \div 8$ f) $45 \div 9$ g) $63 \div 7$ h) $49 \div 7$
i) $13 \div 2$ j) $42 \div 10$ k) $37 \div 6$ l) $28 \div 5$
m) $22 \div 3$ n) $51 \div 8$ o) $60 \div 9$ p) $59 \div 7$

2 A £20 taxi fare is shared equally between 4 people. How much does each person pay?

3 A swimmer gets £80 sponsorship money for swimming 10 lengths.
   How much was she sponsored per length?

4 A packet of 5 pencils costs 45p. How much is this per pencil?

5 48 tins are arranged in 6 rows. How many tins are in each row?

6 A bag of 30 sweets is shared between 4 children. If all the children have to have the same number of sweets, what is the maximum number of sweets each child can have?

7 28 people want to go to a football match. Each car holds 5 people.
How many cars do they need?

8 How many teams can be made for 5-a-side football if there are 29 players?

9 40 people are invited to a wedding reception. Each table seats 6 people. How many tables are needed?

10 An office orders 50 filing trays. They are shared equally between the 8 office clerks. How many filing trays are left over?

b Standard method

When the number to be divided is too large, it is not possible to use times tables or a multiplication grid.
There is a method that breaks the number down.

Example $96 \div 3$

Re-write the sum $3\overline{)96}$ Divide 3 into 9 first: $9 \div 3 = 3$
Put the 3 above the 9

$$\begin{array}{r} 3 \\ 3\overline{)96} \end{array}$$ Then divide 3 into 6: $6 \div 3 = 2$
Put the 2 above the 6

$$\begin{array}{r} 32 \\ 3\overline{)96} \end{array}$$ $96 \div 3 = \mathbf{32}$

Sometimes the numbers do not divide exactly.

Example $57 \div 2$

$2\overline{)57}$ $5 \div 2 = 2$ remainder 1

$$\begin{array}{r} 2 \\ 2\overline{)5^17} \end{array}$$ Put the 2 above the 5 and the 1 in front of the 7.
The 1 is 1 **Ten** so this makes 17.
Divide 2 into 17,
$17 \div 2 = 8$ remainder 1.

$$\begin{array}{r} 28 \text{ r1} \\ 2\overline{)5^17} \end{array}$$ Put the 8 above the 17 then write down the remainder.
$57 \div 2 = \mathbf{28 \ r \ 1}$

Practice

1 Copy and complete these.

a) 2)48	**b)** 3)99	**c)** 2)80	**d)** 5)60
e) 5)75	**f)** 4)92	**g)** 6)78	**h)** 4)76
i) 3)87	**j)** 3)88	**k)** 5)92	**l)** 7)86
m) 8)99	**n)** 4)70	**o)** 3)95	**p)** 6)89

2 How many 5 millilitre doses of medicine can be taken from a 90 millilitre bottle?

3 A doctor allows 5 minutes for each patient.
How many patients can the doctor see in 1 hour (60 minutes)?

4 Four people divide a £68 restaurant bill equally. How much does each person pay?

5 A child's school trip costs £75. The trip is paid for in 3 equal payments.
How much is each payment?

6 A 70 metre length of tape is cut into 5 equal pieces. How long is each piece?

7 75 plants are packed into trays of 6.

   a) How many trays are filled?
   b) How many plants are left over?

8 It is recommended that there is 1 adult to look after every 3 children under the age of 2 in a nursery. How many adults are needed to look after 40 children under the age of 2?

9 A box of 50 pens is shared equally between 4 people.
How many pens are left over?

> ▶ Multiplication and division are **inverse** operations. You can check the result of a multiplication by dividing. If the result of a division is exact, you can check it by multiplying.

In the first example in this section we found that $96 \div 3 = 32$.
To check this, work out 32×3. The answer is 96.
Note that if there is a remainder, you multiply then add the remainder.
The check for the second example is $28 \times 2 = 56 + 1 = 57$.

$$\begin{array}{r} 32 \\ 3\overline{)96} \end{array} \qquad \begin{array}{r} 32 \times \\ 3 \\ \hline 96 \end{array}$$

Check your answers to question **1** by multiplying.

Multiply and divide whole numbers by 10 and 100   N1/L1.4

a Multiply by 10 and 100 in your head

Multiplying (and dividing) by 10 and 100 in your head is useful when you need to estimate answers or work with large numbers.

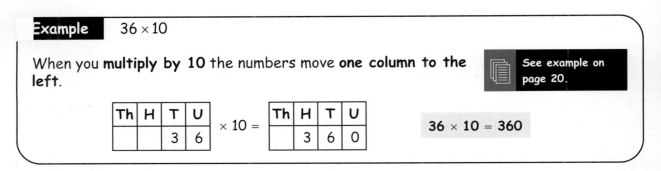

Multiplying by 100 is the same as multiplying by 10 then 10 again.
The numbers move **two columns to the left**. With a whole number this leaves two spaces to be filled by zeros.

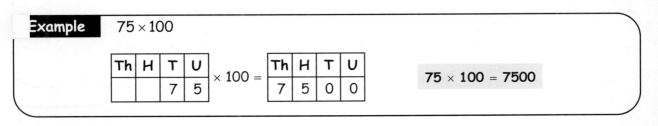

Practice

1 Calculate these in your head.

   a) 13×10 b) 75×10 c) 136×10 d) 202×10
   e) 90×10 f) 190×10 g) 12×100 h) 37×100
   i) 129×100 j) 120×100 k) 303×100 l) 123×100

2 How many pence would you get for a £5 note? (£1 = 100p)

3 How many 10p coins would you get for a £20 note? (£1 = 10 × 10p)

4 There are 10 millimetres in 1 centimetre.
   How many millimetres are there in 66 centimetres?

5 There are 100 centimetres in one metre. How many are there in 15 metres?

6   There are 100 envelopes in one box. How many are there in 25 boxes?

7   A cashier has forty-five £10 notes in the till. How much is this?

8   There are 10 disks in one box. How many disks are there in 50 boxes?

9   100 people each donate £25 to charity. How much money is this altogether?

b Divide by 10 and 100 in your head

When you divide by 10 or 100 the numbers move to the right.

Example $360 \div 10$

Th	H	T	U
	3	6	0

$\div 10 =$

Th	H	T	U
		3	6

$360 \div 10 = 36$

Example $4500 \div 100$

Th	H	T	U
4	5	0	0

$\div 100 =$

Th	H	T	U
		4	5

$4500 \div 100 = 45$

If the number does not end in zero, the answer is a decimal.

Example $365 \div 10$

Th	H	T	U
	3	6	5

$\div 10 =$

Th	H	T	U
		3	6

. 5

$365 \div 10 = 36.5$

Example $4523 \div 100$

Th	H	T	U
4	5	2	3

$\div 100 =$

Th	H	T	U
		4	5

. 23

$4523 \div 100 = 45.23$

If you need an exact answer, give the decimal form (see page 106).
If you do not need an exact answer, you can round the number (see page 107).

Practice

1 Calculate these.

    a) $460 \div 10$ **b)** $4600 \div 10$ **c)** $4600 \div 100$ **d)** $46\,000 \div 100$

    e) $530 \div 10$ **f)** $5300 \div 10$ **g)** $5300 \div 100$ **h)** $53\,000 \div 100$

    i) $9900 \div 10$ **j)** $750 \div 10$ **k)** $57\,000 \div 10$ **l)** $3800 \div 100$

2 A lottery win of £12 000 is shared between 100 people.
How much does each person get?

3 A printer charges £15 for 100 colour copies.
What is the cost per copy? (£1 = 100p)

4 There are 10 millimetres in 1 centimetre.
What is 720 millimetres in centimetres?

5 There are 100 centimetres in 1 metre.
What is 24 000 centimetres in metres?

6 Paperclips are packed in boxes of 100.
How many boxes would 275 000 paper clips fill?

7 Candles are sold in boxes of 10. How many boxes will 3500 candles fill?

8 100 workers in a call centre each answer the same number of calls.
How many does each worker answer out of a total of 17 600 calls?

9 About one out of ten people are left-handed.
How many people out of 150 are likely to be left-handed?

Use multiplication and division

N1/L1.5

Try to do these in your head.

Practice

1 Copy and complete these by putting the missing number in each box.

    a) $4 \times 7 = \boxed{}$ **b)** $5 \times 6 = \boxed{}$ **c)** $5 \times \boxed{} = 50$

    d) $6 \times \boxed{} = 36$ **e)** $\boxed{} \times 8 = 32$ **f)** $9 \times 7 = \boxed{}$

    g) $9 \times \boxed{} = 81$ **h)** $7 \times \boxed{} = 42$ **i)** $\boxed{} \times 7 = 56$

    j) $\boxed{} \times 8 = 64$ **k)** $4 \times \boxed{} = 36$ **l)** $8 \times 6 = \boxed{}$

2   How many 2 pence coins make 20p?

3   There are 6 eggs in a box.
    How many boxes do you need to get 54 eggs?

4   A £72 bill is shared equally between 8 people.
    How much does each person pay?

5   One book costs £9. How much do 7 of these books cost?

6   One box holds 3 light bulbs. How many boxes do I need to buy to
    get 27 light bulbs?

7   I save £8 each week. How many weeks will it take me to save £64?

8   I work 8 hours each day, for 5 days a week.
    How many hours is this altogether?

9   I earn £56 for 7 hours work. How much is this per hour?

Recognise numerical relationships   N1/L1.6

a Multiples

A **multiple** of a number can be divided **exactly** by that number, (see page 000).

Example	18 is a multiple of 2, 3, 6 and 9 because $2 \times 9 = 18$ and $3 \times 6 = 18$

Practice

1 a) Which of these are multiples of 4?   7   12   23   32   37   40
   b) Which of these are multiples of 7?   21   29   36   42   64   70
   c) Which of these are multiples of both 3 **and** 4?
                                                 6   12   17   20   21   24
   d) Which of these are multiples of both 2 **and** 5?
                                                 4   10   15   18   25   30

2 Write down all the multiples below 100 of

   a) 6   b) 8   c) 9.

b Square numbers

A **square** number is made when you multiply any whole number by itself.

> **Example**   25 is a square number as $5 \times 5 = 25$
>
> $\times$ 5
>
> 5

Practice

1 Copy out the multiplication grid on page 20. Shade the square numbers.

2 Which of these are square numbers?

    6   9   20   24   25   32   40   49   54   62   81   100

c Use mental arithmetic to multiply multiples of 10

This is useful for estimation.

> **Example** 5×60
>
> $5 \times 60 = 5 \times 6 \times 10$ ← **Think of 60 as 6 × 10.**
> $= 30 \times 10 = \mathbf{300}$

> **Example** 30×40
>
> **Think of 30 as 3 × 10.**
>
> $30 \times 40 = 3 \times 4 \times 10 \times 10$
>
> **Think of 40 as 4 × 10.**
>
> $3 \times 4 = 12$ $\times 10 = 120$ $\times 10 = 1200$ So $30 \times 40 = \mathbf{1200}$

Practice

1 Work these out in your head.

    a) 3×30 **b)** 4×60 **c)** 7×20 **d)** 9×50

    e) 8×60 **f)** 3×90 **g)** 20×70 **h)** 40×50

    i) 60×70 **j)** 70×50 **k)** 60×60 **l)** 90×80

2 5 people pay £20 each for concert tickets. How much is this altogether?

3 A typist estimates there are 20 words in a line and 40 lines on a page. Approximately how many words are there on a page?

4 It takes 30 payments of £40 each to repay a loan. How much is paid altogether?

5 50 teams of 6 people take part in a quiz. How many people is this altogether?

6 About 80 people per day visit an exhibition. Roughly how many people visit the exhibition in a month of 30 days?

7 A bag of potatoes weighs 30 kilograms. What is the total weight of 90 bags?

8 30 coaches each take 50 people to a rugby match. How many people is this?

9 How many seconds are there in an hour? (1 minute = 60 seconds, 1 hour = 60 minutes)

Multiply and divide large numbers

N1/L1.3

a Multiply large numbers

Break down the numbers so that the **Tens** and **Units** of each number are multiplied together. There are different ways of doing this. Use the method that seems most familiar or straight-forward to you.

Example	32 × 41

Grid Method   This works out the **Tens** and **Units** separately.

×	30	2	
40	1200	80	1280 +
1	30	2	32
			1312

Separate the **Tens** and **Units**.
Multiply 40 × 30 and 40 × 2.
Multiply 1 × 30 and 1 × 2.
Add the answers across then down.

Traditional Method   This works out 32×1 then 32×40, then adds them.

```
    3 2 ×
    4 1
    ─────
    3 2
  1 2 8 0
  ───────
  1 3 1 2
```

Multiply $1 \times 2 = 2$ Put the 2 in the **Units** column.
Multiply $1 \times 3 = 3$ Put the 3 in the **Tens** column.
                            (You have now multiplied 32×1.)
Put a zero in the **Units** first (because you are now multiplying tens).
Multiply $4 \times 2 = 8$ Put the 8 in the **Tens** column.
Multiply $4 \times 3 = 12$ Put this down on the left.
                            (You have now multiplied 32×40.)
Add together the 32 and the 1280 = **1312**

If you prefer, you can start by multiplying 32×40.
The first line in the answer would be 1280 with the 32 underneath.

Example 245×63

Grid Method

×	200	40	5	
60	12 000	2400	300	14 700 +
3	600	120	15	735
				15 435
				1

Separate the **Hundreds**, **Tens** and **Units**.
Multiply 60×200, 60×40 and 60×5.
Multiply 3×200, 3×40 and 3×5.
Add the answers across then down.

Traditional Method   This works out 245×3 then 245×60, then adds them.

Carry numbers

```
      2 4 5 ×
        6 3
      ───────
      7₁ 3₁ 5
  1 4₂ 7₃ 0 0
  ───────────
  1 5 4 3 5
      1
```

Multiply $3 \times 5 = 15$ Put down 5, carry 1.
Multiply $3 \times 4 = 12$ Add the carried 1 = 13. Put down 3, carry 1.
Multiply $3 \times 2 = 6$ Add the carried 1 = 7. Put down 7.
                            (You have now multiplied 245×3.)
Put 0 in the Units column. (To multiply by 60, multiply by 10 then 6.)
Multiply $6 \times 5 = 30$. Put down 0 and carry 3.
(*Some people put carried numbers at the top. Wherever you put them take care not to get carried numbers muddled. You can cross them out when you have finished with them.*)
Multiply $6 \times 4 = 24$ Add the carried 3 = 27. Put down 7, carry 2.
Multiply $6 \times 2 = 12$ Add the 2 carried = 14. Put down 14.
                            (You have now multiplied 245×60.)
Add together the 735 and 14 700 = **15 435**.

If you find the grid method and traditional method difficult, try this last method:

Example 245×63

Lattice Method

Draw a grid with diagonal lines like this.
Put 245 across the top and 63 down the right-hand side.
Multiply the $5 \times 6 = 30$. Split the answer into Tens and Units.
Put 3 in the top of the box and 0 in the bottom.

Do the same with each pair of digits,
e.g. $4 \times 6 = 24$ Put 2 in the top of the box and 4 in the bottom.
To find the answer you now need to add together the numbers in the diagonal lines.
Start with the bottom right hand corner.

5	= 5
$0 + 1 + 2$	= 3
$3 + 4 + 1 + 6$	= 14 (carry the 1)
$2 + 2 + 1$(carried)	= 5
1	= 1

giving the answer **15 435**.

▶ Note each method can be extended for any number of digits and decimal numbers.

Practice

1   Work these out without a calculator, then use a calculator to check.

a) 41×25 b) 60×32 c) 52×43 d) 45×62
e) 38×56 f) 29×43 g) 56×78 h) 57×44
i) 36×70 j) 45×67 k) 54×45 l) 63×49
m) 123×35 n) 632×47 o) 225×57 p) 342×80
q) 512×63 r) 309×42 s) 708×96 t) 573×48

2   A caterer charges £16 per head. How much is the charge for 45 people?

3   There are 48 tins in each tray. How many are there in 35 trays?

4   A coach company charges £27 a ticket for a trip. 42 people buy tickets.
    How much money is this altogether?

5   A school has 36 classes. Each class has 31 children.
    How many children are there at the school?

6   A concert hall has 85 rows of 48 seats. What is the total number of seats?

7 A lorry driver travels about 350 miles a day. Approximately how many miles are travelled in 20 days?

8 A smoker uses 25 cigarettes per day. How many is this in a year (365 days)?

9 Roughly how many days old is a man on his 85th birthday? Assume that there are 365 days in every year.

b Divide large numbers

You can use the standard method to divide large numbers as well as small numbers.

See page 24.

Example   9396 ÷ 4

$$\begin{array}{r} 2\ 3\ 4\ 9 \\ {}^{1\ \ 1\ \ 3} \\ 4\overline{)9\ 3\ 9\ 6} \end{array}$$

9 ÷ 4 = 2 rem 1   Put 2 above the 9.
Carry 1 to make the 3 into 13.

13 ÷ 4 = 3 rem 1   Put 3 above the 3.
Carry 1 to make the 9 into 19.

19 ÷ 4 = 4 rem 3   Put the 4 above the 9.
Carry 3 to make the 6 into 36.

36 ÷ 4 = 9   Put the 9 above the 6.

The answer for 9396 ÷ 4 is **2349**.

Example   18 053 ÷ 9

$$\begin{array}{r} 2\ 0\ 0\ 5\ \text{r}\ 8 \\ {}^{1\ \ \ \ \ \ 5} \\ 9\overline{)1\ 8\ 0\ 5\ 3} \end{array}$$

cannot do 1 ÷ 9 so carry the 1 to make the 8 into 18.

18 ÷ 9 = 2   Put the 2 above the 8.

0 ÷ 9 = 0   Put the 0 above the 0.

cannot do 5 ÷ 9 so put 0 above the 5 and carry the 5 to make 3 into 53.

53 ÷ 9 = 5 rem 8   Put the 5 above the 3.
Write down the remainder.

The answer for 18 053 ÷ 9 is **2005 remainder 8**.

Practice

1 Work these out.

a) 5910 ÷ 6   b) 3240 ÷ 8   c) 7929 ÷ 9

d) 14 608 ÷ 4   e) 29 470 ÷ 7   f) 34 125 ÷ 5

g) 14 508 ÷ 8   h) 62 500 ÷ 6   i) 25 127 ÷ 3

j) 48 950 ÷ 6   k) 50 000 ÷ 9   l) 80 225 ÷ 4

2 A market research company employs 8 people to carry out 2000 interviews. How many people will they each interview if they share the 2000 equally?

3 A bill for £2025 is paid in 9 equal payments. How much is each payment?

4 Tickets for an outdoor event cost £6 each. Altogether £19 326 is taken in ticket sales. How many tickets are sold?

5 At a factory 34 000 ice lollies are packed into boxes of 8. How many boxes are filled?

6 26 000 millilitres of perfume is packed as 5 millilitre samples. How many samples are there?

7 Six people inherit £135 000 to be shared equally between them. How much does each person inherit?

8 £250 000 is divided equally between 4 charities. How much does each charity get?

It is more difficult to divide by a large number. You may need to try out estimates at each stage. Set the working out in either of the ways shown below.

Example   648 ÷ 18

$$\begin{array}{r} 3\ 6 \\ {}^{10} \\ 18\overline{)6\ 4\ 8} \end{array}$$

How many 18s in 64?
There are three 20s in
60 so 3 is a good guess.
18 × 3 = 54
There are 10 left.

$$\begin{array}{r} 3\ 6 \\ 18\overline{)6\ 4\ 8} \\ 5\ 4 \\ \hline 1\ 0\ 8 \\ 1\ 0\ 8 \\ \hline 0 \end{array}$$

Bring the 8 down – this is neater than squeezing the 10 that are left in front of the 8.
There are six 18s in 108.

Rough working

$$\begin{array}{r} 18\ \times \\ 3 \\ \hline 54 \\ {}_2 \end{array}$$

$$\begin{array}{r} 18\ \times \\ 6 \\ \hline 108 \\ {}_4 \end{array}$$

Answer
= **36**

---

9 Work these out. Check your answers on a calculator.

a) 882 ÷ 21   b) 988 ÷ 19   c) 675 ÷ 15   d) 925 ÷ 25
e) 377 ÷ 29   f) 800 ÷ 32   g) 1170 ÷ 18   h) 2312 ÷ 17

10 Calculate the monthly pay if the annual pay is   (1 year = 12 months so divide by 12)

a) £24 480   b) £15 000   c) £35 160   d) £42 984.

Efficient methods of calculating with numbers of any size N1/L2.2

a Multiples, factors and prime numbers

A **multiple** of a number can be divided **exactly** by that number.
e.g.   6, 21 and 30 are all multiples of 3.

A **factor** of a number is something that **divides exactly into it**.
e.g.   2, 3, 4 and 6 are all factors of 12.

A **prime** number has **two factors** – itself and 1.
e.g.   2, 5, 7 and 11 are all prime numbers.

(Note 1 is **not** a prime number. It has only one factor – itself.)

There are some quick ways of checking for factors and multiples.

To check whether 2 is a factor of a number, look at the last digit.
If it is **even**, then **2 is a factor** (i.e. the number is a multiple of 2).
So 2 is a factor of numbers like 74, 348, 74 256, etc.

To check whether 5 is a factor of a number, look at the last digit.
If it is **0 or 5**, then **5 is a factor** (i.e. the number is a multiple of 5).
So 5 is a factor of numbers like 70, 345, 74 250, etc.

To check whether 3 is a factor of a number, add all the digits.
If the total is **divisible by 3**, then **3 is a factor**
(i.e. the number is a multiple of 3).

Example   12 345

$1 + 2 + 3 + 4 + 5 = 15$ then $1 + 5 = 6$
6 is divisible by 3 so 3 is a factor of 12 345
(and 12 345 is a multiple of 3).

Keep adding the digits together.

The same method works for 9.

Example   13 860

$1 + 3 + 8 + 6 + 0 = 18$ then $1 + 8 = 9$
so 9 is a factor of 13 860 (and 13 860 is a multiple of 9).

Practice

1   Which of the numbers listed below are multiples of

   a) 2   **b)** 5   **c)** 3   **d)** 9?

   98,   127,   165,   243,   364,   539,   720,   945,   1603,   25 245

2 **a)** What is the smallest number that is a multiple of both 3 **and** 5?
   b) Find the smallest number that is a multiple of both 4 **and** 6.
   c) What is the largest number that is a factor of both 18 **and** 30?
   d) Find the largest number that is a factor of both 21 **and** 70.

3 **a)** Find the numbers that are factors of 12 and also multiples of 3.
   b) Find 2 factors of 18 that are also factors of 81.

4 **a)** Find a prime number greater than 3 that is a factor of 30.
   b) What is the next prime number after 23?

5 Find a number that is a factor of 15, 171 and 411.

b Calculations with numbers of any size

The standard methods for multiplying and dividing are given earlier. For large numbers it is often quicker and more accurate to use a calculator, but sometimes numbers are too large to fit on the calculator display. It is also useful to be able to do rough checks to make sure the calculator is giving the right answer. Try to use mental arithmetic whenever you can – everything gets easier with practice! Look out for short-cuts.

Example   A £1 500 000 lottery win is shared equally between 30 people. How much does each person get?

To divide by 30, divide by 10 then 3
   $1\,500\,000 \div 10 = 150\,000$
   $15 \div 3 = 5$ So the answer is **£50 000**.

Example   Four charities each receive £125 000. How much is this in total?

          $2 \times 125 = 250$ $250 \times 2 = 500$
   so 4×125 $= 500$ To multiply by 4, double then double again.
   and $4 \times £125\,000 = £500\,000$

Practice

Work these out. Use mental arithmetic when the numbers are easy enough.

1 How much is each payment if a debt of £3600 is paid off in:

   a) 12 equal payments   **b)** 40 equal payments
   c) 100 equal payments?

2   Each month a company sends out 3500 customer account statements.
    How many statements does it send out in a year (12 months)?

3   A mortgage is paid off at £5000 a year for 30 years.
    How much is paid in total?

4   A local paper sells an estimated 32 000 papers. On average
    four people read each paper. How many people read the
    paper altogether?

5   A company doubles its original advertising budget of £750 000.
    What is its budget now?

6   The total salary bill for 8 company directors is £2.4 million. Each director earns the same
    amount. What is each salary? (Give the answer in full.)

7   A builder sells 20 flats for £145 000 each. How much is this in total?

8   Approximately 1.3 million tourists visit a country each year.
    About how many tourists will visit the country during the next 5 years?

9   A company announces spending of £1.5 million over the next 4 years.
    How much is this per year?

10 The table shows the profits made by the three
    sections of a company. The total profit is shared
    equally between two partners.
    How much do they each receive?

Section	Profits
A	£2.46 million
B	−£3.28 million
C	£5.14 million

Number

4 Rounding and Estimation

Approximation and estimation (numbers up to 1000) N1/E3.7, N1/E3.8

a When to estimate

Estimation is used to work out an **approximate** answer.
This is useful if you want to:

● do a quick rough calculation

● check that an answer to a calculation is sensible

● find an approximate figure when you cannot calculate something exactly.

Estimation is **not** used to find an accurate answer.

Example   A shopper has 95p left in his purse.
Can he afford to buy 3 stamps costing 28p each?

28p is nearly 30p. $3 \times 30p = 90p$. **Yes, he can afford the 3 stamps.**

Example   A shopper buys 3 items costing £49 each. The shop charges £196.
Is this approximately correct?

£49 is nearly £50. $3 \times £50 = £150$. **No, the shop has charged too much.**

Example   A businessman needs to arrive at an airport **at least** 2 hours before his
flight departs at 11:30 am. He has to drive 50 miles to the airport.
What time should he leave home?

There is no single correct answer to this problem.
The businessman needs to use his knowledge and experience to work it out.
He might estimate that the journey will take about **2 hours** due to traffic.
He might also allow **another hour** to park and find the check in.
If so, he will estimate that he needs to leave home at 6:30 am to arrive at 9:30 am.

1   In which of these situations would you use estimation?

   a) To work out how much food to buy for a party.
   b) To calculate an employee's pay.
   c) To work out how much spending money to take on holiday.
   d) To measure a dose of medicine.
   e) To measure a piece of glass to fit a frame.
   f) To work out how far it is from London to Edinburgh.
   g) To work out how long it will take to get to the cinema.
   h) To count the number of children on a school trip.
   i) To work out how much paint to buy to decorate a room.
   j) To calculate how much change to give.

b Round to the nearest 10 and 100

Rounding numbers to the **nearest 10** gives whole numbers that end in **zero** (e.g. **10, 20, 30**). This is useful because numbers like 50 and 90 are much easier to work with than numbers like 49 or 93.

Example   Round 74 to the nearest 10

70   71   72   73   **74**   75   76   77   78   79   80

74 lies between 70 and 80. It is nearer to 70, so it is rounded down to **70**.

Example   Round 238 to the nearest 10.

230 231 232 233 234 235 236 237 **238** 239 240

238 lies between 230 and 240. It is nearer to 240, so it is rounded up to **240**.

Example   Round 196 to the nearest 10.

190   191   192   193   194   195   **196**   197   198   199   200

196 is between 190 and 200 it is nearer to 200, so it is rounded up to **200**.

Example   Round 485 to the nearest 10.

480   481   482   483   484   **485**   486   487   488   489   490

485 lies between 480 and 490. It is in the middle.
In maths we use the rule:
If it is in the middle, you should **round up**, in this case to **490**.

▶ **To round to the nearest 10:**
If the Units digit is **less than 5, round down** (e.g. 283 = 280 to nearest 10).
If the Units digit is **5 or more, round up** (e.g. 427 = 430 to nearest 10).
The answers always end in 0.

```
10   11   12   13   14   15   16   17   18   19   20
```

Practice

1 Round each number to the nearest 10.

a) 37	b) 15	c) 22	d) 92
e) 137	f) 215	g) 422	h) 992
i) 412	j) 99	k) 699	l) 313
m) 242	n) 175	o) 368	p) 707
q) 365	r) 811	s) 901	t) 275

Large numbers are often rounded to the nearest 100. Deciding whether to round to the nearest 10 or 100 depends on the size of the number and how accurate you want the answer to be.

Example   Round 370 to the nearest 100.

```
300  310  320  330  340  350  360  370  380  390  400
```

370 lies between 300 and 400. It is nearer to 400 so it is rounded up to **400**.

▶ Any whole number from 350 to 399 would be rounded up to 400.
So numbers like 351, 365, 382 and 399 are all 400 to the nearest 100.

Example   Round 720 to the nearest 100.

```
700  710  720  730  740  750  760  770  780  790  800
```

720 lies between 700 and 800. It is nearer to 700 so it is rounded down to **700**.

▶ Any whole number from 700 to 749 would be rounded down to 700.
So numbers like 706, 721, 736 and 749 are all 700 to the nearest 100.

Example   Round 550 to the nearest 100.

500 510 520 530 540 550 560 570 580 590 600

550 lies between 500 and 600. It is in the middle.
Remember the rule in maths is: **if it is in the middle, round up**, here to **600**.

▶ **To round to the nearest 100:**
If the Tens digit is **less than 5, round down**   (e.g. 427 = 400 to nearest 100).
If the Tens digit is **5 or more, round up**   (e.g. 283 = 300 to nearest 100).
The answers always end in two 0s.

100 110 120 130 140 150 160 170 180 190 200

2 Round each number to the nearest 100.

a) 170	b) 350	c) 620	d) 880
e) 175	f) 357	g) 629	h) 851
i) 383	j) 199	k) 750	l) 749
m) 851	n) 999	o) 235	p) 428
q) 857	r) 810	s) 250	t) 59

c Use estimates to check calculations

You can check whether the answer to a calculation is sensible by rounding the numbers and estimating the answer.

Example   A student calculates that if one CD costs £18 then 3 will cost £34.

A rough check shows this cannot be correct:
£18 rounded to the nearest £10 is £20. 3 × £20 = 60. Therefore the student's answer is not sensible. (The correct answer is £54.)

Example   A saver has £412 in her bank account. She thinks that if she takes out £285 there will be £273 left in the account.

A rough check shows this cannot be correct:
£412 rounded to the nearest £100 is £400 and £285 rounded to the nearest £100 is £300.
£400 − £300 = £100. (The correct answer is £127.)

Practice

1   Use an estimate to check whether each statement is correct.

Quality Menswear – Price list

Jumpers	£25	Jackets	£67
Shirts	£20	Coats	£85
Ties	£8	Suits	£159
Trousers	£29		

Note
Round to numbers you can work out easily

a) The total cost of a jacket and trousers is £136.

b) A suit costs £92 more than a jacket.

c) A jacket and two pairs of trousers cost £125 altogether.

d) A shopper spends £87 on trousers. He has bought 2 pairs.

e) Coats are reduced by £27 in a sale. The sale price is £58.

f) A shopper buys 9 jumpers. The total cost is £225. (Hint: Work out £25 × 10)

g) A man buys 3 suits. Altogether they cost £577. (Hint: Work out £160 × 3)

h) Last year suits cost £115. The price has increased by £64.

2   The table shows the number of pairs of gloves of different sizes sold in a shop.

Size	Number sold
Small	191
Medium	412
Large	286

a) Find the total number sold.

b) How many more medium than large pairs were sold?

Check each answer by rounding the numbers to the nearest hundred.

3   Use the information in the table below to answer the questions.
In each part you will need to carry out a series of calculations.
Use estimates to check each calculation you do.

	Hotel Expensivo – Price List		
	Cost per person, per night £	English breakfast per person £	Continental breakfast per person £
Adult	55	8	6
Child	38	5	3

Find the cost for

a) 2 adults and 1 child, staying 2 nights with English breakfast
(*Note: Work out the cost for 1 night with breakfast, then double it*)

b) 1 adult and 3 children, staying 4 nights with Continental breakfast

c) 2 adults and 4 children, staying 3 nights with Continental breakfast.

Approximate and estimate with large numbers   N1/L1.8, N1/L1.9

a Round to the nearest 1000, 10 000, 100 000, 1 000 000

The method for rounding larger numbers is similar to that for smaller numbers.
For example:

To round a number to the nearest thousand:

- Identify which digit is in the **Thousands** column.

- Look at the Hundreds digit to the right – this is the 'deciding digit'.
  If it is **below 5, round down** so the Thousands digit stays the same.

- If the Hundreds digit is **5 or above, round up** so the Thousands digit increases by one.

- After the thousands digit write 000 (because a number rounded to the nearest **Thousand** will have no Hundreds, Tens or Units).

Example

a) **To round 3 257 432 to the nearest 1000**

Thousand digit   Deciding digit

3 25**7** 432

4 is **less than 5**, so **round down**
The thousands digit, 7, stays the same.

3 257 432 to the nearest thousand is **3 257 000.**

To the nearest **Thousand** means there are no Hundreds, Tens or Units.
The number must end in 000.

b) **To round 3 257 432 to the nearest 10 000**

Ten Thousands digit   Deciding digit

3 2**5**7 432

7 is **more than 5**, so **round up**
The ten thousands digit increases by 1.

3 257 432 to the nearest ten thousand is **3 260 000.**

To the nearest **Ten Thousand** means there are no Thousands, Hundreds, Tens or Units.
The number must end in 0 000.

c) **To round 3 257 432 to the nearest 100 000**

Hundred Thousands digit   Deciding digit

3 **2**57 432

When the deciding digit is **5**, **round up**.
The hundred thousands digit increases by 1.

3 257 432 to the nearest hundred thousand is **3 300 000.**

A number rounded to the nearest Hundred Thousand ends in 00 000.

d) **To round 3 257 432 to the nearest 1 000 000**

Millions digit   Deciding digit

3 256 432   2 is **less than 5**, so **round down**.

3 256 432 to the nearest million is **3 000 000**.

A number rounded to the nearest **Million** ends in 000 000.

Practice

1 Round each number to the nearest 1000.

a) 4562   b) 6500   c) 27 421   d) 30 950
e) 255 756   f) 105 220   g) 951 021   h) 1 365 500

2 Round each number to the nearest 10 000.

a) 29 000   b) 52 000   c) 145 000   d) 209 000
e) 765 900   f) 231 900   g) 684 625   h) 1 909 000

3 Round each number to the nearest 100 000.

a) 480 000   b) 320 000   c) 1 450 000   d) 4 608 000
e) 1 659 000   f) 2 783 540   g) 1 999 000   h) 12 832 359

4 Round the following numbers to the nearest 1 000 000.

a) 2 990 000   b) 3 050 000   c) 6 500 000
d) 15 650 000   e) 4 459 999   f) 1 755 000

Newspapers often use numbers that have been rounded.
They are easier to read and have more impact.

Example

24 989 fans attend football match!   or   25 000 fans attend football match!

The second headline is more likely to grab the reader's attention.

5 Round the numbers in the following headlines:

a) 2 987 000 unemployed

b) Company announces 7018 job losses

c) 12 756 people attend charity event

d) £1 987 649 lottery win

e) 4721 new jobs created

f) 3 005 021 copies of record sold

g) £21 095 000 profits for company

h) 278 650 people to benefit from new laser treatment

Activity

See how many numbers you can find in newspapers that have been rounded.

---

b Use estimates to check calculations

You can use an estimate to check whether the answer to a calculation is about the right size (sometimes said to be 'of the correct order').

Example

	Year 1	Year 2
Company profits	£145 270	£277 650

The chairman of the company says,
'In the second year company profits rose by over £132 000.'
Is this true?

To the nearest £10 000:   £145 270 is approximately £150 000
                           £277 600 is approximately £280 000

$280 - 150 = 130$ so £280 000 − £150 000 = £130 000
The answer is about the right size and the statement is **likely to be true**.

Practice

1 The table below gives the number of employees in the four main sectors of industry in the North East and South East regions of England in 2001.

| | Number of people employed 2001 | | | |
	Manufacturing	Wholesale and retail	Real estate	Health and social work
North East	175 489	167 224	94 564	131 628
South East	491 800	656 808	621 068	390 613

Source: Census 2001 Key Statistics for Health Areas in England and Wales

Use estimates to decide whether each statement is true or false.

a) Approximately 300 000 more people are employed in manufacturing in the South East than the North East. True or False?

b) Approximately twice as many people are employed in real estate in the South East as in the North East. True or False?

c) Nearly three times as many people are employed in health and social work in the South East as in the North East. True or False?

d) Nearly 200 000 more people are employed in wholesale and retail than real estate in the North East. True or False?

e) Roughly 35 000 more people are employed in wholesale and retail than real estate in the South East. True or False?

f) Over 150 000 more people are employed in wholesale and retail than manufacturing in the South East. True or False?

g) Approximately 20 000 more people are employed in manufacturing than wholesale and retail in the North East. True or False?

You will need to carry out a series of calculations with large numbers to solve the following problem. Use estimation to check your answers at each stage.

2 The money taken at a charity concert is listed below in the income table.
The expenditure table shows the costs of putting on the concert.

Income	Total £
2976 tickets @ £25 each	
2204 tickets @ £12 each	
1008 programmes @ £3 each	
592 souvenir mugs @ £8 each	
Total	

Expenditure	Total £
Hire of venue and insurance	17 750
Publicity and printing	4899
8 technicians @ £489 each	
50 security staff @ £175 each	
Performers (donated time)	0
Total	

a) Copy and complete the tables to find the total income and expenditure.

b) Calculate the difference between the total income and expenditure to find out how much money was raised.

Use estimates to check calculations with numbers of any size

N1/L2.2

Use estimates to check whether answers are of an appropriate size i.e. 'of the correct order' even when using a calculator.

Example   The table gives UK cinema admissions (no. of tickets sold)
How many more admissions were there in 1991 than 1990?

1990	97.37 million
1991	100.29 million

100.29 – 97.37 = 2.92 million = **2 920 000**

Check 100 million – 97 million = 3 million
This agrees as 2 920 000 rounded to the nearest million is 3 million.

$$\begin{array}{r} 100.29 - \\ \underline{97.37} \\ 2.92 \end{array}$$

Practice

1 The table gives the number of people who visited cinemas in each year shown.

   a) Use a calculator to find the increase or decrease in cinema admissions between consecutive years shown in the table.
   Give your answers in full.

   b) Use estimation to check that your answers are of the right order.

Cinema admissions (millions)	
1935	912.33
1945	1 585.00
1955	1 181.80
1965	326.60
1975	116.30
1985	72.00
1995	114.56

Source: BFI Film and Television Handbook

2 The table gives the wins in the national lottery.

   a) Use a calculator to find the total prize money.
   b) Use estimates to check your answer to a).

Prize	No. of winners
£9 087 130	1
£115 618	9
£1 947	695
£68	31 248
£10	789 236

Number

5 Ratio and Proportion

Work with ratio and proportion

N1/L1.7

a Ratios

When you dilute drinks or chemicals or follow a ~   ou need to mix ingredients in the correct **ratio** to get the right result. The ~   ven in terms of 'parts'. The size of a 'part' depends on how much of the m~

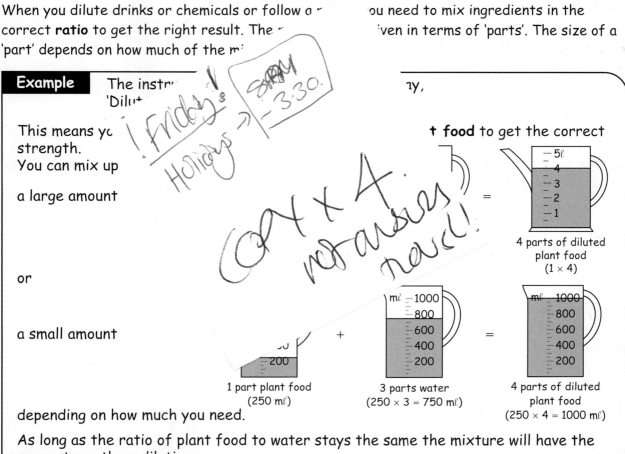

| Example | The instr~ 'Dilu+ | ~y, |

This means yc strength.
You can mix up

a large amount

t food to get the correct

4 parts of diluted plant food (1 × 4)

or

a small amount

1 part plant food (250 mℓ) + 3 parts water (250 × 3 = 750 mℓ) = 4 parts of diluted plant food (250 × 4 = 1000 mℓ)

depending on how much you need.

As long as the ratio of plant food to water stays the same the mixture will have the same strength or dilution.

Example   Instructions for mixing pink paint say "Mix 1 part red with 4 parts white".

a) How much white paint should you mix with 500 mℓ of red paint?
b) How much red paint should you mix with 500 mℓ of white paint?

a) Red paint   1 part = 500 mℓ
   White paint   4 parts = 500 × 4 = **2000 mℓ** or **2 litres**
                                  (1 litre = 1000 mℓ)
b) White paint   4 parts = 500 mℓ
   Red paint   1 part = 500 ÷ 4 = **125 mℓ** $\frac{1\ 2\ 5}{4\overline{)5^{1}0^{2}0}}$

Practice

1 a) How much water should you mix with 50 mℓ of orange squash?

   b) How much water should you mix with 100 mℓ of orange squash?

   c) If you mix the correct amount of water with 200 mℓ of orange squash, how much diluted squash will you have?

Dilute 1 part orange squash with 4 parts water

2 a) How much water should you mix with 250 mℓ of shampoo?

   b) How much water should you mix with 500 mℓ of shampoo?

   c) If the correct amount of water is mixed with 800 mℓ of shampoo, will it fit into a 5 litre (5000 mℓ) bucket?

Mix one part shampoo with six parts warm water

Carpet Shampoo

3

For **standard** mortar mix 1 part cement with 5 parts sand.
For **strong** mortar mix 1 part cement with 3 parts sand

		Cement	Sand
Standard		5 kg	
mortar			50 kg
		15 kg	
Strong		3 kg	
mortar		12 kg	
			60 kg

Hint:
For sand **multiply** by 5 (or 3)
For cement **divide** by 5 (or 3)

Copy and complete the table by giving the missing quantities for sand and cement.

b Direct proportion

Sometimes instructions give the amount of each ingredient rather than using 'parts'. If you need more (or less) of the mixture then you need to increase (or decrease) the quantity of each ingredient **in proportion**.

For example   to **double** the amount, **multiply everything by 2**

to make **five** times as much, **multiply everything by 5**

to make **half** the amount, **divide everything by 2**

to make a **third** of the amount, **divide everything by 3**.

Example

Mushroom Soup (*serves 4*)

225 g mushrooms	1 onion	1 potato
710 mℓ milk	50 g butter	5 mℓ thyme
sprig of parsley	salt & pepper to taste	

How much of each ingredient do you need to make mushroom soup for 8 people?

For twice as many people, you need double the amount of soup. You need to double the amount of each ingredient.

450 g mushrooms   **2 onions**   **2 potatoes**   **1420 mℓ milk**
100 g butter   **10 mℓ thyme**   **2 sprigs of parsley**   **salt & pepper to taste**

> **Example**   The instructions on a bottle of floor cleaner say,
> 'Pour 2 capfuls (30 mℓ) into a bucket with 6 litres of water.'
>
> **a)** How much floor cleaner should you use with 3 litres of water?
> **b)** How much floor cleaner should you use with 1 litre of water?
>
> **a)** The amount of water has been halved (divided by 2), so the amount of floor
> cleaner should be halved. This means you need **1 capful (15 mℓ)** of floor cleaner.
>
> **b)** This is a third of the amount of water in part a.
> You should use a third of the amount of floor cleaner. $15 \div 3 = 5$
> This means you need **5 mℓ (a third of a capful)** of floor cleaner.

Practice

1 a) Rewrite the naan bread recipe to make

  i)   12 breads
  ii)   3 breads.

b) How much milk, flour and yogurt do you need to make 2 breads?

Naan Bread Ingredients

150 mℓ milk	2 teaspoons caster sugar
450 g plain flour	2 teaspoons dried yeast
150 mℓ plain yogurt	½ teaspoon salt
1 egg	1 teaspoon baking powder
	2 tablespoons vegetable oil

Makes 6 breads

---

2 How many teaspoons of gravy granules do you need to make

  a) 560 mℓ (1 pint) of gravy
  b) 140 mℓ (¼ pint) of gravy
  c) 70 mℓ (⅛ pint) of gravy?

Gravy granules
Mix 4 teaspoons of granules with 280 mℓ (½ pint) of water

3 a) How much water should you mix with these amounts of plaster?
  i)   1250 g   **ii)** 500 g   **iii)** 250 g
  (Note: 1 litre = 1 000 mℓ)

b) How much water and plaster should you mix together to cover
  i)   2 square metres   **ii)** 4 square metres?

1 litre of water mixed with 2 500g of plaster will will cover 1 square metre

Calculate ratio and direct proportion

a Simplify ratios and find amounts

The ratio '1 part plant food to 3 parts water' can be written as 1 : 3.
This form is useful for simplifying ratios with large numbers and units of measurement.

> ▶ **To simplify a ratio, divide both sides by the same number.**
> This is like simplifying fractions – see page 87.

Suppose a recipe for pastry uses 100 g of butter and 200 g flour.
The ratio of butter to flour is 100 : 200.

When the units are the same you do not need to write them in the ratio.

In this case, you can divide by 100.
(or by 10 then 10 again, or by 5 then 20)
The ratio of butter to flour is 1 : 2.
This means there is twice as much flour as butter.

1 : 2

This ratio can be applied to any quantity.
The table shows some possibilities.

Butter	Flour
50 g	100 g
75 g	150 g
200 g	400 g

Example   The recipe for a children's cocktail says, 'Mix 75 mℓ of strawberry syrup with 100 mℓ of apple juice and 150 mℓ of mango juice.'

a) Write this as a ratio in its simplest form.
b) How much mango juice and apple juice should you mix with 120 mℓ of strawberry syrup?

strawberry   mango   apple

a) The ratio of the ingredients is   75 : 100 : 150.
To simplify this, divide each number by 25 (or 5 then 5 again).
The ratio of strawberry syrup to mango juice to apple juice is   **3 : 4 : 6.**

b) Using the ratio 3 : 4 : 6   if 3 parts strawberry syrup = 120 mℓ
then 1 part = 120 ÷ 3 = 40 mℓ
4 parts mango juice = 4 × 40 = **160 mℓ**
6 parts apple juice = 6 × 40 = **240 mℓ**

> ▶ **Find one part first, then multiply to find each amount.**

Practice

1 Simplify the ratio in each statement.

  a) The ratio of men to women at a party is 20 : 30.
  b) The ratio of management to staff in a factory is 30 : 150.
  c) In a batch of light bulbs the ratio of good to faulty is 7000 : 500.
  d) The ratio of helpers to children is 12 : 54.
  e) The ratio of home to away supporters at a match is 24 000 : 8000.
  f) The ratio of games won, drawn and lost is 12 : 3 : 18.
  g) The ratio of A, B and C exam grades is 30 : 45 : 75.
  h) The ratio of votes for 3 candidates is 132 000 : 72 000 : 40 000.

> **Note**
> **Keep dividing until you have the smallest possible numbers.**

2 a) Look at the instructions for coffee machines.
    i) Write the ratio of descaler to water in its simplest form.
    ii) How much water should you mix with 100 mℓ of descaler?

  b) Look at the instructions for kettles.
    i) Write the ratio of descaler to water in its simplest form.
    ii) How much water should you mix with 400 mℓ of descaler?

> For coffee machines mix 125 mℓ of descaler with 500 mℓ of water.
>
> For kettles mix 500 mℓ of descaler with 750 mℓ of water.

3 a) *Use the information for velvet green paint.*
    i) Write the quantities of white, moss and leaf green paint as a ratio in its simplest form.
    ii) How much moss and leaf green paint should you mix with 80 mℓ of white paint?
    iii) How much white and leaf green paint should you mix with 1800 mℓ of moss paint?

  b) *Use the information for sepia tint paint.*
    i) Write the quantities of white, beige and chocolate brown paint as a ratio in its simplest form.
    ii) How much beige and chocolate brown paint should you mix with 80 mℓ of white paint?
    iii) How much white and chocolate brown paint should you mix with 180 mℓ of beige paint?
    iv) How much white and beige paint should you mix with 750 mℓ of chocolate brown paint?

Mix and Match Paints
Velvet Green
To make 1 litre (1000 mℓ) mix:
50 mℓ White
450 mℓ Moss
500 mℓ Leaf Green
Sepia Tint
To make 1 litre (1000 mℓ) mix:
200 mℓ White
300 mℓ Beige
500 mℓ Chocolate Brown

▶ Quantities must be in the **same units** before you can simplify the ratio.

Example   The instructions on a bottle of cleaning fluid say,
'Mix 50 mℓ of cleaning fluid with 1 litre of water.'

How much water should you mix with 80 mℓ of cleaning fluid?

The ratio of cleaning fluid to water is 50 mℓ : 1 litre.
It is easier to convert the larger units into the smaller ones.
        1 litre = 1000 mℓ

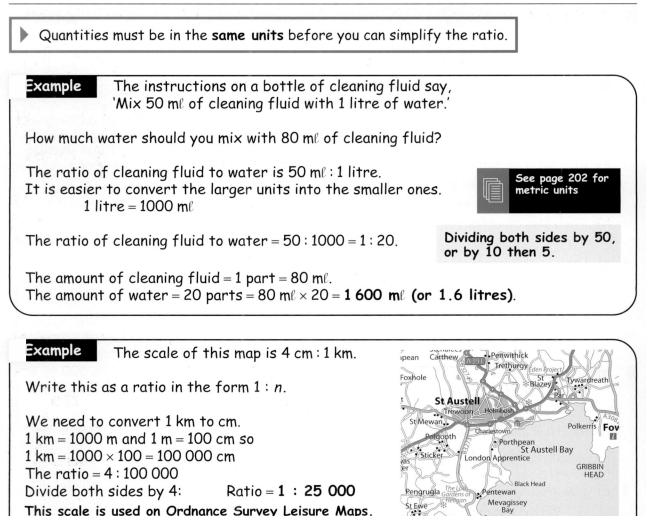

> See page 202 for metric units

The ratio of cleaning fluid to water = 50 : 1000 = 1 : 20.

> **Dividing both sides by 50, or by 10 then 5.**

The amount of cleaning fluid = 1 part = 80 mℓ.
The amount of water = 20 parts = 80 mℓ × 20 = **1 600 mℓ (or 1.6 litres)**.

Example   The scale of this map is 4 cm : 1 km.

Write this as a ratio in the form 1 : *n*.

We need to convert 1 km to cm.
1 km = 1000 m and 1 m = 100 cm so
1 km = 1000 × 100 = 100 000 cm
The ratio = 4 : 100 000
Divide both sides by 4:   Ratio = **1 : 25 000**
This scale is used on Ordnance Survey Leisure Maps.

---

4 Write each ratio in its simplest form.

  a) lawn food : water = 30 mℓ : 1 litre
  b) chocolate : toffee = 1 kg : 800 g
  c) lace trim : ribbon = 25 cm : 1 m
  d) card : stamp = £1.95 : 30p
  e) map : actual distance = 2 cm : 1 km
  f) cost : VAT = £50 : £8.75
  g) cement : lime : sand = 500 kg : 1 tonne : 4.5 tonnes
  h) flour : butter : sugar : dried fruit = 1 lb : 8 oz : 8 oz : 12 oz

Conversions	
1 litre = 1000 mℓ	1 m = 100 cm
1 kg = 1000 g	1 m = 1000 mm
1 tonne = 1000 kg	1 km = 1000 m
1 lb = 16 oz	

5 a) Write the ratio of weedkiller and water in its simplest form.
  b) How much water is needed with 40 mℓ of weedkiller?
  c) How much weedkiller is needed with 2400 mℓ of water?

Weed Killer

Mix 50 mℓ Weed Killer with 4 litres water

6 A pet shop makes 'Small Pet Food Mix' by mixing $1\frac{1}{2}$ kg cereal, 400 g nuts and 200 g seeds.

    a) Write these quantities in the same units as a ratio, then simplify it.   (Note: 1 kg = 1000 g)

    b) The mixture is always made with the ingredients in the same proportion.

        i) What quantity of cereal and nuts are mixed with 20 g of seeds?

        ii) What quantity of nuts and seeds are mixed with 600 g of cereal?

For more practice with scale diagrams and maps see page 180.

7 The scale on a map is 1 : 50 000.

    a) What does 1 cm on the map represent? Give your answer in metres.

    b) What does 2 cm on the map represent? Give your answer in kilometres.

b Make a total amount

Sometimes you need to find the quantity of each ingredient to make a particular total amount.

Example

How much anti-freeze and how much water do you need to make 1 litre (1000 mℓ) of diluted anti-freeze?

The ratio 1 : 3 means
1 part anti-freeze + 3 parts water
= 4 parts diluted anti-freeze.

Add the parts to find the total number of parts.

These 4 parts need to make 1000 mℓ so 1 part = 1000 ÷ 4 = 250 mℓ.

Divide to find one part.

Amount of anti-freeze = 1 part = **250 mℓ**.
Amount of water = 3 parts = 3 × 250 = **750 mℓ**.

Check your answer by adding: 250 mℓ anti-freeze + 750 mℓ water
                            = 1000 mℓ diluted anti-freeze.

Practice

1 The instructions on a bottle of squash say 'Dilute one part orange squash with four parts water.'

How much squash and how much water do you need to make

    a) 1 litre of diluted squash   (Remember 1 litre = 1000 mℓ)

    b) $1\frac{1}{2}$ litres of diluted squash?

2 How much of each colour do I need to make:

    a) 5 litres   **b)** 1 litre of 'Sunny Day' paint?

> **Mix and Match Paints**
>
> To make **Sunny Day** mix
> 1 part Tangerine paint,
> 1 part White paint and
> 3 parts Buttercup paint

3 A health shop mixes ingredients to make bags of muesli.
The amounts for a 1 kg bag are: 600 g cereal, 250 g fruit,
150 g nuts.

    a) Write this as a ratio in its simplest form.
    b) Calculate how much of each ingredient is needed to make
        i) 800 g of muesli   **ii)** 1800 g of muesli.

4 The population of a town consists of 15 000 Afro-Caribbean people, 45 000 Asian people
and 150 000 white people.

    a) Write this information as a ratio and simplify it.
    b) A new company in the town plans to employ 420 people. If the number of employees
        from these ethnic groups is in the same ratio as the population, how many employees
        will be from each group?

5 Ahmed, Ben and Cilla invest £4000, £10 000 and £16 000 in a new business.
They agree to share any profits in the ratio of their investments.

    a) Write the investments as a ratio in its simplest form.
    b) In its first year the company makes a profit of £45 000.
        How much does each person get?
    c) Ben gets £25 000 from the second year's profits.
        What was the total profit for the second year?
    d) Cilla gets £100 000 from the third year's profits.
        What was the total profit for the third year?
    e) Find the total amount received by each person during these 3 years.

c Use ratios to compare prices

You can compare prices by finding the value of a 'part'.

Example

The 200 g jar of coffee costs £2.80
The 300 g jar costs £3.99. Which is better value?

The ratio of the weights of the jars = 200 : 300 = 2 : 3.
The smaller jar has 2 parts and the larger jar has 3 parts
For the smaller jar: Cost of 1 part = £2.80 ÷ 2 = £1.40
For the larger jar: Cost of 1 part = £3.99 ÷ 3 = £1.33
The **larger** jar is the better value.

> ▶ Find the cost of 1 part for each jar.
> (This is the cost per 100 g in this case.)

There are other ways to work out the best value. In the example you could find the cost per 100 g for the smaller jar, then multiply by 3 and compare the result with the cost of the larger jar. You could use this way as a check.

Practice

1 In each case find which is the better value:

a)
Toilet Rolls 9   £2.70
Toilet Rolls 12   £4.20

b)
shampoo 400 ml   £2.90
shampoo 600 ml   £4.20

c)
Corn Flakes 350 g   £2.80
Corn Flakes 450 g   £3.90

d)
Envelopes 100   £1.25
Envelopes 200   £4.50
Envelopes 500   £9.99

e)
99p
£2.25
£5.19

2 A builders' merchant delivers loose sand at £17.50 for 0.5 tonne, £32.50 for 1 tonne or £120 for 5 tonnes. The builders' merchant also sells bags of sand at £1.75 for a 25 kg bag and £2.50 for a 40 kg bag.
A local store charges £1.50 for a 5 kg bag of sand.

a) Calculate the price per tonne in each case.   (Remember 1 tonne = 1000 kg)
b) A builder buys 0.5 tonnes loose sand from the builders' merchant but only uses 0.3 tonnes. He sells the rest at the same rate as he paid for it.
How much money does he get from the sale?
c) What would a 5 kg bag cost if it was charged at the same rate as 5 tonnes of loose sand?

Number

6 Using Formulae

Evaluate expressions and make substitutions in formulae   N1/L2.4

A **formula** is a relationship between quantities. It can be written in words or as an algebraic expression. Formulae are used in many areas such as science, engineering and finance and also for working things out on a spreadsheet.

Suppose when someone hires a church hall, they pay £20 per hour plus a fixed administration fee of £10.
For 2 hours the total charge is $2 \times £20 + £10 = £50$.
For 5 hours the total charge is $5 \times £20 + £10 = £110$.
In general the formula in words for total charge is:

$$\textbf{Total charge = number of hours} \times \textbf{£20 + £10}$$

You can write this formula more neatly using letters. If you use 'C' for the total charge in £s and 'n' for 'the number of hours', the formula becomes:

$$C = n \times \textbf{20 + 10}$$

When using letters, we usually leave out the $\times$ for multiplication to avoid confusing it with the letter x. We also write the number in $n \times 20$ first, so the formula becomes:

$$C = \textbf{20}n + \textbf{10}$$

> **20n means 20 × n**

You can use the formula to work out the charge for hiring the hall for other times.
e.g. to find the charge for 8 hours, **substitute** 8 for n and work out:

$$C = 20 \times 8 + 10 = 160 + 10 = \textbf{£170}$$

Practice

1 **a)** Hiring a hotel conference room for a day costs £15 per delegate plus a fixed charge of £75. Write this as a formula
   i)   in words
   ii) in letters using T for the total cost in £s and d for the number of delegates.

   b) Use your formula to calculate the cost of a day's hire for
   i) 10 delegates   **ii)** 20 delegates   **iii)** 50 delegates.

2 A cookery book gives this formula for the time to roast a joint of meat:
Time in minutes = number of kilograms × 50 minutes + 25 minutes extra.

   a) Write this as a formula in letters using C for the total cooking time in minutes and w for the weight of the joint in kilograms.

   b) Use your formula to find the cooking time for a joint of meat weighing
     i) 2 kg   **ii)** 2.5 kg   **iii)** 0.8 kg.

3 A taxi company charges £0.80 a mile plus a £2 call-out fee.

   a) Write this as a formula using F for the total fare in £s and m for the number of miles.

   b) Use your formula to calculate the total fare for a journey of
     i) 5 miles   **ii)** 12 miles   **iii)** 17.5 miles.

4 Each week a sales assistant earns £2.50 for each customer account he opens plus his basic pay of £180.

   a) Write this as a formula using P for the total pay in £s and a for the number of customer accounts.

   b) Use your formula to find how much he earns in a week when he opens
     i) 4 accounts   **ii)** 10 accounts   **iii)** 15 accounts.

5 A firm uses this formula to work out the cost of producing Christmas cards:

$$C = 0.05n + 30$$

where C is the total cost in £s and n is the number of cards produced.

   a) Find the cost of producing
     i) 200 cards   **ii)** 1000 cards   **iii)** 8000 cards.
   b) What does the number 0.05 in the formula represent?
   c) What happens to the overall cost per card if more cards are produced?

Suppose a church charges £20 an hour for the hire of its hall, £5 an hour for the hire of its kitchen plus a fixed administration charge of £10.
What is the total charge for hiring the hall and kitchen for 3 hours?

The correct answer is £85. Did you get this? How did you work it out?
One way is to add the two charges per hour together first: £20 + £5 = £25
Then multiply by 3 to find the charge for 3 hours: £25 × 3 = £75
Then add the £10 administration charge: £75 + £10 = £85

This arithmetic can be written as one expression: $3 \times (£20 + £5) + £10$
The brackets show the part that is worked out first.

When you do arithmetic it is essential to add, subtract, multiply or divide the numbers in the correct order. The mathematical convention that you must follow is often called **BODMAS**:

Work out brackets first	then ÷ or ×	+ and – last	Note
B	**O** **D** **M**	**A** **S**	'Other' includes
brackets	other divide multiply	add subtract	squares see p. 30 and p. 228.

For example, $8 + 12 \div 4 = 8 + 3 = 11$ (**not** $20 \div 4 = 5$). **Divide** before **adding**.

Scientific calculators are programmed to do calculations in the right order.
Take care – many other calculators are not! Check these on your calculator:

Examples

$3 + 2 \times 3 = 9$ (multiply 2×3 first) $3 \times (3 + 2) = 15$ (add $3 + 2$ first)
$15 - 9 \div 3 = 12$ (divide 9 by 3 first) $(15 - 9) \div 3 = 2$ (take 9 from 15 first)

---

6 Calculate these without a calculator – take care to use the right order.

a) $5 + 2 \times 7$ b) $10 - 2 \times 5$ c) $6 \times 3 + 2$
d) $10 + 12 \div 2$ e) $20 - 8 \div 2$ f) $(20 - 8) \div 2$
g) $2 \times (5 + 7)$ h) $2 \times (3 + 7 + 1)$ i) $5 \times 4 - (6 - 3)$

Check your answers on your calculator.

BODMAS also applies to formulae.

Example

When a car accelerates smoothly the distance in metres it travels is given by
$d = \frac{t(u + v)}{2}$ where u metres per second is its starting speed, v metres per second is its final speed and t seconds is the time taken.

The brackets mean you should add u and v first. Then multiply by t because this is next to the brackets (remember this means x). Finally divide by 2.

So if a car accelerates from 8 metres per second to 12 metres per second in 5 seconds the distance it travels is:

$$d = \frac{5(8 + 12)}{2} = \frac{5 \times 20}{2} = \frac{100}{2} = \textbf{50 metres}$$

This means ÷ 2 after working out the top.

---

7 Use the formula in the above example to calculate the distance d when

a) $t = 10$, $u = 0$ and $v = 10$ b) $t = 3$, $u = 7$ and $v = 11$.

8 A demonstrator earns £6 an hour plus £5 for every sewing machine she sells.

a) Write this as a formula. Use P to represent the total pay in £s, t to represent the number of hours worked and n to represent the number of machines sold.

b) Use your formula to calculate the total pay if she
 i) works 8 hours and sells 3 machines
 ii) works 15 hours and sells 5 machines
 iii) works 40 hours and sells 12 machines.

9 A building society uses the formula $M = 3(A + B)$ to calculate the maximum loan it allows a couple to have.

M is the maximum loan and A and B are their annual incomes in £s.

Calculate the maximum loan the couple can have when:

a) $A = £15\,000$ and $B = £12\,000$ **b)** $A = £20\,000$ and $B = £18\,000$

c) $A = £35\,000$ and $B = £30\,000$ **d)** $A = £54\,700$ and $B = £38\,250$.

10 Use the formula $V = IR$ where V = voltage, I = current in amps and R = resistance in ohms to find V when $I = 2.4$ and $R = 50$.

11 Use the formula $s = \dfrac{d}{t}$ where s = average speed, d = distance and t = time to find s when

a) $d = 150$ miles and $t = 2.5$ hours   **b)** $d = 6$ km and $t = 15$ mins.

12 Skiing tuition costs a fixed charge of £10 for insurance plus £18 per hour for the instructor and £E per hour for equipment hire(depends on the equipment).

a) Write this as a formula using C to represent the total cost in £s and n to represent the number of hours.

b) Use your formula to calculate the cost for
 i) 3 hours when $E = 5$ **ii)** 5 hours when $E = 7$ **iii)** $7\frac{1}{2}$ hours when $E = 10.5$.

13 The formula for calculating the area of a trapezium is

$A = \dfrac{h(a + b)}{2}$ (Assume all the lengths are in cm.)

For more area and volume formulae see page 230 and 235.

Find the area of a trapezium when

a) $a = 6$, $b = 3$ and $h = 4$ **b)** $a = 10$, $b = 7$ and $h = 8$

c) $a = 4.5$, $b = 2.5$ and $h = 3$ **d)** $a = 25$, $b = 13$ and $h = 15$.

14 Use the formula $C = \dfrac{5(F - 32)}{9}$ where C = temperature in °Celsius and F = temperature in °Fahrenheit to find C when

a) $F = 212$ **b)** $F = 77$.

Activity

You can use formulae in a spreadsheet programme to carry out calculations.
If you have access to a computer with a spreadsheet, try this example, then experiment with other numbers and situations.

Example   An employee's time sheet shows the hours she has worked:

Monday 6,   Tuesday 7,   Wednesday 8,
Thursday 7,   Friday 5

She earns £8 an hour. Follow the instructions to find her wage for the week.

● Enter the days of the week in cells A1 to E1.

● Enter the number of hours in cells A2 to E2.

● In cell F2 enter: =8*SUM(A2:E2) and press enter.

(Note the symbol * means multiply so this formulae means 8 × the sum of the amounts in cells A2 to E2.)
Cell F2 should show **£264**, the amount the employee has earned.

Number

7 Mixed Operations and Calculator Practice

Solve problems N1/E3.9

When you use maths to solve real-life problems, take care to choose the correct operations (+, −, × or ÷). Always **check that your answer is sensible**, especially if you use a calculator, as it is easy to press the wrong button.

If you do enter a wrong number, you may be able to correct it by pressing the CE (Clear Entry) button. This deletes the last number you entered, without clearing the whole sum. The C (Clear) button, often in red, clears everything. However, calculators vary – check how your calculator works.

Example A householder buys a new table for £499.

a) She pays £280 deposit. How much is left to pay?
b) She pays the rest in 6 equal instalments. How much is each instalment?

Work it out on paper
a) For the amount left to pay
work out 499 − 280

$$499 - 280 \atop \underline{£219}$$

then check on your calculator
Press
4 9 9 − 2 8 0 =
The calculator will give **219**

b) To find an instalment
work out 219 ÷ 6

$$6\overline{)21^39.^30} = 36.5$$

Carry on the calculation
÷ 6 =
The calculator will give 36.5

See p. 100 for money in decimals

This means **£36.50** ← To show the pence add a zero at the end.

Practice

Work these out on paper, then check with a calculator.

1 Jars of jam are packed in boxes of 72.
How many jars of jam are there in 8 boxes?

2 A prize of £936 is shared equally between six people.
How much do they get each?

3 There are 196 men, 218 women and 372 children staying in a hotel.
a) How many people is this altogether?
b) How many more women than men are there?

4   A householder pays £65 cash plus 6 instalments of £78 for a new cooker.
    a) What is the total of the instalments?
    b) How much does he pay altogether?

5   Two friends book a holiday. The total cost is £994.
    a) They pay a deposit of £99. How much is left to pay altogether?
    b) How much has each friend left to pay? Assume they split the cost equally.

6   A worker earns £17 per hour overtime.
    a) How much does she earn for 9 hours overtime?
    b) Her basic wage is £418 per week. How much does she earn altogether?

7   A new car has a mileage of 278 at the beginning of June and 548 at the end of June.
    a) How many miles has the car travelled in June?
    b) How many miles is this per day? (There are 30 days in June.)

Sometimes working things out without a calculator is easier, especially with small numbers.

Example

Paint is sold in 5 litre, 2 litre and 1 litre tins.
The bigger the tin, the better the value, i.e. the
bigger the tin, the cheaper the price per litre.

A decorator needs 17 litres of red paint.
What tins should she buy?

5 litres   2 litres   1 litre

The 5 litre tins are the best value, so the
decorator should buy most of the paint in these.

$17 \div 5 = 3$ remainder 2

Three 5 litre tins

2 more litres are needed

The decorator should buy **three 5 litre tins and one 2 litre tin**.

Working out $17 \div 5$ on a calculator gives 3.4 (5 goes into 17 'three and a bit times').
This means you need 3 whole 5 litre tins and 0.4 (just under half) of the next 5 litre
tin. If you decide to buy just three 5 litre tins, you must calculate further to see how
much more paint you need:

$3 \times 5 = 15$ $17 - 15 = 2$ i.e. you need another 2 litre tin (as above).

---

8   Find the cheapest combination of tins for

    a) 27 litres   b) 39 litres   c) 128 litres

    This means use a
    calculator for part c).

9   Paper plates can be bought in packs of 10, 25 or 50.
    What combination of packs gives **exactly**

    a) 40 plates   b) 75 plates   c) 275 plates   d) 360 plates?

Example   A sofa costs £785 in cash. You can also buy it on credit with a deposit of £50 and 9 monthly payments of £90. How much extra is this?

9 monthly payments of £90 costs $9 \times £90 = £810$
To find the total cost, add the £50 deposit $£810 + £50 = £860$
Extra cost = difference between the 2 amounts $£860 - £785 = £\textbf{75}$

You can do these calculations on a calculator as follows:

          $9 \times 90 = 810$ $+ 50 = 860$ $- 785 = 75$

▶ **On some calculators you must do 9 × 90 first and then + 50. If you enter 50 + 90 × 9, such calculators add 50 and 90, then multiply the total by 9, giving an answer that is much too big! Check how your calculator works.**

10   Pay £99 cash or £20 deposit and   Pay £690 today or £45 deposit and
     6 payments of £15   9 payments of £75

a)   How much more does it cost to buy the armchair on credit?
b)   How much more does it cost to buy the three-piece suite on credit?

11

The pack of 2 batteries is on special offer.
If you buy 2 packs you get one pack free (so a total of 6 batteries costs £6).

Find the cheapest combination of packs to get

a) 6 batteries   **b)** 8 batteries   **c)** 10 batteries   **d)** 12 batteries.

12

Theme Park Admission Rates	
Standard Price	£25
Children (16 and under)	£15
Family Ticket (2 adults and 2 children)	£75
Group Ticket (10 people of any age)	£200

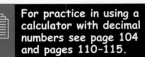

Find the cheapest combination of tickets for

a) 2 adults and one child

b) 1 adult and 5 children

c) 2 adults and 3 children

d) 8 adults

e) 4 adults and 6 children

f) 5 adults and 5 children

For practice in using a calculator with decimal numbers see page 104 and pages 110–115.

Calculate efficiently

N2/L1.11

Calculators are useful for working with large or difficult numbers and problems that involve several stages. It is very easy to enter a number incorrectly, so it is important to check that the answer you get is sensible. You can check your answer using estimation or by reversing the process to take you back to the number you started with.

Example   Two jobs are advertised in a newspaper:

Which job pays the higher **annual** salary and by how much?

Administration clerk's annual salary
= £980 × 12 = £11 760.
Office assistant's annual salary
= £229 × 52 = £11 908.
The **office assistant** has the higher annual salary.
Difference between salaries = £11 908 – £11 760
                        = £**148**.

Checks:
11 760 ÷ 12 = 980

11 908 ÷ 52 = 229

148 + 11 760 = 11 908

Job@lert
Administration Clerk
£980 per month

Office Assistant
£229 per week

If your calculator has a memory, you can store the answer 11 760 so you don't need to enter it again. On most calculators pressing M+ stores the number. When you want to use it again, press MR (Memory Recall).

However, calculators vary – find out how yours works.

Practice

1   Which job pays the higher **annual** salary and by how much?

a) | Sales assistant £5 an hour 20 hours a week | or | Part-time receptionist £450 a month |

b) | Warehouse assistant £240 a week | or | Delivery worker £990 a month |

Check your working using division (as in the example).

2 Use the information in the table.

Hotel	Cost per person for 2 nights (£)	Cost per person per extra night (£)
Grand	199	45
Splendid	227	52
Magnificent	255	63
Supremo	312	71

a) Calculate the cost for 🖩
   i) 2 people spending 3 nights in the Hotel Grand
   ii) 4 people spending 4 nights in the Hotel Splendid
   iii) 4 people spending 5 nights in the Hotel Magnificent.

b) How much more expensive is it for 4 people to spend 4 nights in the Hotel Supremo than the Hotel Magnificent?

Check your working by rounding the numbers and estimating

c) How much more expensive is it for 4 people to spend 7 nights in the Hotel Supremo than the Hotel Grand?

d) A tourist has a budget of £650 for hotel accommodation. How many nights can she stay at
   i) the Hotel Grand   ii) the Hotel Supremo?

Calculate efficiently with numbers of any size   N1/L2.2, N2/L2.10

Negative numbers can be entered into most calculators using the [+/−] button. This changes positive numbers into negative numbers. Some calculators have a [(−)] button instead. Consult your calculator booklet if necessary.

Example

A company has 2 factories. One makes a profit of £0.8 million, the other a loss of £1.5 million. What is the overall profit?

$$0.8 \text{ million} + {-}1.5 \text{ million} = -0.7 \text{ million}$$

There should be a minus sign before the 0.7 showing it is a negative number. The company has made an overall profit of −£0.7 million. This means a loss of £0.7 million.

To enter −1.5 press 1.5 then the [+/−] button. This changes 1.5 into a negative number.

Practice

1 The highest recorded temperature at a weather station was 28.7 °C.
The lowest recorded temperature was −26.9 °C.
What is the difference between these temperatures?

2 The table shows the profit made by a company in three consecutive years.
Calculate the total profit.

	Profit (£)
Year 1	£0.25 million
Year 2	−£0.76 million
Year 3	£1.42 million

3 The table gives the balance in a bank account at the beginning of each day at the end of February.
Calculate the total amount paid into or drawn out of the account each day.

Date	Balance (£)
25th Feb	564.32
26th Feb	−18.49
27th Feb	−835.60
28th Feb	1943.26
1st Mar	−154.42

4 At the beginning of each month Mr Woods pays £38 into his account with a gas company. He receives quarterly bills (at the end of every 3 months) showing the total charge for the gas used. They also show by how much his account is in debit or credit. This amount is then carried forward to the next quarter. The total charge for each quarter in a year is shown below.
Calculate by how much Mr Woods is in debit or credit at the end of each quarter.

1st quarter	£93.95	2nd quarter	£152.70
3rd quarter	£112.10	4th quarter	£87.15

5 a) Copy the table.
  b) Use the information below to write the profits for each year in your table.
  Write the numbers in full (in figures but not in decimal form) and show whether they are positive or negative.

In its first year of trading in 1995 MT Productions made a profit of £1.2 million. Profits fell by £500 000 in the second year, a further £1 million in the third year and £250 000 in 1998. In 1999 profits rose by £450 000 but 2000 brought about fresh disasters with profits falling again by £0.9 million. Profits then increased steadily by £500 000 per year reaching £500 000 in 2003.

Year	Profit (£)
1995	
1996	
1997	
1998	
1999	
2000	
2001	
2002	
2003	500 000

  c) Use your table to find
   i) the difference between the highest and lowest years' profits
   ii) the total profit made by MT Productions from 1995 to 2003.

Scientific calculators have other useful buttons, e.g. brackets.
If you have a scientific calculator, use the brackets buttons to calculate the answers to questions 7, 9, 12, 13 and 14 on page 61.
Also use the x^2 button to answer questions 1–5 on page 228.
For more practice use the questions on page 234.

Number

8 Fractions

Understand fractions

N2/E3.1

a Fractions in words, numbers and sketches

Each fraction has a top called the **numerator** and a bottom called the **denominator**.

These numbers are fractions: $\frac{1}{6}$, $\frac{2}{7}$, $\frac{7}{10}$ ← numerator

← denominator

You can show fractions by shading.

Examples

one sixth	two sevenths	seven tenths

1 out of 6 **equal** parts
$= \frac{1}{6}$

2 out of 7 **equal** parts
$= \frac{2}{7}$

7 out of 10 **equal** parts
$= \frac{7}{10}$

This is a **unit** fraction – it has 1 on the top.

Practice

1 Write these fractions as numbers.

   a) one third   **b)** two fifths   **c)** three eighths   **d)** five twelfths

2 Write these fractions in words.

   a) $\frac{1}{2}$ **b)** $\frac{2}{3}$ **c)** $\frac{3}{4}$ **d)** $\frac{3}{5}$ **e)** $\frac{5}{8}$ **f)** $\frac{7}{9}$

3　What fraction is shaded? Write your answers in words and numbers.

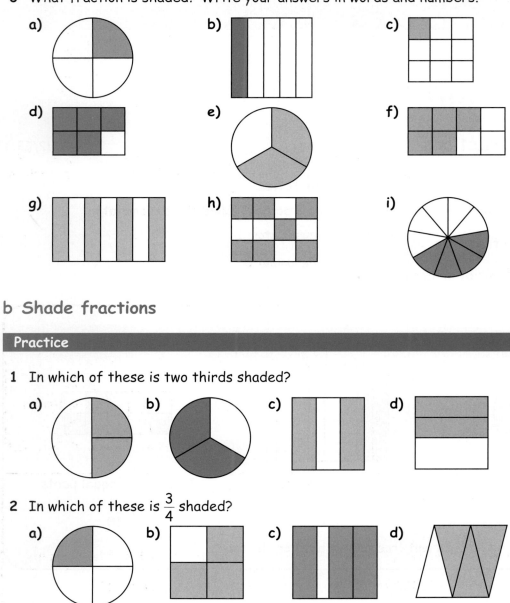

b　Shade fractions

Practice

1　In which of these is two thirds shaded?

a)　　　b)　　　c)　　　d)

2　In which of these is $\frac{3}{4}$ shaded?

a)　　　b)　　　c)　　　d)

3　Copy each sketch. Shade the fraction.

a)　$\frac{2}{5}$

b)　$\frac{3}{10}$

c)　$\frac{7}{8}$

d)　three sevenths

e)　five eighths

f)　eleven twelfths

4 Draw a sketch to show each fraction.

a) $\frac{1}{2}$ b) $\frac{1}{3}$ c) $\frac{1}{4}$ d) $\frac{1}{8}$ e) $\frac{1}{10}$ f) $\frac{4}{5}$

g) $\frac{3}{8}$ h) $\frac{2}{9}$ i) $\frac{6}{7}$ j) $\frac{9}{10}$ k) $\frac{5}{12}$ l) $\frac{11}{15}$

c Read about fractions

Fractions are used in many ways. For example, adverts often use fractions to describe special offers. Government reports and the media sometimes give survey results as fractions. Recipes in cookery books give some amounts in fractions.

Practice

Write down each fraction in words and in numbers.

1 Half price!

One third off!

2

Lentil Patties	
1 cup lentils	1 pint stock
$\frac{1}{4}$ cup peas	1 onion
$\frac{3}{4}$ cup potato	1 clove garlic
$1\frac{1}{2}$ tablespoons oil	$\frac{1}{2}$ tablespoon thyme
1 egg	salt & pepper

3

Investments Magazine

Next, Selfridges Offer U.K. Shoppers Discounts To Boost Sales

January 1, 2003

Next Plc and other British retailers are reducing their prices by as much as two thirds in post-Christmas sales.
Almost a third of the mall's 150 stores started reducing prices before Dec. 25.

4

Social Trends 33

'There were 24.4 million households in Great Britain in 2002, an increase of almost a third since 1971.'
'A quarter of non-married adults in Great Britain were cohabiting in 2000/01.'
'In England and Wales, the average age of women at the birth of their first child increased by one and a half years over the last decade.'
'Half of the men in the UK liked DIY repair work, compared with about one fifth of women. Conversely, three quarters of women surveyed said they liked non-food shopping, compared with just under half of men.'
'Almost three fifths of those aged 70 and over in Great Britain knew most or many of the people in their neighbourhood, compared with just over a third of those aged between 16 and 29.'

Source: www.statistics.gov.uk

Activity

Collect other examples where fractions are used.

Equivalent fractions

N2/E3.2

a Use sketches

Look at the sketches.

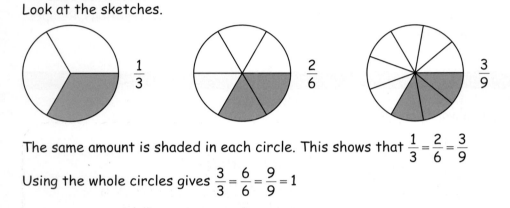

The same amount is shaded in each circle. This shows that $\dfrac{1}{3} = \dfrac{2}{6} = \dfrac{3}{9}$

Using the whole circles gives $\dfrac{3}{3} = \dfrac{6}{6} = \dfrac{9}{9} = 1$

Practice

1 What do these sketches show?

a)

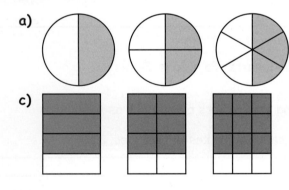

b)

c)

d)

2 Draw sketches to show that

a) $\dfrac{1}{2} = \dfrac{4}{8}$

b) $\dfrac{1}{2} = \dfrac{5}{10}$

c) $\dfrac{1}{4} = \dfrac{3}{12}$

d) $\dfrac{3}{5} = \dfrac{6}{10}$

e) $\dfrac{2}{3} = \dfrac{6}{9}$

f) $\dfrac{2}{5} = \dfrac{6}{15}$

g) $\dfrac{3}{4} = \dfrac{6}{8}$

h) $\dfrac{5}{6} = \dfrac{10}{12}$

i) $\dfrac{4}{5} = \dfrac{16}{20}$

b Find the missing number

Sketches on the last page showed $\frac{1}{3} = \frac{2}{6} = \frac{3}{9}$.

Although these fractions look different, they are the same size.

> ▶ **The size of a fraction is not altered when you multiply or divide the numerator (top) and denominator (bottom) by the same number.**

$$\overset{\times 2}{\underset{\times 2}{\frac{1}{3} = \frac{2}{6}}} \qquad\qquad \overset{\div 3}{\underset{\div 3}{\frac{3}{9} = \frac{1}{3}}}$$

You can find a missing numerator or denominator.

Examples

$$\frac{3}{5} = \frac{?}{10}$$

The bottom has been multiplied by 2
Do the same to the top:

$$\frac{3}{5} = \frac{6}{10}$$

$$\frac{12}{20} = \frac{3}{?}$$

The top has been divided by 4
Do the same to the bottom:

$$\frac{12}{20} = \frac{3}{5}$$

Practice

Find the missing numbers:

1 $\frac{1}{2} = \frac{?}{8}$

2 $\frac{2}{5} = \frac{?}{20}$

3 $\frac{1}{4} = \frac{?}{12}$

4 $\frac{3}{7} = \frac{?}{14}$

5 $\frac{1}{2} = \frac{5}{?}$

6 $\frac{3}{4} = \frac{6}{?}$

7 $\frac{2}{3} = \frac{8}{?}$

8 $\frac{4}{5} = \frac{20}{?}$

9 $\frac{6}{12} = \frac{?}{2}$

10 $\frac{5}{15} = \frac{?}{3}$

11 $\frac{12}{18} = \frac{?}{3}$

12 $\frac{14}{18} = \frac{?}{9}$

13 $\frac{14}{21} = \frac{2}{?}$

14 $\frac{12}{20} = \frac{3}{?}$

15 $\frac{20}{30} = \frac{2}{?}$

16 $\frac{16}{24} = \frac{4}{?}$

17 a) Find the missing numbers: $\frac{1}{7} = \frac{2}{?} = \frac{3}{?}$.

   b) Write down two other fractions that are equivalent to $\frac{1}{7}$.

18 a) Find the missing numbers: $\dfrac{5}{7} = \dfrac{?}{21} = \dfrac{?}{63}$.

  b) Write down two other fractions that are equivalent to $\dfrac{5}{7}$.

19 Find three other fractions that are equivalent to

  a) $\dfrac{3}{8}$ **b)** $\dfrac{2}{5}$ **c)** $\dfrac{4}{11}$ **d)** $\dfrac{7}{9}$.

20 The following fractions are all equal to 1. What are the missing numbers?

$$\frac{?}{2} \qquad \frac{?}{4} \qquad \frac{5}{?} \qquad \frac{7}{?} \qquad \frac{?}{11} \qquad \frac{15}{?} \qquad \frac{20}{?} \qquad \frac{?}{100}$$

c Find equivalent fractions in a list

Practice

1 Which of these fractions are equivalent to $\dfrac{1}{2}$?

$$\frac{2}{4}, \quad \frac{7}{12}, \quad \frac{3}{6}, \quad \frac{1}{6}, \quad \frac{6}{12}, \quad \frac{2}{3}, \quad \frac{3}{4}, \quad \frac{5}{10}, \quad \frac{6}{16}, \quad \frac{4}{8}, \quad \frac{1}{6}$$

2 a) List the fractions below that are equivalent to $\dfrac{1}{3}$.

  b) List those that are equivalent to $\dfrac{2}{3}$.

$$\frac{6}{9}, \quad \frac{6}{18}, \quad \frac{4}{12}, \quad \frac{5}{15}, \quad \frac{8}{12}, \quad \frac{2}{6}, \quad \frac{4}{6}, \quad \frac{12}{18}, \quad \frac{3}{9}, \quad \frac{10}{15}$$

3 a) List the fractions below that are equivalent to $\dfrac{1}{4}$.

  b) List those that are equivalent to $\dfrac{3}{4}$.

$$\frac{6}{16}, \quad \frac{2}{8}, \quad \frac{4}{12}, \quad \frac{5}{20}, \quad \frac{3}{12}, \quad \frac{12}{16}, \quad \frac{4}{16}, \quad \frac{9}{12}, \quad \frac{15}{20}, \quad \frac{6}{8}, \quad \frac{10}{15}$$

4 Copy each diagram. Draw arrows between equivalent fractions.
One arrow has been drawn on the first diagram.

a)

$\dfrac{1}{5}$	$\dfrac{9}{15}$
$\dfrac{3}{4}$	$\dfrac{15}{18}$
$\dfrac{2}{5}$	$\dfrac{15}{20}$
$\dfrac{5}{6}$	$\dfrac{2}{10}$
$\dfrac{1}{3}$	$\dfrac{5}{15}$
$\dfrac{3}{5}$	$\dfrac{6}{15}$

b)

$\dfrac{3}{4}$	$\dfrac{6}{24}$
$\dfrac{2}{3}$	$\dfrac{4}{24}$
$\dfrac{1}{3}$	$\dfrac{9}{24}$
$\dfrac{1}{4}$	$\dfrac{9}{12}$
$\dfrac{3}{8}$	$\dfrac{8}{12}$
$\dfrac{1}{6}$	$\dfrac{8}{24}$

d Write quantities as fractions

Here are some important facts about length, capacity and weight:

1 cm = 10 mm	1 m = 100 cm	1 m = 1000 mm	1 km = 1000 m
1 cℓ = 10 mℓ	1 ℓ = 100 cℓ	1 ℓ = 1000 mℓ	1 kg = 1000 g

You can use these facts to write some quantities as fractions.

Examples

$8 \text{ mm} = \dfrac{8}{10} \text{ cm}$ (8 out of 10)

$\qquad = \dfrac{4}{5} \text{ cm}$

(by dividing top and bottom by 2)

$250 \text{ g} = \dfrac{250}{1000} \text{ kg}$ (250 out of 1000)

$\qquad = \dfrac{25}{100} \text{ kg}$ (dividing by 10)

$\qquad = \dfrac{1}{4} \text{ kg}$ (dividing by 25 or 5 then 5 again)

Practice

1. Write these lengths as fractions of a centimetre.

   a) 5 mm   b) 4 mm   c) 6 mm

2. Write these weights as fractions of a kilogram.

   a) 500 g   b) 750 g   c) 100 g   d) 200 g   e) 600 g

3. Write these lengths as fractions of a kilometre.

   a) 5 m   b) 50 m   c) 500 m   d) 100 m   e) 150 m

4. Write these volumes as fractions of a litre.

   a) 20 mℓ   b) 50 mℓ   c) 200 mℓ   d) 500 mℓ   e) 400 mℓ

5. Write these lengths as fractions of a metre.

   a) 20 cm   b) 50 cm   c) 90 cm   d) 80 cm   e) 5 cm
   f) 100 mm   g) 200 mm   h) 400 mm   i) 600 mm   j) 20 mm

Compare fractions and mixed numbers

N2/L1.1

a Use fraction walls

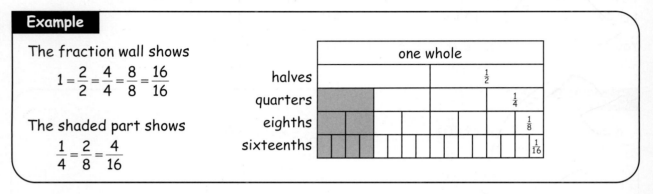

Example

The fraction wall shows
$$1 = \frac{2}{2} = \frac{4}{4} = \frac{8}{8} = \frac{16}{16}$$

The shaded part shows
$$\frac{1}{4} = \frac{2}{8} = \frac{4}{16}$$

	one whole			
halves			$\frac{1}{2}$	
quarters				$\frac{1}{4}$
eighths				$\frac{1}{8}$
sixteenths				$\frac{1}{16}$

Practice

1 Find the missing numbers.

a) $\frac{1}{2} = \frac{?}{4}$

b) $\frac{1}{2} = \frac{?}{8}$

c) $\frac{1}{2} = \frac{?}{16}$

d) $\frac{3}{4} = \frac{?}{8}$

e) $\frac{3}{4} = \frac{?}{16}$

f) $\frac{3}{8} = \frac{?}{16}$

g) $\frac{5}{8} = \frac{?}{16}$

h) $\frac{7}{8} = \frac{?}{16}$

2 Put each set of fractions in order of size. Start with the **smallest**.

a) $\frac{3}{8}, \frac{7}{16}, \frac{5}{16}$

b) $\frac{5}{8}, \frac{9}{16}, \frac{1}{2}$

c) $\frac{13}{16}, \frac{7}{8}, \frac{3}{4}$

3 This fraction wall shows halves, fifths and tenths.
Find the missing numbers.

a) $1 = \frac{?}{5} = \frac{?}{10}$

b) $\frac{1}{2} = \frac{?}{10}$

c) $\frac{1}{5} = \frac{?}{10}$

d) $\frac{2}{5} = \frac{?}{10}$

e) $\frac{3}{5} = \frac{?}{10}$

f) $\frac{5}{5} = \frac{?}{10}$

	one			
halves			$\frac{1}{2}$	
fifths				$\frac{1}{5}$
tenths				$\frac{1}{10}$

4 Put these fractions in order of size, starting with the **largest**.

$$\frac{2}{5}, \frac{7}{10}, \frac{1}{2}, \frac{1}{10}, \frac{9}{10}, \frac{3}{5}, \frac{3}{10}, \frac{1}{5}, \frac{4}{5}$$

$$\frac{4}{10} \quad \frac{7}{10} \quad \frac{5}{10} \quad \frac{1}{10} \quad \frac{9}{10} \quad \frac{6}{10} \quad \frac{3}{10} \quad \frac{2}{10} \quad \frac{8}{10}$$

b Compare fractions

These fractions are all **unit fractions** – they all have 1 in the numerator.

In unit fractions, the larger the denominator, the smaller the fraction.

For example, $\frac{1}{15}$ is smaller than $\frac{1}{10}$.

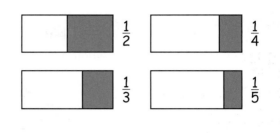

$\frac{1}{2}$ $\frac{1}{4}$ $\frac{1}{3}$ $\frac{1}{5}$

Practice

1 Which is **smaller**?

    a) $\frac{1}{7}$ or $\frac{1}{8}$ **b)** $\frac{1}{10}$ or $\frac{1}{6}$ **c)** $\frac{1}{20}$ or $\frac{1}{19}$ **d)** $\frac{1}{12}$ or $\frac{1}{3}$

2 Which is **larger**?

    a) $\frac{1}{20}$ or $\frac{1}{25}$ **b)** $\frac{1}{19}$ or $\frac{1}{17}$ **c)** $\frac{1}{5}$ or $\frac{1}{50}$ **d)** $\frac{1}{13}$ or $\frac{1}{11}$

3 Write these fractions in order of size. Start with the **smallest**.

    $\frac{1}{4}$, $\frac{1}{12}$, $\frac{1}{2}$, $\frac{1}{5}$, $\frac{1}{10}$, $\frac{1}{15}$, $\frac{1}{3}$, $\frac{1}{6}$, $\frac{1}{20}$

4 Write these fractions in order of size. Start with the **largest**.

    $\frac{1}{8}$, $\frac{1}{11}$, $\frac{1}{21}$, $\frac{1}{14}$, $\frac{1}{9}$, $\frac{1}{16}$, $\frac{1}{13}$, $\frac{1}{7}$, $\frac{1}{17}$

It is more difficult to compare other fractions. Shading parts of equal rectangles helps.

The sketch shows that $\frac{4}{5}$ is larger than $\frac{2}{3}$.

$\frac{2}{3}$

$\frac{4}{5}$

Draw sketches to illustrate your answers to questions 5 to 7.

5 Which is **larger**?

    a) $\frac{3}{4}$ or $\frac{2}{3}$ **b)** $\frac{1}{2}$ or $\frac{2}{5}$ **c)** $\frac{1}{3}$ or $\frac{2}{5}$

6 Which is **smaller**?

    a) $\frac{1}{2}$ or $\frac{4}{7}$ **b)** $\frac{3}{5}$ or $\frac{7}{9}$ **c)** $\frac{5}{6}$ or $\frac{3}{4}$

7 Write these fractions in order of size. Start with the **smallest**.

    $\frac{1}{2}$, $\frac{3}{7}$, $\frac{2}{5}$, $\frac{3}{10}$, $\frac{3}{4}$

c Improper fractions and mixed numbers

An **improper fraction** has a bigger numerator than denominator, e.g. $\frac{5}{4}$.

A **mixed number** is a mixture of a whole number and a fraction, e.g. $1\frac{1}{4}$.

The diagram shows $1\frac{1}{4} = \frac{5}{4}$.

whole one + 1 quarter = one and a quarter

4 quarters + 1 quarter = 5 quarters

$\frac{3}{4}$ is less than $1\frac{1}{4}$.

3 quarters

Practice

1 What do these diagrams show?

For each part give a mixed number and an improper fraction.

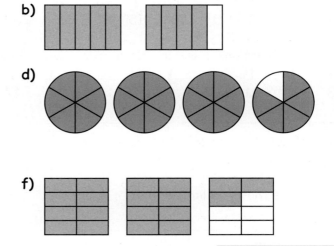

a)

b)

c)

d)

e)

f)

2 Draw diagrams to show that

a) $1\frac{3}{4} = \frac{7}{4}$ b) $2\frac{1}{2} = \frac{5}{2}$ c) $1\frac{2}{3} = \frac{5}{3}$ d) $3\frac{4}{5} = \frac{19}{5}$

> Can you see a quick way to write mixed numbers as improper fractions?

3 a) Draw diagrams to show each of these numbers in eighths.

$\frac{7}{8}$, $1\frac{3}{8}$, $\frac{5}{8}$, $2\frac{1}{8}$, $1\frac{1}{4}$, $\frac{3}{4}$, $1\frac{1}{2}$

b) List the original numbers in order of size, starting with the **smallest**.

d Find or estimate fractions

The first sketch shows a chocolate bar.
The second shows it again after some has been eaten.
What fraction is left?

6 out of 10 squares are left $\dfrac{6}{10} = \dfrac{3}{5}$ (dividing by 2)

You can also imagine the bar divided into 5 parts, as in this sketch.
This also shows that $\dfrac{3}{5}$ is left and $\dfrac{2}{5}$ was eaten.

Use your ruler to measure the lengths of the bars in the diagram:
Length of original bar = 30 mm. Length after some was eaten = 18 mm.
The fraction that is left is $\dfrac{18}{30} = \dfrac{3}{5}$ (dividing top & bottom by 6).

Practice

1   Here are some more chocolate bars. In each case estimate
    i) the fraction that is left   **ii)** the fraction that was eaten.

a)

b)

c)

Use your ruler to check your answers.

2   Use a fraction to describe how much is in each jug.

a)

b)

c)

Hint: You can use a ruler to measure
      the height of the jug and liquid.

3 Here is a water tank. Use a fraction to describe how full it is in each sketch.

a)   b)   c)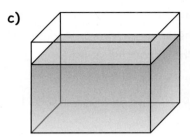

4 Estimate what fraction of the drink is left in each sketch.

a)   b)   c)

5 The sketch shows a pie.
For each part
   i) estimate what fraction of the pie has been eaten
   ii) estimate what fraction of the pie is left.

a)   b)   c)   d)

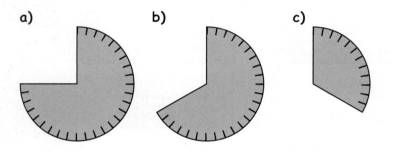

Find a fraction of something

a By dividing when the numerator is 1

To find $\frac{1}{2}$ of something, divide it by 2.

To find $\frac{1}{3}$ of something, divide it by 3.

To find $\frac{1}{4}$ of something, divide it by 4, and so on.

> When the numerator is 1, divide by the denominator.

Example

$\frac{1}{3}$ of 84 kg = 84 kg ÷ 3 = **28 kg**

$$3\overline{)8\,^24}$$
$$2\;8$$

Example   Six partners in a company each get a sixth of the profits of £64 500.

They each get $\frac{1}{6}$ of £64 500.
£64 500 ÷ 6 = £10 750. They each get **£10 750**.

$$6\overline{)6\,4\,^45\,^30\,0}$$
$$1\;0\;7\;5\;0$$

Practice

1 Find

a) $\frac{1}{2}$ of £56   **b)** $\frac{1}{3}$ of 72 cm   **c)** $\frac{1}{6}$ of £546   **d)** $\frac{1}{10}$ of £2500

e) $\frac{1}{4}$ of £84   **f)** $\frac{1}{5}$ of £780   **g)** $\frac{1}{8}$ of 576 m   **h)** $\frac{1}{9}$ of £2574

2 There are 24 students in a class. Half of them are women.
How many are women?

3 A jacket costs £45. This price is reduced by a third in a sale.

a) How much is saved?   **b)** What is the sale price?

Third off

4 Seventy people take a driving test. A fifth of them fail.

a) How many people fail?   **b)** How many people pass?

5 A petrol tank holds 60 litres when full. It is a quarter full.
How many litres of petrol are in the tank?

Empty   Full
FUEL

6 Four friends share a prize of £340 equally between them.
How much do they get each?

7 A sixth of the adults in a town did not vote. There are altogether 21 000 adults.
How many adults   **a)** did not vote   **b)** voted?

8 A chef uses one eighth of a kilogram bag of flour to thicken a sauce.

a) How many grams of flour does he use?   (1 kg = 1000 g)
b) How many grams are left in the bag?

b Finding more than one part

> ▶ When the numerator is not 1, divide by the
>   denominator then multiply by the numerator.

Example   Find $\frac{3}{4}$ of £540.

To find $\frac{3}{4}$ of £540, divide it by 4, then multiply by 3

£540 ÷ 4 = £135

$$4\overline{)5^14^20}$$
$$135$$

	1 3 5
	3 ×
	4 0 5
	1 1

Then £135 × 3 = **£405**

Divide by the denominator.
Then multiply by the numerator.

Practice

1 Find

   a) $\frac{3}{4}$ of £840   b) $\frac{2}{3}$ of £156   c) $\frac{2}{5}$ of 75 m   d) $\frac{3}{5}$ of 250 g

   e) $\frac{5}{6}$ of 420 cm   f) $\frac{2}{7}$ of £1610   g) $\frac{5}{8}$ of £2880   h) $\frac{4}{9}$ of 3285 kg

2 A company has 360 employees. Two-thirds of these are men.
   How many are men?

3 A box contains 45 chocolates.
   Two-fifths of these are dark chocolates.
   How many dark chocolates are there?

4 A firm makes £45 000 profit. The firm spends three quarters of the
   profit on new equipment. How much does the firm spend on new equipment?

5 There are 34 500 spectators at a football match. Nine tenths of these support the home
   team. How many spectators support the home team?

6 Two hundred and seventy five people go to a Christmas pantomime. Three fifths of them
   are children. How many children go to the pantomime?

7 A car costs £6900. The buyer gets a loan for five sixths of the price.
   How much is the loan?

8 A holiday company sells 480 000 holidays during a year. Three quarters of these are
   holidays abroad. How many of the holidays are abroad?

c By combining unit fractions

The sketch shows $\frac{3}{4} = \frac{2}{4} + \frac{1}{4} = \frac{1}{2} + \frac{1}{4}$.

To find $\frac{3}{4}$ of something, you can add $\frac{1}{2}$ and $\frac{1}{4}$

$$\frac{3}{4} = \frac{1}{2} + \frac{1}{4}$$

Example

$\frac{1}{2}$ of £540 = £270

$\frac{1}{4}$ of £540 = £135

So $\frac{3}{4}$ of £540 = £270 + £135

         = **£405**

$\frac{1}{2}$ of £540

$$\begin{array}{r} 2\,7\,0 \\ 2\overline{)5^1 4\,0} \end{array}$$

$\frac{1}{4}$ of £540

$$\begin{array}{r} 1\,3\,5 \\ 4\overline{)5^1 4^2 0} \end{array}$$

$\frac{3}{4}$ of £540

$$\begin{array}{r} 2\,7\,0 \\ 1\,3\,5+ \\ \hline 4\,0\,5 \\ {\scriptstyle 1} \end{array}$$

You can check this by multiplying £135 by 3.

Practice

1 Find

  a) $\frac{3}{4}$ of £1520   **b)** $\frac{3}{4}$ of 56 kg   **c)** $\frac{3}{4}$ of 432 m.

2 a) Draw a sketch to show that $\frac{5}{8} = \frac{4}{8} + \frac{1}{8} = \frac{1}{2} + \frac{1}{8}$.

  b) Find   **i)** $\frac{1}{2}$ of £960   **ii)** $\frac{1}{8}$ of £960   **iii)** $\frac{5}{8}$ of £960.

  c) Check **biii)** by multiplying your answer to **bii)** by 5.

3 a) Draw a sketch to show that $\frac{3}{8} = \frac{2}{8} + \frac{1}{8} = \frac{1}{4} + \frac{1}{8}$.

  b) Find   **i)** $\frac{1}{4}$ of 256 m   **ii)** $\frac{1}{8}$ of 256 m   **iii)** $\frac{3}{8}$ of 256 m.

  c) Check **biii)** by multiplying your answer to **bii)** by 3.

4 a) Draw a sketch to show that $\frac{5}{6} = \frac{3}{6} + \frac{2}{6} = \frac{1}{2} + \frac{1}{3}$.

  b) Find   **i)** $\frac{1}{2}$ of £7200   **ii)** $\frac{1}{3}$ of £7200   **iii)** $\frac{5}{6}$ of £7200.

d Scale up and down

Example

A recipe for macaroni cheese for 6 people includes these ingredients:

300 g cheese   120 g butter   240 g macaroni

Suppose there are only 4 people. You need $\frac{4}{6} = \frac{2}{3}$ of the quantities.

To find what you need, divide each quantity by 3, then multiply by 2:

Cheese: $300 \text{ g} \div 3 = 100 \text{ g}$ $100 \text{ g} \times 2 = \textbf{200 g}$
Butter: $120 \text{ g} \div 3 = 40 \text{ g}$ $40 \text{ g} \times 2 = \textbf{80 g}$
Macaroni: $240 \text{ g} \div 3 = 80 \text{ g}$ $80 \text{ g} \times 2 = \textbf{160 g}$

> Note there is twice as much macaroni as butter in both sets of ingredients.

Note: If there were 9 people, you would need $\frac{9}{6} = \frac{3}{2}$ of the quantities.

In this case you would need to divide each quantity by 2, then multiply by 3.
Check that this gives 450 g of cheese, 180 g of butter and 360 g of macaroni.

Practice

1 The recipe gives the ingredients for leek and potato soup for 6 people.
Find the quantities you need for

a) 4 people   **b)** 8 people.

Leek & Potato Soup (for 6 people)	
270 g potatoes	450 g leeks
750 mℓ milk	150 mℓ stock

2 The main ingredients for a nut loaf for 8 people are

400 g nuts   200 g breadcrumbs   240 g tomatoes   4 onions

  a) What fraction of the quantities do you need for 6 people?
  b) Find the quantities for 6 people.

3 These are the ingredients for 20 almond biscuits.

300 g flour   160 g sugar   140 g butter   60 g ground almonds

  a) What fraction of the quantities do you need for 16 biscuits?
  b) Find the quantities for 16 biscuits.

4 For sandwiches for 20 people a caterer uses

4 loaves of bread   800 g butter   8 tomatoes   2 cucumbers
400 g paté   300 g chicken   500 g cheese   1 lettuce

Find the quantities for sandwiches for
a) 15 people   **b)** 25 people.

Put fractions in order (using a common denominator) N2/L2.1

Comparing fractions is easy if they have the same denominator.

For example, $\frac{3}{5}$ is more than $\frac{2}{5}$

Practice

1 Which is **larger?** a) $\frac{1}{3}$ or $\frac{2}{3}$ b) $\frac{7}{9}$ or $\frac{5}{9}$ c) $\frac{7}{10}$ or $\frac{9}{10}$

2 Put each set of fractions in order. Start with the **smallest.**

a) $\frac{3}{5}, \frac{2}{5}, \frac{4}{5}$ b) $\frac{5}{7}, \frac{1}{7}, \frac{2}{7}, \frac{4}{7}$ c) $\frac{4}{9}, \frac{5}{9}, \frac{2}{9}, \frac{8}{9}, \frac{1}{9}$

Comparing fractions with different denominators is harder.
You can do this by making the denominators the same.

Or see page 77
for another way

Example To compare $\frac{2}{3}$ with $\frac{7}{12}$ write $\frac{2}{3}$ as twelfths: Because 3 divides into 12 we can change the denominator from 3 to 12.
12 is the '**common denominator**'.

$$\overset{\times 4}{\underset{\times 4}{\frac{2}{3} = \frac{8}{12}}}$$

To change the bottom to 12, multiply 3 by 4.
Then do the same to the top.

$\frac{8}{12}$ is bigger than $\frac{7}{12}$ so $\frac{2}{3}$ is **bigger than** $\frac{7}{12}$.

The denominator, 12, is the '**common denominator**' for these fractions.

Example Write $\frac{5}{8}, \frac{7}{10}$ and $\frac{3}{5}$ in order of size, starting with the smallest.

Look for a common denominator – a number that 8, 5 and 10 all divide into.
The best common denominator for these numbers is 40.

Now write all the fractions with 40 as the denominator:

$$\overset{\times 5}{\underset{\times 5}{\frac{5}{8} = \frac{25}{40}}} \qquad \overset{\times 4}{\underset{\times 4}{\frac{7}{10} = \frac{28}{40}}} \qquad \overset{\times 8}{\underset{\times 8}{\frac{3}{5} = \frac{24}{40}}}$$

Other common denominators (e.g. 80)
could be used.
40 is the **best** because it is the **smallest.**

In order of size the fractions are: $\frac{3}{5}, \frac{5}{8}, \frac{7}{10}$.

3 Write each pair with the same denominator, then say which is the **larger**.

a) $\frac{1}{4}$ or $\frac{1}{5}$ b) $\frac{3}{5}$ or $\frac{3}{10}$ c) $\frac{2}{3}$ or $\frac{3}{4}$ d) $\frac{1}{2}$ or $\frac{4}{7}$

4 Write each group in order of size, starting with the **smallest**.

a) $\frac{1}{2}, \frac{5}{8}, \frac{3}{8}$ b) $\frac{2}{5}, \frac{3}{10}, \frac{1}{4}$ c) $\frac{5}{16}, \frac{3}{4}, \frac{7}{8}, \frac{1}{2}$

d) $\frac{5}{6}, \frac{3}{4}, \frac{2}{3}, \frac{11}{12}$ e) $\frac{3}{4}, \frac{1}{2}, \frac{5}{7}, \frac{3}{7}$ f) $\frac{1}{3}, \frac{5}{12}, \frac{1}{4}, \frac{1}{2}, \frac{3}{8}$

5 Write each group in order of size, starting with the **largest**.

a) $\frac{1}{2}, \frac{4}{7}, \frac{2}{7}$ b) $\frac{5}{9}, \frac{2}{3}, \frac{5}{6}$ c) $\frac{1}{2}, \frac{4}{9}, \frac{3}{4}, \frac{2}{3}$

d) $\frac{4}{5}, \frac{2}{3}, \frac{9}{10}, \frac{13}{15}$ e) $\frac{5}{9}, \frac{5}{8}, \frac{4}{9}, \frac{7}{12}$ f) $\frac{3}{5}, \frac{2}{3}, \frac{7}{10}, \frac{13}{15}, \frac{2}{9}, \frac{11}{15}$

To put a mixture of fractions and mixed numbers in order, consider them in groups.

Example   To put $\frac{2}{3}$, $1\frac{3}{4}$, $1\frac{2}{3}$, $2\frac{1}{3}$ and $\frac{5}{6}$ in order

Under 1: $\frac{2}{3}$ and $\frac{5}{6}$ common denominator 6 $\frac{2}{3} = \frac{4}{6}$ is smaller than $\frac{5}{6}$

Between 1 and 2: $1\frac{3}{4}$ and $1\frac{2}{3}$ common denominator 12 $1\frac{3}{4} = 1\frac{9}{12}, 1\frac{2}{3} = 1\frac{8}{12}$

Above 2: $2\frac{1}{3}$ only

In order, starting with smallest: $\frac{2}{3}, \frac{5}{6}, 1\frac{2}{3}, 1\frac{3}{4}, 2\frac{1}{3}$

---

6 Write each group in order of size, starting with the **smallest**.

a) $1\frac{3}{5}, \frac{3}{4}, 2\frac{2}{5}, 1\frac{1}{2}, 2\frac{1}{3}$ b) $\frac{5}{8}, 1\frac{3}{4}, \frac{4}{7}, 1\frac{7}{12}, 1\frac{5}{6}$

c) $\frac{4}{9}, 2\frac{2}{3}, \frac{5}{7}, 2\frac{3}{7}, 1\frac{3}{4}, 2\frac{1}{2}$ d) $1\frac{2}{3}, 1\frac{5}{8}, \frac{1}{4}, 1\frac{11}{12}, 2\frac{1}{8}, 1\frac{5}{6}$

Write one number as a fraction of another

N2/L2.3

a Simplest form

The fractions $\frac{8}{12}, \frac{2}{3}, \frac{4}{6}, \frac{10}{15}$ and $\frac{6}{9}$ are all equal to each other.

$\frac{2}{3}$ is the **simplest form** – its numerator and denominator are the smallest.

▶ **To find the simplest form of a fraction divide the top and bottom by the same number. Repeat this as far as you can.**

Example   Write $\dfrac{240}{320}$ in its simplest form.

Look for numbers that divide into the top and bottom.

$$\dfrac{240}{320} = \dfrac{24}{32} = \dfrac{3}{4}$$

There is more than one way of doing this. Here is another way:

$$\dfrac{240}{320} = \dfrac{120}{160} = \dfrac{60}{80} = \dfrac{3}{4}$$

Finding the simplest form is sometimes called '**cancelling**'.

If you divide by large numbers it is quicker, but it is sometimes easier to divide by small numbers.
Keep going until you are sure there is nothing else you can divide by.

Practice

Write each fraction in its simplest form.

1 $\dfrac{20}{50}$ 2 $\dfrac{12}{16}$ 3 $\dfrac{9}{27}$ 4 $\dfrac{12}{30}$ 5 $\dfrac{80}{100}$

6 $\dfrac{32}{48}$ 7 $\dfrac{200}{400}$ 8 $\dfrac{150}{200}$ 9 $\dfrac{25}{75}$ 10 $\dfrac{72}{96}$

11 $\dfrac{140}{700}$ 12 $\dfrac{81}{270}$ 13 $\dfrac{560}{840}$ 14 $\dfrac{1500}{3500}$ 15 $\dfrac{1320}{2200}$

b Write one quantity as a fraction of another

Example   Write 60 cm as a fraction of a metre.

1 m = 100 cm, so the fraction is $\dfrac{60}{100} = \dfrac{6}{10} = \dfrac{3}{5}$ (dividing by 10, then 2).

> **Example**   Seventy women and fifty-six men work in a factory.
> What fraction of the workers are men?
>
> The total number of workers $= 70 + 56 = 126$.
>
> The fraction that are men $= \dfrac{56}{126} = \dfrac{28}{63} = \dfrac{4}{9}$ (dividing by 2, then 7).

Practice

1 What fraction of an hour is

   a) 15 minutes   **b)** 20 minutes   **c)** 48 minutes?

> Remember metric units:
> 1 kg = 1000 g
> 1 g = 1000 mg
> 1 cℓ = 10 mℓ
> See p 188 and p 207

2 What fraction of a kilogram is

   a) 100 g   **b)** 750 g   **c)** 400 g   **d)** 640 g?

3 Write each of these volumes as a fraction of a centilitre.

   a) 3 mℓ   **b)** 5 mℓ   **c)**   2 mℓ   **d)** 4 mℓ   **e)** 6 mℓ

4 For each of these weights

   a) 50 g   **b)** 500 mg   **c)** 250 g   **d)** 250 mg   **e)** 200 g

   find the equivalent weight from $\dfrac{1}{4}$ g, $\dfrac{1}{2}$ kg, $\dfrac{1}{5}$ g, $\dfrac{1}{50}$ kg, $\dfrac{1}{2}$ g, $\dfrac{1}{4}$ kg, $\dfrac{1}{5}$ kg, $\dfrac{1}{20}$ kg

5 One pound is equal to 16 ounces. What fraction of a pound is

   a) 8 ounces   **b)** 4 ounces   **c)** 12 ounces   **d)** 6 ounces?

6 A photographer has taken 24 photographs on a film of 36.
   What fraction of the photographs have been taken?

7 Neil earns £800 per month. His rent costs £160 per month.
   What fraction of Neil's wage does he spend on rent?

8 During one day at a driving test centre, eighteen people pass their driving test and twelve people fail.
   What fraction of the drivers pass?

9 A car costs £6400 when it is new. It is sold later for £3600.
   What fraction is this of its original value?

10 The table shows the results of a survey at a factory about how employees travel to work.

a) Copy and complete the table.

b) Find the fraction of **i)** men   **ii)** women that travel by each method.
(Hint: Use the total of the Men column for the denominator in part (i))

c) What fraction of the total workforce are
i) men   **ii)** women?

	Men	Women	Total
Car	240	300	
Bus	120	270	
Train	80	100	
Cycle	15	10	
Walk	25	40	
Total			

c Estimate one quantity as a fraction of another

Example

The table gives the number of employees in different departments of a company.

1347 out of the 2054 factory workers are men.

As a fraction this is $\frac{1347}{2054}$ – not a very easy or convenient fraction!

Department	Men	Women	Total
Factory	1347	707	2054
Distribution	59	20	79
Administration	48	196	244
Sales	29	13	42
Total	1483	936	2419

There are several ways of giving a simpler estimate. The best way depends on the numbers in the fraction. In this fraction:

Rounding both numbers to the nearest 1000 gives $\frac{1000}{2000} = \frac{1}{2}$.

This is a much simpler fraction, but not very accurate.

Rounding both numbers to the nearest 100 gives $\frac{1300}{2100} = \frac{13}{21}$.

This is more accurate than $\frac{1}{2}$, but not very simple.

In this case a better method is to round 1347 up to 1400 and 2054 to 2100.

$\frac{1400}{2100} = \frac{14}{21} = \frac{2}{3}$ About two thirds of the factory workers are men.

This fraction is simpler than $\frac{13}{21}$ and is actually more accurate as well.

When estimating fractions, **try to find near numbers that will cancel**.

Practice

Use the table on page 89.

1 By rounding the numbers to the nearest 10, estimate the fraction of the people in Distribution who are
a) women   **b)** men.

2 a) Estimate the fraction of the people in Administration who are women by rounding the numbers
   i) to the nearest 10
   ii) to the nearest 50.

  b) What happens if you round the numbers to the nearest 100?

3 a) Use these methods to estimate the fraction of people in Sales who are men.
   i) Round 29 and 42 to the nearest 10.
   ii) Round 29 to 28, but leave the total as 42.

  b) Which answer do you think gives the most accurate fraction? Why?

4 a) Estimate the fraction of the total work force that work in
   i) Administration   **ii)** Sales   **iii)** Distribution   **iv)** the Factory.

  b) Estimate the fraction of the total work force that are
   i) men   **ii)** women.

5 The number of kilometres travelled by passengers on the railway in one year was 10.1 billion. Of these 7.4 billion kilometres were on ordinary tickets and the rest were on season tickets.

  a) Which of these fractions is the best estimate of the fraction of the distance that was on ordinary tickets?
   i) $\frac{7}{10}$ **ii)** $\frac{3}{4}$

  b) Estimate the fraction of kilometres that were on season tickets.

6 The table shows the amount of different types of energy consumed in the UK in a year.

  a) Find the total consumption.
  b) Estimate the fraction of energy that was
   i) coal
   ii) petroleum
   iii) natural gas
   iv) primary electricity.

Energy type	Amount (tonnes of oil equivalent)
Coal	42 600 000
Petroleum	81 700 000
Natural gas	91 400 000
Primary electricity	21 400 000

Source:
www.dti.gov.uk/energy/inform/energy_stats/
total_energy/1_2inlandenergyconsumption.xls

7 The table shows the amount of waste recycled in England and Wales during a year.
Estimate the fraction of the total that is of each type.

Waste type	Amount (thousand tonnes)
Paper	943
Glass	411
Compost	816
Metal	326
Textiles	44
Cans	27
Other	298

Source: Department for Environment, Food and Rural Affairs/Welsh Assembly Government

---

Activity

Visit government or other websites to find some interesting statistics.
Write the information you find in terms of fractions.
Some suggestions are given below.

- Data for employment, industry, population, leisure and tourism etc. from the National Statistics website (www.stats.gov.uk)
- Transport figures from the Department of Transport (www.dft.gov.uk)
- Information about housing from the Land Registry (www.landreg.gov.uk)
- Information from the Department of Health (www.doh.gov.uk)
- Crime figures from the Home Office website (www.homeoffice.gov.uk)

Add and subtract fractions

N2/L2.4

a Add and subtract fractions with the same denominator

Look at the diagrams.

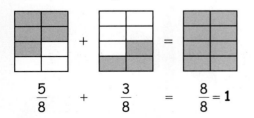

$$\frac{5}{8} + \frac{3}{8} = \frac{8}{8} = 1$$

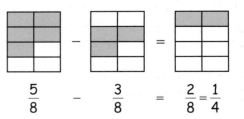

$$\frac{5}{8} - \frac{3}{8} = \frac{2}{8} = \frac{1}{4}$$

When 2 fractions have the same denominator:

To add them, add the numerators.   To subtract them, subtract the numerators.
The denominator stays the same.   Simplify the answer if possible.

Examples

$\dfrac{7}{12} + \dfrac{1}{12} = \dfrac{8}{12} = \dfrac{2}{3}$ (cancelling by 4) $\dfrac{9}{10} - \dfrac{3}{10} = \dfrac{6}{10} = \dfrac{3}{5}$ (cancelling by 2)

Practice

Work these out. Write each answer in its simplest form.

1 $\dfrac{3}{5} + \dfrac{1}{5}$ 2 $\dfrac{3}{5} - \dfrac{1}{5}$ 3 $\dfrac{5}{6} + \dfrac{1}{6}$ 4 $\dfrac{5}{6} - \dfrac{1}{6}$

5 $\dfrac{2}{7} + \dfrac{3}{7}$ 6 $\dfrac{5}{7} - \dfrac{2}{7}$ 7 $\dfrac{5}{8} - \dfrac{1}{8}$ 8 $\dfrac{4}{9} + \dfrac{2}{9}$

9 $\dfrac{9}{10} - \dfrac{1}{10}$ 10 $\dfrac{2}{5} + \dfrac{3}{5}$ 11 $\dfrac{4}{15} + \dfrac{2}{15}$ 12 $\dfrac{7}{8} - \dfrac{3}{8}$

13 A café sells drinks, meals and snacks.

It makes $\dfrac{1}{5}$ of its profits on meals and $\dfrac{2}{5}$ of its profits on snacks.

a) What is the total fraction of its profits that it makes on meals and snacks?
b) What fraction of its profits does it make on drinks?

14 The audience at a pantomine is made up of children, men and women.
Five eighths of the audience are children.
a) What fraction are adults?

One eighth of the audience are men.
b) What fraction are women?

b Add and subtract fractions with different denominators

If 2 fractions have different denominators you cannot
add or subtract them immediately.

▶ **You must change them into equivalent
fractions with the same denominator.**

Look for the **smallest** number that all the denominators
divide into exactly.
(Here 2 and 3 both divide into 6.)
This is called the **common denominator**.

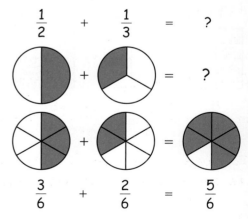

$\dfrac{1}{2}$ + $\dfrac{1}{3}$ = ?

+ = ?

+ =

$\dfrac{3}{6}$ + $\dfrac{2}{6}$ = $\dfrac{5}{6}$

Examples

$$\frac{1}{6} + \frac{3}{8} + \frac{1}{3}$$

6, 8 and 3 all divide into 24
so make 24 the common denominator

$$\frac{1^{\times 4}}{6_{\times 4}} + \frac{3^{\times 3}}{8_{\times 3}} + \frac{1^{\times 8}}{3_{\times 8}}$$

$$= \frac{4}{24} + \frac{9}{24} + \frac{8}{24}$$

$$= \frac{21}{24} = \frac{7}{8}$$

$$\frac{5}{7} - \frac{3}{8}$$

7 and 8 both divide into 56
so make 56 the common denonimator

$$\frac{5^{\times 8}}{7_{\times 8}} - \frac{3^{\times 7}}{8_{\times 7}}$$

$$= \frac{40}{56} - \frac{21}{56}$$

$$= \frac{19}{56}$$

Practice

Work these out. Write each answer in its simplest form.

1 $\frac{3}{5} + \frac{1}{10}$

2 $\frac{4}{5} - \frac{3}{10}$

3 $\frac{2}{3} + \frac{1}{6}$

4 $\frac{1}{2} - \frac{1}{6}$

5 $\frac{2}{3} + \frac{1}{4}$

6 $\frac{3}{4} - \frac{2}{5}$

7 $\frac{3}{4} - \frac{5}{8}$

8 $\frac{5}{9} + \frac{1}{3}$

9 $\frac{2}{3} - \frac{2}{5}$

10 $\frac{4}{7} + \frac{1}{3}$

11 $\frac{2}{5} + \frac{1}{3}$

12 $\frac{9}{10} - \frac{3}{5}$

13 $\frac{1}{4} + \frac{1}{3} + \frac{1}{6}$

14 $\frac{5}{8} - \frac{2}{5}$

15 $\frac{1}{2} + \frac{2}{15} + \frac{1}{3}$

16 $\frac{8}{9} - \frac{5}{6}$

17 $\frac{8}{9} + \frac{1}{3} - \frac{3}{4}$

18 $\frac{9}{10} - \frac{3}{4}$

19 $\frac{9}{10} - \frac{2}{5} - \frac{1}{2}$

20 $\frac{3}{4} + \frac{1}{2} - \frac{3}{8}$

21 A worker spends a quarter of her wages on rent, a third on clothes and a sixth on food.

a) What is the total fraction that she spends?

b) What fraction does she have left?

c Improper fractions and mixed numbers

Sometimes adding gives an **improper** fraction, i.e. a 'top-heavy' fraction.

For example, $\frac{9}{10} + \frac{3}{10} = \frac{12}{10} = \frac{6}{5}$ This is $1\frac{1}{5}$

> A **mixed number** has a whole number and a fraction part.

To change improper fractions to mixed numbers:
Make as many whole numbers as possible – the rest is the fraction part.

Examples

$$\frac{17}{5} = 3\frac{2}{5}$$

$$\frac{19}{7} = 2\frac{5}{7}$$

$$\frac{35}{4} = 8\frac{3}{4}$$

How many 4s in 35? (8)
How many are left? (3)

($\frac{15}{5}$ equals 3

$\frac{2}{5}$ left over)

($\frac{14}{7}$ equals 2

$\frac{5}{7}$ left over)

($\frac{32}{4}$ equals 8

$\frac{3}{4}$ left over)

Also see p. 78

Practice

Write these improper fractions as mixed numbers.

1 $\frac{9}{5}$ 2 $\frac{13}{5}$ 3 $\frac{13}{3}$ 4 $\frac{17}{3}$ 5 $\frac{15}{4}$

6 $\frac{9}{2}$ 7 $\frac{13}{2}$ 8 $\frac{10}{7}$ 9 $\frac{21}{4}$ 10 $\frac{17}{6}$

11 $\frac{19}{3}$ 12 $\frac{33}{5}$ 13 $\frac{23}{8}$ 14 $\frac{37}{10}$ 15 $\frac{40}{9}$

If an answer is an improper fraction, change it to a mixed number.

Examples

$$\frac{5}{8} + \frac{7}{8} = \frac{12}{8} = 1\frac{4}{8} = 1\frac{1}{2}$$

$$\frac{1}{2} + \frac{3}{8} + \frac{1}{3} = \frac{12}{24} + \frac{9}{24} + \frac{8}{24} = \frac{29}{24} = 1\frac{5}{24}$$

Add these. Give your answers as mixed numbers and cancel where possible.

16 $\frac{7}{9} + \frac{5}{9}$ 17 $\frac{11}{14} + \frac{5}{14}$ 18 $\frac{7}{8} + \frac{3}{4}$ 19 $\frac{1}{2} + \frac{2}{3}$

20 $\frac{4}{5} + \frac{7}{10}$ 21 $\frac{4}{7} + \frac{3}{4}$ 22 $\frac{3}{10} + \frac{2}{5} + \frac{1}{2}$ 23 $\frac{5}{6} + \frac{3}{4} + \frac{5}{8}$

d Add and subtract mixed numbers

It is often useful to change mixed numbers into improper fractions.

▶ To change mixed numbers to improper fractions:
   Change the whole number then add the other part.

Examples

$$1\frac{3}{4} = \frac{7}{4}$$ $$2\frac{1}{4} = \frac{9}{4}$$ $$2\frac{3}{5} = \frac{13}{5}$$ $$4\frac{1}{5} = \frac{21}{5}$$

Numerator = $4 \times 5 + 1 = 21$

Denominator stays the same

(1 is 4 quarters   (2 is 8 quarters   (2 is 10 fifths   (4 is 20 fifths

+ 3 quarters   + 1 quarter   + 3 fifths   + 1 fifth

= 7 quarters)   = 9 quarters)   = 13 fifths)   = 21 fifths)

Practice

Write these mixed numbers as improper fractions:

1 $1\frac{1}{2}$ 2 $2\frac{1}{2}$ 3 $3\frac{1}{2}$ 4 $1\frac{2}{3}$ 5 $2\frac{2}{3}$

6 $2\frac{1}{5}$ 7 $3\frac{4}{5}$ 8 $2\frac{1}{6}$ 9 $1\frac{5}{6}$ 10 $2\frac{3}{8}$

11 $2\frac{3}{7}$ 12 $5\frac{7}{8}$ 13 $4\frac{9}{10}$ 14 $3\frac{4}{9}$ 15 $6\frac{2}{7}$

To add or subtract mixed numbers:

either
● **work with the whole numbers and fractions separately**
or
● **change them into improper fractions.**

Choose the method you prefer

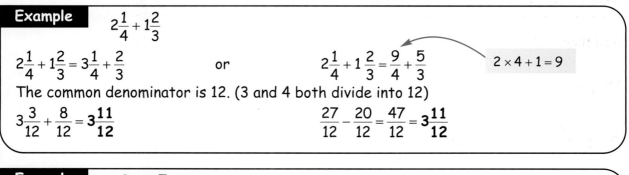

Example

$$2\frac{1}{4} + 1\frac{2}{3}$$

$$2\frac{1}{4} + 1\frac{2}{3} = 3\frac{1}{4} + \frac{2}{3}$$ or $$2\frac{1}{4} + 1\frac{2}{3} = \frac{9}{4} + \frac{5}{3}$$ $$2 \times 4 + 1 = 9$$

The common denominator is 12. (3 and 4 both divide into 12)

$$3\frac{3}{12} + \frac{8}{12} = 3\frac{11}{12}$$ $$\frac{27}{12} - \frac{20}{12} = \frac{47}{12} = 3\frac{11}{12}$$

Example

$$4\frac{2}{5} - 2\frac{7}{10}$$

$$4\frac{2}{5} - 2\frac{7}{10} = 2\frac{2}{5} - \frac{7}{10}$$ or $$4\frac{2}{5} - 2\frac{7}{10} = \frac{22}{5} - \frac{27}{10}$$ $$4 \times 5 + 2 = 22$$

The common denominator is 10. (5 divides into 10)

$$2\frac{4}{10} - \frac{7}{10} = 1\frac{14}{10} - \frac{7}{10} = 1\frac{7}{10}$$ $$\frac{44}{10} - \frac{27}{10} = \frac{17}{10} = 1\frac{7}{10}$$

Work these out. Write each answer in its simplest form.

16 $1\frac{1}{4}+1\frac{1}{2}$ **17** $2\frac{3}{5}-1\frac{3}{4}$ **18** $3\frac{1}{2}+1\frac{5}{6}$ **19** $3\frac{3}{4}-2\frac{1}{3}$

20 $5\frac{1}{2}+2\frac{5}{8}$ **21** $4\frac{1}{3}-1\frac{1}{2}$ **22** $2\frac{3}{4}-1\frac{4}{5}$ **23** $3\frac{7}{10}+2\frac{2}{5}$

24 $5\frac{2}{3}-1\frac{4}{5}$ **25** $3\frac{4}{7}+2\frac{1}{2}$ **26** $4\frac{1}{2}+2\frac{3}{4}$ **27** $2\frac{1}{2}-1\frac{3}{8}$

28 The preparation of food for a meal takes $1\frac{1}{4}$ hours and it takes $1\frac{3}{4}$ hours to cook it. How long does it take altogether?

29 A $1\frac{1}{2}$ pound piece is cut from a cheese that weighs $5\frac{3}{4}$ pounds. What weight of cheese is left?

30 The table shows the hours worked by a part-time hairdresser.

a) Find the total time she worked.
b) How much longer did she work on Friday than on Saturday?
c) How much longer did she work on Friday than on Thursday?

Day	Time worked
Thurs	$3\frac{3}{4}$ hours
Fri	$6\frac{1}{2}$ hours
Sat	$5\frac{1}{4}$ hours

Fractions on a calculator

N2/L1.11, N2/L2.10

Your calculator may be able to calculate with fractions.

The fraction key usually looks like this: $a^{b/c}$. Try the examples below:

	Example	Press	Display	Answer
Entering a fraction	$\frac{2}{3}$	[2] [$a^{b/c}$] [3]	2⌐3 (or 2r3)	
Equivalent fractions – cancelling	$\frac{6}{8}$	[6] [$a^{b/c}$] [8] [=]	3⌐4	$\frac{3}{4}$
Improper fractions to mixed numbers	$\frac{8}{5}$	[8] [$a^{b/c}$] [5] [=]	1⌐3⌐5	$1\frac{3}{5}$
Mixed numbers to improper fractions	$2\frac{3}{4}$	[2] [$a^{b/c}$] [3] [$a^{b/c}$] [4] [d/c]	11⌐4	$\frac{11}{4}$
Finding a fraction of a number ('of' is ×)	$\frac{3}{4}$ of 6	[3] [$a^{b/c}$] [4] [×] [6] [=]	4⌐1⌐2	$4\frac{1}{2}$
Fraction arithmetic use +, −, ×, ÷	$\frac{3}{4} - \frac{2}{3}$	[3] [$a^{b/c}$] [4] [−] [2] [$a^{b/c}$] [3] [=]	1⌐12	$\frac{1}{12}$
Fraction to decimal – do as a division	$\frac{5}{8}$	[5] [÷] [8] [=]	0.625	0.625
Decimal to fraction – use place value then cancel on the calculator	0.35	Put $\frac{35}{100}$ into the calculator [3] [5] [$a^{b/c}$] [1] [0] [0] [=]	7⌐20	$\frac{7}{20}$

Try the earlier fraction questions again using a calculator.

Number

9 Decimals

Understand decimals in context (up to 2 decimal places) N2/E3.3

Decimal numbers have a whole number part and a fraction part.
The **decimal point** separates the two parts.
Read 7.3 as '**seven point three.**'

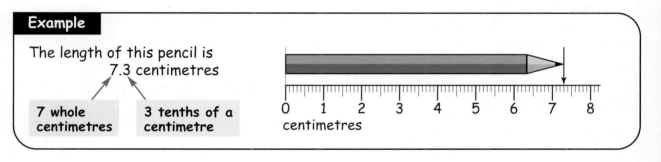

We often use decimals to give lengths.
Look at a ruler or tape measure.

Each centimetre (cm) is divided into 10 equal divisions. Each division is $\frac{1}{10}$ cm.

As a decimal this is 0.1 cm.

2 divisions = $\frac{2}{10}$ cm or 0.2 cm, 3 divisions = $\frac{3}{10}$ cm or 0.3 cm and so on.

Example

The length of this pencil is
7.3 centimetres

7 whole centimetres   **3 tenths of a centimetre**

Practice

1 Write down the length in centimetres marked by each arrow.

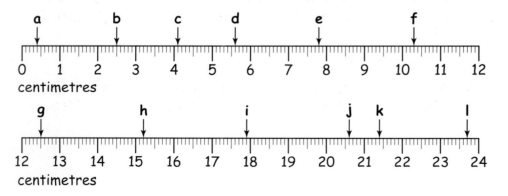

To put lengths in order compare the whole number part, then the fraction part.

Example   The lengths of 5 pencils are: 7.6 cm, 8.1 cm, 6.9 cm, 7.3 cm, 7.9 cm.

Look at the **whole numbers first**.
8 is the largest so the longest pencil is 8.1 cm.
There are three lengths starting with 7   (7.6 cm, 7.3 cm and 7.9 cm).
To put them in order **compare the tenths**:   7.9 cm then 7.6 cm then 7.3 cm.
The shortest pencil is 6.9 cm long.
The answer is: 8.1 cm, 7.9 cm, 7.6 cm, 7.3 cm, 6.9 cm

Whole nos.	tenths
7 .	6
8 .	1
6 .	9
7 .	3
7 .	9

---

2 Put each group in order, starting with the **longest**.

a) Caterpillars: 1.9 cm, 2.4 cm, 1.8 cm, 2.5 cm, 2.1 cm

b) Leaves: 4.5 cm, 3.8 cm, 3.9 cm, 3.4 cm, 4.1 cm, 4.3 cm

c) Twigs: 10.6 cm, 9.9 cm, 11.1 cm, 10.5 cm, 9.6 cm, 10.7 cm

Each length in the last section had **1 decimal place** (1 dp)
i.e. each length had 1 digit after the decimal point.

7.3 cm

↑
1 decimal place

For money we often use **2 decimal places** (2 dp):
There are **100 pence in each pound**
so   £2.31 = 231p (p stands for 'pence').

£2.31 is 2 pounds, 31 pence
↑↑
2 decimal places

Each pence is one hundredth of a pound. $31p = £\frac{31}{100}$ (31 **hundredths** of a £)

---

3 Write each amount in pence.

a) £1.00   b) £2.18   c) £1.09   d) £4.07   e) £0.62
f) £8.24   g) £5.70   h) £9.04   i) £10.17   j) £16.40

4 Write each amount in £ using decimals.

a) 213p   b) 402p   c) 85p   d) 350p   e) 103p
f) 600p   g) 725p   h) 937p   i) 1000p   j) 2409p

To put prices in order, **compare the £ first, then the pence**.

Example   Put these prices in order, starting with the **cheapest**.
£3.45, £2.98, £3.06, £2.80, £2.77

Look at the whole £s first, 2 is less than 3
The prices starting with 2 are £2.98, £2.80 and £2.77
Now compare the pence, the correct order is £2.77, £2.80, £2.98

The prices starting with 3 are £3.45 and £3.06
Now compare the pence, the correct order is £3.06, £3.45

The answer is: £2.77, £2.80, £2.98, £3.06, £3.45

£	pence
3 .	45
2 .	98
3 .	06
2 .	80
2 .	77

5 Put each group in order from cheapest to most expensive.

a) £1.21   £1.37   £1.02   £2.07   £1.46   £1.19   £1.87

b) £74.02   £47.20   £56.78   £66.18   £63.21   £63.02

c) £11.17   £10.08   £11.91   £10.07   £11.01   £10.70

100 centimetres = 1 metre. (See page 169.)
Each centimetre (cm) is **one hundredth** of a metre (m).

15 cm = 0.15 m (just like 15p = £0.15)   and   234 cm = 2.34 m

(Read 0.15 as 'point one five'   **2 metres**   **34 centimetres**
and 2.34 as 'two point three four'.)

Working with m and cm is like working with £ and pence, but with measurements we usually leave off any zero at the end of the decimal part.

Examples

In measurements:	30 cm = 0.3 m	and	750 cm = 7.5 m	**zero removed**
In money:	30p = £0.30	and	750p = £7.50	**zero kept**

6 How many centimetres are there in each of these measurements?

a) 0.22 m   b) 1.07 m   c) 1.73 m   d) 0.74 m   e) 1.33 m
f) 1.12 m   g) 1.15 m   h) 0.67 m   i) 2.6 m   j) 5.4 m

7 Write each measurement in metres using decimals.

a) 154 cm   b) 315 cm   c) 94 cm   d) 120 cm   e) 762 cm
f) 402 cm   g) 70 cm   h) 250 cm   i) 1134 cm   j) 2230 cm

8 The heights of some groups of children are given below.
Put each group in order starting with the **shortest**.

a) 1.5 m	1.67 m	1.72 m	1.8 m	1.55 m	1.63 m	1.74 m
b) 1.32 m	1.26 m	1.39 m	1.28 m	1.31 m	1.3 m	1.4 m
c) 0.72 m	0.99 m	1.02 m	0.88 m	1.01 m	0.84 m	1.03 m

In fractions 50 out of 100 $= \dfrac{50}{100} = \dfrac{1}{2}$ Half of a metre $= 50$ cm $= 0.5$ m

Half of £1 $= 50$ pence, i.e. £0.50   and $3\dfrac{1}{2}$ m $= 3.5$ m

Learn

> ▶ **0.5 in decimals** $= \dfrac{1}{2}$ **in fractions.**

---

9 a) Write these as decimals: **i)** $1\dfrac{1}{2}$ m   **ii)** $7\dfrac{1}{2}$ m   **iii)** $10\dfrac{1}{2}$ m

   b) Write these as mixed numbers: **i)** 2.5 m   **ii)** 6.5 m   **iii)** 15.5 m

Activities

1 Read prices from adverts, price lists etc. Select coins and/or notes to match.

2 Measure some items in cm then write the measurements in m using decimals.

Write and compare decimals up to 3 decimal places N2/L1.4, N2/L2.5

a Place value

Look at the decimal numbers. The headings show the **place value** of each digit.

	Hundreds 100s	Tens 10s	Units 1s	.	Tenths 10ths	Hundredths 100ths	Thousandths 1000ths
14.13		1	4	.	1	3	
7.509			7	.	5	0	9
0.173			0	.	1	7	3

Look at the first decimal 14.13 (fourteen point one three).
It has no hundreds, 1 ten, 4 units, 1 tenth, 3 hundredths and no thousandths.

Note
ten = 10
tenth = $\frac{1}{10}$

In money £14.13 can be made up from 1 ten-pound note, 4 pound coins, 1 ten-pence coin and
3 pence. (10 pence is $\dfrac{1}{10}$ of a £ and 3 pence is $\dfrac{3}{100}$ of a £.)

There is more than one way of writing the decimal part in fractions.

$$14.13 = 14 + \frac{1}{10} + \frac{3}{100} \qquad \text{or} \qquad 14\frac{13}{100}$$

as separate fractions   in a single fraction

This is like having 1 ten-pence coin and 3 one-pence coins or 13 one-pence coins.

Now look at the second decimal in the place value table (on page 101), 7.509.

The **place value** of the **digit** 5 is $\frac{5}{10}$ and the place value of the 9 is $\frac{9}{1000}$.

There are no hundredths, but the zero is important as it keeps the 9 in the thousandths column.

In fractions $7.509 = 7 + \frac{5}{10} + \frac{9}{1000}$ or $7\frac{509}{1000}$ — decimal digits / heading for last digit

The last decimal, 0.173, has no whole number part.

In fractions $0.173 = \frac{1}{10} + \frac{7}{100} + \frac{3}{1000}$ or $\frac{173}{1000}$

Practice

1 a) Draw a place value table. Write the following numbers in it.

i) 116.74	**ii)** 37.54	**iii)** 12.06	**iv)** 4.52
v) 536.09	**vi)** 506.926	**vii)** 67.354	**viii)** 127.063
ix) 107.401	**x)** 231.079	**xi)** 619.102	**xii)** 423.073

b) Write down the place value of each digit that is coloured.

2 Draw a place value table. Write the following numbers in it.

a) Fifty-seven point three two   **b)** Six point nine
c) Twelve point four one   **d)** One hundred point three five
e) Ninety-six point nought seven   **f)** Twelve point five nought six
g) Four hundred and ninety-seven point six four three

3 Write these as fractions or mixed numbers using tenths, hundredths or thousandths (see p. 78 for mixed numbers).

a) 0.7	**b)** 0.06	**c)** 0.003	**d)** 0.04	**e)** 3.05
f) 6.4	**g)** 15.007	**h)** 8.02	**i)** 10.6	**j)** 240.009

4 Write each of these numbers in terms of fractions in **two different ways** (i.e. as separate fractions and as a single fraction).

a) 0.17	**b)** 0.49	**c)** 0.031	**d)** 0.357	**e)** 6.23
f) 8.043	**g)** 42.107	**h)** 1.241	**i)** 502.69	**j)** 17.653

b Write decimals as common fractions

You can simplify fractions by dividing the top and bottom by the same number.

See page 87 for a reminder.

Example Write 0.75 as a fraction.

$$0.75 = \frac{75}{100} = \frac{15}{20} = \frac{3}{4}$$

As a fraction $0.75 = \frac{3}{4}$

dividing top and bottom by 5 then 5 again

Practice

Write these decimals as simple fractions.

1 0.5	**2** 0.2	**3** 0.4	**4** 0.6	**5** 0.8
6 0.15	**7** 0.35	**8** 0.55	**9** 0.25	**10** 0.45

c Put decimals in order of size

▶ Compare the whole number part, then the decimal digits in order of size.

Example

Put 2.97, 3.081, 2.963, 2.79, 2.805, 2.965 in order starting with the largest.

3.081
2.97
2.965
2.963
2.805
2.79

→3rd dp
whole   **2nd dp**
    1st dp

Compare the digits

First look at the whole numbers.
3 is bigger than 2 so 3.081 is the largest.
All the other numbers start with 2.

Look at the 1st decimal place.
9 is the largest, but there are 3 numbers.
To compare 2.97, 2.963 and 2.965:

Look at the 2nd decimal place.
7 is larger than 6 so 2.97 is the largest.
Now to compare 2.963 and 2.965:

Look at the 3rd decimal place.
5 is larger so 2.965 is next, then 2.963
The remaining numbers are 2.79 and 2.805. To compare these:

Go back to the 2nd decimal place.
8 is larger than 7, so 2.805 is next.

The answer is   **3.081   2.97   2.965   2.963   2.805   2.79**

Practice

1 Put each group in order of size starting with the **largest**.

a) 5.02   7.21   6.76   4.32   6.12   5.98   5.03   4.68   7.11
b) 13.1   14.21   12.97   14.26   12.5   13.03   12.43   12.07
c) 26.42   21.5   25.06   26.11   21.8   25.17   21.43   26.47
d) 3.19   7.21   3.5   6.48   3.21   7.84   6.96   4.06   5.74

2 Put each group in order of size starting with the **smallest**.

a) 1.075   0.307   0.003   1.11   1.05   1.761   0.23
b) 12.05   12.502   12.429   12.5   12.121   12.005
c) 20.095   19.16   21.35   19.006   21.101   19.375
d) 604.002 483.562 581.879 581.098 428.003 412.438

3 Put each group of weights in order **largest** first (heaviest).

a) 2.009 kg   1.045 kg   1.762 kg   2.032 kg   1.104 kg
b) 1.7 kg   1.07 kg   1.707 kg   1.007 kg   1.077 kg
c) 0.041 kg   0.405 kg   0.318 kg   0.058 kg   0.201 kg

4 The following times (in seconds) are recorded at a race day.
   Write each group in order, starting with the **shortest** time (quickest).

a) 12.056   12.009   11.909   11.099   12.201   12.037
b) 18.567   19.002   18.411   18.591   18.302   19.041
c) 26.057   25.503   25.601   25.072   26.001   25.021

Use a calculator to solve problems   N2/E3.4

A calculator is useful for working with decimals, but it is easy to press the wrong key.
It is important that you always check the answer.

When using a calculator:

● take care to press the numbers and the decimal point correctly

● include a zero before the decimal point in the answer if there is no whole number

● write down a sensible number of decimal places

● For money use 2 decimal places to give the nearest pence and add a zero if necessary
  (e.g. 3.5 means £3.50)

● write down the units if there are any (e.g. £, m, kg)

● think about whether the answer is sensible

● use estimation, inverse calculations or a different method to check the answer.

Example

Three presents cost £5.99, £2.45 and £3.95.
Using a calculator gives the total: 5.99 + 2.45 + 3.95 = 12.39   Answer = **£12.39**

Check by estimating (to the nearest £): £6 + £2 + £4 = £12

or

There is a choice of ways to check – just use one way.

Check using inverse calculations: 12.39 – 3.95 – 2.45 = 5.99

or

Check by adding in a different order: 3.95 + 2.45 + 5.99 = 12.39

Practice

Use a calculator to work these out. Check each answer.

1 a) 13 + 1.05
b) £1.02 + £3.74
c) 1.5 m + 0.5 m
d) 5.75 + 3.05 + 1.9
e) £4.57 – £0.86
f) £11.00 – £2.19
g) 9 m – 4.5 m
h) 23 – 1.14
i) 5.03 × 3
j) £3.07 × 0.5
k) 5 × 0.2 kg
l) £7.15 × 4
m) 6.45 ÷ 3
n) £3.13 ÷ 4
o) 6 m ÷ 0.3 m
p) 1.35 ÷ 0.2

2 Four friends share the cost of a meal, £18.50. How much do they pay each?

3 A girl spends £1.17 on sweets and her brother spends £4.20.
How much do they spend altogether?

4 A boy saves £3.50 each week. How much does he save in 8 weeks?

5 a) A dressmaker buys 14.75 metres of material. She only uses 9.5 metres.
How much material does she have left?
b) The dressmaker cuts 1.5 metres of ribbon into 5 equal lengths.
How long is each length?

6 A teenager spends £3.09 on magazines each week.
How much does she spend during 6 weeks?

7 A shopper spends £4.07, £1.99 and £2.70.
How much is this altogether?

8 Oliver wins £20. He spends £15.74 of his winnings.
How much does he have left?

Multiply and divide decimals by 10 and 100

N2/L1.6

To multiply by 10 or 100, move the numbers to the **left** so they become **larger**.

Move the numbers as many times as there are zeros in 10 or 100.

One column for 10 (as it has 1 zero). Two columns for 100 (as it has 2 zeros).

To divide by 10 or 100, move the numbers to the **right** so they become **smaller**.

Example 4.1×100

$4.1 \times 100 = 410$

The 4 moves 2 places – it is now 4 hundreds instead of 4 units. The 1 is now worth ten instead of a tenth. Put zero in the units column to keep the numbers in place.

Hundreds 100	Tens 10s	Units 1s	.	Tenths 10ths
		4	.	1
4	1	0	.	

Compare this with page 26 (whole numbers).

Example $32 \div 10$

$32 \div 10 = 3.2$

The 3 and 2 both move 1 place to the right.
The 3 is now 3 units.
The 2 is now 2 tenths.

Tens 10s	Units 1s	.	Tenths 10ths
3	2	.	0
	3	.	2

Practice

Use a place value table to help you work these out.

1 a) 17.4×10 b) 5.63×100 c) 17.12×10
   d) 11.743×10 e) 16.01×100 f) 112.2×100

2 a) $56.22 \div 10$ b) $63.04 \div 10$ c) $1.44 \div 100$
   d) $102.01 \div 10$ e) $57.04 \div 100$ f) $106 \div 100$

3 a) 26.11×10 b) $5.77 \div 10$ c) 1.04×100
   d) $121 \div 100$ e) 47.2×100 f) $566.02 \div 100$

The metric system is based on tens, hundreds and thousands.

£1 = 100p   1 cm = 10 mm   1 m = 100 cm = 1000 mm   1 km = 1000 m
1 kg = 1000 g   1 cl = 10 ml   1 l = 100 cl = 1000 ml

To convert from one unit to another you need to multiply or divide by 10, 100 or 1000.
(Note that for 1000 you need to move 3 columns.)

To convert from **large** units **to small** units **multiply**.

To convert from **small** units **to large** units **divide**.

Examples

4.6 m to cm
4.6 m × 100 = 460 cm

> ▶ There are 100 cm in a metre –
> to convert metres to centimetres
> multiply by 100.

1679 g to kg
1679 g ÷ 1000 = 1.679 kg

> ▶ There are 1000 g in a kilogram
> – to convert grams to kilograms
> divide by 1000.

---

4 Convert these.

a) 30 cm to mm   b) 3.7 m to cm   c) 145 cm to m   d) 45 mm to cm

e) £3.45 to pence   f) 789p to £   g) 0.66 m to cm   h) 65 cℓ to litres

i) 1567 g to kg   j) 18 mm to cm   k) 0.6 km to m   l) 7580 m to km

5 Copy the amounts below. Draw lines between the equivalent amounts.

a)
7500 g	2.3 m
230 cm	0.75 ℓ
2300 g	7.5 kg
75 cℓ	1.25 ℓ
125 cℓ	2.3 kg

b)
0.5 m	750 g
1.2 ℓ	5 mℓ
0.75 kg	50 cm
1.2 cm	120 cℓ
0.5 cℓ	12 mm

> For more
> conversions see
> pages 172, 194
> and 206.

Round decimal numbers and approximate

N2/L1.7, N2/L2.5

To round decimal numbers to whole numbers:

- Look at the **first decimal place** (1st dp).

- If it is **below 5, leave the whole number as it is.**

- If it is **5 or above, round the whole number up by 1**.

> Rounding is used to
> estimate or check
> calculations.

Example

Round 2.47 to the nearest whole number.

Units 1s	.	Tenths 10ths	Hundredths 100ths
2	.	4	7

1st dp   This is the 'deciding digit'

4 is **below 5**
so 2.**4**7 = **2** to the nearest whole number.

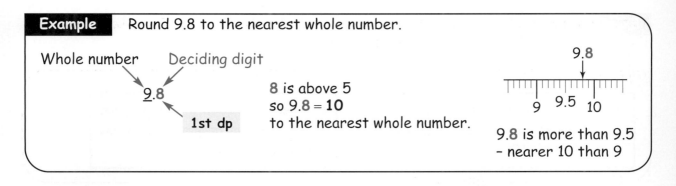

Example Round 9.8 to the nearest whole number.

Whole number Deciding digit

9.8

1st dp

8 is above 5
so 9.8 = **10**
to the nearest whole number.

9.8

9   9.5   10

9.8 is more than 9.5
– nearer 10 than 9

Practice

1 Round each of these to the nearest whole number.

a) 14.7	**b)** 13.1	**c)** 7.4	**d)** 3.8	**e)** 9.7	**f)** 6.21
g) 16.31	**h)** 11.81	**i)** 9.84	**j)** 11.71	**k)** 15.07	**l)** 0.71
m) 4.315	**n)** 5.572	**o)** 0.469	**p)** 26.98	**q)** 249.5	**r)** 99.67

In these questions round values to whole numbers then estimate the answers.

2 Three friends spend £4.96 each. Estimate how much they spend altogether.

3 A dressmaker buys 1.8 m of blue silk, 1.2 m of red silk and 2.9 m of green silk.
Estimate how much material is bought altogether.

4 A shopper buys items costing £4.21, £0.91 and £1.21.
Estimate the total cost.

5 Estimate the total weight of these parcels.

6 Rita says she has £15 in her purse, to the nearest £.
What is the least amount of money she can have?

0.98 kg

1.7 kg

2.5 kg

To round a decimal to **one decimal place, look at the** second decimal place.
If this is **5 or above, round the first decimal place up**.

Example Round 7.26 to 1 decimal place.

Deciding digit

7.26

1st dp   **2nd dp**

6 is above 5
so 7.26 = **7.3** to 1 decimal place.

To round to **two** decimal places look at the **third** decimal place. If this **is 5 or above, round the second decimal place up** (otherwise leave it as it is).

Example   Round 3.084 to 2 decimal places.

Deciding digit

3.0<u>8</u>4

2nd dp   3rd dp

4 is below 5 so leave the 2nd dp as it is.
3.0<u>8</u>4 = 3.08 to 2 decimal places.

Example   Round 8.297 to 2 decimal places.

Deciding digit

8.2<u>9</u>7

2nd dp   3rd dp

7 is above 5 so round 29 up to 30
8.2<u>97</u> = 8.30 to 2 decimal places.
This is like rounding £8.297 to the nearest pence.

To round to **three** decimal places look at the **fourth** decimal place and so on.

7 Round these numbers to 2 decimal places.

a) 5.678   b) 16.591   c) 11.325   d) 21.898   e) 155.793
f) 16.224   g) 131.076   h) 6.749   i) 121.903   j) 1.891
k) 2.396   l) 16.7081   m) 15.9152   n) 13.5618   o) 1.0065

8 Round these amounts to 2 decimal places.

a) £1.273   b) 2.726 kg   c) £12.158   d) 17.415 m   e) 22.567 km
f) 14.725 g   g) 16.194 cm   h) £9.6439   i) 0.473 ℓ   j) 15.098 km

9 Round these.

a) £15.39 to the nearest pound   b) 13.606 kg to the nearest kg
c) 5.1128 litres to 2 dp   d) £31.566666 to 2 dp
e) £7.165431 to the nearest pence   f) 6.597 m to 2 dp

10 A student is asked to give answers correct to 1 dp. Round these to 1 dp.

a) 9.533333   b) 12.3567   c) 13.17098   d) 6.6974   e) 121.79311
f) 5.7217   g) 91.7508   h) 151.90854   i) 65.0911   j) 73.64842

11 Round the following numbers to three decimal places.

a) 5.79241   b) 16.9376   c) 3.74912   d) 0.97386   e) 4.03189
f) 16.7701   g) 12.08051   h) 27.90109   i) 1.54973   j) 17.6999

Activity

Find out how to round decimals on your calculator or on a spreadsheet.
Use this method to check your answers to the questions above.

Add and subtract decimals

N2/L1.5, N2/L2.6

▶ **To add or subtract decimals, line up the decimal points.**

See pages 10 and 13 for a reminder of + and − methods

You can check your answer by:

● rounding to the nearest whole numbers and estimating the answer
● using inverse (opposite) calculations (see page 14)
● using a calculator.

Example   15.07 + 3.1

```
  15.07
+  3.10
  18.17
```

Check (estimating)
```
   15
 +  3
   18
```

Check (inverse)
```
  18.17
−  3.10
  15.07
```

Example   24.3 − 3.75

```
  24.30
−  3.75
  20.55
```
← Fill gaps with 0s

Check (estimating)
```
   24
 −  4
   20
```

Check (inverse)
```
  20.55
+  3.75
  24.30
```

Practice

Calculate and check these without a calculator.

1 a) 5.2 + 3.9
   b) 4.9 − 2.1
   c) 10.4 + 12.96
   d) 72.34 − 49.67
   e) £204.07 − £196.30
   f) £137.60 − £107.06
   g) £18.99 + £108.17
   h) 2.1 m − 0.75 m
   i) 57.06 + 106.1
   j) 13.12 − 12.07
   k) 105.17 + 22.4
   l) 49.35 + 107.19

Work these out, then check with a calculator.

2   A saver has £354.60 in the bank. She withdraws £217.74.
    What is her new balance?

3   Two friends book a holiday costing £980.89. They pay a deposit of £98.08.
    How much is left to pay?

4   A shopper receives £13.49 change from a twenty pound note.
    How much has he spent?

5   A worker earns £1120.09. He spends £875.42. How much does he have left?

6   A student buys three books costing £55.44, £13.62 and £17.29.
    What is the total cost?

7   The interest on a loan of £1500 is £427.61. What is the total amount owed?

8   A factory has 476.5 m of material in stock. It uses 326.25 m. How much is left?

9   A householder receives bills for £372.15, £32.07 and £11.19.
    How much is this altogether?

10 A farmer wants to fence some land. The lengths of the sides are 65.8 m, 67.75 m, 78.95 m
    and 96.5 m. Add these lengths to find the perimeter.

11 The table shows the time in seconds taken by
    each swimmer in two relay teams.

    a) Find the total time taken by each team.
    b) Which team won and by how many seconds?

	Team A	Team B
1st swimmer	21.42	22.56
2nd swimmer	25.58	23.10
3rd swimmer	24.17	24.78
4th swimmer	19.96	20.34

Work these out without a calculator then use rounding to check.

12 a) $2.396 + 5.274 + 2.821$ b) $9.08 - 2.765$ c) $3.24 + 6.382 - 5.493$

13 In a race the fastest time is 43.456 seconds and the slowest time is 59.572 seconds.
    What is the difference between these times?

Multiply decimals

N2/L1.5, N2/L2.6

To multiply decimals:

See pages 21 and 31 for a reminder.

- Ignore the decimal points and use your usual method to multiply the figures.

- Count the total number of decimal places (dp) in **both** numbers being multiplied.
  Starting at the end of the answer, count the same number of decimal places and insert the decimal point.
  (Add zeros to the front if needed, e.g. $0.3 \times 0.2 = 0.06$)

- Round the answer to a sensible number of figures (e.g. money to the nearest £ or pence).

- Check the answer.

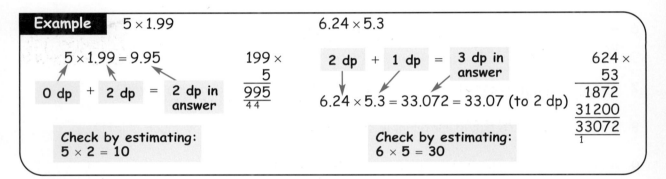

Example 5×1.99 6.24×5.3

$5 \times 1.99 = 9.95$

0 dp + **2 dp** = **2 dp in answer**

$$199 \times$$
$$\underline{5}$$
$$995$$
$$\small 44$$

Check by estimating:
$5 \times 2 = 10$

2 dp + **1 dp** = **3 dp in answer**

$6.24 \times 5.3 = 33.072 = 33.07$ (to 2 dp)

$$624 \times$$
$$\underline{53}$$
$$1872$$
$$31200$$
$$\underline{33072}$$
$$\small 1$$

Check by estimating:
$6 \times 5 = 30$

Practice

1 Calculate these without a calculator. Round answers to 2 dp where necessary.
   Use estimation to check each answer.

   a) 0.6×4 **b)** 0.2×0.1 **c)** 7×0.05 **d)** 0.3×0.4

   e) 3.65×4 **f)** 19.7×3 **g)** 11.22×0.5 **h)** 165×0.09

   i) 40.7×0.8 **j)** 85.7×0.06 **k)** 5.01×2.1 **l)** 1.8×0.69

   m) 5.19×7.3 **n)** 7.43×1.08 **o)** 18.1×3.66 **p)** 4.25×3.07

Work these out, then check with a calculator.

2 A dressmaker wants to make 4 dresses. Each dress uses 3.75 m of material.
   How much material is needed altogether?

3 James buys 6 bottles of wine containing 0.75 litres each.
   How many litres of wine is this altogether?

4 A shop assistant's hourly wage is £5.95.
   How much does he earn for 37.5 hours?

5 An office puts in an order for stationery.
Copy and complete the table by working out the prices and total cost.

Order No	Item description	Price of item	Quantity	Price
PHF/1357	A4 paper	£3.99	5	
PHF/1359	A3 paper	£4.75	3	
ZL/129	Box black pens	£0.85	8	
FL/376	White board pens	£1.02	6	
GH/76P	Chrome stapler	£4.50	3	
GH/76L	Staples	£0.49	12	
		Total cost of all items		

6 A rectangular lawn is 43.6 m long and 28.4 m wide.
What is its area to the nearest square metre?

See page 225.

L2 **7** Calculate these without a calculator. Use estimation to check each answer.

  a) 3.725×8 **b)** 1.864×0.9 **c)** 5.209×4.3

8 A tourist is going to China. She changes £400 to yen.
The exchange rate is £1 = 189.112 yen. How many yen does she get?

9 A cuboid is 3.6 m × 1.7 m × 5.8 m. Multiply these to work out its volume to 1 dp.

10 A circular fish pond has a diameter of 3.2 m.
Find its circumference and area to 1 dp. Use $\pi = 3.142$.

See pages 227 and 228 for the formulae.

Divide decimals

N2/L1.5, N2/L2.6

To divide a decimal by a whole number:

- Divide the figures as usual.

- Keep the decimal points in line.

- Round the answer to a sensible number of figures (where necessary).

- Check the answer.

See page 34 for a reminder.

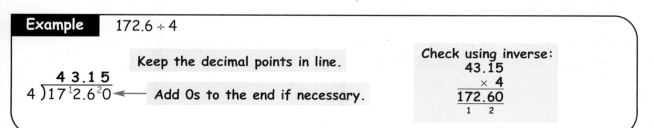

Example $172.6 \div 4$

Keep the decimal points in line.

$$4 \overline{\smash{)}17^12.6^20} \quad \begin{array}{c} 4\,3.1\,5 \end{array}$$

Add 0s to the end if necessary.

Check using inverse:
$$\begin{array}{r} 43.15 \\ \times\ 4 \\ \hline 172.60 \\ \end{array}$$

Practice

1   Do these without a calculator. Check each answer.

a) $49.2 \div 4$ b) $33.78 \div 3$ c) $79.9 \div 5$ d) $232.47 \div 7$
e) $137.88 \div 9$ f) $67.08 \div 6$ g) $423.06 \div 3$ h) $301.14 \div 8$

To divide a decimal by a decimal:

● Change the number you are dividing by into a whole number.
  Do this by multiplying by 10 or 100 or 1000.

● Do exactly the same to the number you are dividing.

● Divide to find the answer.

| **Example** | $7.4 \div 0.05$ |

$7.4 \div 0.05 = 740 \div 5$ Multiply 0.05 by 100 to make it into the whole number 5.
Do the same to 7.4

$$\begin{array}{r} 1\ 4\ 8 \\ 5\,\overline{)7^2 4^4 0} \end{array}$$ Answer = 148   Check by inverse on calculator:
148 × 0.05 = 7.4

| **Example** | Find $31.52 \div 2.4$ to 2 decimal places. |

$31.52 \div 2.4 = 315.2 \div 24$ Multiply 2.4 by 10 to make it into the whole number 24.
Do the same to 31.52

$$\begin{array}{r} 1\ 3.\ 1\ 3 \\ 24\,\overline{)31^7 5.^3 2^8 0} \end{array}$$ Answer = 13.13

This is very difficult!   e.g.   2 4
                                                                  × 3
● Try out some values in rough when you need to.   7 2
                                                                   1
● For the last figure, you need to decide which is nearer to 80:
  $24 \times 3 = 72$ or $24 \times 4 = 96$ 3 is nearer
  (Alternatively you could work it out to   Check by estimating:
  3 decimal places then round your answer.)   30 ÷ 2 = 15

---

2   Calculate these without a calculator. Give the answer to 2 dp when not exact.
    Check each answer.

a) $0.8 \div 0.2$ b) $1.5 \div 0.5$ c) $0.4 \div 0.02$ d) $1.8 \div 0.9$
e) $3.9 \div 0.03$ f) $6.8 \div 0.2$ g) $13.25 \div 0.5$ h) $10.8 \div 0.03$
i) $2.5 \div 0.04$ j) $34 \div 0.7$ k) $74.16 \div 0.06$ l) $43.2 \div 1.2$
m) $56.9 \div 3.1$ n) $90.1 \div 5.3$ o) $115.2 \div 0.12$ p) $35 \div 0.25$
q) $5.75 \div 1.1$ r) $120 \div 7.9$ s) $14.3 \div 4.6$ t) $101.52 \div 2.16$

3 A total of 8.4 mm of rain fell in a week. What was the average rainfall per day?

4 Three friends share the cost of a taxi between them as equally as they can.
The taxi cost £6.50 How much do they each pay?

5 A roll of ribbon is 20 metres long.
How many pieces of length 0.4 metres can be cut from the roll?

6 A drinks company sells cola in 0.33 litre cans.
How many cans can be filled from 2000 litres of cola?

7 Calculate these without a calculator (Note: You will need to × 1000 this time).
Check each answer.

    a) $9.7 \div 0.005$ **b)** $0.378 \div 0.012$ **c)** $0.48 \div 0.025$ **d)** $14.2 \div 0.125$

8 A holidaymaker buys a present costing 18 euros. The exchange rate is 1.414 euros to the pound. How much does the present cost to the nearest pound?

9 A tourist returns from America with $200. The exchange rate is $1.601 to the pound. What will she receive? Give your answer to the nearest pound.

Here is a mixture of calculations to try.

10 Estimate the answers, then work them out accurately to 2 decimal places.
    a) $15.435 + 16.586$ **b)** 3.791×1.9 **c)** $21.452 - 7.693$
    d) $11.924 \div 2.1$ **e)** 5.798×7.1 **f)** $19.687 - 7.132$
    g) $9.687 + 2.763$ **h)** $9.782 \div 2.5$ **i)** 5.7×3.793

11 The table shows a caterer's vegetable order.

Item	Weight	Price per kg
Potatoes	50 kg	£0.28
Carrots	25 kg	£0.36
Sprouts	12.5 kg	£0.52
Mushrooms	6.4 kg	£2.35

    a) Find the total cost.
    b) He is given a discount of a third of the price.
        How much does he pay?

12 It takes 25 lengths of wallpaper, each 3.2 m long to cover a room.
The decorator allows an extra 0.25 m per length for matching the pattern.
Rolls of wallpaper are 10.05 m long.
How many rolls does the decorator need to cover the room?

Number

10 Percentages

Understand percentages and find percentage increase and decrease

N2/L1.8

a Understand percentages

Percent means out of 100. It is also written using the sign %.

100% of something = the whole amount

This grid has been split into 100 squares:

30 out of 100 are white.   30% are white.
37 out of 100 are grey.   37% are grey.
18 out 100 are orange.   18% are orange.
15 out of 100 are black.   _15%_ are black.
         The total % = 100%

Practice

1 Look at the coloured squares in this grid.

   a) Write down the percentage for each colour.
   b) Check that the total % is 100%.

2 Draw a grid of 100 squares.

   a) Colour in these percentages: 34% red, 16% green,
       21% blue, 19% black.
   b) What % of the squares are not coloured?

Every % can be written as a fraction.

9% means 9 out of 100.   As a fraction this is $\frac{9}{100}$.

53% means 53 out of 100.   As a fraction this is $\frac{53}{100}$.

---

3 Write these percentages as fractions (out of 100).

   a) 3%   **b)** 63%   **c)** 13%   **d)** 57%
   e) 27%   **f)** 11%   **g)** 91%   **h)** 39%

4 Write these fractions as percentages.

a) $\dfrac{7}{100}$ b) $\dfrac{19}{100}$ c) $\dfrac{41}{100}$ d) $\dfrac{73}{100}$

e) $\dfrac{99}{100}$ f) $\dfrac{81}{100}$ g) $\dfrac{1}{100}$ h) $\dfrac{49}{100}$

There are 100 pence in a pound.

10 pence out of a pound = 10% of £1   90 pence out of a pound = 90% of £1

---

5 Write these amounts as percentages of £1.

a) 20 pence   b) 45 pence   c) 16 pence   d) 85 pence

6 The following are percentages of £1. Write each amount in pence.

a) 17%   b) 99%   c) 22%   d) 51%

b Percentage increase and decrease

Wage and price rises are often given as percentages.

Example

A 5% pay rise means that you get an extra 5p for every £1 you earn.
If you earn £6 an hour, a 5% increase is 6 × 5p = 30p per hour
If you earn £9 an hour, a 5% increase is 9 × 5p = 45p per hour
The more you earn, the higher your wage rise.

Example

A price rise of 3% means that the new price is 3p higher for every £1 of the old price.
If the old price was £129, the new price is 129 × 3p higher.
The price rise = 387p = £3.87

$$\begin{array}{r} 1\ 2\ 9 \\ \times\ 3 \\ \hline 3\ 8\ 7 \\ \scriptstyle 2 \end{array}$$

Practice

1 a) Find the increase from a 5% wage rise when the rate per hour is
   i) £5   ii) £8   iii) £7   iv) £10   v) £11.

b) Repeat part a) for a 2% wage rise.

c) Repeat part a) for a 3% wage rise.

2 The table shows the weekly wage of each assistant in a shop before they all get a pay rise of 4%.
Find how much extra each worker gets per week.

Worker	Weekly Wage
Jan	£230
Kate	£185
Luke	£217
Wes	£194

3 A hotel manager increases all the prices in her hotel by 6%.
Find the price increase on each of these.

a) Breakfast £5   **b)** Lunch £12   **c)** Evening meal £25
d) Single room £57 per night   **e)** Double room £89 per night

---

When shops have a sale they often advertise price reductions as percentages.

Example

'20% off' means a reduction of 20p in every pound.
If an item costs £10 the reduction is 10 × 20p = 200p = £2.

Discounts are also price reductions, often given as percentages.

Example

'12% off for cash', means a 12p reduction in every pound.
If a job costs £90 the discount is 90 × 12p = 1080p = £10.80.

---

4 a) A shop reduces its prices by 10%. Find the reductions on these prices.
   i) £2   **ii)** £7   **iii)** £6   **iv)** £4   **v)** £5
   vi) £8   **vii)** £9   **viii)** £10   **ix)** £17   **x)** £18

   b) Repeat part a) for a reduction of 8%.
   c) Repeat part a) for a reduction of 30%.
   d) Repeat part a) for a reduction of 15%.

5 Find each reduction.

   a) 20% off £50   **b)** 10% off £39   **c)** 50% off £16
   d) 40% off £35   **e)** 15% off £60   **f)** 25% off £8
   g) 12% off £36   **h)** 75% off £20   **i)** 6% off £125

6 A supplier offers a discount of 12% for early payment.
Find the discounts on these amounts.

   a) £600   **b)** £1250   **c)** £3768   **d)** £27 854

Find percentages of quantities and measurements   N2/L1.9, N2/L2.8

1 square out of the 100 in this grid is black.

$1\% = 1 \text{ out of } 100 = \dfrac{1}{100}$

> ▶ **To find 1% of something, divide it by 100.**

Example

1% of £750 = **£7.50**

Example

1% of 20 m = 0.20 m = **0.2 m**

See page 106 for help with ÷ 100.

Practice

1 Find 1% of these.

    a) 500   **b)** 630 km   **c)** 894 g   **d)** £30   **e)** £480   **f)** £26

Multiply to find other percentages.

Example   Find 3% of 250 kg

1% of 250 kg = 2.5 kg   (dividing by 100)

$\overset{\times 3}{}$

3% of 250 kg = $\underset{1}{\underline{7.5}}$ **kg**   (multiplying by 3)

2 Find 3% of these.

    a) 400   **b)** £540   **c)** 80 km   **d)** £50   **e)** 35 kg   **f)** £17

3 Find 4% of these.

    a) 7000   **b)** 450 m   **c)** 750 g   **d)** 95 km   **e)** £360   **f)** £32

For other percentages the multiplying is more difficult.

There are quicker ways for some percentages.

Look at the grid at the top of this page. 50 out of the 100 squares are orange.

This is half of the grid.

$50\% = 50 \text{ out of } 100 = \dfrac{50}{100} = \dfrac{1}{2}.$ **Learn**   ▶ $50\% = \dfrac{1}{2}$

To find 50% of something, divide it by 2.

Example   Find 50% of 8 m

$8 \div 2 = 4$ m   so 50% of 8 m = **4 m**

Example   Find 50% of £15

$15 \div 2 = 7.5$ so 50% of £15 = **£7.50**

$$2\overline{)15^1.0}^{\,7.5}$$

---

4   Find 50% of these.

   a) £160   **b)** 50 m   **c)** 96 km   **d)** £15   **e)** 780 kg   **f)** 900 g

5   This recipe is for fruit crumble for four people.

   a) Find 50% of each ingredient.
   b) How many people would the new amount of crumble feed?

> **Fruit Crumble**
> 250 g plain flour
> 120 g butter
> 90 g sugar
> 280 g blackberries
> 200 g redcurrants
> 150 g strawberries

Look at the grid on page 119 again. 10 of the 100 squares are grey.
This is a tenth of the grid.

$10\% = 10$ out of $100 = \dfrac{10}{100} = \dfrac{1}{10}$ **Learn** ▶ $10\% = \dfrac{1}{10}$

▶ **To find 10% of something, divide it by 10.**

Example   10% of £150 = **£15**

Example   10% of £3.50 = **£0.35**

📄 See page 106 for help with ÷ 10.

---

6   Find 10% of these.

   a) £450   **b)** 90 m   **c)** £2400   **d)** 54 cm   **e)** 62 kg   **f)** 325 m
   g) £4.20   **h)** £8   **i)** £23.70   **j)** £105   **k)** 2.8 tonnes   **l)** 0.7 km

▶ **To find 20%, find 10% then double it.**

Example   Find 20% of 80.

10% of 80 = 8   (because 80 ÷ 10 = 8)
20% of 80 = 8 × 2 = **16**   **20% = 10% × 2**

▶ **To find 30%, find 10% then multiply by 3.**

Example   Find 30% of £3.20.

10% of £3.20 = £0.32   (because £3.20 ÷ 10 = £0.320 = £0.32)
                    ×3
30% of £3.20 = **£0.96** or **96p**   **30% = 10% × 3**

▶ **To find 40%, find 10% then multiply by 4.**

Example   Find 40% of 68 kg.

10% of 68 kg =   6.8 kg   (because 68 ÷ 10 = 6.8)
                    ×4
40% of 68 kg = **27.2 kg**   **40% = 10% × 4**
              3

You can use a similar method for other multiples of 10% (e.g. 60%, 70%).

7 Find these using the method shown above.

a) 20% of 120 g   b) 30% of 170 kg   c) 60% of 560 g   d) 40% of 960 m
e) 20% of 54 kg   f) 40% of £160   g) 20% of £574   h) 30% of £12
i) 70% of £63.20   j) 80% of 91 m   k) 90% of 14.2 kg   l) 60% of 18.5 kg

▶ **To find 5% of something, find 10% then halve it.**

Example   Find 5% of 270 kg

10% of 270 kg = 27 kg
5% of 270 kg = **13.5 kg**

5% = 10% ÷ 2

$$\frac{13.5}{2)27.^{1}0}$$

▶ **To find 15%, find 10% then 5% and add them together.**

Example   Find 15% of £18

10% + 5%:
10% of £18 = £1.80 +
5% of £18 = £0.90
15% of £18 = **£2.70**

15% = 10% + 5%

$$\begin{array}{r} 0.90 \\ 2\overline{)1.^180} \end{array}$$

You can find lots of others by combining the methods,
e.g. for 35% find 10%, multiply by 3 for 30%, then find 5% and add it on.

Example   Find 35% of £90

10% of £90 = £ 9

30% + 5%:
30% of £90 = £27 +
5% of £90 = £ 4.50
35% of £90 = **£31.50**

35% = 30% + 5%

$$\begin{array}{r} 4.5 \\ 2\overline{)9.^10} \end{array}$$

8 Use the methods above to find these.

a) 5% of 80 kg   b) 5% of £45   c) 5% of £62.40   d) 5% of 436 m
e) 15% of 110 kg   f) 15% of 46 m   g) 15% of £96   h) 25% of 20 m
i) 25% of 400 g   j) 35% of £200   k) 45% of 160 litres l) 55% of 60 kg
m) 65% of 125 m   n) 95% of 90 m   o) 35% of 7 680 kg   p) 85% of £16 520

9 A couple pay a 15% deposit on a house costing £129 900. How much is the deposit?

10 35% of the proceeds from ticket sales for a concert go to charity.
Ticket sales total £4300. How much of this goes to the charity?

11 A holiday costs £1870. The travel agent asks for a 25% deposit.
How much is the deposit?

There are other ways of finding 25% of something.

▶ **To find 25%, you could halve (to find 50%), then halve again.**

Example   **Find 25% of £80**   **Find 25% of 8.4 km**

so
50% of £80 = £40
25% of £80 = **£20**

so
50% of 8.4 m = 4.2 km
25% of 8.4 m = **2.1 km**

> ▶ Another way to find 25% is to ÷ by 4.   Learn **25%** = $\frac{1}{4}$

Example   Find 25% of £80   Find 25% of 8.4 km

$$80 \div 4 = 20$$
so   25% of £80 = **£20**

$$8.4 \div 4 = 2.1$$
so   25% of 8.4 km = **2.1 km** $\begin{array}{r} 2.1 \\ 4\overline{)8.4} \end{array}$

---

12 Find 25% of these by halving, then halving again.

a) £60   b) 94 m   c) 12.8 m   d) £24.80   e) 766 m   f) 19 cm
g) £150   h) £27.40   i) 15.9 kg   j) 99 m   k) 45 km   l) £6.60

Check your answers by dividing each quantity by 4.

> ▶ To find 75%, you could halve to find 50% then halve again to find 25%, then add the two together.

Example   Find 75% of 240 m.

50% of 240 m = 240 ÷ 2 = 120
25% of 240 m = 120 ÷ 2 = 60
50% + 25%   **75% of 240 m =**   <u>**180 m**</u>

75% = 50% + 25%

> ▶ Another way to find 75% is to divide by 4 (to find 25%) then multiply by 3.

Example   Find 75% of 240 m

25% of 240 m = 240 ÷ 4 = 60
75% of 240 m = 60 × 3 = **180 m**

Learn **75%** = $\frac{3}{4}$

---

13 Find 75% of these by the first method given above.

a) £180   b) 96 m   c) 360°   d) 520 m   e) 170 kg   f) £96.80
g) £12.80   h) 124 cm   i) 4.8 m   j) 18.48 kg   k) 20.8 g   l) £66.40

Use the second method to check your answers.

Use 2 different methods to answer each of these.

14 A carpenter has 90 metres of skirting board. He needs
    50% more. What extra length does he need?

15 A coat priced at £120 is reduced by 50% in a sale.
    What is the reduction?

16 Last year 300 people came to the school play. This year they
    have sold 25% more tickets. How many more tickets have they sold?

17 There are 60 seats on a coach. 75% of these are taken. How many seats are taken?

18 A social club has 320 members. 25% of the members are men. How many are women?

19 James buys 480 tiles. 75% of these are blue. How many blue tiles are there?

L2 Sometimes you need to round the answer.   N2/L2.8

> ▶ **Leave rounding until the end** – this gives a more accurate answer.

Example   Find 15% of £63.35.

           10% of £63.35 = £6.335 +   3.1 6 7 5 | See p 107 for
            5% of £63.35 = £3.1675   2)6.3¹3¹5¹0 | rounding decimals
10% + 5%   15% of £63.35 = £9.5025 = **£9.50 to nearest pence**

---

20 Find each of these to 2 decimal places.

   a) 30% of £19.95   **b)** 75% of 107.3 m   **c)** 50% of £65.95
   d) 35% of £621.35   **e)** 25% of 133.35 m   **f)** 70% of £19.99

21 An account holder has £565.79 in the bank. The interest rate is 5% per annum.
    How much interest does she earn in a year?

22 The items in a shopper's basket cost £4.99, £17.95 and £19.99. The shop gives a 25%
    discount on the total bill. What is the discount?

23 A nurse earns £1575.49 per month. He gets a 5% pay rise.
    How much extra does he earn per month?

24 An insurance agent sells a policy for £449.99. His commission is 7.5%
    How much commission does he make? (Hint: 7.5% is half of 15%)

Work out VAT

N2/L2.8

Value Added Tax (VAT) at 17.5% is charged on most of the items you buy.

> ▶ To work out VAT, find 10%, halve this to find 5%, then halve again to find 2.5%.
> Then add all these together

Example Work out the VAT on a television set costing £250.

$$10\% \text{ of } £250 = £25$$
$$5\% \text{ of } £250 = £12.50 \ +$$
$$2.5\% \text{ of } £250 = £\ \ 6.25$$
$$VAT = 17.5\% \text{ of } £250 = \mathbf{£43.75}$$

VAT = 17.5%
= 10% + 5% + 2.5%

Example A radio costs £26.99 without VAT. How much is the VAT?

$$10\% \text{ of } £26.99 = £2.699$$
$$5\% \text{ of } £26.99 = £1.3495 \ +$$
$$2.5\% \text{ of } £26.99 = £0.67475$$
$$VAT = 17.5\% \text{ of } £26.99 = £4.72325 = \mathbf{£4.72}$$

$$\begin{array}{r} 1.34\,9\,5 \\ 2\overline{)2.69^19^10} \\ \hline 0.6\,74\,7\,5 \\ 2\overline{)1.3^149^15^10} \end{array}$$

Practice

1 Work out the VAT at 17.5% on each of these.

   a) £900   b) £2400   c) £180   d) £360   e) £98   f) £46
   g) £25.80 h) £9.60   i) £22.40 j) £96.80 k) £120.82 l) £27.56
   m) £82.84 n) £49.90 o) £24.98 p) £59.96 q) £7.95   r) £119.99

2 Work out the VAT at 17.5% on these.

   a) sofa costing £980   b) stereo costing £249
   c) coat costing £59.90   d) shoes for £69.50
   e) toaster at £14.95   f) electronic game £59.99

Percentage increase and decrease

N2/L1.10, N2/L2.7

To find the new amount after a % change, you need to **add the increase** or **subtract the reduction**.

Example An employee who earns £7 per hour gets a 6% increase.
What is his new rate of pay?

6% is 6p in the £, so the increase is 7 × 6p = 42p.
New rate of pay = £7 + 42p = **£7.42**

Example   A coat that costs £89.90 is reduced by 30% in a sale.
Find the sale price.

Find the reduction:
10% of £89.90 = £ 8.99
                           ×3
30% of £89.90 = £26.97

Check: 9 × 3 = 27

then take it away:
                £89.90 −
                £26.97
Sale price = £62.93

Check: 90 − 30 = 60

Practice

1   For each price, find the sale price after a reduction of: **a)** 20%   **b)** 25%

   i) £120   **ii)** £500   **iii)** £1200   **iv)** £1500   **v)** £1050   **vi)** £892

2   For each price, find the new price after an increase of: **a)** 10%   **b)** 15%

   i) £780   **ii)** £120   **iii)** £80   **iv)** £64   **v)** £1070   **vi)** £644

> Use your working from **a**

3   A saver has £600 in the bank. The interest rate is 5% per annum.
    How much will the saver have in the bank after a year?

4   A dressmaker needs 67m of material. She decides to buy 10% extra in case of mistakes.
    How much material does she buy altogether?

5   A dress in a shop window is priced at £65. This is reduced by 15% in a sale.
    What is the sale price?

6   A stationery shop gives a 5% discount to students.
    How much does a student pay for goods priced at £20?

7   The number of tickets available for a play is 900. Only 70% of these tickets are sold.

   a) How many tickets are sold?   **b)** How many tickets are left?

8   There are 120 sweets in a bag. 40% have been eaten. How many sweets are left?

9   A television is priced at £199.
    The assistant offers a 10% discount for cash.
    What is the discounted price?

10   A deposit of 25% has been paid on a holiday costing £1040.
     How much is there left to pay?

L2 **11** For each price, find the sale price after a reduction of 7%.

    i) £120   **ii)** £500   **iii)** £1200   **iv)** £1500   **v)** £1050   **vi)** £892

12 For each price, find the new price after an increase of 8%.

    i) £780   **ii)** £120   **iii)** £80   **iv)** £64   **v)** £1070   **vi)** £644

13 The prices of some items before VAT are shown below.
Find the prices including VAT.

14 The old design of a greenhouse costs £320. A new design costs 12.5% more.
How much is the new design?

Another way to increase or decrease by a percentage   N2/L2.7

You can add or subtract the % from 100% first.

> **Example**   A worker who earns £9 an hour gets a 4% wage rise.
> The new wage is **100%** + **4%** = **104%** of the old wage.
> 1% of the old wage = £9 ÷ 100 = £0.09 = 9p
> New wage = 104% = 104 × 9p = 936p = **£9.36**
>
> *Add the % increase to 100%.*

> **Example**   A coat costing £85 is reduced by 20% in a sale.
> The sale price is **100%** − **20%** = **80%** of the original price.
> 10% of the original price = £85 ÷ 10 =   £8.50
>   ×8
> Sale price = 80% of the original price = **£68.00**
>   4
>
> *Subtract the % decrease from 100%.*

Practice

1 A worker who earns £8 an hour gets a 3% wage rise. What is his new wage rate?

2 A shop makes 10% profit on confectionery. The cost price of some items are shown below.
   Find how much it sells these goods for.

3 A jacket costing £56 is reduced by 30% in a sale. What is the sale price?

4 A car bought for £6500 loses 20% of its value in a year.
   How much is it worth at the end of the year?

Check your answers to some of the questions in the last exercise using this method.

Equivalent fractions, decimals and percentages   N2/L1.3, N2/L2.2

a Write percentages as decimals

Fractions, decimals and percentages all represent parts of something.
(Fractions and decimals are part of 1, percentages are part of 100.)

> See page 000 for a reminder of how to ÷ 100.

> ▶ **To change a percentage to a decimal,
>   divide the percentage by 100**

| Examples | 75% = **0.75**   70% = 0.70 = **0.7**   7% = **0.07** |

Practice

1 Change these percentages to decimals.

   a) 25%   b) 35%   c) 40%   d) 30%   e) 80%   f) 5%
   g) 10%   h) 15%   i) 4%   j) 8%   k) 3%   l) 9%

L2

Examples   23% = **0.23**   12.5% = **0.125**   7.5% = **0.075**

2 Write these percentages as decimals:
   a) 16%   b) 32%   c) 49%   d) 95%   e) 64%   f) 52%
   g) 17.5%   h) 62.5%   i) 37.8%   j) 3.6%   k) 2.5%   l) 1.25%

b Write decimals as percentages

> ▶ To change a decimal to a percentage,
>   multiply the decimal by 100

See page 106 for a reminder of how to × 100.

Examples   0.2 = **20%**   0.45 = **45%**   0.02 = **2%**

Practice

1 Change these decimals to percentages.

   a) 0.75   b) 0.25   c) 0.65   d) 0.6   e) 0.06   f) 0.1
   g) 0.01   h) 0.5   i) 0.05   j) 0.9   k) 0.09   l) 0.99

L2

Examples   0.87 = **87%**   1.2 = **120%**   0.175 = **17.5%**   0.038 = **3.8%**

2 Write these decimals as percentages;
   a) 0.29   b) 0.57   c) 0.43   d) 1.5   e) 2.5   f) 0.875
   g) 0.325   h) 0.065   i) 0.005   j) 0.205   k) 0.168   l) 2.45

c Write percentages as fractions

> ▶ To write a percentage as a fraction,
>   write it over 100, then cancel if possible.

For a reminder of cancelling see page 87.

Examples $30\% = \dfrac{30}{100} = \dfrac{3}{10}$ $75\% = \dfrac{75}{100} = \dfrac{3}{4}$ $7\% = \dfrac{7}{100}$

   (÷10)   (÷25)   (doesn't cancel)

Practice

Write each percentage as a fraction in its simplest form.

1 a) 10%   b)   20%   c)   40%   d)   80%   e)   30%   f)   90%
    g) 50%   h) 25%   i) 5%   j) 15%   k) 45%   l) 3%

2 a) 19%   b) 64%   c) 95%   d) 8%   e) 86%   f) 72%

L2

Sometimes you need to multiply the top and bottom to give whole numbers.

Examples

$$4\tfrac{1}{2}\% = \frac{4\tfrac{1}{2}}{100} \xrightarrow{\times 2} \frac{9}{200}$$

$$33\tfrac{1}{3}\% = \frac{33\tfrac{1}{3}}{100} \xrightarrow{\times 3} \frac{100}{300} = \frac{1}{3}$$

> Remember this one – it is used a lot e.g. in sales.

$$7.5\% = \frac{7.5}{100} \xrightarrow{\times 10} \frac{75}{1000} = \frac{3}{40}$$

$$1.25\% = \frac{1.25}{100} \xrightarrow{\times 100} \frac{125}{10\,000} = \frac{5}{400} = \frac{1}{80}$$

3   Write each percentage as a fraction in its simplest form.

a) $1\tfrac{1}{2}\%$ b) 2.5% c) 6.4% d) $12\tfrac{1}{2}\%$ e) 8.5% f) 62.5%

g) 37.5% h) 10.5% i) 8.75% j) $66\tfrac{2}{3}\%$ k) 12.8% l) $3\tfrac{3}{4}\%$

d Write fractions as decimals and percentages

> ▶ **To write a fraction as a decimal, divide the top by the bottom.**
> **You can then change it to a percentage by multiplying by 100.**

Example

$$\frac{3}{4} = 3 \div 4 = \mathbf{0.75} \text{ as a decimal}$$

$$= \mathbf{75\%} \text{ as a \%}$$

$$\begin{array}{r} 0.\ 7\ 5 \\ 4\overline{)3.\,^30^20} \end{array}$$

> To change decimals to fractions see page 103.

Add 0s if needed

Practice

1   Change these fractions to decimals and then to percentages.

a) $\dfrac{1}{10}$ b) $\dfrac{1}{5}$ c) $\dfrac{2}{5}$ d) $\dfrac{4}{5}$ e) $\dfrac{3}{10}$ f) $\dfrac{9}{10}$

2 Copy and complete these tables.

Fraction	Decimal	%
$\frac{1}{2}$		
$\frac{1}{4}$		
$\frac{3}{4}$		
$\frac{1}{10}$		
$\frac{1}{5}$		
$\frac{1}{3}$		$33\frac{1}{3}\%$

Fraction	Decimal	%
	0.4	
	0.7	
	0.35	
		60%
		90%
		15%

Learn those in the first table.

3 Write these fractions as decimals, then percentages.

a) $\frac{9}{20}$ b) $\frac{5}{8}$ c) $\frac{7}{8}$ d) $\frac{27}{40}$ e) $\frac{7}{25}$ f) $\frac{2}{3}$ (to 2 dp)

4 Put each group in order of size, starting with the **smallest**.
(Hint: Change them to the same type.)

a) 0.76   78% $\frac{3}{4}$

b) $\frac{1}{2}$ 0.49   51%

c) 24% $\frac{1}{4}$ 0.22

d) 0.21   19% $\frac{1}{5}$

e) $\frac{5}{9}$ 50%   0.58

f) $\frac{8}{9}$ 88%   0.9

g) 59%   0.56 $\frac{7}{12}$

h) $\frac{7}{16}$ 0.49   45%

Use a calculator to find percentages   N2/L1.11, N2/L2.10

Two methods of using a calculator to work out percentages are given below.

Method A

- Divide the amount by 100 to find 1%.

- Multiply by the required percentage.

- Add or subtract the result if necessary (i.e. if you need the final amount).

> ▶ Your calculator may have a % key. The way this works varies from one calculator to another – consult your instruction booklet to find out how yours works and use it if you wish.

Method B

- Divide the % by 100 to write it as a decimal.

- Multiply the decimal by the amount.

- Add or subtract the result if necessary
  (i.e. if you need the final amount).

Example   VAT is charged at 17.5% on a bill for £19.99.

Find   **a)** the VAT amount   **b)** the total amount charged.

a)

Method A

1% of £19.99 = £19.99 ÷ 100 = £0.1999

17.5% of £19.99 = £0.1999 × 17.5

                = £3.49825 = **£3.50**

Method B

17.5% = 17.5 ÷ 100 = 0.175

0.175 × £19.99 = £3.49825

              = **£3.50**

b) Total amount = VAT + original amount = £3.49825 + £19.99

                       = £23.48825 = **£23.49**

Carry on the working on your calculator

Whichever method you use:

- Think about whether the answer is sensible.

- Carry out a check – you could use the other method or find an estimate.

Practice

Use a calculator to work these out. Round answers to 2 dp where necessary.
Use one method to work out the answer, then another method to check.

1 Calculate these.

a) 22% of 65	**b)** 37% of £170	**c)** 41% of 12 m	**d)** 82% of £520
e) 19% of 25 kg	**f)** 36% of 920 g	**g)** 28% of 94	**h)** 11% of 46 cm
i) 14% of 16 litres	**j)** 17% of 154 m	**k)** 72% of £672	**l)** 9% of 178
m) 63% of 74 km	**n)** 15% of £45	**o)** 1% of 85	**p)** 7.5% of 120 cm
q) 8.2% of £165	**r)** 68% of 13 m	**s)** 28% of 6.25 m	**t)** 0.5% of £6350

2 The prices shown below do not include VAT. Find each price including VAT at 17.5%.

3 Two shops sell the same stereo.

Work out the prices to find out which is the better buy.

4 A worker who earns £19 000 a year gets a 3.5% wage rise. What is her new salary?

5 A car costs £6900 when new. It is resold later for 65% of this.
How much is it sold for?

6 This table shows the annual percentage rate (APR) for loans from 4 different lenders.

Lender	Bayleys	Anchor	Rock Solid	Direct
APR	6.6	6.5	6.3	6.7

Work out the interest charges from each lender for one year on loans of

a) £1000   **b)** £2500   **c)** £1750   **d)** £3225   **e)** £12 500   **f)** £0.8 million.

7 A photocopier can enlarge or reduce the
dimensions of anything it copies.
Find the new length and width of a copy of this
picture when the photocopier is set at

a) 75%   **b)** 125%   **c)** 133%   **d)** 141%.

6 inches

4 inches

Remember you can increase or decrease the % first to find the final amount.

Example   VAT is charged at 17.5% on a bill for £19.99.
Find the total amount charged.

See page 132. "for methods A and B"

100% plus 17.5% VAT = 117.5%
Total amount = 117.5% of £19.99 = £0.1999 × 117.5 = **£23.49** (method A)
or 1.175 × £19.99 = **£23.49** (method B)

---

8 Find the final amounts:

a) 22% discount on £42   **b)** 105 g plus an 8% increase
c) 600 m plus a 15% increase   **d)** 42 cm minus 19%
e) 24 km increased by 32%   **f)** 106 kg minus 12%
g) 57 m plus 15%   **h)** 25 litres minus 35%
i) £14 increased by 60%   **j)** 25% wage rise on £7 an hour

9 A shopper buys the following goods:
a radio for £21.99   3 DVDs at £14.99 each   a DVD rack for £14.95.
These prices do not include VAT.
What is the total price of the goods including VAT at 17.5%?

Write one number as a percentage of another   N2/L2.9

- Write the information as a **fraction** and **simplify** if possible.
- **Divide the top by the bottom** to write the fraction as a **decimal**.
- **Multiply by 100** to change into a percentage.

See page 129.

Example   9 students out of a class of 24 have blonde hair.

The fraction having blonde hair is $\frac{9}{24} = \frac{3}{8}$

As a decimal this is 0.375.
The % who have blonde hair = 0.375 × 100 = **37.5%**.

Check on calculator
9 ÷ 24 = 0.375
0.375 × 100 = 37.5

Practice

1 In a class of 20 students, 12 are men.
What % of the students are   **a)** men   **b)** women?

2 Ten chocolates in a box of twenty-five are soft centred. What % is this?

3   The table shows the marks a student gets in his
    course assignments.
    Find his % mark for each assignment.

Asst	1	2	3	4
Mark	18	56	52	66
out of	30	70	80	120

▶ Quantities must be in the **same units**.

Example   What is 75p as a % of £2.50?

Write £2.50 in pence.

As a fraction 75p out of 250p is $\dfrac{75}{250} = \dfrac{3}{10}$

As a decimal this is 0.3. As a % it is **30%**.

---

4   a) What is 450 g as a % of 900 g?   b) What % of £60 is £20?
    c) What % of £6 is 30p?   d) What % of 1 kg is 250 g?
    e) What is 50 mm as a % of 1 m?   f) What is 33 cl as a % of 1 litre?

5   A water company is laying 2 km of pipe. In the first week it lays 160 m of the pipe.
    What % is this?

6   A bank loan of £5000 is repaid over 3 years at
    £150 a month.
    What is the % interest rate?

▶ **Note: Write the interest as
    a % of the** original amount

7   £1000 is invested in a savings account and receives interest of £3.75 per month.

    a) How much is the money worth after a year?   b) What is the % interest rate?

8   Out of 75 people who take a driving test, 45 pass. What % is this?

9   A new car is bought for £8000 and sold one year later for £7000.
    What is the % loss?

10 There is £600 in a bank account before a withdrawal of £168 is
    made.
    What percentage is withdrawn?

Use a calculator for the rest.
Give answers to 2 dp when not exact.

11 There are 150 houses in Sherbourne Close.

   a) 102 houses are lived in by families. What % are **not** families?
   b) A survey carried out in Sherbourne Close shows that 21 of the households are vegetarian. What % is this?
   c) 86 of the houses have satellite TV. What % is this?

12 In one month a travel company sells 780 holidays. 520 of these are in Europe.

   a) What % of the holidays are   **i)** in Europe   **ii)** outside Europe?
   b) Check your answers to part **a** by adding the %. The total should be 100%.

13 A school has 378 pupils. 203 of these are blonde. What % are not blonde?

14 In a college with 1254 students 358 students are part-time.

   a) What percentage are part-time?
   b) 25 of the 358 part-time students study maths. What % is this?

15 If you order this meal for two between 6 pm and 7 pm, it costs £19.
   What % do you save?

Set meal for 2	
Onion Bhajee	£2.20
Chicken Chat	£2.45
Balti Chicken	£6.45
Chicken Tikka Masala	£5.99
Aloo Gobi	£1.95
Pilau Rice	£1.80
Keema Nan	£1.30

Sometimes you may just want a rough %, or you may want to estimate a % to check an answer from a calculator.

Example   1546 out of 6012 students in a college are full-time.

This gives the fraction $\frac{1546}{6012}$.

Rounding to the nearest hundred gives $\frac{1500}{6000} = \frac{1}{4}$.   **Round to numbers that simplify.**

The % of students who are full-time is approximately **25%**.

Note: Rounding to the nearest 1000 gives 33% – this is not as accurate.

16 Estimate these.

    a) What % of 587 is 294?   **b)** What % of 1960 is 978?

    c) What % of 987 is 254?   **d)** What % of £124 is £27?

17 In the 20 162 crowd who watch a football match, there are 4213 women and 4936 children. The rest of the crowd are men.

    a) Estimate the % of the crowd that are
        i) women   **ii)** children   **iii)** men.

    b) Check your answers by adding these % together.

18 The table shows a householder's gas bills during a year.

    a) What is the total for the year?

    b) Approximately what % of this total was for
        i) spring   **ii)** summer
        iii) autumn   **iv)** winter?

    c) Check your answers to part **b** by adding the % together.

Season	Bill
Spring	£79.94
Summer	£31.63
Autumn	£81.80
Winter	£126.26

Measures, Shape and Space

1 Money

Add and subtract sums of money

MSS1/E3.1

a Line up the £s and pence

To add or subtract money, line up the decimal points.

Examples

£2 + £1.20 + 5p

£		p	
2	.	00	+
1	.	20	
0	.	05	
£3	.	25	

£5 – 75p

£		p	
5	.	00	–
0	.	75	
£4	.	25	

For writing money as decimals see page 99.

If less than 10p, put 0 here.

Practice

1 Write these in columns, lining up the decimal points. Work out the answers.

a) £5.80 + 45p + 6p
b) £16.50 + 25p + 5p
c) £2 + 60p + 7p
d) £5 + 5p + 35p
e) 75p + £2 + 50p + £1.10
f) £3.99 – 54p
g) £5.50 – 45p
h) £5 – £2.40
i) £5 – £3.99
j) £5 – £1.49
k) £2.76 + £5.80 + £17
l) £80.05 – £15.99

2 A boy has £5 in his pocket. He finds 50p, then meets a friend who gives him £2.50. What is the total amount of money he has now?

3 A girl has £5. She spends £1.05 on a bus ticket. How much does she have left?

4 a) A workman buys a beefburger, chips and a cup of coffee at the burger bar. The prices are in the list. What is the total cost?

   b) He pays with a £10 note. How much change should he get?

Burger Bar Prices

Beefburger £1.29
Cheeseburger £1.75
Chips 85 pence

Tea 60 pence
Coffee 95 pence
Fruit juice 75 pence

b Use a calculator to add and subtract money

	Parts of a £1	
	Before the point	After the point
	£	● 10p 1p

£3 . 4 2

3 pounds → (4)
40 pence → (4)
2 pence → (2)

Either work in £s using decimals

£1.20 + 60p – 5p   enter 1.2   [+]   0.6   [–]   0.05   [=]   **answer**
                                                                    1.75

£1   2 × 10p   £0   6 × 10p   £0   0 × 10p   5 × 1p

Remember to include the £ sign   £1.75

or work in pence (using £1 = 100p).

£1.20 + 60p – 5p   enter 120   [+]   60   [–]   5   [=]   **answer**
                                                                175

Remember to include the pence sign   175p

Do not use both the £ and p signs. Your answer is in £s or p. It cannot be in both.

£1.75 ✓   175p ✓   £1.75p ✗

> For more money
> calculations see
> page 105
> (Decimals section).

Practice

1   Add these amounts together using a calculator.
    Give the answer in £ if it is 100p or more.
    Check your answers using another method.

> **Note**
> Add a zero to the end if the calculator gives
> just 1 decimal place when you work in £.
> e.g. 4.5 means £4.50

a) £1.50 + 50p + 5p   b) £2.25 + 35p – 10p   c) £2.54 + 42p + 2p
d) 60p + 42p + £2   e) £3.13 + 35p – 9p   f) 50p + 3p + 4p + 40p
g) £3.30 + 3p – 50p   h) 5p + 90p + £2 + £1.50   i) £1.10 – 8p – 40p – 3p
j) £3 + 65p + £2.50 + 10p k) £18.37 – 90p – £4.49   l) £7.48 – £3.96 + £9

Round money to the nearest 10p or £   MSS1/E3.2

a Round to the nearest 10p

The rounding rule is:

> ▶ If the **amount ends in 5p or more**, round up to the next 10p above.
> ▶ If the **amount ends in less than 5p**, round down to the 10p below.

Examples

Look at the grid below:

54p ends in **4**, which is **less than 5**. **Round down** to **50p**.

68p ends in **8** which is **more than 5**. **Round up** to **70p**.

Round amounts in the **unshaded** area **down**. Round amounts in the **shaded** area **up**.

	1p	2p	3p	4p	5p	6p	7p	8p	9p	
0										10p
10p										20p
20p										30p
30p										40p
40p										50p
50p		Round down		54						60p
60p								68	Round	70p
70p									up	80p
80p										90p
90p										£1.00

Practice

1 Find where each amount is on the grid, then round it to the nearest 10p.

a) 12p   **b)** 27p   **c)** 34p   **d)** 41p   **e)** 85p   **f)** 59p

g) 25p   **h)** 62p   **i)** 46p   **j)** 77p   **k)** 90p   **l)** 3p

2 Round these to the nearest 10p.

a) £2.13   **b)** £4.43   **c)** £5.71   **d)** £7.24   **e)** £6.93   **f)** £9.11

g) £5.69   **h)** £4.18   **i)** £3.33   **j)** £8.85   **k)** £18.04   **l)** £27.97

3 Round the cost of each item to the nearest 10p.
Then add to find the approximate total cost for each person.

	Val			Yui			Carl	
a)	pen	43p	**b)**	pen	29p	**c)**	pen	39p
	ruler	27p		ruler	33p		ruler	28p
	pencil	<u>38p</u>		pencil	<u>54p</u>		pencil	<u>45p</u>

b Round to the nearest £

The rounding rule is:

▶ If the **amount ends in 50p or more, round up** to the £ above.

▶ If the **amount ends in less than 50p, round down** to the £ below.

Examples

£5.42 = **£5** to the nearest £   (because **42p** is less than 50p)
£62.59 = **£63** to the nearest £   (because **59p** is more than 50p)

Practice

1 Round each amount to the nearest £.

a) £2.60   b) £3.10   c) £4.80   d) £5.20   e) £6.90   f) £7.30
g) £8.20   h) £9.40   i) £1.70   j) £0.50   k) £10.00   l) £19.70

2 Round these figures to the nearest £.

a) £12.13   b) £34.43   c) £15.71   d) £27.24   e) £336.93   f) £9.11
g) £25.69   h) £24.18   i) £13.33   j) £228.85   k) £76.50   l) £76.49

3 **a)** Round the cost of each item to the nearest pound, then add to estimate the total cost.

i)   Veg   £1.99   ii) Cake   £2.49   iii) Files   £4.10
      Cheese   £2.27   Coffee   £3.05   Paper   £3.89
      Meat   £5.90   Milk   99p   Calculator £5.10

b) Use a calculator to find the exact totals.

Activity

Round each amount on a shopping receipt (or bank statement, payslip etc.) to the nearest £ and find the total. Use a calculator to add the exact amounts and compare the results.

For more work on rounding decimals see page 107.

Add, subtract, multiply and divide sums of money   MSS1/L1.1

a Understand place value of £s and pence

Two hundred and forty-six pounds, thirty-five pence is written in numbers as £246.35.

The 2 represents £200
The 4 represents £40
The 6 represents £6
The 3 represents 30p
The 5 represents 5p

WHOLE POUNDS				PARTS OF A £	
£			•	PENCE	
Hundreds of £s	Tens of £s	Single £s	DECIMAL POINT	Tenths of a £ 10p	Hundredths of a £ 1p
2	4	6	.	3	5

Practice

1 What does the 3 represent in each amount?

   a) £531.42   **b)** £26.43   **c)** £143.15   **d)** £84.32   **e)** £306

2 What does the 9 represent in each amount?

   a) £92.12   **b)** £20.96   **c)** £119.20   **d)** £45.59   **e)** £931.45

3 Write these amounts in numbers.

   a) one hundred and ten pounds   **b)** twenty-five pounds, twenty pence
   c) twelve pounds and fifty pence   **d)** thirty pounds, five pence
   e) two hundred and thirty pounds, fifteen pence
   f) four hundred and thirteen pounds, twenty-five pence
   g) three hundred and three pounds, three pence
   h) three hundred and twenty-five pounds

4 List these amounts in numbers, starting with the **smallest**.
   seven hundred and thirty-two pounds, sixty-one pence
   seven hundred and forty-one pounds, twelve pence
   seven hundred and thirty-six pounds, two pence
   seven hundred and thirty-one pounds, thirty-four pence

5 Write these amounts in words.

   a) £10.50   **b)** £5.99   **c)** £12.50   **d)** £505.00
   e) £2.15   **f)** £410.04   **g)** £45.49   **h)** £209.09

6 Put these amounts in order, starting with the **largest**.
   £324.14   £234.41   £324.41   £342.14   £234.14   £342.41

b Add, subtract, multiply and divide money

Use the decimal methods given in Section 1, Chapter 9 (pages 110–115).

▶ To **add** or **subtract**, **line up the decimal points**.

Examples

$£125 + £1.25$

$$
\begin{array}{r}
125.00 \\
1.25 \\
\hline
£126.25
\end{array} +
$$

$£125 - £1.25$

$$
\begin{array}{r}
125.00 \\
1.25 \\
\hline
£123.75
\end{array} -
$$

Fill the gaps with 0s.

Line up the decimal points.

Example

To multiply,
multiply the numbers
then count the decimal places

£4.15 ← 2 decimal places in the question.
×3
£12.45 ← 2 decimal places in the answer.

To divide by a whole number

7.23
2)£14.46   = **£7.23**

Divide as usual, keeping the decimal points in line.

If the answer has one decimal place (e.g. £4.2) add a zero to show the pence (£4.20).

Practice

1   Work these out without a calculator, then use a calculator to check.

a) £14.59 + £4.15 + 69p
b) £6.95 × 4
c) £14.99 × 6
d) £2.99 + £30 + 99p
e) £20 − £6.99
f) £18 ÷ 4
g) £25.80 ÷ 5
h) £15 − £2.79
i) £50 − £3.76 − £14.99
j) 7 × £15.40 + £8.75
k) £7.80 ÷ 3 − 50p
l) 57p × 9 − £4.30

2   a) A student's course costs £34.50 for one term.
        How much does it cost for three terms?
    b) The exam fee is £28.60. What is the total cost of the three term course and the exam?

3   A student pays £114.60 for a course for the full year. There are three equal terms.
    How much is the course per term?

4   A student pays £26.97 for a shirt and tie. He returns the tie
    and gets a refund of £8.99. How much did the shirt cost?

 For more money calculations see pages 110-115 (Decimals section).

Activities

Use a catalogue to find the total cost for a list of goods, or work out what you can buy for £100.
Fill in an expenses claim form.
Check bills or wage slips.

Convert between currencies

MSS1/L2.1

To find exchange rates, look on the Internet, or in the daily papers.

Country/area	Currency name	Bank SELLING rate £1 =	Bank BUYING rate £1 =
Australia	Dollar ($)	$2.42	$2.48
Europe	Euro (€)	€1.43	€1.46
India	Rupee	76.92 rupees	79.81 rupees
Japan	Yen	189.65 yen	193.83 yen
South Africa	Rand	11.74 rand	12.05 rand
USA	Dollar ($)	$1.69	$1.73

If you want foreign currency, the bank SELLS it to you at the SELLING rate.

Examples   For each £ you get €1.43 (euros), or 189.65 Japanese yen.

£ —— **MULTIPLY by selling rate** ——▶ Foreign Currency

If you exchange £500:   for euro you get $500 \times 1.43 = €715$

for Japanese yen you get $500 \times 189.65 = 94\ 825$ yen

Practice

1   The table shows a bank's customers for foreign currency one day.
Copy and complete the table using the rates given above.

	£s to exchange	Currency Type	Currency Amount
Mr Blank	£900	US dollars	
Mrs Smith	£750	Australian dollars	
Mr Hashan	£600	Euro	
Miss Patten	£1200	South African rand	
Ms Chang	£2000	Japanese yen	
Mr Davies	£150	Indian rupee	
Miss Bailey	£87 500	Euro	

If you want to change foreign currency back to £s, the bank BUYS it from you at the BUYING rate.

Examples

Foreign Currency —— **DIVIDE by buying rate** ——▶ £

For: $300 (Australian)   you get $300 \div 2.48 = £120.97 = £121$ (nearest £)

10 000 rupees   you get $10\ 000 \div 79.81 = £125.30 = £125$ (nearest £)

2   A bank has customers returning from holiday who want to convert their foreign currency back into £s. Copy and complete the following table to show to the nearest £ what they should receive.

	Amount	Currency type	£
Mr Wragg	$720	US dollars	
Miss Yen	$950	Australian dollars	
Mr Ennis	3400	Japanese yen	
Ms Masters	5600	Indian rupees	
Miss Dank	€1200	Euro	
Mr Caine	256 000	Japanese yen	
Ms Wright	350	South African rand	

3   A couple used 500 litres of petrol at 1.25 euro per litre whilst touring Europe.
The exchange rate they received was 1.45 euro to the pound.
How much did the petrol cost them to the nearest pound?

Travel agents and banks often charge a commission for changing currency.

For the following questions assume the commission charged is £3 for exchanges up to £200 and $1\frac{1}{2}\%$ on amounts over £200. Assume that the customer only receives the whole units of currency (e.g. he would only get €642 of €642.73).

---

4   **a)**   A businessman changes £250 into US dollars for a trip to America.
How many dollars does he receive? (Use the rates given on p. 144)
   b)   The businessman is ill, and has to cancel his trip. He changes the dollars back into £s.
How much does he get?
   c)   Altogether how much does he lose because of the cancellation?

5   **a)**   A family changed £1200 into Australian dollars at 2.14 dollars to the £ when they booked a flight to Australia. How many dollars did they get?
   b)   The exchange rate later rose to 2.42. How much, in dollars, would they have gained if they had waited to exchange their money?
   c)   The family returns from Australia with 85 dollars. How much do they receive after paying commission when they exchange these dollars for pounds at a rate of 2.45 dollars to the £?

Activity

Use information from the Internet or holiday brochures to cost a holiday.
Decide how much money you would take and estimate what foreign currency you would receive.

Measures, Shape and Space

2 Time

Read and record dates

MSS1/E3.3, MSS1/L1.2

	Month	Abbreviated form
1	January	Jan
2	February	Feb
3	March	Mar
4	April	Apr
5	May	May
6	June	Jun
7	July	Jul
8	August	Aug
9	September	Sep
10	October	Oct
11	November	Nov
12	December	Dec

There are different ways to write the date.

Full date   16th November 2004

Medium date   16/Nov/2004

Use the abbreviated month

Short date   16/11/04

Nov. is the 11th month

04 is 2004 (83 is 1983)

Practice

Fill in the missing words:

1 a) January is the _____ month of the year.

b) _____ is the second month of the year.

c) March is the _____ month of the year.

d) April is the _____ month of the year.

e) _____ is the 5th month of the year.

f) _____ is the sixth month of the year.

g) _____ is the 7th month of the year.

h) The eighth month of the year is _____.

i) The 9th month of the year is _____.

j) October is the _____ month of the year.

k) The 11th month of the year is _____.

l) The 12th month of the year is _____.

2 What is today's date? Write it in all 3 ways.

3 a) A student was born on 02/04/79. Write her birth-date in full.
   b) Her friend was born on 22nd February 1978. Write this is in the short date format.

4 Alexander Bell made the first ever telephone call on 10th March 1876. Write this in the medium date format.

5 The first test-tube baby was born on 25/07/78. Write this date in full.

Activities   Essential

1 You need a list of the months of the year and a list of college term dates.
   a) Write the college term dates by the correct month on the list.
        Use the short date format.
   b) i) Write in your family's birthdays in the medium date format.
      ii) Ask members of the class for their birthdays (they can make up any year).
         Use the medium date format.
   c) Add any other special dates to your list.

2 You need a blank calendar with the bank holidays marked.
   a) Which year is your calendar for?
   b) Find which days of the week these are on
      i) Christmas Day i.e. 25th December
      ii) New Year's Day i.e. 1st January
     iii) May Day i.e. 1st May
     iv) May 17th
      v) October 25th.
   c) Find the dates of
      i) Good Friday
      ii) Easter Monday
     iii) the August bank holiday.
   d) Write these on your calendar
      i) your birthday
      ii) your name by today's date
     iii) the days your college terms begin and end
     iv) any other dates that are important to you.

Read, measure and record time   MSS1/E3.3

a am and pm

8:30 could be when you get up in the morning, or when you watch T.V. in the evening.
To tell us which it is, the day is split into two halves: **am** and **pm**.

← am →		← pm →	
12:00 am	1:00 am 2:00 am 3:00 am 4:00 am 5:00 am 6:00 am 7:00 am 8:00 am 9:00 am 10:00 am 11:00 am	12:00 pm	1:00 pm 2:00 pm 3:00 pm 4:00 pm 5:00 pm 6:00 pm 7:00 pm 8:00 pm 9:00 pm 10:00 pm 11:00 pm	12:00 am
midnight	night morning	midday lunchtime noon	afternoon evening	midnight

9:30 in the morning = 9:30 am   9:30 in the evening = 9:30 pm

Practice

1 Write these times in numbers using am or pm.

- **a)** 7:00 in the morning
- **b)** 4:00 in the afternoon
- **c)** 11:30 before lunch
- **d)** 5:00 when the shops are closing
- **e)** 1:00 when most people are asleep
- **f)** 8:45 the morning rush hour

2 Match the times to the events.

- **a)** Waking up with a bad dream
- **b)** Football kick off time
- **c)** Coffee break
- **i)** 7:45 pm
- **ii)** 11:00 am
- **iii)** 1:00 am

3 Suggest activities for the following times.

- **a)** 9:00 am   **b)** 12:00 pm   **c)** 5:30 pm   **d)** 7:45 am

4 How many hours are there from

- **a)** 3:00 am to 3:00 pm
- **b)** 5:30 am to 6:30 pm
- **c)** 4:15 am to 9:15 pm
- **d)** 10:00 am to 7:30 pm
- **e)** 8:00 pm Mon to 7:00 am Tue
- **f)** 7:00 pm Tue to 6:30 am Wed?

b Read and record time to the nearest 5 minutes

The **short** hand is the **hour** hand.
The **long** hand is the **minute** hand.

There are **60 minutes** in **an hour**.
There are **30 minutes** in **half an hour**.
There are **15 minutes** in a **quarter of an hour**.

There are **5 minutes** between each number and the next.

On the clock, the hour hand has gone past 5.
The minute hand has gone round from 12 to 3. This means it is 15 minutes past.
The time is five fifteen. This is written as 5:15. (We also say 'quarter past five'.)

Look at these clocks. The times are given underneath.

Examples

10 minutes past 7
or

7:10

30 minutes past 9
or

9:30

or half past nine

40 minutes past 3
or

3:40

1   Write each time in two different ways.

a)   b)   c)   d)

When the minute hand has gone past 30, we can count minutes **to the next hour.**

We often read the time to the nearest 5 minute mark.
To the nearest 5 minutes, this clock says **20 minutes to 10**

▶ **To the nearest 5 minutes means to the nearest number marked on the clock.**

Look at these clocks.

They both say 50 minutes past 1
or
10 minutes to 2.

1:50

2 Write the time to the nearest 5 minutes in three ways.

a)   b)   c)   d)

e)   f)   g)   h)

Use the 12 and 24 hour clock

a The 12 hour and 24 hour clock

The 24 hour clock is used for timetables, videos, digital clocks and other timers.

The hours are numbered up to 24 instead of using am and pm.

hours   colon (2 dots)   minutes

4 digits are used to give times __ : __

It is easy to write am times as 24 hour clock times:

| **Example** | 6:20 am = **06:20** | 10:35 am = **10:35** |

Timetables often omit the colon.

It is more difficult with pm times – usually you need to add 12 hours:

Example Write 4:36 pm in 24 hour time.

hours:minutes

4:36 (remove the pm)

Add 12 hours to pm times.   add 12 hours   +12:00

4:36 pm is   **16:36**

Example Write quarter to seven in the morning as a 24 hour clock time.

15 minutes before 7 = 45 minutes past 6 = **06:45**
(For quarter to seven in the evening add 12 hours to give 18:45.)

Take care near midnight and midday   12:15 am = 00:15
12:15 pm = 12:15

Practice

1 Write these as 24 hour clock times.

a) 3:50 pm   **b)** 7:00 am   **c)** 9:15 am   **d)** 10:26 pm   **e)** 3:42 pm   **f)** 1:30 pm
g) 6:45 am   **h)** 12:05 am   **i)** 7:40 pm   **j)** 6:59 pm   **k)** 6:42 am   **l)** 8.25 pm

2 Write these as 24 hour clock times.

a) quarter past 3 in the morning   **b)** quarter to 5 in the evening
c) half past 7 in the morning   **d)** 10 to 9 in the morning
e) 10 past 11 at night   **f)** midday
g) 5 to 4 in the afternoon   **h)** quarter to 8 in the morning
i) 25 to 6 in the evening   **j)** 10 to 3 in the afternoon
k) 5 past 4 in the afternoon   **l)** 10 past 11 in the morning

3 Write these times in figures as 24 hour clock times.

a) six minutes past four in the afternoon
b) fifteen minutes past three in the afternoon
c) eleven minutes past eight in the morning   **d)** fifteen minutes to ten in the morning
e) ten minutes to seven in the evening   **f)** twenty five minutes to midnight
g) five minutes to eleven in the morning   **h)** twelve minutes past midday
i) twenty minutes past nine in the evening   **j)** half past six in the evening

> **Example**   Write 07:15 as a 12 hour clock time
>
> Remove the 0 and write am (morning time)   **7:15 am**

> **Example**   Write 23:50 in 12 hour time
>
> 23:50
> subtract 12 hours   − 12:00
> 2350 =   **11:50 pm**   (evening time, so write pm)
>
> ▶ **Subtract 12 hours to find the pm time.**

4   Write these 24 hour clock times using am or pm.

a) 23:30   b) 06:45   c) 07:12   d) 16:45   e) 12:10   f) 01:10
g) 12:16   h) 14:10   i) 00:00   j) 06:05   k) 13:46   l) 09:15

5   Match the times.

a) 15:52   14 minutes to 4 in the morning   5:05 pm
b) 03:46   9 minutes past 7 in the evening   11:54 pm
c) 17:05   28 minutes to 5 in the afternoon   3:46 am
d) 23:54   8 minutes to 4 in the afternoon   4:32 pm
e) 19:09   6 minutes to midnight   3:52 pm
f) 16:32   5 minutes past 5 in the afternoon   7:09 pm

b Use timetables

Most timetables are in 24 hour clock time. The colon is often omitted.

> **Example**   Find the first train leaving Bournville for Birmingham.
>
>
>
> 1   **Look down the 1st column – find Bournville.**
>
> 2   **Read along the row. The 1st train leaves Bournville at 0622.**
>
> 1
> ↓ **Extract from the Redditch – Birmingham timetable**
>
> | Redditch | d | | | | 0628 | | | 0658 |
> |---|---|---|---|---|---|---|---|---|
> | Longbridge | d | 0615 | 0623 | 0633 | 0644 | 0654 | 0702 | 0713 |
> | Kings Norton | d | 0620 | 0627 | 0637 | 0649 | 0658 | 0707 | 0719 |
> | Bournville 2—d▶ | | 0622 | 0630 | 0640 | 0651 | 0701 | 0710 | 0721 |
> | Five Ways | d | 0629 | 0638 | 0648 | 0659 | 0708 | 0718 | 0729 |
> | Birmingham | a | 0633 | 0642 | 0652 | 0703 | 0713 | 0722 | 0733 |
>
> 3   **Check for any further information, e.g. a = arrival (the train arrives at 0633), d = departure.**
>   **With some timetables, trains only run on certain days.**

Practice

1 Use the timetable above to answer these questions. Give answers as 24 hour clock times.

   a) **i)** When is the first train from Redditch to Birmingham?

      ii) When does this train arrive in Birmingham?

   b) When is the first train after 7 o'clock in the morning to leave from Longbridge?

   c) **i)** When does the first train leave from Kings Norton?

      ii) At what time does this train arrive in Birmingham?

   d) Which is the latest train from Bournville that you can catch if you want to be in Birmingham by 7 o'clock in the morning?

   e) Which is the latest train you can catch from Kings Norton if you want to be in Birmingham by half past 7 in the morning?

   f) A commuter arrives at Kings Norton at half past six in the morning.

      i) Which is the next train she can catch?

      ii) When does this train depart from Five Ways?

2 This timetable gives the bus times going in both directions. It uses 12 hour clock time. Give your answers as am or pm times.

EASY RIDER 629		Woodgate Valley North – Selly Oak			
From	Woodgate Valley North	8:45	10:10	1:55	3:15
Woodgate	Moat Meadow	8:53	10:18	2:03	3:23
	Quinbourne Centre	9:00	10:25	2:10	3:30
	Onneley House	9:15	10:40	2:25	3:45
to	Harborne, High Street	9:25	10:50	2:35	3:55
	Old Tokengate	9:39	10:55	2:40	4:00
	Queen Elizabeth Hospital	9:40	—	2:45	4:05
Selly Oak	Selly Oak	9:50	—	3:00	4:10
From	Selly Oak	—	12:20	4:10	
Selly Oak	Queen Elizabeth Hospital	—	12:30	4:20	
	Old Tokengate	—	12:40	4:25	
	Harborne, High Street	11:25	12:45	4:30	
to	Onneley House	11:35	12:55	4:40	
	Quinbourne Centre	11:50	1:10	4:50	
	Moat Meadow	11:57	1:17	4:55	
Woodgate	Woodgate Valley North	12:05	1:25	5:00	

   a) When does the first bus leave Woodgate Valley North?

   b) When does the first bus return from Selly Oak to Woodgate Valley North?

   c) **i)** Which is the first bus from Quinbourne Centre after 10 am to go to Selly Oak?

      ii) When does this bus arrive at Selly Oak?

   d) Which is the first bus from Moat Meadow to go to Queen Elizabeth Hospital?

   e) You are at Queen Elizabeth Hospital at midday.
      What is the earliest time you could get to Harbourne High Street by bus?

   f) **i)** You are at Onneley House. Which bus should you catch to be at Queen Elizabeth Hospital by ten thirty in the morning?

      ii) If you leave the hospital at quarter to twelve, when will you catch your bus back to Onneley House?

      iii) When would you get back to Onneley House?

   g) You are at Moat Meadow. You are due to meet friends at the Old Tokengate at 3 pm. What is the latest bus you could catch?

Units of Time   MSS1/L1.3, MSS1/L2.2

60 seconds = 1 minute   52 weeks = 1 year
60 minutes = 1 hour   365 days = 1 year
24 hours = 1 day   366 days = 1 leap year (a leap year has an extra day)
7 days = 1 week   100 years = 1 century
12 months = 1 year   1000 years = 1 millennium

Practice

1 Copy and complete these.

   a) $\frac{1}{2}$ minute = _____ seconds   b) $\frac{1}{4}$ year = _____ months
   c) $\frac{1}{2}$ hour = _____ minutes   d) 2 centuries = _____ years
   e) $\frac{1}{4}$ hour = _____ minutes   f) 1 millennium = _____ years
   g) $\frac{1}{2}$ year = _____ months   h) 2 years = _____ weeks
   i) 2 weeks = _____ days   j) $\frac{1}{2}$ year = _____ weeks

   ---

   Do you know this poem?

   30 days have September, April, June and November
   All the rest have 31
   Except February alone, which has 28 days clear and 29 each leap year.

   ---

2 a) How many days are there in i) June   ii) November   iii) February in a leap year?
   b) How many days are there altogether in i) July and August   ii) March and April?

3 Which unit of time would you use to measure the following events?

   a) Boil an egg   b) 100 metre sprint
   c) The time taken for 2nd class mail delivery
   d) A holiday abroad   e) Flying to Europe
   f) Travelling by boat to Australia
   g) The natural age of an oak tree

   | seconds? minutes? |
   | hours?   days? |
   | weeks?   months? |
   | years?   centuries? |

4 Copy and complete these.

   a) $3\frac{1}{2}$ minutes = _____ seconds   b) 180 seconds = _____ minutes
   c) $4\frac{1}{2}$ hours = _____ minutes   d) 300 minutes = _____ hours
   e) 3 years = _____ months   f) 30 months = _____ years
   g) 7 weeks = _____ days   h) 35 days = _____ weeks
   i) $4\frac{1}{2}$ centuries = _____ years   j) 500 years = _____centuries
   k) 3 millennia = _____ years   l) 10 000 years = _____ millennia

5 How many millennia have there been since the birth of Christ?

> ▶ **per annum** means **per year**   ▶ **per quarter** means $\frac{1}{4}$ **of a year**

6 A workman's wage is £15 000 per annum. How much is this each month?

7 A hospital patient has to wait 28 days to hear the results of a test.
   How many weeks is this?

8 The instructions say, 'Cook the food in a microwave for $2\frac{1}{2}$ minutes', but the microwave works in seconds. Write the cooking time in seconds.

9 It takes $1\frac{3}{4}$ hours to cook a chicken in the microwave. What is this in minutes?

10 How many weeks are there in 1 quarter?

11 A student's phone bill is £26 per month. What is the phone bill for

   a) a quarter of the year   **b)** a full year?

Calculate time
MSS1/L1.3, MSS1/L2.2

a Add and subtract time in hours, minutes and seconds

> ▶ **Remember   60 seconds = 1 minute   60 minutes = 1 hour**

Example   1 minute + 40 seconds + $1\frac{1}{2}$ minutes

min	sec	
1	00 +	1 minute
	40	40 seconds
1	30	1 minute 30 seconds
2	70	70 seconds = 1 minute + 10 seconds

(Write $\frac{1}{2}$ minute as 30 seconds)

(Change 70 seconds to minutes and seconds)

2 min + 1 min + 10 sec = **3 minutes 10 seconds**

Example   4 hours 36 minutes – 49 minutes

h	min	
4	36 –	
	49	

can't take 49 from 36 so
change an hour to minutes

4 h 36 min = 3h 36 min + 1 hour = 3h 36 min + 60 min

h	min	
3	96 –	
	49	
3	47	**3 hours 47 minutes**

Practice

1 Add these times together.

   a) 3 hours 20 minutes + $1\frac{3}{4}$ hours + 15 minutes
   b) $6\frac{1}{2}$ minutes + $2\frac{1}{4}$ minutes + 12 seconds
   c) $2\frac{1}{2}$ minutes + 40 seconds + 25 seconds
   d) $3\frac{3}{4}$ minutes + 30 seconds + 2 minutes
   e) 7 hours 40 minutes + 35 minutes + $1\frac{1}{2}$ hours
   f) $1\frac{1}{2}$ hours + 40 minutes + 1 hour 55 minutes

2 Subtract these times.

   a) $3\frac{1}{4}$ hours − 55 minutes   **b)** $2\frac{1}{4}$ hours − 35 minutes
   c) $2\frac{1}{4}$ minutes − 55 seconds   **d)** $1\frac{1}{2}$ minutes − 38 seconds
   e) $4\frac{1}{4}$ hours − 40 minutes   **f)** 2 minutes 10 seconds − 49 seconds

3 a) Cooking instructions for a curry in the microwave say, 'Cook for $6\frac{1}{2}$ minutes, stand for 3 minutes, then cook for a further $1\frac{1}{2}$ minutes.' What is the total time?
   b) For rice, the cooking time is $4\frac{1}{2}$ minutes, followed by 2 minutes standing, then another 45 seconds cooking. Altogether how long does it take to cook the rice?

4 A decorator takes altogether $1\frac{1}{2}$ hours to paint a window. He spends 35 minutes preparing the wood and the rest of the time painting. How long does he spend painting?

b Find the difference between times by adding on

Example   How long is it from 09:45 to 11:30?

Start time	09:45		
Number of minutes to the next hour	09:45 ⟶ 10:00 =	15 minutes	
Number of hours	10:00 ⟶ 11:00 = 1 hour		Add
Number of minutes after the hour	11:00 ⟶ 11:30 =	30 minutes	

Time from 09:45 to 11:30 = **1 hour 45 minutes**

To check this, round to the nearest hour: 10:00 to 12:00 is 2 hours

Practice

1 Find the time from: (also check by rounding the times)

   a) 04:55 to 07:36   **b)** 06:42 to 09:24   **c)** 09:45 to 12:30
   d) 08:42 to 10:15   **e)** 07:26 to 11:14   **f)** 06:35 to 10:25
   g) 9:55 am to 2:10 pm **h)** 7:50 am to 4:26 pm **i)** 8:35 am to 12:16 pm
   j) midday to 17:50   **k)** 2:15 pm to midnight **l)** 2:15 am to midnight

Example   A part-time worker starts work at 11:15 am and finishes at 3:45 pm. For how long does he work?

Start time   11:15
Number of minutes to the next hour   11:15 ⟶ 12:00 =   45 minutes
Number of hours   12:00 ⟶ 3:00 = 3 hours   **Add**
Number of minutes after the hour   3:00 ⟶ 3:45 =   45 minutes
                          Time between 1:15 and 5:45 = **3 hours 90 minutes**

▶ **Remember 60 minutes = 1 hour**

3 hours + 1 hour 30 minutes
He works 4 hours 30 minutes

2 Find the time worked by each worker.

	Started	Finished		Started	Finished		Started	Finished
a)	9 am	12:30 pm	b)	10:15	16:30	c)	12:10 pm	5:40 pm
d)	14:30	18:45	e)	7:30 pm	1 am	f)	22:45	06:30

3 Find each journey time.

	Departure	Arrival		Departure	Arrival		Departure	Arrival
a)	0615	1136	b)	1305	1723	c)	1910	2316
d)	1024	1436	e)	0816	1251	f)	1513	1726
g)	0822	1054	h)	1212	1436	i)	1806	2131
j)	1825	2134	k)	0628	1042	l)	2102	2314

c Find the difference between times by subtracting

Example   A journey starts at 10:15 am and ends at 1:46 pm. How long does it take?

Put the times into 24 hour clock time (if necessary)   10:15 to 13:46
Start with the final time   13:46 −
Subtract the start time   10:15   **Subtract**
                                    Time for the journey =   3:31   **3 hours 31 minutes**

Example   How long is it from 7:55 am to 2:10 pm?

You can't take 55 from 10, so change an hour into 60 minutes.

In 24 hour clock time this is 07:55 to 14:10
Start with the final time   14:10 −   13:10 + 1 hour
Subtract the start time   07:55

                  13:10 + 60 =   13:70 −
                                 07:55
           Time between =   6:15   **6 hours 15 minutes**

Practice

1   Find the time taken for these journeys.

   a) 1:15 pm to 3:42 pm   **b)** 11:26 am to 1:55 pm   **c)** 2:36 pm to 3:49 pm
   d) 1:26 pm to 2:59 pm   **e)** 7:24 am to 2:50 pm   **f)** 6:54 am to 1:05 pm
   g) 11:43 am to 1:32 pm   **h)** 9:43 am to 1:28 pm   **i)** 7:49 pm to 9:16 pm
   j) 11:56 am to 4:13 pm   **k)** 3:33 pm to 5:13 pm   **l)** 10:44 am to 9:13 pm

2   The timetable below is for Eurostar.

London	Brussels
0609	1001
0653	1037
0822	1210
0827	1210
1022	1405

London	Calais
0614	0856
0619	0856
1148	1431
1153	1431
1518	1756

London	Paris
0922	1329
0927	1329

   a)   How long do these journeys take?
   i)   0822 from London to Brussels   **ii)**   1022 from London to Brussels
   iii) 1153 from London to Calais   **iv)**   0922 from London to Paris

   b)   What is the difference in journey time between the 0614 and the 0619 from London
   to Calais?

Activity

   Plan a journey, a concert or an evening watching TV.
   Write down the times for the start and end of each part/programme.
   Work out how long each part takes.

Use timers

Alarm clocks can be set for any time. They use 12 or 24 hour clock time, with an analogue or
digital display. **Analogue** means on a clock or scale.
These clocks have all been set to ring at 7 pm (to wake a nightshift worker).

The alarm hand is usually a
different colour

(12 hour)

(24 hour)

Practice

1 For each part sketch 3 clocks like these.

Show the alarm time on each clock.

a) 10:30 pm **b)** 6 am
c) 11:15 pm **d)** 8:30 am

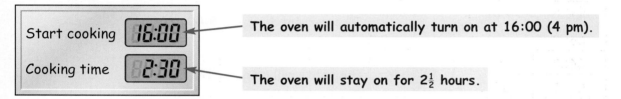

(12 hour)   (24 hour)

Ovens often have timers – generally in 24 hour clock time. The diagram shows one type.

| Start cooking | 16:00 | ← The oven will automatically turn on at 16:00 (4 pm). |
| Cooking time | 2:30 | ← The oven will stay on for 2½ hours. |

The meal will be cooked by 18:30, i.e. 6:30 pm.

Example A meal takes 1 hour 20 minutes to cook. It must be ready by 18:00 (6 pm).

To find the time it needs to start cooking:

$$18:00 - 1:20 = 16:40$$

The cooker times are as shown.

| Start cooking | 16:40 |
| Cooking time | 1:20 |

Meal ready for 18:00 (6 pm)

---

2 Copy the cooker display for each part. Fill in the times needed.

a) You want a meal to be ready for 19:00.
It takes 1½ hours to cook.
b) You want a meal to be ready at 17:30.
It takes 2¼ hours to cook.
c) A meal takes 1 hour 40 minutes to cook. You want it to be ready at 20:15.
d) A meal takes 1¾ hours to cook. You want it to be ready at 7 pm.

| Start cooking | |
| Cooking time | |

Video recorder displays show the date, channel and the start and end times of programmes to be recorded. Time displays are in 24 hour clock time.

Date 4/12   Start 19:30

Channel 3   Finish 20:55

Day and month is shown.

The video will start recording Channel 3 at 7:30 pm on 4th December and end at 8:55 pm.

Activity

You need a listing of television programme times. Pick four programmes you would like to video. Write down the information you would need to set a video recorder.

Some timers use a **24 hour analogue clock**, e.g. automatic central heating and light switches. They have on/off mechanisms that are attached to the dial. The dial moves clockwise round a marker on the socket. The marker shows the current time.

The current time is 16:00.

The lights will go on at 17:00 and stay on until 22:00.
They will go on again at 07:00 and off at 08:30.

3 When will the lights go on and off with these automatic timers?

a)   b)

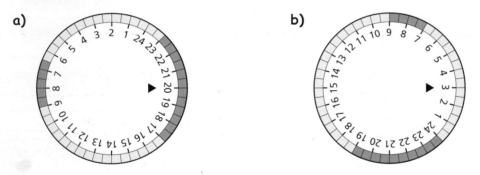

4 Draw dials similar to these and show the settings for the following times.

a) Central heating on between 06:00 and 08:30 and on again between 17:00 and 22:30.

b) Lights on between 07:15 and 09:30 and again between 16:30 and 22:15.

Some digital timers (such as stopwatches) show minutes and tenths and hundredths of a second.

The tenths and hundredths of a second are usually shown with smaller numbers.

For example, these show the times for runners in a race:

1st `01:05 20` 1 minute, 5 seconds and 2 tenths of a second (1 min 5.20 s)

2nd `01:15 32` 1 minute, 15 seconds and 32 hundredths of a second (1 min 15.32 s)

3rd `01:16 02` 1 minute, 16 seconds and 2 hundredths of a second (1 min 16.02 s)

5 The times for the rest of the runners are given below. Write them in words and figures.

a) `01:16 47`   b) `01:21 05`   c) `01:16 59`

d) `01:22 20`   e) `01:17 08`   f) `01:22 40`

L2 **Example**

The times of the first and second runners in a race are as shown. How much quicker is the winner?   `03:56 23` `04:02 38`

longer time first	minutes		seconds	can't take 56.23 from 2.38, so change a minute to seconds	minutes		seconds	
	4	:	02.38		3	:	62.38 –	
	3	:	56.23		3	:	56.23	subtract
					0		6.15	

The winner is **6.15 seconds** quicker.

6 Find the difference between each pair of times.

a) `01:25 31` `01:27 52`   b) `02:43 03` `02:42 47`   c) `01:58 23` `02:00 38`

d) `05:10 24` `04:59 56`   e) `04:36 01` `04:22 49`   f) `13:57 30` `14:22 32`

7 The times for the swimmers in the six swimming lanes in a race are given below.

`02:34 05`   `02:49 30`   `02:16 43`   `03:01 09`   `03:00 24`   `02:44 51`

Put the times in order, then find the difference between each time and the next.

Measures, Shape and Space

3 Length

Understand distance: kilometres and miles

MSS1/E3.4

In Britain we use **miles** to measure long distances on the roads.
In the rest of Europe, long distances are measured in **kilometres**.

km stands for kilometres.   1 km = 1000 m (metres)
1 mile is longer than 1 km.   1 km is about $\frac{2}{3}$ of a mile.

It takes about 30 minutes to walk 1 mile. It takes about 20 minutes to walk 1 km.

Practice

1 A **City 10 miles**   B **3 km**   C **City 5 km**   D **1 mile**

   a) Which of the signs above might you see in Britain?
   b) Which might you see in other parts of Europe?

2 Copy and complete the table below. You will need to:

   ● estimate how far in miles you travel to get to each place (starting from home)
   ● estimate how far it is in kilometres
   ● say how you would get there
   ● estimate how long it takes to get there.

	Journeys			
	Approximate distance in miles	Approximate distance in kilometres	Do you use the car, bus, bike or walk?	How long does the journey take?
Class				
Shops				
Dentist				
Bus stop				
Work				
The nearest hospital				

3 For each journey choose an approximate distance.

  a) 1 hour by car   **b)** 40 minutes walking   **c)** 15 minutes walking
  d) 30 minutes walking **e)** 1 hour by bike   **f)** 20 minutes walking
  g) 1 hour by train

  | 50 miles | 1 km | 80 miles | 1 mile | 2 km | 10 miles | $\frac{1}{2}$ mile |

Find the distance

MSS1/L1.5

a Use distances marked on a map

This is a sketch map of part of Somerset. The towns are shown with dots.
The numbers give the distances in miles between the towns by road.

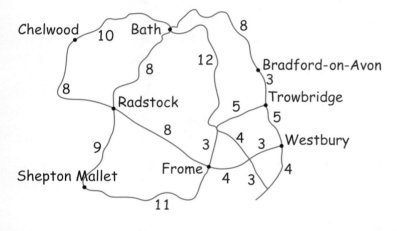

Practice

1 Find the shortest distance by road in miles between

  a) Radstock and Bath   **b)** Bradford-on-Avon and Bath
  c) Chelwood and Radstock   **d)** Shepton Mallet and Bath
  e) Chelwood and Frome   **f)** Westbury and Shepton Mallet
  g) Trowbridge and Bath   **h)** Frome and Bath.

2 A taxi driver starts from Shepton Mallet. He travels to Frome, then Westbury and then
  Trowbridge by the most direct route. How far does he travel altogether?

3 A travelling salesman starts from Westbury and travels to Trowbridge.
  He then goes via Bradford-on-Avon to Bath and finally to Chelwood.
  How far does he travel altogether?

b Use a mile/kilometre chart

Distances in miles

Aberdeen						
216	Carlisle					
129	92	Edinburgh				
146	95	43	Glasgow			
261	45	137	140	Kendal		
84	132	45	62	177	Perth	
227	371	284	296	416	239	Thurso

To find the distance from Carlisle to Perth

Look down from Carlisle
Look across from Perth

Distance = **132 miles**

Practice

1 Find the distance between

a) Aberdeen and Kendal

b) Edinburgh and Thurso

c) Carlisle and Glasgow

d) Thurso and Perth

e) Perth and Aberdeen

f) Thurso and Kendal.

Some charts show both kilometres and miles like the chart below.
Check which side of the chart you need to look at.

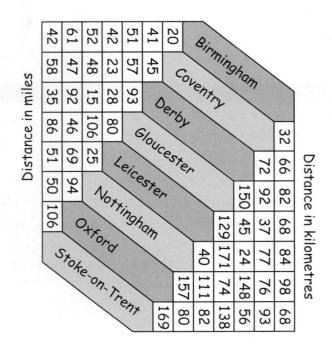

2 Use the chart above to answer the following questions.

  a) What is the distance in kilometres from Birmingham to Oxford?
  b) What is the mileage between Gloucester and Nottingham?
  c) How many miles are there between Coventry and Derby?
  d) How many kilometres are there between Leicester and Stoke-on-Trent?
  e) What is the mileage from Coventry to Nottingham?
  f) How much longer, in miles, is the journey from Birmingham to Nottingham than the journey from Birmingham to Derby?
  g) How many more kilometres do you travel to get from Oxford to Derby than you travel to get from Oxford to Coventry?
  h) You travel from Birmingham to Oxford and then to Nottingham. How many kilometres do you travel altogether?

> **Activity**
>
> Use a road atlas to find the distance in miles from your home town to other towns in England. List the towns in order of distance from your home town.

Measure length in metric units   MSS1/E3.5, MSS1/L1.4, MSS1/L2.3

a Measure in millimetres and centimetres

A **millimetre** is about the width of this fullstop •

It is the smallest measurement most people use.
The width of your little finger is probably about a **centimetre**.

This ruler measures centimetres (cm) and millimetres (mm)   **10 mm = 1 cm**

Which is the best way to measure the length of the needle?

A

cm 1   2   3   4

B

cm 1   2   3   4

C

cm 1   2   3   4

C is the best way.

The needle is **3 cm** long to the **nearest cm**.
More accurately, it is **28 mm** long.

Practice

On the ruler below, the measurement marked by **a** is **1 cm to the nearest cm** and   **13 mm to the nearest mm**.

▶ Use the **numbered marks** for **the nearest cm**.

▶ Use the **other marks** for the **nearest mm**.

a   b   c   d e   f   g h

0   1   2   3   4   5   6   7   8   9   10   11   12

1   Write down the measurements marked by each of the other letters.
   Give each answer   **i)** to the nearest cm   **ii)** to the nearest mm.

▶ The ruler shows that **10 mm = 1 cm** so   to change mm to cm, divide by 10.
   to change cm to mm, multiply by 10.

---

2   Copy and complete these.

a) 20 mm = _____ cm   **b)** 3 cm = _____ mm   **c)** 50 mm = ____ cm
d) 7 cm = _____ mm   **e)** 60 mm = _____ cm   **f)** 8 cm = _____ mm
g) 40 mm = _____ cm   **h)** 9 cm = _____ mm   **i)**   120 mm = ____ cm

---

▶ You can write lengths using decimals.
   10 mm = 1 cm means **1 mm = 0.1 cm**

cm 1   2   3   4

The needle's length = 28 mm or 2 cm 8 mm
This is the same as 2.8 cm

Also see page 98.

| **Examples** | 42 mm = **4.2 cm**   1.7 cm = **17 mm** |

3 Copy and complete these.

    a) 15 mm = ____ cm   **b)** 1.2 cm = _____ mm   **c)** 26 mm = ____ cm

    d) 1.3 cm = _____ mm   **e)** 14 mm = ____ cm   **f)** 2.1 cm = _____ mm

    g) 84 mm = ____ cm   **h)** 3.9 cm = _____ mm   **i)** 125 mm = ____ cm

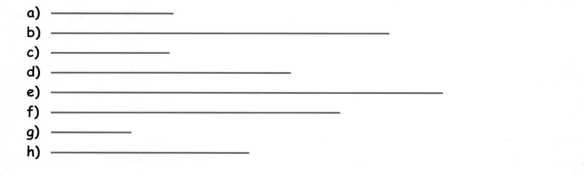

Check that the length of this line is 57 mm

This is the same   as   5 cm 7 mm

                      or   5.7 cm

The first decimal place gives mm.

4 Measure each line. Give each measurement in 3 different ways.

    a) ————————————

    b) ———————————————————————

    c) ——————————

    d) ———————————————

    e) —————————————————————————

    f) ————————————————————

    g) ————————

    h) ——————————————————

5 List the lines in question 4 in order of size, longest first.

Example

The distance between the rods is 36 mm or 3 cm 6 mm or 3.6 cm

6 Measure the distance between each pair of rods. Write each distance in three ways.

    a)

    b)

    c)

L1

7 Measure the length of each item to the nearest mm. Write each answer in 3 ways.

a) 3   4   5   6   7   8   9   10

.... cm

b) 3   4   5   6   7   8   9   10

.... cm

c) 1   2   3   4   5   6   7   8

.... cm

d) 10   11   12   13   14   15   16   17

.... cm

e) 15   16   17   18   19   20   21   22

.... cm

f) 3   4   5   6   7   8   9   10

.... cm

g) 7   8   9   10   11   12   13   14

.... cm

Activities

1 Copy and complete the following table.
Estimate, then measure, each object to the nearest centimetre.
Measure the items more accurately in centimetres then millimetres.

Item	Estimate to nearest cm	Measurement to the nearest cm	Measurement in mm
Length of this book			
Length of the fire exit notice			
Width of the fire exit notice			
Length of a piece of paper			
Width of a piece of paper			
Length of your pencil			
Length of an eraser			

2 You will need a collection of nails, screws, screw plugs and pieces of wood.

   a) Measure the length and pin head width of each nail, screw and plug.
        Label each nail, screw and plug with its measurements.
   b) Sort the nails and screws in order of length starting with the shortest.
   c) Sort the nails and screws again, this time in order of pinhead width.
   d) Match each screw with a plug.
   e) Sort the screws depending on the width of screwdriver they need.
   f) Measure the thickness of each piece of wood. Label them.
   g) Find the nails and screws that are the best for each piece of wood.

3 Without using a ruler, draw lines that you think are 1 cm, 2 cm, 3 cm, 4 cm and
    5 cm long. Measure your lines with a ruler to see how accurate they are.

b Measure in metres, centimetres and millimetres

Part of a long tape measure is shown below. It is labelled in centimetres and millimetres.
A tape measure like this can be used for measuring distances like the length of a room.

This is 93 cm
or 930 mm

1 metre

This is 105 cm
or 1 m 5 cm
or 1050 mm
or 1 m 50 mm

The tape measure shows that

▶ **1 m = 100 cm = 1000 mm.**

Here is another tape measure near 1 m marked in a slightly different way.
The measurement at **a** on the tape is **98 cm** or **980 mm. b** is at **111 cm** or **1110 mm.**

1000 mm

1110 mm

a   c   **1 m**   d   e   f   g   b   h

98 cm
or 980 mm

Remember 1 cm = 10 mm.

111 cm
or 1110 mm

The mark at **a** is **98 cm** which is the same as **0.98 m**
The measurement at **b** can also be written as: **1 m 11 cm** or **1.11 m**

The first 2
decimal places
are cm.

Practice

1   Write the measurement at each of the other letters in cm then in mm.

2   Write the measurement in metres using decimals at each of the other letters (on the ruler at the bottom of p. 169).

The diagram below shows part of a tape measure labelled in centimetres.
To the **nearest cm**   a is at **365 cm** or **3.65 m**   and   b is at **367 cm** or **3.67 m**.

3   i)   Give the measurement at each of the other letters to the nearest cm.
    ii) Write each measurement in m using decimals.

L1

You can use the small divisions on the tape measure to give lengths more accurately.
a is at **364.8 cm**. In millimetres this is **3648 mm** (multiplying by 10).
You can write this using metres as **3 m 648 mm** or **3.648 m**. ← The first 3 decimal places are mm
b is at **367.4 cm** or **3674 mm** or **3 m 674 mm** or **3.674 m**.

4   Write the measurement at each of the other letters in these 4 different ways.

Activity

1   Copy the table. Use a tape measure, ruler, and/or a trundle wheel to complete it.

	Length in m	Length in cm	Length in mm	Width in m	Width in cm	Width in mm
Room						
Window						
Table						

2   Measure your height in metres, then centimetres to the **nearest centimetre**.
    Copy and extend the table. Fill it in for yourself and other members of your group.

Name	Height in m	Height in cm	Height in mm

3   List everyone in your group in height order, starting with the tallest.

Estimate lengths between marked divisions

MSS1/L2.3

Some rulers are marked only in centimetres.
You have to estimate the number of millimetres.

Imagine the millimetres between 3 and 4.

The length of the rod is about 4 cm.
A more accurate estimate is 3 cm 7 mm or 3.7 cm.

Practice

1 a) Estimate the length of each rod below
       i)   to the nearest cm
       ii) to the nearest mm.
   b) Measure the lengths accurately.

2 Here is a plan of a group of houses.
Each house has its own plot of land.

Scale: 1 mm to 1 m

Copy and complete the following table.

	Measurements on the plan				Actual measurements			
	House length	House width	Plot length	Plot width	House length	House width	Plot length	Plot width
House A								
House B								
House C								
House D								

3 This drawing shows the front of a house.

The scale is 10 mm to 1 m

a) On the drawing, measure in mm the heights of points A, B, C and D above the ground.

b) Use the scale 10 mm to 1 m, to find the actual heights of points A, B, C and D.

c) Copy and complete the table below by measuring from the plan in mm and then working out the actual measurements.

	Measurement on drawing in mm	Actual measurement
i) The length of the house		
ii) The width of the downstairs window		
iii) The width of the smaller upstairs window		
iv) The width of the larger upstairs window		
v) The height of the downstairs window		
vi) The height of the upstairs windows		
vii) The width of the front porch		

Maps often show the scale like this.
Use your ruler to measure the length of the line
representing 10 km.
It is 2 cm long.
On this map the scale is 1 cm to 5 km.
You can use this scale to measure
distances on the map.

Example

Use a ruler to measure the
distance between Harrogate and
Otley. It is 2.8 cm.

The **direct** distance between
Harrogate and
Otley = 2.8 cm × 5 = 14 km.

Sometimes you might want to measure distances that are not straight.

Example

To estimate the distance **along the road** from
Leeds to Pudsey lie a piece of cotton (or string)
along the road.

Then lie it along the scale.
The actual distance is 11 km or (7 miles).

If the distance is too long to lie along the scale, measure the length of the cotton
with your ruler. Then use the scale 1 cm to 5 km.

4 a) Use a ruler to find the **direct** distance in kilometers between
  i) York and Tadcaster **ii)** Leeds and Garforth
  iii) Harrogate and York **iv)** Garforth and Tadcaster.

b) Find the distance in kilometres **along the road** from
  i) Leeds to Wetherby **ii)** Tadcaster to York
  iii) Selby to Wetherby **iv)** Wetherby to Harrogate.

5 A tutor uses this map when visiting college sites at A, B, C and D.

Scale: 1 cm to 500 m

Copy and complete the table:

	Length on map (cm)	Actual distance (km)
Tutor's home to A		
Tutor's home to B		
Tutor's home to C		
Tutor's home to D		

Use ratios on scale drawings   MSS1/L2.10

A scale of **1 : 20** on a plan means **actual measurements are 20 times those on the plan.**
So   5 cm on the plan   represents $20 \times 5 = 100$ cm (i.e. 1 m)   in real life.
Another way of giving this scale is **5 cm to 1 m.**

Example

The plan of a shop has a scale of 1 : 500. On the plan the shop is 12 cm long and 9 cm
wide. What are its actual dimensions?

Length $= 500 \times 12 = 6000$ cm   Width $= 500 \times 9 = 4500$ cm
       $= \textbf{60 m}$ $= \textbf{45 m}$

**Multiply by 500 to
find the real length.**

**Divide by 100 to
change cm to m.**

Practice

1   Some of the other measurements from the plan of the shop are given below.
    Use the scale 1 : 500 to find the actual measurements.

   a) Length of car park 10 cm   **b)** Width of car park 6 cm
   c) Length of stockroom 5 cm   **d)** Width of stockroom 4 cm
   e) Length of office 2 cm   **f)** Width of office 1.2 cm
   g) Length of display area 3.2 cm   **h)** Width of display area 2.3 cm

2   The plan of a flat has a scale of 1 : 200.

   a) Copy and complete the table to give
           the actual measurements of the
           rooms.
   b) What does 1 cm on the plan
           represent?
           Give your answer in metres.

Room		on plan	actual
Lounge	Length	30 mm	
	Width	25 mm	
Kitchen	Length	18 mm	
	Width	14 mm	
Bathroom	Length	15 mm	
	Width	12 mm	
Bedroom	Length	24 mm	
	Width	16 mm	

3 Here is a plan of the downstairs layout of a house.

a) Measure the dimensions (i.e. length and width) of Rooms A, B and C and the hallway D on the plan.

b) Find the actual dimensions.

4 This is a plan of a garden.
Find the **actual**

a) length of the patio
b) width of the patio
c) length of the shed
d) width of the shed
e) length of the greenhouse
f) width of the greenhouse
g) length of the whole garden
h) width of the whole garden.

5 This map has a scale of 1 : 25 000.
Copy and complete the table below.
Measure the distances by road on the map as accurately as you can.
(Places are shown by black dots.)

Distance	On map	Actual
a) The Minster – Hospital		
b) The Minster – Cemetry		
c) Snow Close Farm – Hospital		
d) College – The Minster		
e) Snow Close Farm – The Minster		
f) Schools – Hospital		
g) Studley – The Minster		

▶ **To write a scale** like 4 cm to 1 km **as a ratio scale** you must **make the units the same**, then **simplify the ratio** (if possible).

Example

$4 \text{ cm} : 1 \text{ km} = 4 \text{ cm} : 1 \times 1000 \times 100 \text{ cm}$
$= 4 : 100\,000$
$= \mathbf{1 : 25\,000}$

> ▶ **1 km = 1000 m**
> **1 m = 100 cm**

This is the scale used on some Ordnance Survey maps.

6 Write each of these scales as a ratio.

a) 1 cm to 1 m   b) 2 cm to 1 m   c) 5 cm to 1 m   d) 1 cm to 20 m
e) 1 cm to 500 m   f) 2 cm to 5 km   g) 5 cm to 8 m   h) 4 cm to 5 km
i) 1 mm to 1 m   j) 5 mm to 1 km   k) 1 mm to 0.5 cm   l) 1 mm to 2.5 m

▶ **Drawing a plan or map**
  If the scale of a plan or map is $1 : n$, then you need to divide actual distances by n to find the corresponding distances on the plan or map.

Example   A drive is 20 m long. How long is it on a plan with a scale of 1 : 500?

Length of drive = 20 m.
In cm 20 × 100 = 2000 cm.

> ▶ It is more convenient to **work in cm for lengths on a plan or map**.

On a plan with a scale of 1 : 500, the length of the drive $= \dfrac{2000}{500} = 4$ cm.

7 In each part draw lines to represent the given distances to the given scale.

a) Using scale 1 : 10, draw lines to represent   i) 60 cm   ii) 1.3 m
b) Using scale 1 : 500, draw lines to represent   i) 16 m   ii) 24 m
c) Using scale 1 : 200, draw lines to represent   i) 26 m   ii) 17.4 m
d) Using scale 1 : 1000, draw lines to represent   i) 70 m   ii) 43 m
f) Using scale 1 : 10 000, draw lines to represent   i) 450 m   ii) 360 m
g) Using scale 1 : 20 000, draw lines to represent   i) 840 m   ii) 1.8 km
h) Using scale 1 : 50 000, draw lines to represent   i) 3.5 km   ii) 5.7 km

8 The sketch shows the dimensions of an office.
It contains

a) a computer desk   1 m by 1.5 m
b) a table   1.2 m by 0.6 m
c) a filing cabinet   60 cm by 50 cm
d) a shelf   40 cm wide.

Draw a scale diagram using a scale of 1 : 25.

Activities

1   Use Ordnance Survey maps or maps from the internet to work out actual distances.

2   Measure a room and the largest items in it (e.g. a classroom, lounge, kitchen or bedroom). Draw a scale diagram of the room.

Measure lengths in imperial units

MSS1/L1.4, MSS1/L2.3

The imperial units for measuring are **inches**, **feet**, **yards** and **miles**.
This ruler is marked in inches. Each inch is divided into 16 parts, called $\frac{1}{16}$ths.

Screws, nails and wood thickness are sometimes measured in inches.
The length of this nail $= 2\frac{4}{16}$ inches $= 2\frac{1}{4}$ inches.
This can be written as $2\frac{1}{4}$ in or $2\frac{1}{4}''$.

See page 73 for equivalent fractions.

Practice

1   Measure these screws and nails in inches.

> ▶ Longer lengths, such as the length of a room, are measured in feet or yards.
> **1 foot = 12 inches**   3 feet 6 inches can be written as 3 ft 6 in or 3' 6"
> **1 yard = 3 feet**   4 yards can be written as 4 yd

Activities

1 Estimate your height in feet and inches then measure it to the nearest inch.
   Estimate, then measure the heights of other students in your group.
   Put your results in a table.

2 a) Measure the length and width of the room in feet and inches.
   b) Write each measurement in yards, feet and inches.

Convert imperial lengths

MSS1/L2.5

> ▶ 12 inches = 1 foot   3 feet = 1 yard   1760 yards = 1 mile

$$\text{inches} \xrightarrow{\div 12} \text{feet} \xrightarrow{\div 3} \text{yards} \xrightarrow{\div 1760} \text{miles} \qquad \text{miles} \xrightarrow{\times 1760} \text{yards} \xrightarrow{\times 3} \text{feet} \xrightarrow{\times 12} \text{inches}$$

Examples

Convert:

72 inches to yards
72 inches ÷ 12 = 6 feet
6 feet ÷ 3 = 2 yards
so **72 inches = 2 yards**

1 mile to inches
1 mile × 1760 = 1760 yards
1760 yards × 3 = 5280 feet
5280 feet × 12 = 63 360 inches
so **1 mile = 63 360 inches**

4' 6" to inches
4' × 12 = 48 inches
48 + 6 = 54 inches
so **4' 6" = 54 inches**

Practice

1 How many inches?

   a) 5 yards   **b)** 6'   **c)** 28 feet   **d)** 16 feet
   e) 2 yards   **f)** 12 yards   **g)** 9 feet 5 inches   **h)** $4\frac{1}{2}$ feet

2 How many feet?

   a) 2 yards   **b)** 80 yards   **c)** 30 inches   **d)** 144"
   e) 5 yards   **f)** 60"   **g)** $1\frac{1}{3}$ yards   **h)** 28 inches

3 How many yards?

a) 72 inches   b) 15′   c) 4 miles   d) 144 inches

4 How many miles?

a) 5280 yards   b) 15 840 yards   c) 17 600 yards   d) 10 560 yards

5 A room measures 9′ 9″ by 12′ 9″. What is the perimeter of the room

a) in feet   b) in yards?

> See page 222 for perimeter.

6 Three children measure their heights in inches:

     Jan 58 inches   Imran 65 inches   Carl 73 inches

Write each height in feet and inches.

Convert between metric and imperial lengths   MSS1/L2.6

a Approximate metric/imperial conversions

> ▶ **1 inch ≈ 2.5 cm**   **1 foot ≈ 30 cm**   **1 m is slightly more than 1 yard**

cm $\xrightarrow{\div 2.5}$ inches   feet $\xrightarrow{\times 30}$ cm

inches $\xrightarrow{\times 2.5}$ cm   cm $\xrightarrow{\div 30}$ feet

> ▶ ≈ means approximately equal to.

Example	This pencil is 4 inches long. How many cm?

1 inch ≈ 2.5 cm   so   4 inches ≈ 4 × 2.5 = 10 cm.   The pencil is about **10 cm** long.

Practice

1 Copy the tables below, then use approximate conversions to fill the gaps.
Remember to write the measurement carefully, e.g. 3 yd 2 ft, not 3.2 yd

inches	centimetres
2 in	
6 in	
8 in	
	7.5 cm
7 in	
	25 cm
	80 cm
18 in	
	100 cm

yards/feet	centimetres	metres
2 ft		
$2\frac{1}{2}$ ft		
	90 cm	
	105 cm	
$4\frac{1}{2}$ ft		
	150 cm	
	210 cm	
2 yd 2 ft		
3 yd		

> This is $\frac{2}{10}$ of a yard.
> 2 feet = $\frac{2}{3}$ of a yard.

▶ **5 miles ≈ 8 km**

1 km ≈ $\frac{5}{8}$ mile or 0.6 miles   1 mile ≈ $\frac{8}{5}$ km or 1.6 km

km ⟶ miles   miles ⟶ km
    ÷ 8, then × 5   ÷ 5, then × 8

Examples

Convert:
40 km to miles   **30 miles to km**
40 km ÷ 8 = 5 then 5 × 5 = **25 miles**   30 miles ÷ 5 = 6 then 6 × 8 = **48 km**

Alternative method
1 km ≈ 0.6 miles   **1 mile ≈ 1.6 km**
40 km ≈ 40 × 0.6 = **24 miles**   30 miles ≈ 30 × 1.6 = **48 km**

Not quite the same as before, but both 24 miles and 25 miles are good **estimates**.

---

2 **a)** Convert these distances to miles.   **i)** 80 km   **ii)** 208 km   **iii)** 30 km
   b) Convert these distances to kilometres. **i)** 60 miles **ii)** 240 miles **iii)** 30 miles

3   The table below gives the distances between pairs of European cities.
    Copy the table, then use approximate conversions to fill the gaps.

		miles	km
a)	Paris to Boulogne	159	
b)	Brussels to Calais		216
c)	Berlin to Cherbourg	847	
d)	Brussels to Dieppe		310
e)	Paris to Dunkerque	174	
f)	Frankfurt to Amsterdam	283	
g)	Munich to Boulogne		944
h)	Turin to Ostend		967
i)	Zurich to Calais	476	
j)	Warsaw to Dieppe		1675

Give answers to the
nearest whole number.

b More accurate conversions

Some more accurate conversion factors are given below.

▶ **1 inch = 2.54 cm   1 yard = 0.914 m   1 mile = 1.61 km**

To convert, either multiply or divide by the conversion factor.

Look carefully at the examples below. Use your calculator to check the answers.

> ### Examples
>
> **Convert:**
>
> | **6 inches to cm** | **5 yards to metres** | **4 miles to km** |
> |---|---|---|
> | 6 inches × 2.54 = 15.24 cm | 5 yards × 0.914 = 4.57 m | 4 × 1.61 = 6.44 km |
>
> | **15 cm to inches** | **5 m to yards** | **6 km to miles** |
> |---|---|---|
> | 15 cm ÷ 2.54 = 5.91 inches | 5 m ÷ 0.914 = 5.47 yards | 6 km ÷ 1.61 = 3.73 miles |
> | | | (rounded to 2 decimal places) |

Practice

1 Change these into cm. (First change into inches if necessary.)

   a) 4 inches   **b)** 9 inches   **c)** 10.5 inches   **d)** 1 ft   **e)** 1 foot 6 inches

2 Change these into metres. Give the answers to 2 decimal places.

   a) 10 yards   **b)** 6 yards   **c)** $4\frac{1}{2}$ yards   **d)** 7 ft   **e)** 180 inches

3 Change these into inches. Give the answers to 2 decimal places.

   a) 15 cm   **b)** 45 cm   **c)** 24.8 cm   **d)** 2.5 m   **e)** 3 m

4 Change these distances to miles. Give the answers to 1 decimal place.

   a) 48 km   **b)** 16 km   **c)** 40 km   **d)** 30 km   **e)** 23.5 km

5 Change these distances to km. Give the answers to 1 decimal place.

   a) 15 miles   **b)** 25 miles   **c)** 42 miles   **d)** 30 miles   **e)** $9\frac{1}{2}$ miles

6 **a)** A map says it is 640 miles from Berlin to Calais. How many kilometres is this?
   b) Rome to Cherbourg is 1090 miles. How many kilometres is this (to the nearest km)?

7 How many miles is this (to the nearest mile)?

   > Cologne
   > 160 km

8 The maximum speed limits on a road in Europe are 120 km per hour and 100 km per hour.
   What are these speeds in miles per hour? Give answers to the nearest mile per hour.

Measures, Shape and Space

4 Weight

Measure weight in metric units

MSS1/E3.6, MSS1/L1.4, MSS1/L2.3

a Know metric units of weight

The common metric units for weight are **grams** (g) and **kilograms** (kg).

1 g is about the weight of 10 matchsticks.

A bag of sugar weighs 1 kg.

> ▶ **1 kg = 1000 g**

The weight of very small items like tablets is measured in **milligrams** (mg).

> ▶ **1 g = 1000 mg**

Practice

1 Which unit would you use to measure the weight of
  a) a packet of tea
  b) a bag of flour
  c) a small tin of tuna
  d) a packet of crisps
  e) a frozen chicken
  f) a pill?

b Weigh on balance scales

Here are some weights that can be used with balance scales:

You can use more than one of each.

Example

To measure 750 g of flour you could use these weights:
500 g + 200 g + 50 g

Pour in flour until the scales are level.

Put a 500 g, a 200 g and a 50 g weight in this pan.

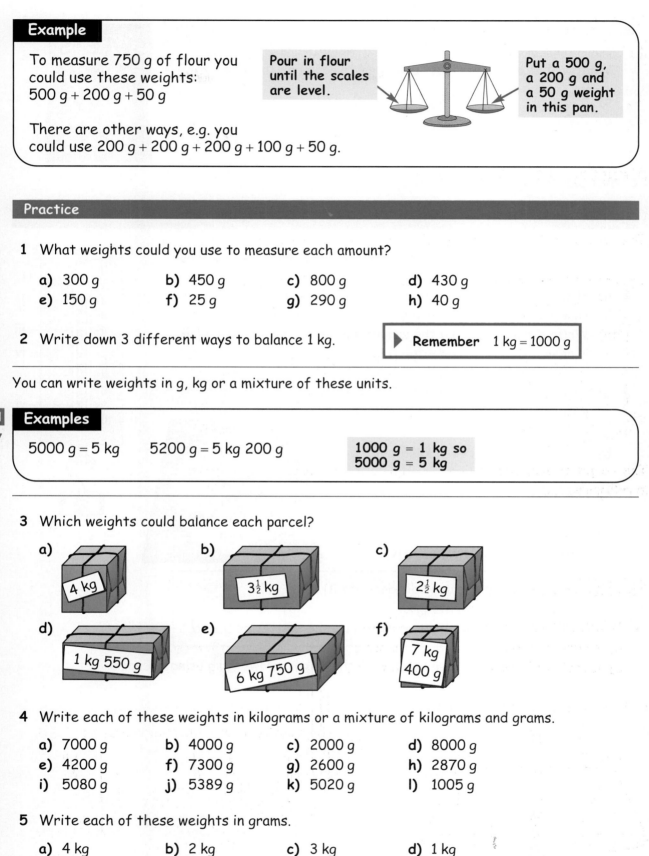

There are other ways, e.g. you could use 200 g + 200 g + 200 g + 100 g + 50 g.

Practice

1 What weights could you use to measure each amount?

a) 300 g   **b)** 450 g   **c)** 800 g   **d)** 430 g

e) 150 g   **f)** 25 g   **g)** 290 g   **h)** 40 g

2 Write down 3 different ways to balance 1 kg.

> ▶ **Remember**   1 kg = 1000 g

You can write weights in g, kg or a mixture of these units.

L1

Examples

5000 g = 5 kg   5200 g = 5 kg 200 g   1000 g = 1 kg so
5000 g = 5 kg

3 Which weights could balance each parcel?

a) 4 kg

b) $3\frac{1}{2}$ kg

c) $2\frac{1}{2}$ kg

d) 1 kg 550 g

e) 6 kg 750 g

f) 7 kg 400 g

4 Write each of these weights in kilograms or a mixture of kilograms and grams.

a) 7000 g   **b)** 4000 g   **c)** 2000 g   **d)** 8000 g

e) 4200 g   **f)** 7300 g   **g)** 2600 g   **h)** 2870 g

i) 5080 g   **j)** 5389 g   **k)** 5020 g   **l)** 1005 g

5 Write each of these weights in grams.

a) 4 kg   **b)** 2 kg   **c)** 3 kg   **d)** 1 kg

e) $1\frac{1}{2}$ kg   **f)** $1\frac{1}{4}$ kg   **g)** $2\frac{1}{2}$ kg   **h)** $3\frac{3}{4}$ kg

6 Each bag of sweets should weigh 1 kg.
Some bags are only partly filled. Their weights are given below.
What weight of sweets must be added to each bag to make 1 kg?

a) 500 g	**b)** 300 g	**c)** 470 g	**d)** 780 g
e) 250 g	**f)** 970 g	**g)** 840 g	**h)** 580 g
i) 360 g	**j)** $\frac{1}{4}$ kg	**k)** $\frac{1}{2}$ kg	**l)** $\frac{3}{4}$ kg

c Measure in grams and kilograms

Practice

This spring balance weighs up to 10 kg.

1 a) How many parts is each kilogram divided into?
 b) How many grams does each small division represent?
 c) Write down in kg and g the weight shown by each arrow i, ii, iii, iv, v, vi.

2 a) What is the maximum number of kilograms that you can weigh on these scales?
 b) How many parts is each kilogram divided into?
 c) How many grams are represented by each small division?
 d) Write down in kg and g the weight shown by each arrow i, ii, iii, iv, v.

> Each kg on the scale is divided into 10 parts.
> Each part represents $\frac{1}{10}$ kg = 0.1 kg. (= 100 g)
> So the weight shown by arrow (v) can be written as 5.2 kg.

 e) Write the weight shown by each of the other arrows in kg using decimals.

3 Some scales weigh light objects like letters at a post office.

 a) What is the maximum weight these scales can measure?

 b) What weight is shown by each arrow?

Look at the scale below. The first arrow is nearer 1 kg than 2 kg.
This means the first reading is 1 kg **to the nearest kilogram**.

The second arrow is nearer 3 kg than 2 kg.
The second reading is 3 kg **to the nearest kilogram**.

4 Write down the rest of the readings, giving each reading to the nearest kilogram.

> Each small division on the scale represents 100 g = $\frac{1}{10}$ kg = 0.1 kg.
> So the weight shown by arrow (vi) can be written as 9 kg 300 g or 9.3 kg.

5 Write the weight shown by each of the other arrows

   a) in kg and g   **b)** in kg using decimals.

6 Look carefully at this scale.

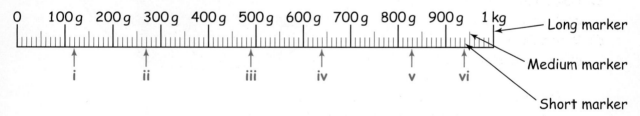

There is 100 g between each long marker and the next.

   a) What weight is between a long marker and the next medium marker?
   b) What weight is between each short marker and the next short marker?
   c) What is the weight shown by each arrow?

7 a) Write down, in kilograms, the weights shown by each arrow on this scale.

   b) What is the difference in weight between:
      i) A and B   **ii)** C and D   **iii)** E and F?

8

a) What do the medium markers show on this scale?
b) How many grams do the smallest divisions represent?
c) Write down the weights at A, B, C, D, E and F.
Give your answers in kilograms and grams.
d) What is the difference in weight between
   i) A and B   **ii)** C and D   **iii)** E and F?

Estimate weights between marked divisions   MSS1/L2.3

Some kitchen scales look like this.
You have to estimate between the
labelled divisions.

1 a) Estimate the weight of each bag as accurately as you can.
   b) Estimate the difference in weight between

   i) bags A and B   **ii)** bags C and D   **iii)** bags E and F
   iv) bags A and F   **v)** bags C and E   **vi)** bags B and D.

   c) How much needs to be added to bags A, B and C if they should each weigh $1\frac{1}{4}$ kg?
   d) How much needs to be added to bags D, E and F if they should each weigh $2\frac{1}{2}$ kg?
   e) There is also a bag G. The total weight of the seven bags is 10 kg.
   What is the weight of bag G?

Activities

1 Write down an estimate of the weight of 10 items in grams or kilograms.
   Use a table like this.
   Use scales or a spring balance to weigh each item accurately.

Item	Estimated weight	Measured weight

2 Estimate your weight in kg. Weigh yourself. How accurate was your estimate?
   Ask other people you know if you can weigh them.
   (Remember people are often sensitive about their weight.)
   Put your results in a table.

3 Use a set of kitchen scales to weigh 100 g of sugar. Put it in a bag.
   Weigh 100 g of paper.
   Find a book you think weighs about 100 g. Weigh the book as accurately as you can. How close was it to 100 g?

4 Choose 10 objects that you have not weighed before.
   (For example you could use things like a bunch of 5 pens.)
   Estimate the weight of each object to the nearest 50 g.
   Weigh the objects. Record your results in a table.
   Now list the objects in order of their weights, starting with the lightest.

Choose units and instruments   MSS1/E3.8, MSS1/L1.4, MSS1/L2.3

Practice

1 Copy this list of items. For each item choose a likely weight.

   a) Medium tin of beans   b) Packet of crisps
   c) Bag of potatoes   d) Yoghurt
   e) Bag of flour   f) Egg
   g) Packet of butter   h) Box of 160 tea bags
   i) Bag of sugar

   25 g, 250 g, 410 g, 5 kg, 50 g   125 g, 500 g, 1 kg 500 g, 1 kg

2 Items are often weighed to the nearest **gram**, **10 grams**, **100 grams** or **kilogram**.
   How accurately would you weigh these items?

   a) A bag of concrete mix   b) Airmail letters
   c) Sugar for a recipe   d) Your weekly weight loss during a diet
   e) Mushrooms

3 a) Which of these scales would be the best to
weigh each parcel?

9 kg   4 kg 400 g   8 kg 500 g   5 kg 400 g

b) Put the parcels in order of weight, lightest first.

c) A postman weighs a parcel on scale A and says it
weighs 3 kg 500 g.
He then measures it on scale B and says it weighs 3 kg 600 g.
Which answer do you think is likely to be more accurate? Why?

Convert between metric weights

MSS1/L1.7, MSS1/L2.5

▶ **1000 mg = 1 g**   **1000 g = 1 kg**   **1000 kg = 1 tonne**

To convert between these units you need to multiply or divide by 1000.

$$\text{from } \mathbf{mg} \xrightarrow{\div 1000} \mathbf{g} \xrightarrow{\div 1000} \mathbf{kg} \xrightarrow{\div 1000} \mathbf{tonnes} \qquad \text{from } \mathbf{tonnes} \xrightarrow{\times 1000} \mathbf{kg} \xrightarrow{\times 1000} \mathbf{g} \xrightarrow{\times 1000} \mathbf{mg}$$

Examples	**Convert:**

5000 mg to g
$5000 \div 1000 = 5$ g

6700 g to kg
$6700 \div 1000 = 6.7$ kg

200 kg to tonnes
$200 \div 1000 = 0.2$ tonnes

1.5 g to mg
$1.5 \times 1000 = 1500$ mg

0.625 kg to g
$0.625 \times 1000 = 625$ g

0.08 tonnes to kg
$0.08 \times 1000 = 80$ kg

The first 3 figures after the point are grams.

Practice

1 How many kilograms?

  a) 4000 g   **b)** 6500 g   **c)** 5485 g   **d)** 34 500 g

  e) 800 g   **f)** 250 g   **g)** 300 000 g   **h)** 750 000 mg

  i) 4 tonnes   **j)** 3.54 tonnes   **k)** 0.5 tonnes   **l)** 0.25 tonnes

2 How many grams?

  a) 7 kg   **b)** 4.5 kg   **c)** 8.268 kg   **d)** 16.4 kg

  e) 3.05 kg   **f)** 0.3 kg   **g)** 0.06 kg   **h)** 1.025 kg

  i) 2000 mg   **j)** 7500 mg   **k)** 500 mg   **l)** 0.001 tonne

3 How many milligrams?

a) 44 g   b) 30.5 g   c) 3.3 g   d) 0.83 g

e) 12.3 g   f) 0.07 g   g) 0.05 kg   h) 3.75 kg

4 How many tonnes?

a) 503 000 kg   b) 42 000 kg   c) 4500 kg   d) 589 000 g

5 Copy and complete these.

a)   3 tonnes = _____ kg   b)   0.5 g = _____ mg   c) 1.5 kg = _____ g

d) 0.5 tonnes = _____ kg   e) 7 tonnes = _____ kg   f) 0.25 g = _____ mg

g)   750 kg = _____ tonnes   h) 5000 kg = _____ tonnes   i)   10 kg = _____ g

6 Put each group in order of size, starting with the **smallest**.

a) 450 g   0.4 kg   4 000 000 mg   0.4 tonnes   450 kg

b) ½ kg   0.25 kg   330 g   25 600 mg   0.45 kg

Calculate using metric weights   MSS1/L1.6, MSS1/L2.5

a Kilograms and grams

Parts of a kilogram

Units	.	Tenths	Hundredths	Thousandths
kg	.	$\frac{1}{10}$th kg	$\frac{1}{100}$th kg	$\frac{1}{1000}$th kg
1000 g	.	100 g	10 g	1 g

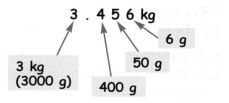

The first 3 dp are grams.

3 . 4 5 6 kg

3 kg (3000 g)   400 g   50 g   6 g

= 3 kg 456 g or 3456 g

Example   1.5 kg + 400 g + 30 g + 5 g

Either **work in grams**:

1.5 kg + 400 g + 30 g + 5 g = 1500 + 400 + 30 + 5 = **1935 g** or **1.935 kg**

× 1000 = 1500 g

Remember the units.

```
1500 +
 400
  30
   5
————
1935
```

or **work in kilograms using decimals**:

1.5 kg + 400 g + 30 g + 5 g = 1.5 kg + 0.4 kg + 0.03 kg + 0.005 kg

= **1.935 kg**

Remember the units.   4 × 100 g   3 × 10 g   5 g

Use a calculator to check.

```
1.5   +
0.4
0.03
0.005
—————
1.935
```

Practice

1   Work these out. Give the answer in kilograms if it is more than 1000 g.
    Check your answers using a calculator or another method.

a) 3 kg + 500 g + 2 kg + 200 g   b) 2.5 kg + 500 g + 75 g
c) 700 g + 2 kg + 400 g + 50 g   d) 1.5 kg + 500 g + 0.25 kg
e) 1 kg + 750 g + 20 g + 2 kg   f) 4 kg + 20 g − 1.75 kg
g) $5\frac{1}{2}$ kg − 800 g   h) 2.5 kg − 900 g
i) 4 kg − 60 g   j) 2 kg − 400 g + 25 g
k) 2 kg − 100 g − $\frac{1}{4}$ kg l) 4 kg + 40 g + 4 g
m) 2 kg + 300 g + 40 g + 5 g   n) 1 kg − 4 g

See page 110 to revise decimals

2   Find the difference in weight between

a) 1.75 kg and 5 kg   b) 3.5 kg and 1.75 kg   c) 475 g and 6.5 kg.

3   Three parcels weigh 2.75 kg, 2.5 kg and 800 g. What is their total weight?

4   How much flour must be added to 285 g to make 570 g?

5   A bag of frozen peas holds $2\frac{1}{2}$ kg. A chef uses 700 g. What weight is left?

6   A piece of cheese weighs 1.2 kg. Two pieces, each weighing 120 g are used for lunch packs.
    What weight of cheese is left? Give the answer in grams.

7   A cook makes a cake. She uses 150 g flour, 150 g butter, 150 g sugar, 250 g mixed dried
    fruit, 100 g fruit peel and 50 g chopped cherries.
    What is the total weight of these ingredients?

8   A fruit grower picks 2.4 kg of strawberries and 1.75 kg
    of raspberries.

a) How many more grams of strawberries than
   raspberries does she pick?
b) She uses 500 g of strawberries and 400 g of
   raspberries in a fruit pudding.
   What total weight of strawberries and raspberries
   are left?
   Give your answer in kg.

L2 b Mixed calculations

Practice

1 A caterer buys 10 kg of potatoes, $1\frac{1}{2}$ kg of tomatoes, $1\frac{1}{4}$ kg of carrots and $1\frac{3}{4}$ kg of apples. What is the total weight of the shopping?

2 Small pots hold 50 g of salt. How many pots can be filled from a $\frac{1}{2}$ kg bag?

3 A shopper buys $\frac{1}{2}$ kg of carrots, 2.5 kg of potatoes, $\frac{1}{4}$ kg of onions and a bag of mushrooms weighing 360 g. How heavy is the shopping?

4 A tin of beans weighs 440 g. How much do 6 tins of beans weigh in kilograms?

5 A box weighs 420 g. A second box is 4 times as heavy. What is the total weight of the 2 boxes? Give the answer in kilograms.

6 A bag of 12 oranges weighs 4.2 kg. Find the average weight per orange.

7 How many 300 g bags of sweets can be made from 4.5 kg of sweets?

8 360 g of cake mix is divided equally between 24 small cake papers. How much cake mix is in each cake paper?

9 2.5 kg of tobacco is put into 50 g packets. How many packets are there?

10 A crate holds 17 kg biscuits. The biscuits are in packets each holding 340 g. How many packets are there in the crate?

L2 c Kilograms and tonnes

▶ **Remember 1000 kg = 1 tonne**

Practice

1 A hospital uses 125 kg potatoes each day. How long will a 2 tonne delivery of potatoes last?

2 A tonne of grain is divided into 2.5 kg bags. How many bags are there?

3 A diesel locomotive weighs 100 metric tonnes. A car transporter train carries 60 motor cars. Each car weighs 800 kg. The cars travel on 15 car transporter trucks, each of which weighs 20 tonnes.

   a) Find the total weight of the cars on the train in tonnes.
   b) i)   Which is the greater weight: the cars or the diesel locomotive?
       ii) Work out the difference in weight in tonnes.
   c) What is the total weight of the car transporter trucks?
   d) What is the total weight of the locomotive, transporter trucks and cars?

Weigh with metric and imperial units

MSS1/L1.4, MSS1/L2.3

Grams (g) and **kilograms** (kg) are **metric** units

▶ **1000 g = 1 kg**

Ounces (oz), **pounds** (lb) and **stones** (st) are **imperial** units.

▶ **16 oz = 1 lb   14 lbs = 1 st**

Many scales show both metric and imperial units.

Activities

1   Use grams, then ounces to weigh some items.
    e.g. a book, a dictionary, a pencil case or a bag.

2   Use kilograms, then pounds to weigh some items.
    e.g. a rubbish bin, 5 books, a chair, yourself.

Convert imperial weights

MSS1/L2.5

▶ **16 oz = 1 lb   14 lb = 1 st   2240 lb = 1 ton**

(Note: This is different from the metric tonne.)

$$\overset{\div 16}{\quad} \quad \overset{\div 14}{\quad}$$

ounces   pounds   stones   tons   tons   stones   pounds   ounces

$$\div 2240 \qquad\qquad \times 2240$$

$$\overset{\times 14}{\quad} \quad \overset{\times 16}{\quad}$$

Examples   Convert:

3 st to lb	**2 lb 4 oz to oz**	**64 oz to lb**	$\frac{1}{2}$ **ton to lb**
$3 \times 14 = $ **42 lb**	$2 \times 16 = 32$ oz	$64 \div 16 = $ **4 lb**	$2240 \div 2 = $ **1120 lb**
	$32 + 4 = $ **36 oz**		

Practice

1   Convert these to oz.

   a) 2 lb   **b)** 4 lb 6 oz   **c)** 6 lb 4 oz   **d)** 12 lb   **e)** 4 lb 8 oz
   f) 3 lb 7 oz   **g)** $\frac{1}{4}$ lb   **h)** $\frac{1}{2}$ lb   **i)** $\frac{3}{4}$ lb   **j)** $2\frac{1}{2}$ lb

2   How many lb are there in each of these?

   a) 16 oz   **b)** 96 oz   **c)** 48 oz   **d)** 128 oz   **e)** 80 oz
   f) 2 st   **g)** 4 st   **h)** $2\frac{1}{2}$ st   **i)** 2 tons   **j)** $1\frac{1}{2}$ tons

Take care with mixed imperial weights.

Example To convert 72 oz to lb and oz:

Find how many whole pounds first $72 \div 16 = 4$ whole lbs
Find how many ounces are used $4 \times 16 = 64$ oz
Find how many ounces are left   72 oz
                                       $-$ 64 oz
                                           8 oz

so 72 oz = **4 lb 8 oz**

You can do this by long division, but take care if you use a calculator.
This gives 4.5 lb. The 0.5 is half of a pound, **not** 5 ounces.

---

3 How may lb and oz are there in each of these?

  a) 56 oz   **b)** 82 oz   **c)** 38 oz   **d)** 73 oz
  e) 44 oz   **f)** 20 oz   **g)** 55 oz   **h)** 81 oz

Calculate using imperial weights

MSS1/L2.5

Practice

1 Brian weighs 183 lb. What is this in stones and pounds?

2 Bill weighs 115 lb. What is this in stones and pounds?

3 How much lighter is Bill than Brian?

  a) in pounds   **b)** in stones and pounds

4 Paul's weight is half way between Brian and Bill. How much does Paul weigh?

  a) in pounds   **b)** in stones and pounds

5 What is the average weight of Brian, Bill and Paul?

6 **a)** Brian decides to lose weight. He starts at 183 lb and loses 4 lbs in the first week of his diet. Copy and complete his weight chart.

	Week 1	Week 2	Week 3	Week 4	Week 5	Week 6
Weight lost	4 lb	4 lb		3 lb		2 lb
New weight in stones and pounds					11 st 11 lb	
New weight in pounds	179 lb		171 lb			

  b) How much did Brian lose altogether during these six weeks?

  c) How much more weight must he lose to reach his target of 10 st 7 lb?

Convert between metric and imperial weights

a Approximate metric/imperial conversions

Activity

Essential

Weigh some items in ounces and then in grams.
(Some suggestions are given in the table.)

Item	Weight in oz	Weight in g
Calculator		
5 pens		
A pad of paper		
Pencil case		

▶ **1 oz ≈ 25 g   1 lb ≈ 450 g**

An ounce is about the same as 25 grams.
If your pencil case weighs 4 oz, it should weigh about 100 g ($4 \times 25 = 100$).
Check your measurements in the table in the same way.

Approximate **conversion factors** between metric and imperial units of weight are given below.
Use them to answer the questions that follow.

Approximate conversion factors

▶ 1 lb is just under $\frac{1}{2}$ kg (about 450 g)   1 kg is just over 2 lb   1 oz ≈ 25 g

Remember this sign means 'approximately equal to'.

Examples $4\frac{1}{2}$ kg ≈ $4\frac{1}{2} \times 2 = $ **9 lb**   360 g ≈ 360 ÷ 25 = **14 oz** (nearest oz)

Practice

1 Which is the correct answer?

a) 4 oz is approximately   5 g   2 kg   100 g   50 g
b) 1 kg is _____ than 2 lb?   more   less

2 A recipe has the following ingredients. Convert each weight into ounces (to the nearest ounce).

a) 375 g fresh suet   b) 250 g currants   c) 560 g raisins
d) 280 g peel   e) 480 g breadcrumbs   f) 720 g flour

3 Pineapple cake has the following ingredients.
Give approximate conversions into grams (to the nearest 5 grams).

a) 14 oz pineapple rings in juice   **b)** 1 oz coconut

c) 5 oz chopped butter   **d)** 8 oz self-raising flour

e) 4 oz brown sugar   **f)** $3\frac{1}{2}$ oz melted butter

g) $2\frac{1}{2}$ oz plain flour   **h)** $7\frac{1}{2}$ oz caster sugar

b More accurate conversions

▶ **1 kg = 2.2 lb**   **1 oz = 28 g**

To convert, multiply or divide by the conversion factor.

Example	Convert 5 kg to lb	Convert 6 lb to kg

Example   Convert 5 kg to lb   Convert 6 lb to kg

$5 \text{ kg} = 5 \times 2.2 = \textbf{11 lb}$

$6 \text{ lb} = 6 \div 2.2 = \textbf{2.73 kg}$ (to 2 dp)
(using a calculator)

You can check using inverse calculations:
$11 \div 2.2 = 5$

$2.73 \times 2.2 = 6.006$
(near 6, the difference caused by rounding)

Practice

1 Use the conversion 1 kg = 2.2 lb to find the missing values.

a) 4 kg = ____ lb   **b)** 22 lb = ____ kg   **c)** 9 kg = ____ lb   **d)** 12 lb = ____ kg

2 Use the conversion 1 oz = 28 g to find these missing values.

a) 4 oz = ____ g   **b)** 140 g = ____ oz   **c)** 15 oz = ____ g   **d)** 70 g = ____ oz

Activity

Use conversions to check weights in recipe books.

Measures, Shape and Space

5 Capacity

Measure capacity and volume

MSS1/E3.7, MSS1/L1.4, MSS1/L2.3

a Know metric measures

The amount of liquid a container holds when full is its **capacity**.
Volume is the amount of space something fills.
The metric unit we use for capacity and volume of liquids is a **litre** (ℓ).

Many fruit juice drinks and squashes are sold in bottles that hold 1 litre.
Even large volumes, like the amount of water in a swimming pool are measured in litres.

Activities   Essential

1   You need:

-   a 5 litre plastic bottle (the sort used by campers)
-   a $\frac{1}{2}$ litre measuring jug.

Measure $\frac{1}{2}$ litre water and pour it into the bottle.
Mark the $\frac{1}{2}$ litre level on the bottle.
Measure another $\frac{1}{2}$ litre water and pour it into the bottle.
Mark and label this level as 1 litre.
Repeat this until you have the bottle marked every $\frac{1}{2}$ litre up to 5 litres.

2   Collect together some large containers, e.g. bowls, saucepans, tins.
Estimate, then measure, how much each container holds.
Put your results in a table with the headings shown below.

Container	Estimate to nearest $\frac{1}{2}$ litre	Measure to nearest $\frac{1}{2}$ litre

---

We measure small amounts of liquid in **millilitres** (mℓ).

1 mℓ is just a few drops.
5 mℓ is the capacity of a medicine spoon/teaspoon.

Measuring jugs are often labelled in millilitres.

> ▶ **1000 mℓ = 1 litre**

Practice

1

a) How many jugs A are needed to fill this litre jug?
b) How many jugs B are needed to fill this litre jug?
c) How many jugs C are needed to fill this litre jug?

2 How many millilitres are there in

a) 1 litre   b) $\frac{1}{2}$ litre   c) $\frac{1}{4}$ litre   d) $\frac{3}{4}$ litre   e) 1 litre 500 mℓ?

3 How many litres are equal to

a) 3000 mℓ   b) 5000 mℓ   c) 9000 mℓ   d) 12 000 mℓ   e) 4500 mℓ?

b Measure in litres and millilitres

Practice

1 This jug measures 2 litres.
Each division represents 200 mℓ.

a) Write down the amount shown by each arrow.
Give your answers in mℓ.

> 200 mℓ is the same as 0.2 litres, so each division on the
> scale measures 0.2 litres.
> The volume shown by arrow v can be written as 1.6 litres.

b) Write the amount shown by each of the other arrows in litres using decimals.

2 a) What is the maximum volume this jug can measure?
b) How many millilitres are represented by the large labelled divisions?
c) How many millilitres are represented by the small unlabelled divisions?
d) Write the measurements shown by each arrow.
e) How many millilitres are there in $\frac{1}{2}$ litre?

3 a) What is the greatest volume this cylinder can measure?
b) How many large divisions are there between 100 mℓ and 200 mℓ?
c) How many mℓ does each large division represent?
d) How many mℓ does each small division represent?
e) Write the measures shown by the arrows.

Estimate between marked divisions

MSS1/L2.3

Sometimes you need to estimate between the divisions on a scale.

Arrow i is about half way between 350 mℓ and 400 mℓ.

An estimate of this reading is **375 mℓ**.

Practice

1 Estimate the readings shown by the other arrows as accurately as you can.

2 Here is another measuring jug.

a) What is the greatest volume this jug measures?
b) Write the measures shown by the arrows as accurately as you can.

Activities

1 You will need a measuring jug marked in hundreds of millilitres to 1 litre.
You also need a cup and some water.

a) How many cupfuls of water do you need to fill the jug to the 1 litre mark?
b) How many cupfuls do you need to fill to the $\frac{1}{2}$ litre level?

L1

2 Collect some bottles, jars and pots.
Estimate then measure how much each container holds.
Put your results in a table.

3 Pour 300 mℓ water into a measuring jug.
Put a stone in the jug.
Make sure it is covered with water.
Measure the level of the water again as accurately as
you can.
The difference between the 2 measurements is the
volume of the stone.

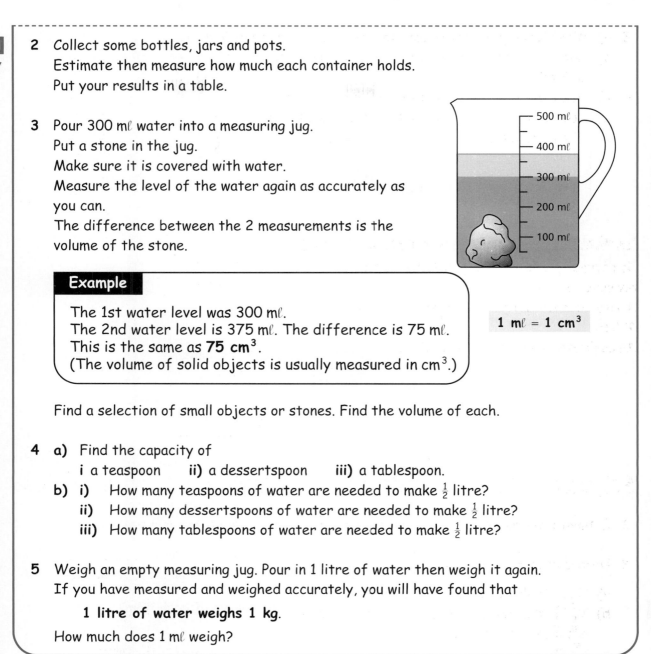

500 mℓ
400 mℓ
300 mℓ
200 mℓ
100 mℓ

Example

The 1st water level was 300 mℓ.
The 2nd water level is 375 mℓ. The difference is 75 mℓ.
This is the same as **75 cm³**.
(The volume of solid objects is usually measured in cm³.)

$1 \text{ mℓ} = 1 \text{ cm}^3$

Find a selection of small objects or stones. Find the volume of each.

4 a) Find the capacity of
   i a teaspoon   ii) a dessertspoon   iii) a tablespoon.
  b) i)   How many teaspoons of water are needed to make $\frac{1}{2}$ litre?
     ii)   How many dessertspoons of water are needed to make $\frac{1}{2}$ litre?
     iii) How many tablespoons of water are needed to make $\frac{1}{2}$ litre?

5 Weigh an empty measuring jug. Pour in 1 litre of water then weigh it again.
If you have measured and weighed accurately, you will have found that

   1 litre of water weighs 1 kg.

How much does 1 mℓ weigh?

Choose units and instruments

MSS1/E3.8, MSS1/L1.4,MSS1/L2.3

Practice

1 Which unit, litres or millilitres, would you use to measure these?

  a) The volume of water in a bath   b) The capacity of a baby bottle
  c) The capacity of a wine glass   d) The volume of water used to wash a car
  e) The capacity of a water butt   f) The water a rabbit drinks in a day

2   Which measuring container is most suitable to measure each amount?

a) The volume of car shampoo to wash a car
b) The volume of gin in a gin and tonic
c) The capacity of a jam jar
d) The volume of paint to decorate a bedroom
e) The capacity of a saucepan

3   Which measuring container would you use to measure each volume?

a) 1.8 litres   b) 300 mℓ   c) 600 mℓ   d) 1500 mℓ
e) 3½ litres   f) 2.5 litres   g) 1400 mℓ   h) 500 mℓ

L1

4   Which level of accuracy would you use to measure the volume of each item?
Choose from the nearest **1 mℓ**, **10 mℓ**, **100 mℓ** or **1 litre**.

a) Kettle   b) Indoor watering can   c) Medicine
d) Sauce jar   e) Fish tank   f) Saucepan
g) Concentrated plant food to mix with 1 litre of water

Convert between millilitres, litres and centilitres

MSS1/L1.7, MSS1/L2.5

Litres and millilitres are the most common metric units for capacity.

▶ **1 litre = 1000 mℓ**

To convert between litres and millilitres, multiply or divide by 1000.
You can use millilitres, litres or a mixture of these.
For example, 1400 mℓ is the same as 1.4 litres or 1 litre 400 mℓ

$$\text{litres} \xrightarrow{\times 1000} \text{mℓ}$$
$$\text{mℓ} \xrightarrow[\div 1000]{} \text{litres}$$

Examples

Convert: 4 litres to mℓ
4 × 1000 = 4000 mℓ

2.5 litres to mℓ
2.5 × 1000 = 2500 mℓ

4875 mℓ to litres
4875 ÷ 1000 = 4.875 litres

or 4 litres and 875 millilitres (the first 3 dp are mℓ)

Practice

1 Write these in millilitres.

a) 5 ℓ
b) 2.6 ℓ
c) 12.5 ℓ
d) 3.625 ℓ
e) 0.682 ℓ
f) 1.85 ℓ
g) 5.063 ℓ
h) 0.75 ℓ
i) 0.083 ℓ
j) 0.04 ℓ

2 Write these in litres, using a decimal point where necessary.

a) 6000 mℓ
b) 3500 mℓ
c) 11 000 mℓ
d) 1100 mℓ
e) 65 400 mℓ
f) 330 mℓ
g) 250 mℓ
h) 425 mℓ
i) 7300 mℓ
j) 5320 mℓ

3 Write these in millilitres.

a) 3 litres 400 mℓ
b) 6 litres 250 mℓ
c) 3 litres 630 mℓ
d) 8 litres 760 mℓ

4 Write these as   **i)** litres and millilitres   **ii)** litres using a decimal point

a) 1200 mℓ
b) 3830 mℓ
c) 4935 mℓ
d) 5769 mℓ
e) 15 800 mℓ
f) 5098 mℓ

5 Find the matching volumes.

a) 100 mℓ
b) 10 mℓ
c) 250 mℓ
d) 50 mℓ
e) 2550 mℓ
f) 500 mℓ
g) 0.1 litre
h) 0.05 litre
i) 0.5 litre
j) 2.55 litres
k) 0.01 litre
l) 0.25 litre

6 Put the bottles in order of size, starting with the **greatest** capacity.

A   1.1 litres
B   94 mℓ
C   1.650 ℓ
D   875 mℓ

Another unit that is used for measuring wine or spirits is the **centilitre** (cℓ).

▶ **1 cℓ = 10 mℓ** (like cm and mm)   **1 litre = 100 cℓ** (like m and cm)

To convert units you need to multiply or divide by 10, 100 or 1000.

$\div 10$ $\div 100$

from mℓ   cℓ   ℓ

$\div 1000$

$\times 100$ $\times 10$

from litre   cℓ   mℓ

$\times 1000$

Examples	Convert:

320 mℓ to cℓ
$320 \div 10 = 32$ cℓ

45 cℓ to litres
$45 \div 100 = 0.45$ litres

3.45 litres to cℓ
$3.45 \times 100 = 345$ cℓ

---

7 How many litres are the same as

a) 300 cℓ   b) 250 cℓ   c) 3050 cℓ   d) 740 cℓ
e) 50 cℓ   f) 33 cℓ   g) 75 cℓ   h) 3210 cℓ?

8 How many centilitres are the same as

a) 30 mℓ   b) 500 mℓ   c) 250 mℓ   d) 85 mℓ
e) 3.5 litres   f) 1.75 litres   g) $\frac{1}{2}$ litre   h) 0.46 litres?

Calculate using metric units of capacity   MSS1/L1.6, MSS1/L2.5

a Litres and millilitres

Parts of a litre

The first 3 dp are mℓ.

Units	.	Tenths	Hundredths	Thousandths
litres	.	$\frac{1}{10}$th litre	$\frac{1}{100}$th litre	$\frac{1}{1000}$th litre
1000 mℓ	.	100 mℓ	10 mℓ	1 mℓ

3 . 4 5 6 litres

6 mℓ
50 mℓ
400 mℓ
3 ℓ (3000 mℓ)

= **3456 mℓ**

Example

Either **work in millilitres**:

$2.4\,ℓ + 200\,mℓ + 15\,mℓ = 2400 + 200 + 15 = \mathbf{2615\ mℓ}$ or **2.615** ℓ

$\times 1000 = \mathbf{2400\ mℓ}$

Remember the units.

```
 2400 +
  200
   15
 2615
```

or **work in litres using decimals**:

$2.4\,ℓ + 200\,mℓ + 15\,mℓ = 2.4\,ℓ + 0.2\,ℓ + 0.015\,ℓ = \mathbf{2.615}\ ℓ$

$2 \times 100\ mℓ$ $10\ mℓ$ $5\ mℓ$

Use a calculator to check.

```
 2.4   +
 0.2
 0.015
 2.615
```

Practice

1 Work these out. Give the answer in litres if it is more than 1000 mℓ.
   Check your answers with a calculator.

   a) 3 litres + 650 mℓ + 50 mℓ
   b) 1 litre + 2 litres + 400 mℓ + 25 mℓ
   c) 7 litres + 2 litres + 75 mℓ
   d) 3.6 litres + 850 mℓ + 80 mℓ
   e) 400 mℓ + 1.64 litres + 40 mℓ
   f) 4.7 litres + 2 litres + 50 mℓ
   g) 150 mℓ + 5 mℓ + 50 mℓ
   h) 10 litres – 4 litres – 40 mℓ
   i) 5 litres – 2 litres – 340 mℓ
   j) $7\frac{1}{2}$ litres – 3.2 litres + 75 mℓ

2 A caterer mixes together 2.5 litres lemonade, 2 litres orange juice, 1.25 litres
   apple juice and 750 mℓ pineapple juice. How much liquid is this altogether?

3 A student buys 2 litres milk. He drinks 350 mℓ then gives 30 mℓ to the cat. How much milk
   is left?

4 Give the answers to these in litres. Check with a calculator.
   a) 6.2 litres + 600 mℓ + 3 cℓ
   b) 50 mℓ + 43 cℓ + 0.6 litre
   c) 5 litres – 43 cℓ
   d) 10 litres – 1 litre – 1 cℓ

5 For each part assume you start with 1 litre of fruit juice.
   How much is left after pouring out the drinks described?

   a) 2 cups holding 250 mℓ each
   b) 3 glasses holding 200 mℓ each
   c) 4 glasses holding 150 mℓ each
   d) 2 tumblers holding 420 mℓ each

6

1.6 ℓ	870 mℓ	950 mℓ	1.25 ℓ
A	**B**	**C**	**D**

   a) What is the total capacity of the 4 jars?
   b) What is the difference in capacity between the largest and the smallest jars?
   c) Which 2 jars have a total capacity of 2.12 ℓ?
   d) A new jar has half the capacity of A? How much does it hold?
   e) Another jar holds 4 times as much as D. What is its capacity?

L2 b Mixed calculations

Practice

1 **a)** A 5 mℓ dose of medicine is taken 4 times a day. What is the total dose per day?
   b) The medicine bottle holds 140 mℓ. How many days will the medicine last?

2 A water butt holds 100 litres of water. A watering can holds 5 litres.
   How many times can you fill the can from the water butt?

3 Water drips from a tap at a rate of 400 mℓ every 5 minutes.
   How much water drips from the tap in an hour?

Questions 4 to 9 are about a child's birthday party.

4 **a)** 24 children go to the party. Each child drinks two 200 mℓ glasses of cola.
       How much cola do they drink altogether?
   b) A bottle holds 1.5 litres. How many bottles are used at the party?

5 The cake recipe needs 3 tablespoons of oil. The cook doesn't have a tablespoon, but she
   does have a teaspoon. She knows a tablespoon holds 15 mℓ and a teaspoon holds 5 mℓ.
   How many teaspoons of oil does she need to use?

6 **a)** Each packet of chocolate whip needs 300 mℓ milk.
       How much milk is needed for 6 packets?
   b) The whip is divided between the 24 children.
       How much milk does each child get in their whip?

7 Each jelly dish holds 850 mℓ. How much will 5 jelly dishes hold?

8 One party game has a large bucket of water. A 750 mℓ jug is used to fill
   the bucket. The jug is filled 8 times. How much water is in the bucket?

9 A cocktail is made for the adults. The recipe for 4 needs
   60 mℓ orange juice,   80 mℓ lemonade,   30 mℓ rum,   and   20 mℓ tequila.

   a) There are 10 adults at the party. How much of each ingredient is needed?
   b) How much fruit cocktail is made altogether?

10 **a)** How many people are in your maths group?
   b) If everyone has a 200 mℓ drink, how much liquid is needed altogether?
   c) A drink recipe is: $\frac{1}{3}$ lemonade, $\frac{1}{4}$ orange juice, $\frac{1}{6}$ apple juice
                        $\frac{1}{6}$ grapefruit juice and $\frac{1}{12}$ lemon juice
       How much of each do you need to make the drink for your group?

Measure with metric and imperial units   MSS1/L1.4, MSS1/L2.3

Many measuring jugs and other containers show both metric and imperial measures.

The common metric units are millilitres and litres.

> ▶ **1000 mℓ = 1 litre**

The common imperial units are fluid ounces (fl oz),
pints (pt) and gallons (gal)

> ▶ **1 pt = 20 fl oz   1 gal = 8 pt**

Activities

1   Fill a pint milk bottle with water.
    Pour the water into a measuring jug similar to the one shown above.
    Does the milk bottle hold   **a)** more or less than 1 litre
                                 b) more or less than $\frac{1}{2}$ litre?

2   Collect some containers that hold less than 1 pint, e.g. cup, mug, small jug, egg cup.
    Estimate, then measure, the capacity of each container in appropriate metric and
    imperial units. Record your results in a table like this:

	Imperial		Metric	
Container	Estimate	Measurement	Estimate	Measurement

3   Collect some containers that hold more than 1 pint, e.g. tin, bowl, saucepan.
    Add these to your table and compare the imperial and metric measurements.
    Can you see that a litre is a bit less than 2 pints?

Convert imperial units of capacity   MSS1/L2.5

> ▶ **1 pint = 20 fluid ounces   1 gallon = 8 pints**

To convert units multiply or divide by the conversion factor.

$$\text{fl oz} \xrightarrow{\div 20} \text{pt} \xrightarrow{\div 8} \text{gal} \qquad\qquad \text{gal} \xrightarrow{\times 8} \text{pt} \xrightarrow{\times 20} \text{fl oz}$$

Examples   Convert:

80 fl oz to pints   **2.5 gallons to pints**
80 ÷ 20 = 4 pints   2.5 × 8 = 20 pints

Practice

1 Convert these to pints.

a) 60 fl oz   b) 40 fl oz   c) 70 fl oz   d) 150 fl oz

e) 4 gallons   f) 1.5 gallons   g) $\frac{1}{2}$ gallon   h) $\frac{1}{4}$ gallon

2 Convert these to gallons.

a) 24 pints   b) 2 pints   c) 60 pints   d) 140 pints

3 Convert these to fluid ounces.

a) 2 pints   b) 0.1 pint   c) $\frac{1}{2}$ pt   d) $\frac{1}{4}$ pt

Calculate using imperial units of volume

MSS1/L2.5

Practice

1 A recipe needs the following ingredients:
1 pt lemonade, $\frac{1}{2}$ pt orange juice, $\frac{1}{4}$ pt apple juice,
$\frac{1}{8}$ pt lemon juice, $\frac{1}{10}$ pt tequila.

a) Write each volume in fluid ounces.
b) What is the total volume in fluid ounces?

2 Sixty guests have $\frac{1}{10}$ pint punch each. How many gallons is this?

3 a) Five gallons of milk are poured into pint bottles.
How many bottles are filled?
b) Pints of milk are sold for 44p each. At the end of the day only 6 pints remain unsold.
How much money is taken?

4 A bottle of concentrated disinfectant holds $1\frac{1}{5}$ pints. The disinfectant is diluted by mixing
4 fluid ounces with 1 gallon of water. How many gallons of water is mixed with the
concentrated disinfectant?

5 A day centre orders milk. There are 5 groups in the centre with 16 people in each group.
Each person drinks 1 pint of milk per day.

a) How many pints of milk are needed
i) each day   ii) each week   iii) each year?   (Assume 365 days in 1 year)
b) Convert each of your answers to part a) into gallons.

Convert between metric and imperial measures

a Approximate metric/imperial conversions

There's a rhyme about the approximate conversion between litres and pints.

'A litre of water's a pint and three quarters.'

This means ▶ **1 litre ≈ $1\frac{3}{4}$ pints**

Other useful approximations are:

▶ **1 fl oz ≈ 30 mℓ**   **1 pint ≈ $\frac{2}{3}$ litre**   **1 gallon ≈ $4\frac{1}{2}$ litres**

Practice

1 Which is larger   **a)**   a pint or a litre   **b)** $\frac{1}{2}$ litre or 1 pint?

2 Copy and complete these.

a) 2 litres ≈ ____ pt   **b)** 3 pt ≈ ____ litres   **c)** 120 mℓ ≈ ____ fl oz
d)   45 ℓ ≈ ____ gal   **e)** 4 gal ≈ ____ litres   **f)** 8 fl oz ≈ ____ mℓ

3 $\frac{1}{2}$ pint is poured out of a litre bottle. How much is left?

4 **a)** Which petrol can holds more: 2 gallon   or   10 litre?
b) Which yoghurt pot holds more: 6 fl oz   or   120 mℓ?

b More accurate conversions

▶ **1 fl oz = 28.4 mℓ**   **1 pt = 568 mℓ**   **1 gallon = 4.55 litres**   **1 litre = 0.22 gallons**

To convert units, multiply and/or divide by the conversion factor(s).

Example   Convert 5 fl oz to mℓ Convert 330 mℓ to fl oz.

5 fl oz = 5 × 28.4 = **142 mℓ**   330 mℓ = 330 ÷ 28.4 = **11.6 fl oz** (to 1 dp)

Check: 142 ÷ 28.4 = 5   **Check: 11.6 × 28.4 = 329.44**
                    (near 330, the difference due to rounding)

Example   A water tank holds 500 litres of water. Use the conversion
10 litres = 2.2 gallons to find its capacity in gallons.

Capacity = 500 ÷ 10 × 2.2 = 50 × 2.2 = **110 litres**

Practice

Use a calculator when the calculations are very difficult.

1 Use the conversion 1 pint = 0.57 litres to find the missing values.

    a) 2 pt = ____ litres   **b)** 2.85 litres = ____ pt
    c) 8 pt = ____ litres   **d)**   4 litres = ____ pt

2 Use the conversion 1 gallon = 4.55 litres to find the missing values.

    a) 5 gal = ____ litres   **b)** 500 litres = ____ gal
    c) 9 gal = ____ litres   **d)**   36 litres = ____ gal

3 Use 2.2 gallons = 10 litres for each part.

    a) A water container holds 20 litres. How many gallons is this?
    b) How many litres does a 12 gallon petrol tank hold?

4 A medicine bottle holds 3 fl oz. How many mℓ is this? (1 fl oz = 28.4 mℓ)

5 a) A pond holds 80 gallons water. How many litres is this? (1 gallon = 4.55 litres)
    b) The pond loses 2.5 litres each day from a leak at the bottom of the
        pond, how many gallons of water are lost each week?
    c) How long will it take for the pond to be empty? Give your answer to the nearest week.

Use conversion scales and tables
MSS1/L2.6

There are other ways to convert between metric and imperial
units of length, weight and capacity.
Side by side scales like this are often given on maps. They can
be used to convert distances between miles and kilometres.

about 2.5 miles

4 km to 1 cm

Example   This scale shows 4 km ≈ 2.5 miles

Practice

1 a) Use the scale above to complete these.
      i)   10 miles ≈ _____ km   **ii)**   8 km ≈ _____ miles
      iii)   8 miles ≈ _____ km   **iv)** 12 km ≈ _____ miles

    A map of the Shetland Islands uses the scale shown above. (i.e. 4 km to 1 cm)

    b) On the map the islands are 17 cm north to south.
        Write the actual distance in   **i)** km   **ii)** miles.
    c) On the map the islands are 14.8 cm east to west.
        Write the actual distance in   **i)** km   **ii)** miles.

2 Copy the following table. Use the ruler to complete the table using the nearest markers.

Length in inches	1	2		$3\frac{1}{2}$			$4\frac{3}{4}$	$5\frac{1}{4}$		
Length in cm	2.5		8		10	11.5			13.7	14.3

3 Write the value marked by each **orange** line or arrow in both metric and imperial units.

4 You can also use this table to convert lengths.
For example, 3 miles = 4.828 km and 3 km = 1.864 miles.

a) A taxi journey is 5 km.
How many miles is this?

b) A student cycles 6 miles to college and 6 miles back each day. How many km is this in a 5 day week?

c) A postman walks 8 miles each day.
How many km is this in a 6 day week?

d) A delivery person makes three calls.
She travels 6 km to the first call, 3 km to the second and 9 km to the third.
How many miles is this altogether?

km	miles/km	miles
1.609	1	0.621
3.219	2	1.243
4.828	3	1.864
6.437	4	2.485
8.047	5	3.107
9.656	6	3.728
11.265	7	4.350
12.875	8	4.971
14.484	9	5.592
16.093	10	6.214

Measures, Shape and Space

6 Temperature

Measure temperature

MSS1/E3.9, MSS1/L1.4, MSS1/L2.4

Temperature is measured using a thermometer.
There are many different types.
Temperature is usually measured in degrees Celsius (°C).

This is a **medical thermometer**.
It is placed under a patient's arm or tongue.
The level of the liquid in the tube shows the patient's
temperature.

The large divisions on the thermometer go up in full
degrees Celsius.

The enlarged section shows each degree is divided into 10 small divisions.
After 35°C, the markers show 35.1°, 35.2°, 35.3°, ..., up to 35.9° (just before 36°C).

Practice

1 a) What is the highest temperature the medical
        thermometer above can measure?
    b) What is the lowest temperature it can measure?
    c) Write down the temperatures shown by each arrow.

2 **Room thermometers** often look like this:

    a) What is the highest temperature that it can show?
    b) What is the lowest temperature it can show?
    c) Write down the temperatures shown by each arrow.

3 a) What is the highest temperature that this
        thermometer measures?
    b) What is the lowest temperature that it measures?
    c) What does each small division on the scale show?
    d) Write down the temperature shown by each arrow.

4 For each part find the number of degrees the temperature rises.

   a) 15°C → 24°C   **b)** 25°C → 32°C   **c)** 3°C → 11°C
   d) 5°C → 21°C   **e)** 9°C → 33°C   **f)** 12°C → 39°C

5 For each part find the number of degrees the temperature falls.

   a) 21°C → 12°C   **b)** 27°C → 9°C   **c)** 34°C → 27°C

6 For each part choose a likely temperature from the list below.

   a) sauna   **b)** cool workroom   **c)** the surface of the sun
   d) hotel room   **e)** ice cube   **f)** sunny summer day

   0°C,   11°C,   20°C,   28°C,   54°C,   6 000°C

Temperatures below freezing point   MSS1/L1.4

The Celsius scale has **negative** numbers **below the freezing point of water**.

   0 = freezing point   −1 = getting colder   −2 = colder still   −3 = even colder

Practice

1 a) What is the highest temperature this thermometer measures?
   b) What is the lowest temperature it measures?
   c) Write down the temperature shown by each arrow.
   d) From your answers to part **c)** write down
     i) the warmest temperature
     ii) the coldest temperature.

2 The cool fridge in the supermarket should be at −4°C.
Which phrase describes the cool fridge with the
temperature shown?

   a) too cold
   b) the right temperature
   c) too warm

3 For each part put the temperatures in order, starting with
the **warmest**.

   a) −21°C   21°C   2°C   −12°C   −2°C   12°C
   b) −4°C   23°C   0°C   −2°C   14°C   4°C
   c) 7°C   1°C   −2°C   5°C   −7°C   3°C

4 For each part find the number of degrees the temperature rises.

a) –5°C to 4°C   b) –2°C to 12°C   c) –3°C to 11°C   d) –6°C to 10°C

e) –9°C to 13°C   f) –12°C to 29°C   g) –7°C to –2°C   h) –20°C to –3°C

5 For each part find the number of degrees the temperature falls.

a) 21°C to –2°C   b) 17°C to –9°C   c) 14°C to –7°C   d) 15°C to –3°C

e) 22°C to –4°C   f) 18°C to –1°C   g) –1°C to –10°C   h) –4°C to –18°C

6 This chart shows the temperature over a period of 10 days.

a) What was the   **i)** highest temperature   **ii)** lowest temperature?

b) On which days was the temperature below freezing point?

c) What was the range of the temperatures over the 10 days?

For range see page 294.

7 The table below shows the central heating settings in a house.
The differences between the inside temperatures and those outside the house are missing.
Fill in these missing values. The sitting room has been done for you.

Central heating settings		Difference between the inside and outside temperature when the outside temperature is:		
Room	Temperature	11°C	6°C	–3°C
Sitting room	21°C	10°C	15°C	24°C
Dining room	20°C			
Kitchen	16°C			
Bedroom 1	19°C			
Bedroom 2	16°C			
Bedroom 3	13°C			

For more work on temperature, see pages 7-8 and 17-18.

Activity

1 a) Use a medical thermometer to take your temperature.
   b) Take the temperature of some other people. Make sure you wash the
       thermometer after each person has used it. Record your results in a table.

2 Make a copy of a thermometer.
   Mark and label the scale to show the following descriptions that weather forecasters
   use: Very hot 30°C, Warm 20°C, Mild 15°C, Cold 5°C.

3 Estimate the temperature for different places, e.g. room, corridor, outside, window
   sill or the top of a heater.
   Place a room thermometer in each place for 2 minutes.
   Record your estimates and the temperatures in a table.

4 **Digital thermometers** like this one are often used in hospital to take a patient's
   temperature. The units used on this thermometer are **degrees Fahrenheit (°F)**.

   Generally only the numbers are shown, not the °C or °F sign.
   Use a digital thermometer to find temperatures, e.g. a warm drink, cup of tea, your
   temperature, the room, a sock or outside. Record your results in a table.

Celsius and Fahrenheit

MSS1/E3.9, MSS1/L1.4, MSS1/L2.4

Ovens measure temperatures in Celsius, Fahrenheit or Gas marks.
This chart gives equivalent temperatures and a description for cooking.

°C	°F	Gas mark	Description
110	225	$\frac{1}{4}$	Cool
120/130	250	$\frac{1}{2}$	
140	275	1	Very low
150	300	2	
160/170	325	3	Low/moderate
180	350	4	Moderate/warm
190	375	5	Moderately hot
200	400	6	Hot
210/220	425	7	
230	450	8	
240	475	9	Very hot

Practice

1 **a)** Which °C settings should you use for
   i) a hot oven   **ii)** a warm oven   **iii)** a cool oven?
   b) Repeat part **a)** for °F.

2 **a)** A roasting temperature for meat is 180°C. What is this in °F?
   b) The roasting temperature for poultry is 50°F higher than for other meats.
         What is the temperature in °F for roasting poultry?
   c) Draw dials like those shown below.

On each dial show the temperature for cooking   **i)** meat   **ii)** poultry.

Use scales to convert temperatures

MSS1/L2.4

Many thermometers like the one on the right show
temperatures in both Celsius and Fahrenheit. You can use
the scales to compare and convert temperatures.

Office temperatures should be at least 16°C.
The scales show that this is also 61°F.

The table gives these and other useful temperatures:

Minimum office temperature

Description	Celsius	Fahrenheit
Office temperatures should not fall below	16°C	61°F
Chilled food in shops should be below	8°C	46°F
Frozen food in shops should be kept below	−18°C	0°F
Most house plants like a temperature over	18°C	64°F
Body temperature	37°C	98.6°F

Use the scales to check the other temperatures in the table.

Practice

1 The freezing point for water is 0°C. What is this in °F?

2 Use the scales to convert these temperatures to Fahrenheit.
Give your answers to the nearest degree.

a) 30°C **b)** 45°C **c)** 23°C **d)** –10°C **e)** –15°C **f)** –6°C

3 Use the scales to convert these temperatures to Celsius.
Give your answers to the nearest degree.

a) 80°F **b)** 50°F **c)** 42°F **d)** 18°F **e)** 105°F **f)** –4°C

Use formulae to convert temperatures

N1/L2.4

This rhyme might help you remember how to convert between Celsius and Fahrenheit.

If C to F confuses you $\dfrac{9C}{5}$ **+ 32 is all you have to do.**

▶ $F = \dfrac{9C}{5} + 32$

For work on formulae see pages 58-61.

Example **Convert:** 40°C to °F

$$F = \frac{9C}{5} + 32 = \frac{9 \times 40}{5} + 32 = \frac{360}{5} + 32 = 72 + 32 = \textbf{104°F}$$

Practice

1 Below are some of the temperatures taken in capital cities around the world.
Convert each temperature to °F.

a) Alexandria 20°C **b)** Barbados 30°C **c)** Toronto 5°C
d) Belgrade 15°C **e)** Berlin 10°C **f)** Algiers 25°C
g) London 12°C **h)** New York 14°C

To convert from °F to °C use ▶ $C = \dfrac{5(F - 32)}{9}$

Example **Convert:** 86°F to °C

$$C = \frac{5(86 - 32)}{9} = \frac{5 \times 54}{9} = \frac{270}{9} = \textbf{30°C}$$

2 Here are some more temperatures from capital cities. Convert these temperatures into Celsius. (Round to the nearest degree.)

a) Amsterdam 52°F **b)** Athens 66°F **c)** Bahrain 93°F
d) Belfast 48°F **e)** Hong Kong 81°F **f)** Moscow 55°F
g) Paris 59°F

Measures, Shape and Space

7 Perimeter, Area and Volume

Perimeter

MSS1/L1.8, MSS1/L2.7

The **perimeter** of a shape is the distance all the way round it.

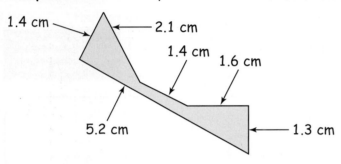

1.4 cm   2.1 cm
1.4 cm   1.6 cm
5.2 cm   1.3 cm

Perimeter =
1.4 + 2.1 + 1.4 + 1.6 + 1.3 + 5.2 = **13 cm**

Practice

1 For each shape use a ruler to measure each side, then calculate the perimeter.

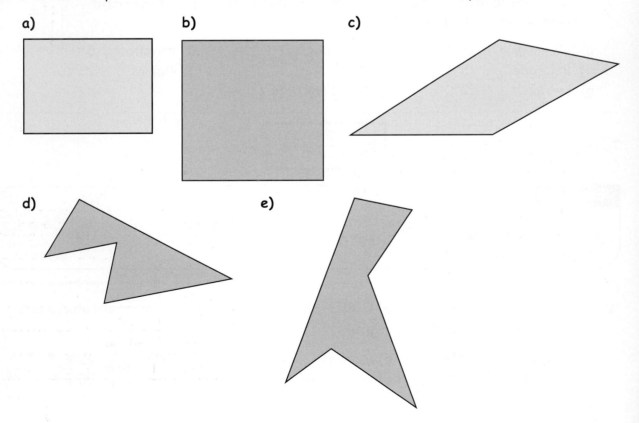

a)

b)

c)

d)

e)

2 A builder needs coving to go round these ceilings.
Work out the total length he needs for each ceiling.

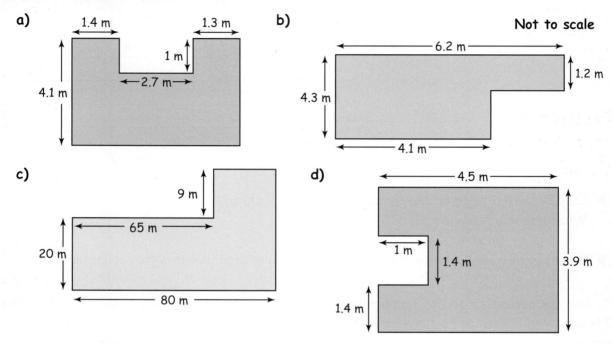

a) 1.4 m, 1.3 m, 1 m, 2.7 m, 4.1 m

b) Not to scale, 6.2 m, 1.2 m, 4.3 m, 4.1 m

c) 9 m, 65 m, 20 m, 80 m

d) 4.5 m, 1 m, 1.4 m, 3.9 m, 1.4 m

3 Find the length of sealant needed to go round the base of the shower shown in the diagram.

1.4 m, 1.1 m

4 The sketch shows a loft hatch.

1.1 m, 80 cm

Find the length of draft excluder needed to go round it.
(Note: You will need to use the same units for each side.)

5 The table gives the lengths and widths of some rectangles.
Copy and complete the table.

Length	Width	Perimeter
6 cm	2 cm	
10 mm	6 mm	
20 cm	6.2 cm	
4.5 m	3 m	
20 mm	15 mm	
2.7 m	2.25 m	

6 Copy the table. Complete it by giving the length and width of two possible rectangles for each perimeter.

Perimeter	Rectangle 1		Rectangle 2	
	length	width	length	width
a) 14 cm				
b) 20 cm				
c) 18 cm				
d) 28 cm				
e) 32 cm				

7 A rectangular field is 400 m long and 250 m wide. What is its perimeter?

8 Lace is needed to go round the perimeter of a 80 cm square table cloth. What length of lace is needed?

9 A rectangular rabbit run is 2 m 40 cm long and $1\frac{1}{2}$ m wide. What is its perimeter?

To find the perimeter of the rectangular shapes in questions 3 and 4 you have added together 2 lengths and 2 widths. This can be written as a formula:

▶ **Perimeter of rectangle = 2 × (length + width)**

Note that length and width are sometimes called **dimensions**.

In letters the perimeter formula is

▶ $P = 2(l + w)$

See Formulae
pages 58–61.

Use this formula to check your answers to the previous questions.

Area
MSS1/L1.9, MSS1/L2.7

a Measuring in square units

Area is the amount of surface covered by a 2-D shape (flat shape).
We measure area in **square units** e.g. **square centimetres** (cm^2) or **square metres** (m^2).

▶ This is 1 cm^2
1 cm wide
1 cm long

The area of this shape is 4 cm^2.

Practice

1 Write down the area of these shapes.

a)   **b)**   **c)**

2 On cm squared paper, draw 4 different shapes, each with an area of 12 cm².

b Area of a rectangle

> **Example**   Find the area of a rectangular room that is 6m long and 3m wide.
>
> You can sketch a rectangle and count the squares.
> The area of the room is 18 m².
>
> You can also find the area without drawing the squares.
> The area of the room is $6 \times 3 = 18$ m².

Practice

1 Find the area of these rectangles.

▶ **Use the same units for both sides.**

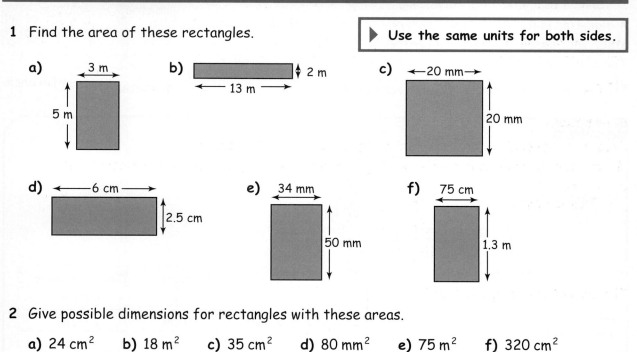

a)   3 m, 5 m

b)   13 m, 2 m

c)   20 mm, 20 mm

d)   6 cm, 2.5 cm

e)   34 mm, 50 mm

f)   75 cm, 1.3 m

2 Give possible dimensions for rectangles with these areas.

   a) 24 cm²   **b)** 18 m²   **c)** 35 cm²   **d)** 80 mm²   **e)** 75 m²   **f)** 320 cm²

L2 The formula for the area of a rectangle is

In letters this is

> **Area = length × width**
> **A = l × w or A = lw**

3 A rectangular lawn is 9 metres long and 6 metres wide.

a) What is the area of the lawn?

b) A gardener spreads fertiliser on the lawn. He uses 20 grams per square metre. How much fertiliser does he use?

4 A rectangular bathroom is being decorated. It is 2.2 m long and 2 m wide.

a) A piece of lino 2 m wide and 2.2 m long is bought for the floor at a price of £9.99 per square metre. What is the cost of the lino?

b) The wall is re-tiled along the length and width of the bath.
The length of the bath is 1.7 m.
The width of the bath is 0.7 m.
The height of the wall above the bath is 1.8 m.
What is the area that is re-tiled?

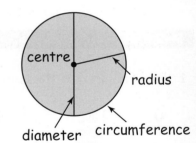

Circles

a Circumference

A **radius** is a straight line from the centre of a circle to the edge.

A **diameter** is a straight line from one side of the circle to the other that passes through its centre.
The diameter is twice the length of the radius.

The perimeter of a circle is called its **circumference**.

Activity

You can find the circumference of a coin by rolling it along a ruler.

6.28 cm

Do this with the coins listed in the table.
Check all the measurements given.

Coin	Diameter	Circumference
1p	2 cm	6.3 cm
2p	2.5 cm	7.9 cm
5p	1.7 cm	5.3 cm

Divide the circumference of each coin by its diameter.
What do you find?

You should find that circumference ÷ diameter is always a bit more than 3.
A more accurate result is 3.14 (to 2 decimal places) or 3.142 (to 3 decimal places).
The exact answer is a never-ending decimal called **pi** and usually written as π.
Your calculator might have a key for π. If so, press it – you should get the number 3.14159265 ...

The relationship between the diameter and the circumference gives these formulae:

> **Circumference** = $\pi \times$ **diameter**
> $C = \pi d$

or

> **Circumference** = $2 \times \pi \times$ **radius**
> $C = 2\pi r$

Example Find the circumference of a circular pond whose radius is 3 m.

$C = 2\pi r = 2 \times \pi \times 3 = 18.84955 ... = 18.8$ m (using the π key on a calculator)
or $2 \times 3.14 \times 3 = 3.14 \times 6 = 18.84 = 18.8$ m (without a calculator)
(rounded to 1 decimal place)

Practice

Give your answers to questions 1 to 3 to 1 decimal place.

1 **a)** Measure the diameter of these coins.   **i)** 10p   **ii)** £1   (in centimetres)
  b) Multiply the diameter by π to find the circumference of each coin.
  c) Check your answers to **b)** by measuring.

2 Find the circumference of each circle. Use 3.14 for π.

  a) diameter 10 cm   **b)** radius 7 cm   **c)** diameter 1.5 m
  d) radius 0.8 m   **e)** diameter 45 m   **f)** diameter 30 m.

  Check using your calculator key for π.

3 Copy and complete the table.

  Use 3.14 or your calculator key for π.

Radius	Diameter	Circumference
2 cm		
	30 mm	
	6 m	
1.2 m		
		15.7 cm
		75.4 mm

4 A wheel has a radius of 24 cm. How far does the wheel travel in one full turn (to the nearest cm)?

5 A circular window needs insulating. The diameter of the window is 80 cm.
  What length of insulation tape is needed to go around the window (to the nearest cm)?

b Area of a circle

The formula for the area of a circle in letters is:

> ▶ **A = πr^2**   **r^2 means r × r**

In words this means: **Area of a circle = π × radius × radius**

Example   Find the area of a circular pond whose radius is 3 m.

$A = \pi \times 3^2 = \pi \times 3 \times 3 = 28.2743 \ldots = $ **28.3 m²** (using the π key on a calculator)
or $3.14 \times 9 = 28.26 = $ **28.3 m²** (without a calculator)
(rounded to 1 decimal place)

Practice

In each question use 3.14 or your calculator key for π.
Round answers for questions 1 to 3 to 1 decimal place.

1 Find the area of each circle.

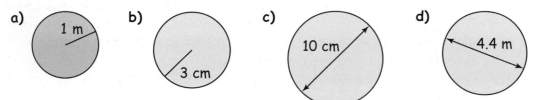

a) 1 m   b) 3 cm   c) 10 cm   d) 4.4 m

2 Find the area of a circle whose radius is

a) 7 cm   b) 2 m   c) 8 mm   d) 12 mm   e) 15 cm   f) 1.4 m.

3 Find the area of a circle whose diameter is

a) 8 cm   b) 20 mm   c) 11 cm   d) 2.5 m   e) 14 mm   f) 80 cm.

4 A circular flower bed has a diameter 0.75 m. Find the area in cm² to the nearest 10 cm².

5 a) What is the diameter of the mirror including the frame?
  b) Find the area of the mirror including the frame.
  c) Find the area of the glass.
  d) What is the area of the frame to the nearest cm²?

8 cm

15 cm

Areas of composite shapes

MSS1/L2.8

Sometimes the area of a shape can be found by splitting it into parts.

Example

Area of A = 1×3 = 3 m²
Area of B = 2×3 = 6 m²
Area of C = 6×5 = 30 m²
Total Area = **39 m²**

Sometimes you can make a rectangle around the shape and subtract part of it.
Here is the same shape again.

Area of large rectangle = $9 \times 5 = 45$ m²
Area of small rectangle = $3 \times 2 = 6$ m²
Area of shape = 45 –
6
Area of shape = **39 m²**

Practice

1   Find the area of each room.

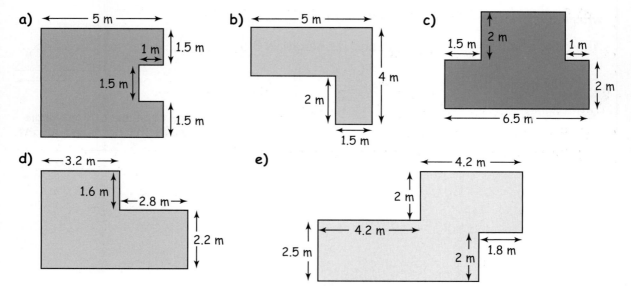

a) 5 m, 1 m, 1.5 m, 1.5 m, 1.5 m

b) 5 m, 4 m, 2 m, 1.5 m

c) 1.5 m, 2 m, 1 m, 2 m, 6.5 m

d) 3.2 m, 1.6 m, 2.8 m, 2.2 m

e) 4.2 m, 2 m, 4.2 m, 2.5 m, 2 m, 1.8 m

2 The sketch shows the layout of a garden.

a) Find the area of
   i) the patio
   ii) the flowerbed
   iii) the pond (to 2 dp)
   iv) the lawn.

b) Fertiliser is spread onto the flowerbed at a rate of 20 g per square metre. How much fertiliser is used to the nearest 10 grams?

c) Weedkiller is spread onto the lawn at a rate of 50 g per square metre.
   How much weedkiller is used to the nearest 10 grams?

3 A room is 3.6 m long and 3 m wide. The walls are 2.2 m high. The door is 0.8 m by 2 m and the window is 1.5 m by 1.2 m.

a) What is the area of the ceiling?
b) Find the total area of walls by adding together the area of the walls and then subtracting the area of the door and window.
c) The walls and ceiling need painting. Each litre of paint covers 12 m². Is a 2.5 litre tin of paint enough to paint this room?

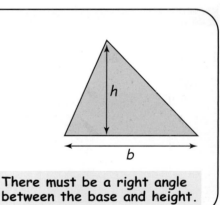

Use formulae to find areas

MSS1/L2.8

Example

The formula for the area of a triangle is $A = \dfrac{bh}{2}$

where b is the base of the triangle and h is its height.

The base of this triangle is 5 cm and its height is 3.6 cm.

The area of the triangle is $\qquad A = \dfrac{5 \times 3.6}{2} = \dfrac{18}{2} = \textbf{9 cm}^2$

There must be a right angle between the base and height.

Practice

1 Use the formula given above to find the area of these triangles.

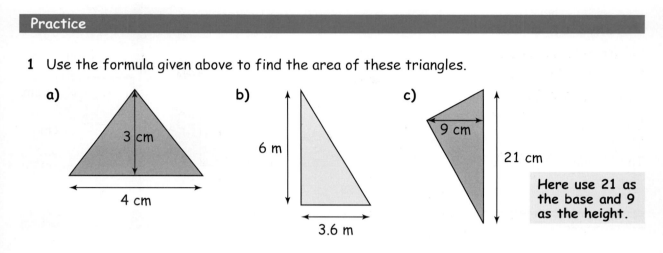

a)

3 cm

4 cm

b)

6 m

3.6 m

c)

9 cm

21 cm

Here use 21 as the base and 9 as the height.

2 A triangular sign has a base 1.5 m long and its height is 1.4 m.
What is the area of the sign?

3 The formula for the area of a kite is $A = 0.5wl$
where w is the width and l is the length.
A kite is 80 cm wide and 1.2 m long.
What is its area? (Remember to use the same units for each length.)

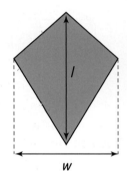

l

w

4 This shape is called a trapezium.

The formula for its area is $A = \dfrac{h(a+b)}{2}$.

Find the area when $h = 12$, $a = 11$ and $b = 19$ (all in cm).

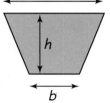

a

h

b

5 The formula for the area of this shape is $A = \dfrac{\pi ab}{4}$.

A pond of this shape is 2.2 m long and 1.3 m wide.
Use your calculator to find the area of the pond.
(Use 3.14 or the special key on your calculator for π.)
Give your answer to 1 decimal place.

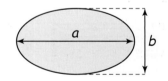

a

b

6 A formula that estimates the area of this window is

$$A = hd + \dfrac{3d^2}{8}$$

Find the area when h is 1.6 (metres) and d is 2 (metres).

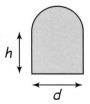

h

d

Volume of a cuboid

MSS1/L1.10, MSS1/L2.9

Volume is the space taken up by a 3-D shape (a solid) or liquid.
We measure volume in **cubic units**. This is 1 cubic centimetre.

To find the volume of a shape, you need to
find the number of unit cubes that fill it.
The shape of a box is called a **cuboid**.
The volume of this cuboid is 3 cm^3.

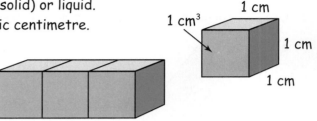

Practice

1 Write down the volume of each cuboid. Assume each of the cubes is 1 cm^3.

a)   b)   c)   d)

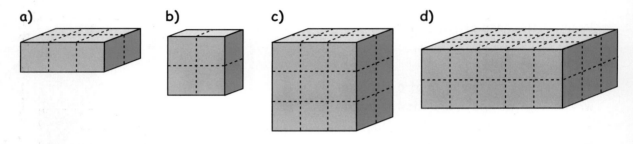

You can find the volume of a cuboid without drawing and counting the cubes.

Look at the cuboid in 1d again. It is 5 cm long, 3 cm wide and 2 cm high.
Its volume is $5 \times 3 \times 2 = 30$ cm^3.

Volume of a cuboid = length × width × height

2 Find the volume of each cuboid.

▶ **Use the same units for all the sides.**

a)   b)   c)

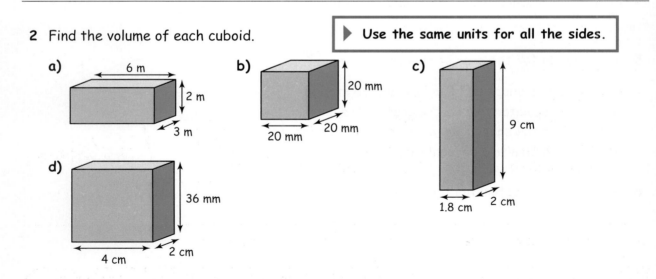

3 Copy and complete this table:

Length	Width	Height	Volume
2 cm	4 cm	5 cm	
3 m	3.4 m	3.5 m	
4 mm	2.5 mm	6 mm	
9 cm	6.2 cm	8 cm	

4 A box has a 1 m square base and it is $\frac{1}{2}$ m high. What is the volume of the box?

5 What is the volume of a box that is 50 cm long, 10 cm wide and 8 cm high?

6 A carton of fruit juice has a volume of 1 litre (i.e. 1000 cm^3).
Find possible dimensions for the length, width and height of the carton.

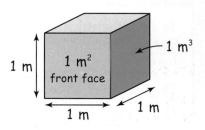

7 A sand pit is 100 cm long, 75 cm wide and 15 cm high.
What is the volume of sand it holds when full?

8 Each side of a dice is 25 mm long. What is its volume?

9 The diagram shows a cube with edges of length 1 metre.
  a) What is the length of each edge in cm?
  b) What is the area of each face in cm^2?
  c) What is the volume of the cube in cm^3?

L2

The formula for the volume of a cuboid is

The formula for the volume of a cube is

▶ $V = l \times w \times h = lwh$

▶ $V = l \times l \times l = l^3$

---

10 The diagram shows a podium made from three
cuboids. Each cuboid is 40 cm wide.

  a) Find the volume of each cuboid in m^3.
  b) What is the total volume of the podium?

To find one dimension divide the volume by the product of the others.

Example	If a cuboid has length 5 cm, width 4 cm and volume 120 cm^3 its height is
	$120 \div (5 \times 4) = 120 \div 20 = \mathbf{6\ cm}$

11 Copy and complete this table:

Length	Width	Height	Volume
4 m	2 m		24 m³
3 cm		8 cm	48 cm³
	3 m	9 m	54 m³
4 cm	4 cm		64 cm³

Volume of a cylinder
MSS1/L2.9

The formula for the **volume of a cylinder** is $V = \pi r^2 h$.
This means $V = \pi \times r \times r \times h$

When finding volumes remember:

- the same units must be used for each measurement
- the volume units are cubed, e.g. 4 **cm³** or 35.6 **m³**
- you can convert volume to litres using **1 litre = 1000 cm³**.

Example   This pipe is 0.8 m long and has a diameter of 40 mm.

To find the volume we need r and h in the same units.
Here it is sensible to use cm: $r = 20$ mm = 2 cm and
$h = 0.8$ m = 80 cm

The volume is $V = \pi \times r \times r \times h = \pi \times 2 \times 2 \times 80 = 1005$ cm³ (using a calculator).
If the pipe is filled with water it will hold just over 1 litre.

Practice

In each question use the π key on your calculator or $\pi = 3.14$.
Give answers to Questions 1 and 2 to 1 dp.

> ▶ **Use the same units for r and h.**

1 Find the volume of the following cylinders.

2 Calculate the volume of a cylinder with

    a) radius 1.2 m and height 2 m   **b)** radius 6 cm and height 9 cm
    c) radius 3 m and height 2.2 m   **d)** radius 3 m and height 1.6 m
    e) diameter 12 cm and height 2.5 cm   **f)** diameter 1 m and height 0.5 m.

3 Find the volume of each cylinder. (Give your answers **b** and **c** in cm³ and the rest in m³ to
    2 decimal places.)

    a) diameter 4 m and height 30 cm   **b)** diameter 2.5 cm and height 16 mm
    c) radius 1.2 cm and height 6 mm   **d)** radius 70 cm and height 0.6 m
    e) radius 0.3 m and height 40 cm   **f)** diameter 1.2 m and height 50 cm

4 A paddling pool has a radius of 60 cm and a depth of 30 cm.
    How much water does it hold when full? Give your answer in m³.

Use formulae to find volumes

The volume formulae for a cuboid and
cylinder are similar – in both formulae:

volume = area of base × height

Shapes like these are called **prisms**.
Some of the shapes in the following
questions are also prisms.

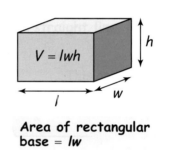

$V = lwh$

Area of rectangular base = lw

$V = \pi r^2 h$

Area of circular base = πr²

Practice

1 The sketch shows a triangular prism.

    The formula $V = \dfrac{bhl}{2}$ gives its volume.

    Find the volume when $b = 10$, $h = 8$ and $l = 30$ (all measured in cm).

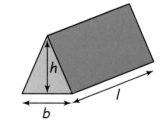

2 The diagram shows the shape of a plant box.

    The formula $V = \dfrac{hl(a + b)}{2}$ gives its volume.

    a) Find V if $h = 25$ cm, $l = 120$ cm, $a = 20$ cm and $b = 30$ cm.
    b) A gardener buys compost in 40 litre bags.
        How many bags does he need to fill the plant box?

▶ **1 litre = 1000 cm³**

Activities

1 Cut out 10 crosses like that labelled **a** (below) from squared paper.
Fit them together to form a tessellation. Repeat this with shapes b, c and d.

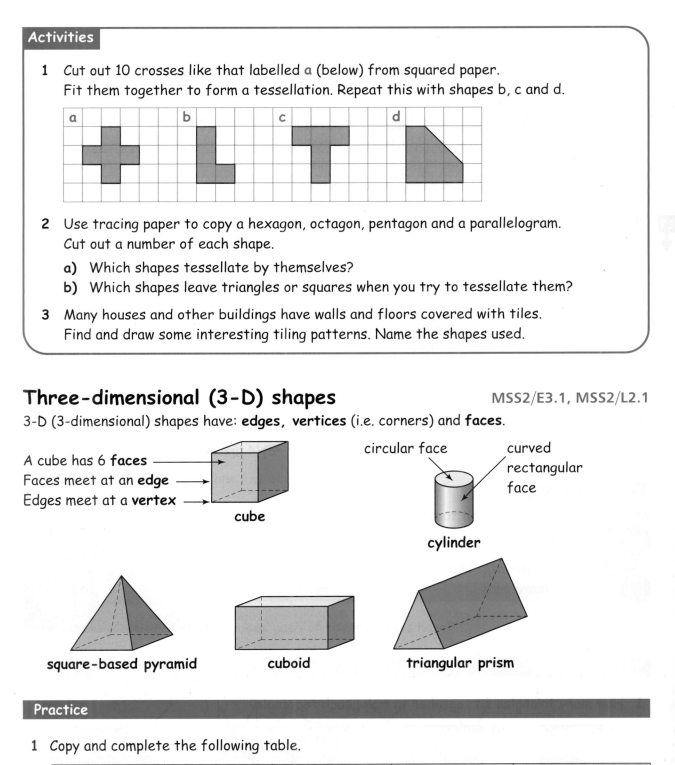

2 Use tracing paper to copy a hexagon, octagon, pentagon and a parallelogram.
Cut out a number of each shape.

a) Which shapes tessellate by themselves?
b) Which shapes leave triangles or squares when you try to tessellate them?

3 Many houses and other buildings have walls and floors covered with tiles.
Find and draw some interesting tiling patterns. Name the shapes used.

Three-dimensional (3-D) shapes

MSS2/E3.1, MSS2/L2.1

3-D (3-dimensional) shapes have: **edges**, **vertices** (i.e. corners) and **faces**.

A cube has 6 **faces**
Faces meet at an **edge**
Edges meet at a **vertex**

cube

circular face   curved
rectangular
face

cylinder

square-based pyramid   cuboid   triangular prism

Practice

1 Copy and complete the following table.

	Shape of faces	Number of faces	Number of edges	Number of vertices
Cube				
Cuboid				
Cylinder				
Square-based pyramid				
Triangular prism				

Activity

Collect together a number of each 3-D shape.

a) Which shapes stack together easily on a shelf?
b) Which shapes are difficult to stack? Why?

Nets
MSS2/L2.1

Folding the 2-D patterns gives the 3-D shapes. The patterns are called **nets**.

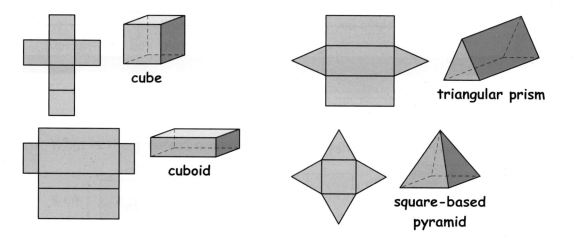

cube

triangular prism

cuboid

square-based
pyramid

Activities

Use graph paper.

1 Draw four different nets for a cube.

2 Draw three different nets for a triangular prism.

3 Draw three different nets for a cuboid.

4 Make a net for
   a) a pyramid with a 5 cm square base and triangular faces of height 7 cm
   b) a prism of length 12 cm, with triangular ends of width 6 cm and height 5 cm.

5 Make a net for a cube with a pyramid on top.

Solve problems involving 2-D and 3-D shapes
MSS2/L2.1, MSS2/L2.2

When some dimensions of an item are given on a diagram, you can often work
out others by adding, subtracting, multiplying or dividing the given lengths.

Handling Data

1 Extracting and Interpreting Information

Information from lists, tables, diagrams, pictograms and bar charts
HD1/E3.1, HD1/E3.2, HD1/L1.1, HD1/L2.1

a Find information from lists

Lists are often used to give information. Examples can be found in books, catalogues, newspapers, magazines, maps and web sites.

Lists can be arranged

- in alphabetical order – as in a phone book
- numerically – a list of instructions are often numbered
- using dates – as in bank statements
- in categories, i.e. grouped by type – as in sales catalogues
- randomly – some shopping lists are written this way.

Practice

1 Look at this list.

   a) How is the list ordered?
   b) Why do you think it is ordered like this?
   c) Write down the school's phone number.
   d) Write down the dentist's phone number.
   e) Whose phone number is 778887?

Name	Phone number
After school club	453521
Child minder	797654
Dentist	787652
Doctor	778887
Fire station	773774
Police station	776431
Railway station	768998
School	791455
Work	798976

2 Here is a list of important events.

a) How is this list ordered?
b) What is happening on April 17th?
c) On what date is the wedding anniversary?
d) When is the school play?
e) The parent's evening is on April 19th.
   Where would this go in the list?

School play	17/03
Party	11/04
Joe's birthday	13/04
Dental appointment	15/04
Dinner date	17/04
Wedding anniversary	20/04

3 Here is a shopping list.

a) How is this list arranged?
b) How many cans of beans are on the list?
c) How many loaves of bread are on the list?
d) What kind of milk do they want?

$\frac{1}{2}$ dozen eggs
Shampoo
Washing powder
Beans × 4
Family pack crisps
Ham
Semi-skimmed milk

4 **a)** How are words in a dictionary arranged?
b) How are events ordered in a diary?
c) How are items ordered on a credit card or bank statement?
d) How are items ordered in an index?
e) How are items ordered in the Yellow Pages?

Lists on the Internet

A **search engine** looks for information on the Internet. When you type in a subject the search engine gives you a list of websites in order of relevance. **Relevant** means closely linked to your search word or words. The list you get depends on the words you use.

Suppose you wanted to find a cinema in Reading.
Typing 'cinema Reading' into a search engine gave these websites:

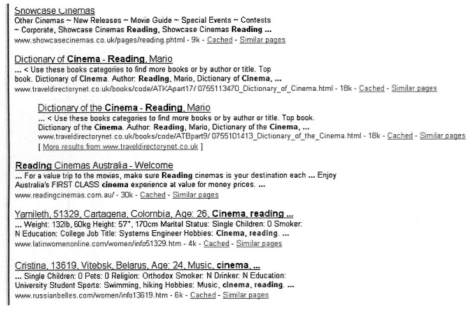

Which of these websites do you think are relevant?

Which are not relevant? Why?

Typing in 'cinema Reading Berkshire' gives more relevant results – try this if you can.

Activities

(If necessary ask your tutor or teacher for help.)

1   Use a dictionary to find the following words.
     evaluate   proportion   integer   frequency

2   Use the Yellow Pages to find the address and phone number of a plumber, a gardener, a taxi and a vet.

3   Use a search engine to find a list of websites that have information on a subject you find interesting. Type in just one word and look at the list of the first ten websites the search engine finds.
     Do you think the first website is the most relevant on the list?
     Do you think the tenth website is the least relevant on the list?

     Carry out another search using more than one word.
     Do you get more relevant results?
     Investigate further, using different combinations of words.
     Find out how to use quotation marks ("...").

b Find information from tables

This table shows the number of men and women in some college evening classes:

This table has a *title* at the top to tell us what the table is about.

title

heading

row

column

Number of students in evening classes

Evening class	No. of women	No. of men
Local History	10	7
Cookery	11	5
Italian	8	9
Do-It-Yourself	4	15

Each column has a **heading**. The first column's heading tell us that this column gives the evening classes. The other column headings show that these columns give the number of women and men in each class. Without the title and headings we would not understand what the table is about.

Practice

1 Use the table above to answer these questions.

   a) How many women are there in the Cookery class?
   b) How many men are there in the Local History class?
   c) How many more men than women are there in the Do-It-Yourself class?
   d) Altogether how many students are in the Italian class?
   e) Which class has the most students?

2 Use the Film Prices table to answer these questions.

   a) How much is a Thriller on video?
   b) How much is a Western on DVD?
   c) Is Comedy cheaper on video or DVD?
   d) Which is more expensive – a Horror DVD or a Comedy DVD?
   e) How much more is a Sci-fi film on DVD than on video?

Film Prices

Genre	Video price	DVD price
Action	£12.00	£15.99
Sci-fi	£10.99	£14.00
Thriller	£11.00	£13.99
Comedy	£9.00	£12.00
Horror	£11.99	£15.00
Western	£9.00	£11.99

L1

3 Use the information in the Car Hire table to answer the questions.

Car Hire

Vehicle type	Hire period		
	3 days	7 days	14 days
Fiat Punto	£110	£190	£330
Ford Fiesta	£115	£185	£355
Ford Ka	£150	£190	£360
Ford Focus	£190	£260	£470
Vauxhall Tigra	£210	£290	£499
Volkswagen Golf	£135	£220	£399

a) How much does it cost to hire
   i) a Ford Ka for 7 days   ii) a Volkswagen Golf for 14 days?
b) You pay £470 to hire a car.
   i) Which car is it?   ii) How long have you hired it for?
c) What is the cheapest car you can hire for 3 days?
d) How much does it cost to hire a Fiat Punto for 7 days?
e) Which car is the most expensive to hire?
f) How much more does it cost to hire a Tigra than a Fiesta for 7 days?

4

Flight Information

Route	Flight number	Departure–Return Days	Outward times		Return times	
			Depart	Arrive	Depart	Arrive
Heathrow – Split	453/65S	Sat–Sat	16:50	21:00	14:30	17:40
Gatwick – Split	789/45S	Fri–Fri	10:00	13:50	21:00	23:50
Manchester – Split	791/75S	Sat–Sat	19:00	22:50	18:10	21:00
Heathrow – Pula	465/71P	Thurs–Thurs	11:30	15:20	12:20	15:30
Gatwick – Pula	781/31P	Fri–Fri	07:00	11:10	06:30	09:20
Manchester – Pula	867/91P	Sat–Sat	18:00	21:50	17:10	20:00

a) What is the flight number of the flight from Manchester to Split?
b) What time is the flight from Gatwick to Pula due to arrive?
c) What time does the return flight for flight number 781/31P leave?
d) Which route does flight number 781/31P fly?
e) What day of the week does the flight from Manchester to Pula fly?

5 a) What is missing from the table below?

Altea	H/Esplendia	7	HB	750	FB	1010	14	HB	1076	FB	1568
Benidorm	H/Fantastica	7	HB	600	FB	950	14	HB	989	FB	1300
Malaga	H/Luxuriosa	7	HB	570	FB	900	14	HB	976	FB	1286
Salou	H/Fabulosa	7	HB	500	FB	845	14	HB	855	FB	1015

b) Redraw the table. Put in the missing items.

c) How much does it cost to stay in Hotel Luxuriosa for 14 nights full board?

d) How much does it cost to stay in Hotel Fabulosa for 7 nights half board?

e) Your hotel costs £1010.

    i) Where are you staying?   **ii)** Is it half board or full board?

    iii) How many nights are you staying there?

f) How much more does it cost to stay full board for 7 nights in Hotel Fantastica in Benidorm than in Hotel Fabulosa in Salou?

L2

6 The table below gives insurance premiums for travel insurance.
Children under 2 years old are covered for free.

Age	2–15 years		16–64		65 or over	
No. of nights	Europe	Outside Europe	Europe	Outside Europe	Europe	Outside Europe
6–9	£18.20	£33.90	£24.30	£44.50	£30.60	£55.25
10–17	£21.80	£38.25	£28.40	£51.20	£35.25	£63.75
18–23	£24.75	£42.50	£33.20	£56.25	£41.75	£70.50

Find the total premium for each of these families who are going on holiday.

a) 14 nights in Europe

    Mr Bell   Age 28

    Mrs Bell   Age 26

    Ben   Age 4

    Julie   Age 1

b) 21 nights outside Europe

    Mr Khan   Age 38

    Mrs Khan   Age 39

    Imran   Age 14

    Mr Khan (senior)   Age 67

Activities

1 Choose a holiday from a brochure.
Use information from the brochure to find out the total cost and the flight times.

2 Look up prices in tables in catalogues.

3 Find the distance between cities from a road atlas table. (See page 164.)

c Find information from diagrams

There are many types of diagrams that give information.

One of the most common is a map. Here is a sketch map of a town centre.

A student from Fripton asks for directions to the college.

One possible route is given below:

Coming into town from Fripton, turn right after the supermarket, turn right again at the T-junction (taking the road to Gatley), then first left. Follow this road past the school and round a left-hand bend. The college is further along on the right.

Practice

1 Write down directions to the college for a student from

   a) Copham   **b)** Edgeley   **c)** Dalton
   d) Gatley   **e)** Barfield   **f)** Appleby.

2 Write down directions to go from

   a) the college to the post office   **b)** the school to the petrol station
   c) the gym to the fish and chip shop   **d)** the cinema to the supermarket
   e) the swimming pool to the pub   **f)** the cinema to the swimming pool.

For more work
with diagrams see
page 177.

d Find information from pictograms

A **pictogram** uses pictures or symbols to represent data.

CD sales in Ramsgate's shops on Saturday — The pictogram's **title** tells you what it is about.

Music Box

George's Records — This is roughly half a symbol. It represents about 50 CDs.

Hot Discs

CD Ramsgate

These are called **categories**.

This is the **key**. It tells you what each symbol represents. ⊙ = 100 CDs

When each symbol represents a number of items, you can only estimate how many are in each category when parts of symbols are used.

Practice

1 Use the pictogram to answer these questions.

   a) How many CDs were sold in George's Records?
   b) Which shop sold   i) the most CDs   ii) the least CDs?
   c) How many more CDs did CD Ramsgate sell than Hot Discs?
   d) How many CDs were sold altogether?

2 The pictogram shows how much a householder spends on his bedroom.

Amount spent on bedroom

Curtains
Bed linen
Carpet
Furniture
Decorating

Key [£20] **represents £20**

   a) Which category of goods cost   i) most   ii) least?
   b) Estimate how much he spends   i) on each category   ii) altogether.

e Find information from bar charts

Bar charts use vertical or horizontal bars to give data.

The bar chart below shows the type of morning drinks chosen by the workers in a factory. The main features are labelled. Note 'decaff' means decaffeinated.

This is the **vertical axis**.

The **title** tells you what the chart is about.

These lines are called **gridlines**.

There are **gaps** between the bars

This is the **horizontal axis**.

Each small division represents one worker.

The **labels** tell you what each bar shows.

The **scale** on the vertical axis tells you how many workers had each type of drink. The first bar shows 25 workers had tea. The second bar shows 12 workers had decaffeinated tea.

Practice

1 a) Copy this table. Use the bar chart to fill in the missing numbers.

Use the table to answer these questions then use the bar chart to check.

Type of drink	Number of workers
Tea	25
Decaff tea	12
Coffee	
Decaff coffee	
Water	
Fruit Juice	

b) How many more workers had tea than decaffeinated tea?

c) How many more workers had fruit juice than water?

d) Altogether how many workers had decaffeinated drinks?

e) How many workers were there altogether?

In a survey people are asked which type of TV programmes they like best. This bar chart shows the results. The label on the vertical axis shows that the number of people is also called the **frequency**. Frequency means how often something happens – in this case how often people chose each type.

Can you see what each division on the vertical axis represents this time?

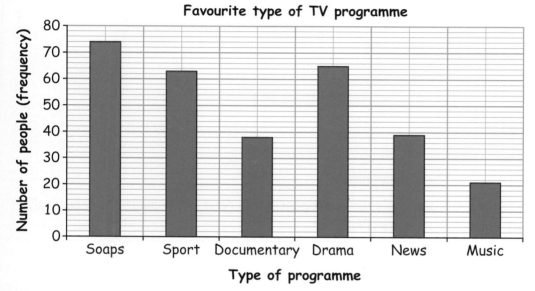

Each division represents 2 people.
The number of people who like soaps best is 74.
The top of the bar for sport lies between 62 and 64 – this means the number of people who like sport best is 63.

2 Use the bar chart above to answer these questions.

a) How many people chose
   i) documentaries   ii) drama   iii) news   iv) music?
b) Which is
   i) the most popular type   ii) the least popular type?
c) How many more people chose documentaries than music?
d) Altogether how many people took part in the survey?

This bar chart shows the population of some countries in Europe.
Can you see what each division on the horizontal axis represents?

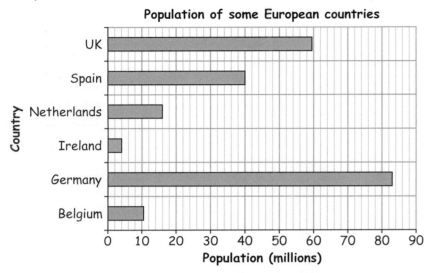

Each division represents 2 **million** people. It is not possible to read the populations accurately, but you can estimate them to the nearest million.

3   Use the bar chart above to answer these questions.

a) Which of these countries has
   i) the largest population   **ii)** the smallest population?
b) Write down the population of each country. Give your answers to the nearest million.
c) **i)** How many more people live in Germany than in the UK?
   ii) How many more people live in the UK than in the Netherlands?
d) What is the total population of the UK and Ireland?

The bar chart below shows the height of each student in a class. Their names are given in a **key** because it is difficult to fit them along the horizontal axis.
What does each division on the vertical axis represent?

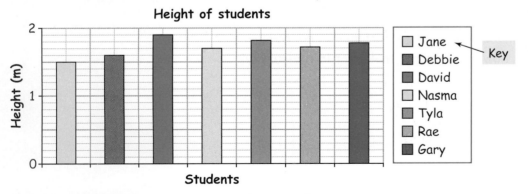

Each division represents 0.1 metres (or 10 cm).
Some of the tops of the bars lie between two gridlines.
Using the **nearest gridline** gives the height to the **nearest 0.1 m**.
For example, Gary's height is 1.8 m to the nearest 0.1 m.

4 a) Copy this table.
Use the bar chart to fill in the missing heights,
correct to the nearest 0.1 m.

b) Who is the shortest student?

c) Who is the tallest student?

d) Who is taller: Nasma or Rae?

e) Who is shorter: Tyla or Gary?

Use the bar chart for b to e.

Student	Height (m)
Jane	
Debbie	
David	
Nasma	
Tyla	
Rae	
Gary	1.8

5 A café sells baked potatoes with a choice of fillings.
The bar chart shows the number of each type of filling bought in one day.

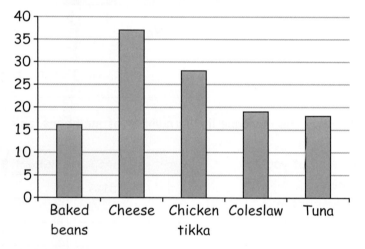

a) What is missing from the bar chart?

b) Which was the **most** popular filling?

c) Which was the **least** popular filling?

d) Draw a table giving the frequency for each type of filling.
Give your answers as accurately as you can.

e) How many baked potatoes were sold altogether?

f) How many more potatoes were filled with cheese than were filled with tuna?

L1 These two charts both show the same information.

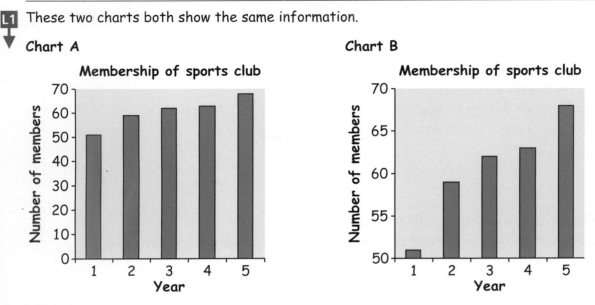

Chart A

Chart B

Changing the scale on an axis changes the impression a chart gives.
Starting at a non-zero value also makes it look different.

6 a) Look at the charts. Which chart makes the increase in the number of members look
       more dramatic?

   b) The charts do not have any gridlines, but you
      can estimate the number of members.
      Look at Chart A, the number of members in
      Year 1 is just above 50. A reasonable estimate
      is 51. This has been entered into the table.

      i)   Copy the table and use Chart A to complete
           the second column.

      ii) Use Chart B to complete the last column of
           your table.

      iii) Which chart was easier to use when estimating the number of members?

Year	Chart A	Chart B
1	51	
2		
3		
4		
5		

> Note
> To emphasise that an axis has a non-zero
> starting value you can start the axis with
> a zig-zag line like this:

The chart below is a **comparative** bar chart. It gives a comparison between the number of full-time and part-time students on vocational courses at a college.

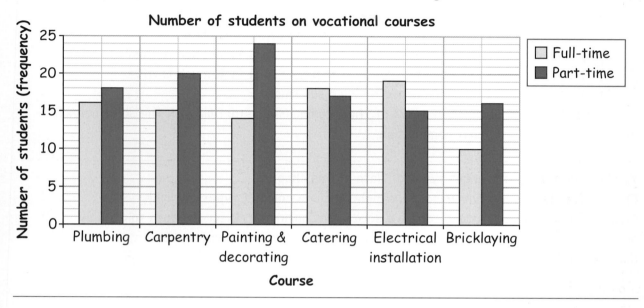

Number of students on vocational courses

7 Use the chart to answer these questions.

a) On which courses are there more full-time than part-time students?

b) How many more part-time students than full-time students are doing
   i) carpentry   ii) plumbing   iii) painting and decorating?

c) Find the total number of students who are doing
   i) bricklaying   ii) catering   iii) electrical installation.

d) Find the total number of
   i) full-time students   ii) part-time students.

The chart below is a **component** bar chart. It shows how the amount each salesman in a car showroom earns in a week. The amount earned is the total of basic pay and commission.

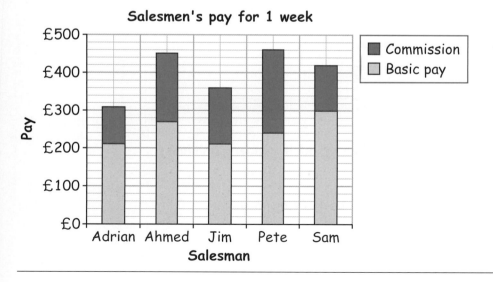

Salesmen's pay for 1 week

8 Use the bar chart above to answer these questions.

a) i) Who earned the **most**? **ii)** How much did he earn?
b) i) Who earned the **least**? **ii)** How much did he earn?
c) Write down the amount earned by each of the other salesmen.
d) i) Who has the highest basic pay? **ii)** How much is this?
e) i) Which salesmen have the same basic pay? **ii)** How much is it?
f) i) Find the commission earned by each salesman.
   ii) List the salesmen in order of their commission, starting with the salesman who earned the **most** commission.

L2 You have met many different types of data in this chapter.
Qualitative data is not numerical – examples include colours, types of drink.
Quantitative (numerical) data can be discrete or continuous. **Discrete** data takes only particular values, for example shoe sizes or number of children in families.
Continuous data can take any value in a given range, for example heights, weights, time to complete a task and other things that you measure.

---

9 Give 3 examples of

a) qualitative data **b)** discrete data **c)** continuous data.

10 Each year a National Readership Survey is carried out to find out what people have read. The chart shows estimates of the number of adults who read a selection of TV magazines in one year.

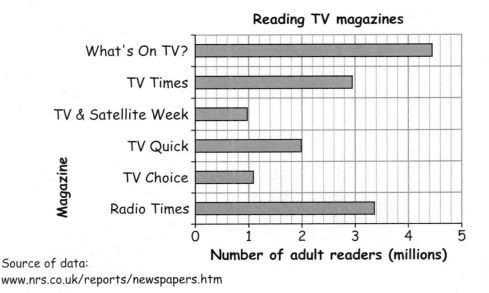

Reading TV magazines

Source of data:
www.nrs.co.uk/reports/newspapers.htm

Estimate the number of adult readers of each TV magazine.
Give each answer

a) to the nearest million **b)** to the nearest 100 000.

11 The chart shows the grades achieved by the candidates in some A level exams one year.

a) Which subject had the biggest % of grade As?

b) Every grade except U is a pass grade.
Which subject had the best pass rate?

c) Draw up a table to give the % in each grade for each subject. Estimate values to the nearest %.

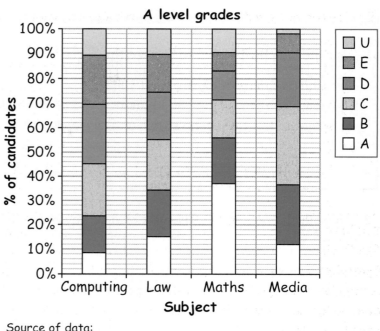

Source of data:
www.qca.org.uk

Information from pie charts and line graphs   HD1/L1.1, HD1/L2.1

a Find information from pie charts

Pie charts show how something is divided into parts.
The pie chart below shows how a student spends a typical day.

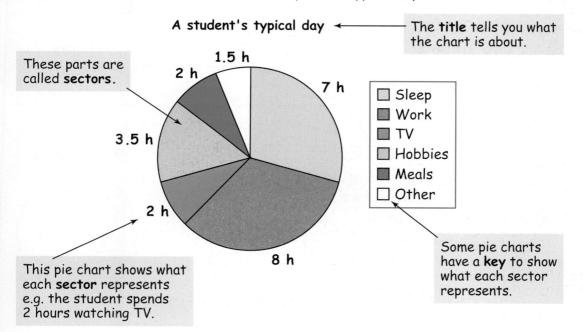

Practice

1 Use the pie chart above to answer these questions.

    a) Which activity took the most time?

    b) How much longer did the student spend on hobbies than on watching TV?

    c) What is the total time shown on the pie chart? Why?

▶ **Some pie charts give information as percentages.**

See page 116 for a reminder.

2 This pie chart shows the results of a survey about how people travel to work.

    a) Which is

        i) the most popular way of getting to work

        ii) the least popular way of getting to work?

    b) What fraction of the people

        i) travel to work by bus   **ii)** walk to work

        iii) travel to work by train   **iv)** drive to work

        v) cycle to work?

    c) Altogether 400 people took part in the survey. Find how many travelled by each method.

Travelling to work

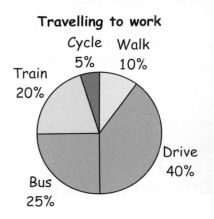

Cycle 5%   Walk 10%
Train 20%
Drive 40%
Bus 25%

Sometimes pie charts do not give the number or the percentage of items in each sector.
You can **estimate** the fraction or percentage from the size of the sector.
If you are told the total number of items you can estimate how many are in each category.
For example, if a pie chart represents altogether 100 people, then half of the circle represents 50 people.

---

3 This pie chart shows the grades given to students for an exam.

    a) Estimate the fraction of the students who got each grade.

    b) Altogether 48 students took the exam. Estimate how many got each grade.

Exam grades

4 The pie chart shows the proportion of each type of property a developer builds on a new estate.

Types of property on development

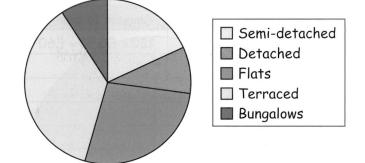

Legend:
- ☐ Semi-detached
- ▨ Detached
- ▨ Flats
- ☐ Terraced
- ■ Bungalows

a) Say which of the following statements are true and which are false.
   i) More than a quarter of the properties are flats.
   ii) There are more bungalows than flats.
   iii) There are approximately the same number of bungalows as detached houses.
   iv) There are more terraced properties than any other type.

b) Put the types of property in order of the numbers built by the developer, starting with the largest.

For more accurate values you need to measure the angles of the pie chart with a **protractor**.

To measure an angle:

1 Put the centre of your protractor on the centre of the pie chart.

2 Lie the zero line of the protractor over one side of the angle.

3 Follow the scale round the edge of the protractor to the other side of the angle.

4 Read the size of the angle.
Take care to use the correct scale!

4. Read angle   108°   3. Follow scale

1. Centres   2. Zero line

There are 360° in a circle. To find accurate information from a pie chart you must find the connection between the angles and the data.

For example, the following pie chart shows how a telephone bill of £180 is shared between 5 flat mates.

$$360° \text{ represents } £180 \quad \text{so} \quad 1° \text{ represents } \frac{£180}{360} = £0.50 \text{ (i.e. 50p)}$$

Measure the angle that shows Bev's share.
The angle is 120°. So Bev's share of the bill = 120 × £0.50 = £60.

---

b Find information from line graphs

Line graphs are often used to show how something changes as time goes by.

The **title** and **labels** on this line graph show that it is about the temperature at a weather station during a day.

The **crosses** show the temperatures that were recorded. The **lines** that join them show how the temperature went up and down during the day.

Practice

1   Use the line graph above to answer these questions.

   a) What does each small square represent on
      i)   the horizontal axis
      ii) the vertical axis?
   b) How often was the temperature measured?
   c) i)   What was the **highest** temperature measured?
      ii) When was this reading taken?
   d) i)   What was the **lowest** temperature measured?
      ii) When was this reading taken?
   e) i)   When was the temperature **measured** as 0°C?
      ii) **Estimate** the other times when the temperature was 0°C.
   f) Between what times was the temperature
      i)   rising
      ii) falling?
   g) When was the temperature rising most quickly?

2 Use this line graph to answer the questions that follow.

Source of data www.met-office.gov.uk

a) What does each small division represent on the vertical axis?

b) i) In which month did the **most** rain fall?
  ii) Estimate how much rain fell in this month.

c) i) In which month did the **least** rain fall?
  ii) Estimate how much rain fell in this month.

d) How much more rain fell in December than in June?

e) Estimate the total rainfall for the year.

3 These graphs both show the profit made by a company over a 5-year period.

a) i) Which graph gives the best estimates of the yearly profits?
  ii) Use this graph to estimate the profit each year.

b) Explain why graph B may be misleading.

This line graph is a **conversion graph**. You can use it to convert gallons to litres and vice versa.

Look at the scales.
What does a small square represent on each axis?

The arrows show that:
14 gallons ≈ 64 litres
16 litres ≈ 3.5 gallons.

> ▶ **Note:** ≈ means 'approximately equal to'.

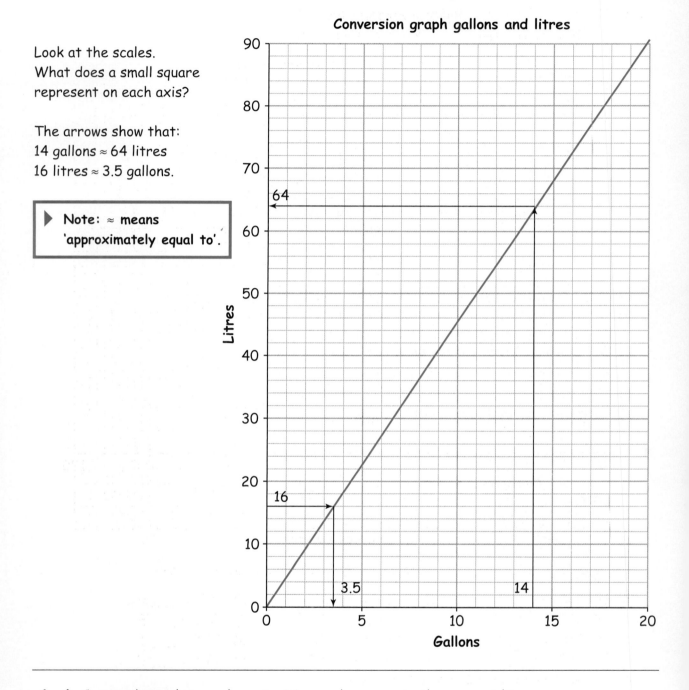

Conversion graph gallons and litres

4 **a)** Copy and complete each part, giving each answer to the nearest litre.
   i) 10 gallons ≈ ____ litres
   ii) 5 gallons ≈ ____ litres
   iii) 18 gallons ≈ ____ litres
   iv) 7.5 gallons ≈ ____ litres
 b) Copy and complete each part, giving each answer to the nearest 0.5 gallon.
   i) 40 litres ≈ ____ gallons
   ii) 72 litres ≈ ____ gallons
   iii) 24 litres ≈ ____ gallons
   iv) 67 litres ≈ ____ gallons
 c) The petrol tank of a car holds 15 gallons. How many litres is this?
 d) There are 82 litres of water left in a tank. How many gallons is this?

5 The graph below converts temperatures from Celsius to Fahrenheit and vice versa.

a) What does each small square represent on
  i) the horizontal axis   **ii)** the vertical axis?

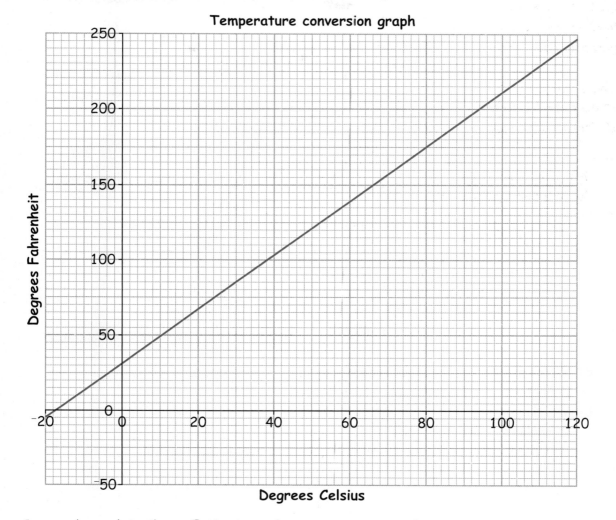

Temperature conversion graph

Copy and complete these. Estimate each answer as accurately as you can.

b) i) 20°C ≈ ____°F   **ii)** 48°C ≈ ____°F   **iii)** 75°C ≈ ____°F
   iv) 27°C ≈ ____°F   **v)** −10°C ≈ ____°F   **vi)** −7°C ≈ ____°F
c) i) 50°F ≈ ____°C   **ii)** 140°F ≈ ____°C   **iii)** 75°F ≈ ____°C
   iv) 205°F ≈ ____°C   **v)** 184°F ≈ ____°C   **vi)** 28°F ≈ ____°C
d) Water freezes at 0°C and boils at 100°C.
   What are these temperatures in Fahrenheit?

> ▶ Line graphs can be used to show **more than one set of data**.

L2

6 The graph below shows the number of hours per day sunshine over the course of a year in Scotland and in England.

Hours per day of sunshine

Source of data www.met-office.gov.uk

a) Which month had the **most** sunshine in
   i) England   ii) Scotland?
b) Which month(s) had the **least** sunshine in
   i) England   ii) Scotland?
c) How much more sunshine was there in England than in Scotland in
   i) January   ii) July?
d) How much more sunshine was there in August than November in
   i) England   ii) Scotland?
e) Write a paragraph to explain what the graph shows.

7 The graph shows the amount of coal, petroleum and natural gas consumed in the UK over the course of a year.

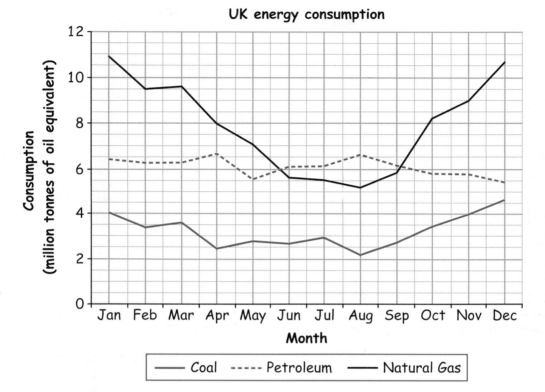

UK energy consumption

a) In which months did the UK consume the **most**
   i) coal   ii) petroleum   iii) natural gas?
b) In which months did the UK consume the **least**
   i) coal   ii) petroleum   iii) natural gas?
c) Estimate the difference in natural gas consumption between January and August.
d) Estimate the total consumption of coal, petroleum and natural gas in
   i) January   ii) June.
e) Describe the way in which natural gas consumption varied over the course of the year. Suggest reasons for this variation.

Activities

1. Look for examples of charts, graphs and diagrams in newspapers, books and magazines. Explain what they show.

2. Find the latest edition of Social Trends on the government's statistics website at www.statistics.gov.uk.
   Print some of the information given in charts and graphs and discuss what they show. Find other information including charts and graphs on the internet.

Handling Data

2 Collecting and Illustrating Data

Record information using a tally chart

HD1/E3.3

How could you find out which type of pet is most popular?

One way is to carry out a survey asking people which pets they have.

The more people you ask, the more representative the results.

The best way of organising the information you collect is in a **tally chart**.

Here is a tally chart from a survey about pets.

The question asked was: **Which types of pet do you own?**

Type of Pet	Tally	Frequency
Dog	JHT JHT JHT I	16
Cat	JHT JHT JHT IIII	
Rabbit	JHT	
Bird	JHT II	
Fish	JHT I	
Reptile	II	
Other	JHT JHT I	
None	JHT JHT III	

A **tally mark** / is put into the table whenever a person says they have a particular type of pet. The fifth tally mark is drawn across the first four to make a group of five. This makes it easier to count the total.

The total number of people for each pet is the **frequency**.

Practice

1 a) The frequency for dogs is 16.
Write down the frequency for each other type of pet.

b) Which is the most popular type of pet?

c) List some types of pet that could be in the 'Other' category.

2 The pet survey also asked people how many pets they had. The answers were:
0, 1, 3, 1, 2, 1, 0, 6, 4, 3, 1, 1, 0, 1, 3, 1, 1, 0, 1, 6, 1, 2, 1, 3, 1, 0, 0, 1, 2, 1,
1, 2, 4, 1, 0, 3, 2, 1, 1, 0, 3, 1, 0, 2, 5, 1, 1, 2, 1, 3, 1, 0, 0, 1, 2, 1, 0, 1, 2, 0

a) This tally chart has been started to show the results. It shows the first 4 answers. Copy and complete it.

Number of pets	Tally	Frequency
0	I	
1	II	
2		
3	I	
4		
5		
6		

b) How many people had
   i) no pets   **ii)** 3 pets   **iii)** more than 3 pets?
c) How many people took part in the survey?

3 The tally chart below shows the grades awarded to students on a course.

a) Copy and complete the table.
b) How many students were on the course?
c) What fraction of the students got
   i) a distinction   **ii)** a merit?
d) What percentage of the students failed the course?

Grade	Tally	Frequency
Distinction	IHT II	
Merit	IHT IHT IIII	
Pass	IHT IHT IHT IIII	
Fail	IHT IHT	

4 A college library's records show the number of books taken by each student who borrowed books during one lunch hour. This data is given below.

1	3	4	1	2	5	4	1	3	1	2	5	1	3	1	2	2	4	1	1	4
2	1	1	6	3	6	1	5	2	1	3	1	2	1	1	4	1	3	1	5	2
1	4	3	3	1	1	2	1	6	4	1	3	4	2	5	6	3	2	3	1	1
5	2	1	3	4	1	5	1	1	2	3	2	1	4	1	5	3	2	1	4	2

a) Draw a tally chart to show these results.
b) What was the most common number of books borrowed?
c) How many students borrowed books during this lunch hour?
d) What % of students borrowed more than 4 books?

Illustrate data using a pictogram or bar chart

HD1/E3.4, HD1/L1.2, HD1/L2.2

a Using a pictogram

A **pictogram** uses simple pictures or symbols to illustrate data (see page 253).
When drawing a pictogram you should:

- Choose a **simple symbol** that is easy to draw.
- Decide how many items each symbol stands for.
- Work out how many symbols you need for each category.
- Draw the pictogram. Use squared paper – this makes it easier to line up the symbols. Try to keep the symbols the same size (except when only part of a symbol is needed).
- Give the pictogram a **title** saying what it is about.
- Include a **key** showing what each symbol stands for.

Practice

1   The table shows the number of hours of sunshine at a seaside resort each day during a week in August.
    Draw a pictogram to show this data.

    Use ☼ to represent 2 hours of sunshine.

    Use ◖ to represent 1 hour of sunshine.

Day	Hours of sunshine
Monday	6
Tuesday	4
Wednesday	3
Thursday	5
Friday	8
Saturday	10
Sunday	9

2   The table shows the number of houses sold by an estate agent in the first six months of a year.
    Draw a pictogram to show this information.

    Use ⌂ to represent 10 houses.

    You will have to decide how much of the symbol to use when you need to show less than 10 houses.

Month	No. of houses
January	25
February	30
March	45
April	52
May	60
June	57

L1

3   A car manufacturer keeps records of the colours of the cars sold. The table gives the results for one model.

Choose a symbol to represent 100 cars and draw a pictogram.

Colour	No. of cars sold
Red	650
Black	425
White	386
Blue	541
Green	150

b Using a bar chart

A **bar chart** uses vertical or horizontal bars to illustrate data (see page 254).

When drawing a bar chart you should:

● Use **squared** or **graph** paper.

● Use an **easy scale**, i.e. make each small square an easy value to use.
  (e.g. 1, 2, 5, 10, 20, 50, 100, 200, 500 are easier than 3, 4, 7, 8, 9, 30, 40, ...)

● Aim for a large chart that is easy to read.

● Use a ruler and sharp pencil to draw the chart. Leave gaps between the bars.

● Give the bar chart a **title** saying what it is about.

● **Label** the axes (give **units** if necessary). Use a pen to do this if you wish.

Practice

1   The pizza toppings ordered in a snack bar during one day are shown in the table.

   a) Draw a bar chart to show this information. Use vertical bars.
   b) Use your chart to answer these questions.
      i)   Which topping is **most** popular?
      ii) Which topping is **least** popular?

Topping	No. of pizzas
Cheese & tomato	15
Seafood	8
Ham & mushroom	12
Pepperoni	18
Roasted vegetable	11

2   The table gives the type and number of fruit trees in an orchard.

   a) Draw a bar chart to show this information. Use horizontal bars.
   b) Use your chart to answer these questions.
      i)   Which is the **most common** type of fruit tree?
      ii) How many more plum trees than pear trees are there?

Type of tree	No. of trees
Apple	36
Cherry	12
Pear	18
Plum	25

3 A company offers holiday homes for rent in some European countries.
The table shows the number of properties it has in each country.

Country	No. of properties
Belgium	15
France	63
Germany	42
Greece	27
Italy	36
Spain	54

a) Draw a bar chart to show this data.
b) In which country does the company have the **most** properties?
c) How many more properties does the company have
   i) in France than in Belgium   ii) in France than in Spain?

Also draw bar charts of the data given in the **tally chart** and **pictogram** sections.
(Page 272)   (page 274)

L1

4 A video rental shop records the number of films rented from different categories.
The table shows the results for one week.

Film type	No. of films
Adventure	340
Children's	276
Comedy	125
Horror	205
Musical	83
Sci-fi	107
Thriller	194

a) Draw a bar chart to show this data.
b) Which category was **most** popular?
c) Which category was **least** popular?
d) List the categories in order of popularity, starting with the most popular.

5 A newsagent records the number of newspapers delivered to the houses he supplies. The results for one day are given in the table.

No. of newspapers	No. of houses
1	324
2	191
3	54
4	27
5	8

a) Draw a bar chart to show this data.
b) Describe briefly what the chart shows.

L2

6 The table shows estimates of the number of people who read daily newspapers.

Newspaper	No. of readers (thousands)
Daily Express	2168
Daily Mail	5564
Daily Star	1460
Daily Telegraph	2235
Guardian	1024
Mirror	5733
Sun	9591
Times	1575

a) Draw a bar chart to show this data.
b) Which of these newspapers is
   i) **most** popular   ii) **least** popular?
c) List the newspapers in order of popularity, starting with the most popular.

Source: National Readership Survey 2000/2001 (www.nrs.co.uk)

7 The table gives the life expectancy of men and women in eight countries.

a) Draw a comparative bar chart to illustrate this data.

b) In which of these countries is
   i)   male life expectancy **greatest**
   ii) female life expectancy **lowest**?

c) i)   Briefly compare male and female life expectancy.
   ii) In which country is the difference between male and female life expectancy greatest?

d) Briefly compare life expectancy in the eight countries.

| Country | Life expectancy (years) | |
	Male	Female
Afghanistan	41.1	43.7
Angola	34.1	38.3
Brazil	65.5	72.0
China	69.8	72.7
India	60.0	61.7
Russia	58.9	72.3
UK	75.1	79.9
USA	74.3	79.5

Source: World Health Report 2002

8 The table below shows the number of men and women employed in UK service industries.

| Industry | Number of employees (thousands) | | |
	Male	Female	Total
Hotels & restaurants	3288	3575	
Transport & communication	1319	489	
Finance & business	3053	2659	
Education & health	2204	4890	
Other	861	923	

Source: Labour Market Statistics 2003

a) Copy and complete the table by filling in the totals.

b) Draw a component bar chart to illustrate the data.

c) Which service industry has
   i)   the greatest total number of employees
   ii) the greatest number of male employees
   iii) the greatest number of female employees?

Activities

Collect some data. Then use a pictogram or bar chart to illustrate it and describe what your illustration shows. Here are some suggestions:

1 Use a tally chart to record the colours (or ages) of cars in a car park.

2 Use a tally chart to record the type of vehicles travelling along a road.

3 Keep a record of how long you watch each TV channel during a week.

4 Record how much time you spend on different activities
   (e.g. hobbies, shopping, housework, work) during a week.

5 Carry out a survey using tally charts to record the information you collect.
   Ask students questions such as 'What is your favourite sport?',
   'What type of programmes do you like most?', 'What is your favourite hobby?'

6 Take some measurements from students in your group
   (e.g. height, length of right hand, length of stride, time taken to recite the alphabet).

L2 Use a comparative or component bar chart to show the results for male and female students from activity 5.

Illustrate data using a pie chart   HD1/L1.2, HD1/L2.2

Pie charts show how something is divided into parts. (See page 261.)
A pie chart is the best way to show the **proportion** (or fraction) of the data that is in each category.

To draw a pie chart:

● Find the **total** of the data (unless it has been given).

● **Divide 360° by the total** to find how many degrees represent each item.

● **Multiply this by the number of items** in each category to find the **angle** for each category. **Check** the total angle is 360°.

● Write a **title** to say what information the pie chart gives.

● Use a **compass** to draw a circle and a **protractor** to measure the angles needed.

● **Label** each sector of the pie chart or give a **key** to show what each sector represents.

Example

The table shows the percentage of students on a course who got each grade.

Grade	% of students
Distinction	13%
Merit	31%
Pass	45%
Fail	11%

As the data are percentages, the total must be 100% (but check to make sure).

Each % will be represented by:

$$\frac{360°}{100} = 3.6°$$

The table shows how the angle is worked out for each grade. Use your calculator to check the working in the table.
Here the total angle is 361°.

Grade	% of students	Angle (nearest °)
Distinction	13%	$13 \times 3.6 = 47°$
Merit	31%	$31 \times 3.6 = 112°$
Pass	45%	$45 \times 3.6 = 162°$
Fail	11%	$11 \times 3.6 = 40°$
Total	100%	361°

The rounding has given an extra degree. When this happens take 1° away from the largest angle, here the angle for the Pass grade should be changed to 161°.

Practice

1 a) Draw a pie chart to show the proportion of students who got each grade.
b) According to your chart which grade had
  i) the smallest proportion of students   **ii)** the largest proportion?

2 A group of students have lunch at a snack bar The table shows what the students eat.

Lunch	No. of students
Sandwich	6
Pasta	5
Baked potato	8
Salad	4
Pizza	1
Total	

a) How many students are there altogether?
b) In a pie chart how many degrees represent each student?
c) Copy the table and add an extra column to show how you work out the angles.
d) Draw a pie chart to illustrate the data.

3 The table shows the number of cars owned by households in the UK.

Number of cars	% of households
0	26
1	46
2	22
3 or more	6

a) Draw a pie chart to illustrate this.
b) What is the most common number of cars owned by households?
c) Do more or less than a quarter of households have no car?

Source: www.transtat.gov.uk

4 The table gives estimates of the number of cars produced in each region during a year.

a) Use the data to draw a pie chart.
b) Which region produces the greatest proportion of cars?

Region	No. of cars (millions)
Western Europe	14.5
Eastern Europe	2.4
Asia	12.7
North America	8.3
Other	2.1

Source: www.autoindustry.co.uk

L2

5 The total amount spent on different types of advertising is given in the table.

a) Draw a pie chart to illustrate this data.
b) Use your chart to answer these questions.
   i) What type of advertising takes the greatest share of the money?
   ii) Does advertising by post earn more or less than advertising in newspapers and magazines?
   iii) Is it true that more than a third of the total amount spent on advertising is spent on TV adverts?

Type of advertising	Amount (£millions)
Post	2049
Newspapers & magazines	3979
Radio	595
Television	4646
Transport & outdoor	823
Other	985

Source: www.adassoc.org.uk

6 The table gives the population and area of each country in the UK.
Draw a pie chart for each set of data and write a paragraph explaining what your charts show.

Country	Population (millions)	Area (000 km²)
England	49.1	130.4
N. Ireland	1.7	13.6
Scotland	5.1	78.1
Wales	2.9	20.8

Source: Office for National Statistics

Draw graphs

HD1/L1.2, HD1/L2.2

a Draw a line graph

A **line graph** is often used to show how something changes as time goes by. (See page 266.)

To draw a line graph:

- Use **squared** or **graph** paper.
- Use an **easy scale**, i.e. make each small square an easy value to use.
  (e.g. 1, 2, 5, 10, 20, 50, 100, 200, 500 are easier than 3, 4, 7, 8, 9, 30, 40, ...)

- Aim for a **large graph** that fills most of the page.
- Use a ruler and sharp pencil to draw the graph.
- Give the graph a **title** saying what it is about.
- **Label** the axes (give **units** if necessary). Use a pen to do this if you wish.
- (L2) If your graph has more than one line, label each line or use a key to show what each line represents.

Practice

1   Students on a college course can attend an extra drop-in class for help.
    The number of students who go to this class each week is shown in the table.

Week	1	2	3	4	5	6	7	8	9	10
No. of students	1	0	6	9	5	8	12	15	10	7

   a) Draw a line graph to illustrate this data. Put the week number on the horizontal axis
       and the number of students on the vertical axis.
   b) Use your graph to answer these questions.
       i)   In which week did the **greatest** number of students attend the class?
       ii)   In which week did the **least** number of students attend the class?
       iii) Describe how the attendance varied over the weeks shown.

2   The table shows the number of
    computers owned by a school
    between 1980 and 2000.

Year	1980	1985	1990	1995	2000
No. of computers	5	12	30	60	120

   a) Draw a line graph.
   b) Estimate how many computers the school had in   i) 1982   ii) 1994.
   c) Estimate the year when the school had   i) 50 computers   ii) 100 computers.

3   The table below shows how the number of motoring offences detected by camera
    increased between 1996 and 2001.

Year	1996	1997	1998	1999	2000	2001
No of offences (thousand)	313	390	447	551	768	1071

   Source: www.homeoffice.gov.uk

   a) Draw a line graph and describe what it shows.
   b) If the trend continued how many motoring offences would be detected by camera in
       2002?

L2

4 A health and safety officer records the noise level in a factory in decibels (dB) every hour. The results are given in the table below:

Time	8 am	9 am	10 am	11 am	noon	1 pm	2 pm	3 pm	4 pm	5 pm
Noise (dB)	40	65	85	89	82	74	84	83	72	54

a) Use these results to draw a line graph.
b) Use your graph to estimate the times when the noise level is exactly 80 decibels.
c) Estimate the total time when the noise level is over 70 decibels.
d) Describe briefly how the noise level varies during the day.
   Suggest reasons for high and low values.

5 The table below gives the number of licensed motorcycles in the UK between 1980 and 2000 and the number of deaths and serious injuries to motor-cyclists in this period.

Year	Number of motorcycles (thousands)	Number of deaths & serious injuries
1980	1372	22 697
1982	1370	22 689
1984	1225	20 009
1986	1065	16 467
1988	912	12 654
1990	833	11 121
1992	684	7338
1994	630	6666
1996	609	6208
1998	684	6442
2000	825	7374

▶ Note: It is often difficult to plot large, but accurate numbers such as those given in the last column. You may find it easier if you round the values to the nearest 50 or 100 first (depending on your choice of scale).

Source: www.transtat.gov.uk

a) Draw line graphs to show
   i) the number of licensed motorcycles between 1980 and 2000
   ii) the number of deaths and serious injuries to motor-cyclists between 1980 to 2000.
b) Describe what your graphs show.

6 A clothing company has shops in London and Manchester. The table below gives the value of sales at these shops during the months of a year.

Month		Jan	Feb	Mar	Apr	May	Jun	Jul	Aug	Sep	Oct	Nov	Dec
Sales	Lon	385	143	162	189	221	254	207	198	240	262	376	437
(£000s)	Man	258	124	138	142	196	205	212	186	193	187	256	328

a) Draw a graph with two lines showing the sales in London and Manchester.

b) For each shop write down
   i)   the month when sales were **highest**
   ii) the month when sales were **lowest**
   iii) the months in which sales were above £300 000.

c) In which month was the difference between the London and Manchester sales
   i) **greatest**   ii) **least**?

d) Briefly describe how sales varied in each shop over the course of the year. Describe any similarities and differences in the sales patterns.

7 The table below gives the average temperature in England and Wales, Scotland and Northern Ireland during each month of a year.

Month		Jan	Feb	Mar	Apr	May	Jun	Jul	Aug	Sep	Oct	Nov	Dec
Average temp (°C)	E&W	5.3	6.6	7.2	8.8	11.4	13.9	15.4	16.5	13.9	9.8	8.2	5.4
	Scot	4.2	3.6	5.0	7.0	9.5	11.8	12.5	14.0	11.8	6.8	6.2	3.5
	NI	6.1	5.6	6.8	8.3	10.6	12.9	13.6	15.0	13.0	8.6	7.8	4.9

Source: www.met-office.gov.uk

a) Draw a graph with a line for each set of data.

b) For each set of data write down
   i)   the **highest** average temperature and the month when it occurred
   ii) the **lowest** average temperature and the month when it occurred
   iii) the months when the average temperature was below 6°C.

c) Describe how the temperature varied in these countries over the course of the year. Describe any similarities and differences.

8 A nurse measures the temperature of a patient every three hours. The results are given in the table below:

Time	7 am	10 am	1 pm	4 pm	7 pm	10 pm	1 am	4 am
Temp (°F)	99.8	101.2	102.9	103.7	103.6	102.9	101.1	99.3

a) Draw a line graph to illustrate these results. Show times from 7 am to 7 am on the horizontal axis and temperatures from 98°F to 104°F on the vertical axis.

b) A patient has a fever when his temperature is 100°F or more. Use your graph to estimate how long this patient's fever lasted.

c) This patient has a normal temperature of 98.5°F. Use your graph to estimate the time when this patient's temperature returns to normal.

Activities

Collect some data and use a pie chart or line graph to illustrate it.
Then describe what your chart or graph shows. Here are some suggestions:

Pie charts
- Keep a record of how you spent the time during one day.
- Collect data from your class, e.g. hair colour, eye colour, method of travel to college.

Line graphs
- Record the outside temperature over the course of a day.
- Use the Internet or teletext to find out how currency exchange rates or share prices change over a period of time.

Visit government (and other) websites
Carry out searches to find some information you are interested in (e.g. sport).
The addresses of some useful government websites are given below.

www.statistics.gov.uk   All sorts of data on population, employment, leisure and tourism, etc.

www.homeoffice.gov.uk   Home Office website giving crime data.

www.odpm.gov.uk   Office of the Deputy Prime Minister for information on housing, etc.

b Draw and use conversion graphs

A **conversion graph** is used to convert units from one system to another (see page 268).
When drawing a conversion graph you should use graph paper, choose scales and label in the same way as for other line graphs. But before you can do this you need to work out values for some points on the graph.

Example

Using 1 inch = 2.54 cm gives this table:
Note only 3 points have been found – 2 points are enough to give the line; the 3rd point acts as a check.

inches	0	5	10
cm	0	12.7	25.4

5 × 2.54   10 × 2.54

Now a sensible scale is needed on both axes.
One possible graph is shown below.

Practice

1 a) Write down what a small square represents on each of the axes on this graph.

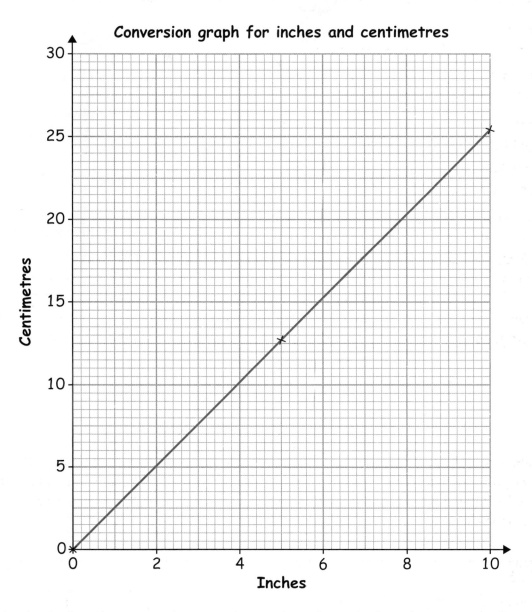

Conversion graph for inches and centimetres

Centimetres (vertical axis)

Inches (horizontal axis)

b) Check that the points shown on the graph agree with the values given in the table above.

c) Use the graph to complete these.

i) 6 in ≈ ____ cm	**ii)** 9 in ≈ ____ cm
iii) 2.6 in ≈ ____ cm	**iv)** 4.3 in ≈ ____ cm
v) 10 cm ≈ ____ in	**vi)** 25 cm ≈ ____ in
vii) 18 cm ≈ ____ in	**viii)** 12.5 cm ≈ ____ in

Check your answers by calculation.

2 **a)** Use the approximation 1 kg ≈ 2.2 lb to draw a conversion graph for kilograms and pounds up to 20 kg.

   b) Use your graph to complete the following, then check by calculation.

   i)   15 kg ≈ ____ lb   **ii)** 9 kg ≈ ____ lb   **iii)** 12.5 kg ≈ ____ lb
   iv) 30 lb ≈ ____ kg   **v)**   14 lb ≈ ____ kg   **vi)** 38.5 lb ≈ ____ kg

---

Activities

1 Draw a conversion graph for miles and kilometres. Find the distance between your home town and major cities such as Birmingham and Manchester from a road atlas. Use your conversion graph to convert the distances to kilometres.

2 Draw a conversion graph for grams and ounces and/or pints and litres. Use your graph(s) to convert the amounts given in recipes.

3 Use a spreadsheet to draw charts and graphs – use the data given in the questions or that you find on the Internet. Much of the data from government websites is available in spreadsheet form.

Handling Data

3 Averages and Range

Find the mean

An **average** is a representative or 'typical' value. There is more than one type of average.

The **mean** is the **arithmetical average**. To find the mean add all the values together, then divide by how many there are.

▶ **Mean** $= \dfrac{\textbf{Sum of data values}}{\textbf{Number of values}}$

Sum means total
(ie add up the values)

Example

The number of goals scored by a footballer in the games he played this season were: 2   0   1   1   0   3   1   2   3   1

Sum of data values $= 2 + 0 + 1 + 1 + 0 + 3 + 1 + 2 + 3 + 1 = 14$

Number of values $= 10$ Mean score $= \dfrac{14}{10} = \textbf{1.4}$ goals per match

Check by reverse calculation: mean × no. of items should equal the total
1.4 × 10 = 14

Practice

1   Find the mean of each set of data. Check each answer.

   a) The number of students absent from a class each week of a term:
          0   1   2   2   1   4   3   0   2   3
   b) The number of calls a student makes on her mobile phone each day in a week:
          5   2   4   0   8   12   11
   c) The ages of the children in a family: 12   10   6   4   1
   d) The number of letters delivered to each house in a street:
          4   5   2   0   4   5   8   6
   e) The weights of puppies in a litter:
       0.41 kg, 0.36 kg, 0.32 kg, 0.36 kg, 0.41 kg, 0.39 kg
   f) Prizes in a lottery:
          £10   £10   £10   £250   £10   £10   £10   £10

Note in part **f** the mean is **distorted** by the large win of £250. *It is not a good representative value.*

2 The table shows the scores of five batsmen in four cricket matches.

a) Find the mean score for each batsman. Check each answer.

b) Which batsman has
   i) the **best** mean score
   ii) the **worst** mean score?

Player	Match			
	1	2	3	4
Andy	112	16	3	49
Imran	0	–	68	43
Mark	–	11	–	37
Stuart	40	33	17	25
Tim	35	27	54	43

Note: – means 'did not play'.

3 Four clerks in an office each earn £5 per hour.
Their manager earns £15 per hour.

a) Find the mean wage.   b) Is this mean a 'typical' value?

4 The table below shows the number of tickets sold for a concert.

Day	Weekdays					Weekend	
	Mon	Tues	Wed	Thurs	Fri	Sat	Sun
Ticket sales	126	205	167	152	298	324	282

Find the mean number of tickets sold

a) per day at the weekend   b) per weekday (i.e. Mon to Fri).

5 The chart shows the rates of pay earned by six students in part-time work.

a) Write down the rate of pay for each student.
b) Calculate the mean rate of pay.
c) Which students get more than the mean rate of pay?

Also find the mean for each set of data given in the questions listed below:

Using a pictogram, page 274, questions 1, 2
Using a bar chart, page 275, questions 1, 2, 3, 4, 6
Draw a line graph, page 281, questions 1, 3, 4, 5, 6

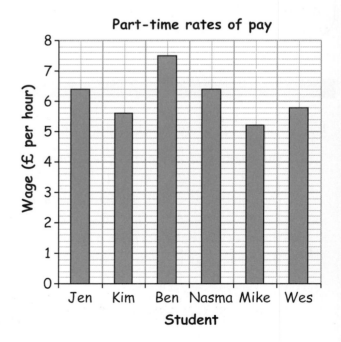

Part-time rates of pay

L2 When data is given in a frequency table it is more difficult to find the mean.

Example

A survey investigates the number of occupants in a block of flats.
The table gives the results.

The mean number of occupants per flat

$$= \frac{\text{total number of occupants}}{\text{total number of flats}}$$

The total number of flats is the sum of the 2nd column, i.e.
$1 + 6 + 12 + 7 + 3 + 0 + 1 = 30$

Number of occupants	Number of flats
0	1
1	6
2	12
3	7
4	3
5	0
6	1

Take care with the number of occupants, the total is **not** just $0 + 1 + 2 + \cdots$
Think about what each row in the table means:

No occupants in 1 flat	= 0 occupants
1 occupant in each of 6 flats	= 6 occupants
2 occupants in each of 12 flats	= 24 occupants
3 occupants in each of 7 flats	= 21 occupants

and so on.

Total number of occupants $= 0 \times 1 + 1 \times 6 + 2 \times 12 + 3 \times 7 + 4 \times 3 + 5 \times 0 + 6 \times 1$
$\qquad\qquad\qquad\qquad\quad = 0 + 6 + 24 + 21 + 12 + 0 + 6 = 69$

A table can be used to show this working neatly.

Here x represents the number of occupants and f, the frequency, is the number of flats.

Mean number of occupants per flat $= \dfrac{69}{30} = \mathbf{2.3}$

x	f	Multiply	xf
0	1	0×1	0
1	6	1×6	6
2	12	2×12	24
3	7	3×7	21
4	3	4×3	12
5	0	5×0	0
6	1	6×1	6
Total	30		69

The method can be written as a formula:

Total number of flats

Total number of occupants

> ▶ **Mean from a frequency table** $= \dfrac{\textbf{Sum of (value} \times \textbf{frequency)}}{\textbf{Sum of frequencies}}$
>
> or in letters $\qquad$ **mean** $= \dfrac{\Sigma\, xf}{\Sigma f}$ $\quad$ where Σ means 'add up'.

6 A trainee secretary has her work checked to see how many errors she makes. The table shows the results for one document she prepares.

   a) How many pages are in the document?
   b) Find the mean number of errors per page.

Number of errors	Number of pages
0	9
1	8
2	0
3	2
4	1

7 A health visitor notes the number of children in each of the families she visits.
The table shows her results.

   a) Find the mean number of children.
   b) How many families had more than the mean number of children?

Number of children	Number of families
1	2
2	8
3	4
4	4
5	1
6	1

8 A rail company records the number of trains on a particular route that arrive late each day.
The table gives the results for June.

   a) Find the mean number of late trains per day.
   b) Five trains travel on this route per day. What % of the trains were late in June?

Number of late trains	Number of days
0	8
1	11
2	9
3	1
4	1

9 The table gives the ages of students on a carpentry course.

   a) How many students are over 20 years old?
   b) Find the mean age.

Age (years)	Number of students
16	5
17	7
18	3
19	4
20	3
21	2
22	1

10 The table below gives the number of goals scored by a football team in home and away matches.

No. of goals		0	1	2	3	4	5	6
No. of games	Home	2	4	3	0	2	0	1
	Away	4	6	0	1	1	0	0

a) Find the mean number of goals scored per match   i) at home   ii) away.

b) Is the team better at scoring goals at home or away?

Find the mode and median
HD1/L2.3

The mean is not the only type of average – there are two others.

> ▶ The **mode** is the **most common value** in a data set.

Sometimes there is more than one mode (when 2 or more values are equally common).
Sometimes there is no mode (when all values occur just once).

> ▶ The **median** is the **middle value** in an ordered list.

If there are two middle values, add them together and divide by 2. This gives the value halfway between them.

Example

The number of tracks on a band's CDs are:

    15   12   14   12   12   14   10   13

Putting these in order gives: ⟵ middle values

    10   12   12 | 12   13 | 14   14   15

The modal number of tracks is **12** – this is the value that occurs most often.

There are 2 middle values, 12 and 13. The median number of CDs is **12.5**.

Also the mean $= \dfrac{10 + 12 + 12 + 12 + 13 + 14 + 14 + 15}{8} = \dfrac{102}{8} = \mathbf{12.75}$

Often one of the averages is a better representative of the data than the others.
In this case the mode is the only average that gives a number of tracks that is possible, so you could argue that the mode is the best average to use.

Some of the advantages and disadvantages of each average are given below:

● The mean has the advantage of **using all the data values**. A disadvantage is that **abnormally high or low data values can make it 'distorted'**. Also the mean is **not usually one of the values in the dataset**.

● The mode is **always one of the values in the dataset**. It is **useful to manufacturers** who want to know the most common size. However, sometimes there is **no mode** or **a lot of modes**. The mode **may be at one end of the distribution**.

● Being in the middle means the median is **not affected by abnormal values**. However, if there are 2 middle values, it **may not be a one of the values in the dataset**.

In the end which average you choose to use will depend on which of these characteristics you think are most important. Opinions may differ about this.

Practice

1 Find the mode, median and mean of each set of data.
Decide which is the best representative value – the mean, the mode or the median.
In each case explain your choice.

a) The number of pints of milk delivered to a house each day in a week:
   2   1   1   0   1   6   0

b) The number of students attending a class each week during a term:
   18   17   17   17   18   16   16   15   12   16

c) The ages of the players on a football team:
   19   18   18   20   29   34   18   18   18   21   19

d) The time taken in minutes by students to complete a test:
   32   28   28   30   27   25   36   27   31   33   30   28

e) Heights of a group of children:
   1.24 m   1.26 m   1.18 m   1.21 m   1.17 m   1.19 m

Find the mode and median for each set of data given in this question:
Find the mean, page 287, question 1

Look back at the scores given for the batsmen in:
Find the mean, page 288, question 2
What happens if you try to find the mode for each batsman?
Find the median for each batsman.
Why do you think the mean is usually used to compare batsmen rather than the median or mode?

▶ To find the **mode** from a **frequency table**, look for the **value with the highest frequency**.

Example

The results of the survey done in a block of flats are shown again in the first two columns of the table below. The **highest frequency** (number of flats) is 12.
This means that the **modal number of occupants per flat** is **2**.
(More flats had 2 occupants than any other number of occupants.)

It is more difficult to find the **median**. It helps if you add another column to the table to show **cumulative frequency**, i.e. a 'running total' of the frequencies.

Number of occupants	Number of flats	Cumulative frequency	
0	1	1	
1	6	7	← 1 + 6 = **7**
2	12	19	← 7 + 12 = **19**
3	7	26	← 19 + 7 = **26**
4	3	29	
5	0	29	
6	1	30	← Total number of flats

There are altogether 30 flats. If the number of occupants for all of these flats were written in a line there would be two middle values – the 15th and 16th.

$$15^{th} \quad 16^{th}$$

0 1 1 1 1 1 1 2 2 2 2 2 2 2 ② ② 2 2 2 3 3 3 3 3 3 3 4 4 4 6

↑ Middle

(Whenever there is an even number of data values, there are two middle values.)

Look at the cumulative frequency column in the table. The 15th and 16th values are both after the 7th value, but before the 19th. This means the 15th and 16th values are both 2. The median is **2 occupants**.

---

2 The table shows the ages of the children left in a creche one morning.

a) Find
  i) the mode
  ii) the median
  iii) the mean.

b) Which value found in part a) do you think is the best representative value?

Age	Number of children
1	1
2	5
3	6
4	8

3 A clothes shop keeps records of the sizes of dresses it
sells. The table shows the results for one style of dress.

Size	Number sold
8	2
10	8
12	10
14	13
16	5
20	2

a) Find
  i) the mode
  ii) the median
  iii) the mean.
b) Which of these averages do you think is most useful
to the shop manager?

Find the mode and median for each set of data given in these questions:
Find the mean, page 288–291, questions 3, 6, 7, 8, 9, 10
Compare your answers with the means you found earlier.
In each question say which average you think is most appropriate and why.

4 In a survey new drivers are asked how many
attempts they needed to pass their driving test.
The table gives the results.

Number of attempts	Number of drivers	
	Men	Women
1	9	7
2	7	8
3	3	2
4	0	2
5	1	1

a) What is the mode for
  i) the men   **ii)** the women?
b) What is the median for
  i) the men   **ii)** the women?
c) Calculate the mean for
  i) the men   **ii)** the women.
d) Which group do you think were the better learners and why?

Find the mean, mode and median for the data given in this question:
Using a bar chart, page 276, question 5
Which of the averages do you think is the best representative? Why?

Find the range

> ▶ **Range = highest value − lowest value**

It gives a measure of how spread out the values are in a set of data.

Example

The table gives the marks achieved
by two students in assignments.

Assignment	1	2	3	4
Bernie	76%	65%	54%	69%
Matt	71%	58%	45%	75%

The range of Bernie's marks = 76% − 54% = 22%
The range of Matt's marks   = 75% − 45% = 30%
Matt's marks are more spread out than Bernie's.
Bernie is the more **consistent** student and Matt is the more **variable**.

Practice

1 The table gives the prices of tins of fruit in a number of supermarkets.

	Penny-Saver	Sam's Store	Low-Price	Super-Food
Apricots	58p	62p	55p	73p
Grapefruit	61p	67p	59p	71p
Peaches	42p	50p	42p	75p
Pineapple	65p	74p	70p	69p

a) Find the price range for each type of fruit.
b) Which type of fruit has
  i)   the most consistent price
  ii) the most variable price?

2 The table below gives the scores of six snooker players in the last ten games they have played.

Player	Scores in the last 10 games									
Alex	38	0	56	83	12	64	21	34	54	71
Cilla	34	56	27	39	42	35	50	76	57	29
Kath	63	19	27	32	60	55	48	85	94	87
Paul	76	58	32	103	67	82	59	147	96	49
Rhona	25	92	147	120	45	62	0	76	15	83
Steve	93	21	47	56	109	74	23	37	88	43

a) Find the mean and range for each player.
b) Who do you think is the best player and why?
c) Who do you think is the most consistent player and why?

Find the range for each set of data given in these questions:
Find the mean, page 287–288, questions 1, 2, 3, 4, 5
Find the mode and median, page 292, question 1

3 A student has drawn the bar chart below to show how long he spent on his computer last week. Each time is shown to the nearest five minutes.

a) Find the mean time per day.
b) Find the range of the times.

L2 You can also find the range from a frequency table, but **take care to use the correct values**.

Example

The results of the survey done in a block of flats are shown again in the table.
The highest number of occupants is 6 and the lowest number is 0.

The range = 6 − 0 = **6**

Note: When the data is given in a frequency table **watch out for zero values** in the frequency column. If the last two values in the second column had been the other way round, the highest number of occupants would have been 5 rather than 6.

Number of occupants	Number of flats
0	1
1	6
2	12
3	7
4	3
5	0
6	1

---

4 A doctor records the number of home visits he makes to patients each day. His results are given in the table.

a) What is the range of the number of visits?
b) What is the modal number of visits?

Number of visits	Number of days
0	0
1	4
2	6
3	10
4	7
5	2
6	1

5 The table shows the ages of the children on a summer camp.

Age (years)	Number of:	
	Boys	Girls
8	3	0
9	5	2
10	12	5
11	6	8
12	5	6
13	2	2
14	0	2
15	1	0

a) What is the range of ages for
   i) boys   ii) girls?
b) What is the modal age for
   i) boys   ii) girls?
c) Use your answers to a) and b) to compare the age distribution of the girls and boys.

Find the range for each set of data given in these questions:
Find the mean, page 291–292, questions 6, 7, 8, 9, 10
Find the mode and median, page 294–295, questions 2, 3, 4

6 The chart shows the number of license penalty points awarded by a court to drivers convicted of driving offences.

a) For the data for men find
   i)   the mode
   ii) the median
   iii) the mean
   iv) the range.
b) Repeat part a) for the women.
c) Compare your results for parts a) and b).

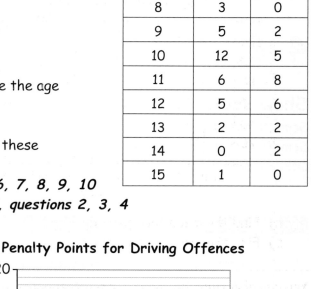

Penalty Points for Driving Offences

Activities

Collect data from your class or from the Internet, teletext, newspapers, etc.
Find and compare averages and ranges. Some suggestions are given below:

From your group: ages, number of pets, heights, time spent on homework, etc.
From other sources: Temperature or rainfall at two or more places
                      Prices of cars of different makes and/or ages.
                      Prices of houses, electrical equipment, CDs, DVDs, etc.

Use a spreadsheet to work out the MODE, MEDIAN, AVERAGE (i.e. MEAN), RANGE.

Handling Data

4 Probability

Show some events are more likely than others HD2/L1.1

Some things are **certain** to happen, e.g. 10 am is certain to come after 9 am.
Some things are **impossible**, e.g. if you empty a bucket the water can't flow uphill.
Other things may or may not happen – these '**events**' may be **likely** or **unlikely**.

Practice

1 Say whether each of these **events** is **impossible**, **unlikely**, **likely** or **certain**.

   a) You will watch television tonight.
   b) You will win a prize with the next raffle ticket you buy.
   c) You will meet a dinosaur on your way home.
   d) It will get dark tonight.
   e) A relative will visit you next week.

Activities

Essential

1 Toss a penny ten times. Record your results in a table like that shown below.
   After each toss work out the % of tosses that have been heads.

Toss number	1	2	3	4	5	6	7	8	9	10
Result										
Total number of heads										
% of heads										

   Compare your results with those of other students in your group.
   Add the number of heads for all the students in your group together.
   Find the % of all the tosses that were heads.

2 Toss a drawing pin ten times. Use a table like that in Activity 1 to record whether the
   drawing pin lands point up or point down. After each toss work out the % of times the
   drawing pin has landed point up. Again compare your results with those of other
   students and find the % of tosses that were point up for the whole group.

3 Throw a dice thirty times and record the results in a tally table. (see p 272)
Work out the % of throws that gave

a) five   **b)** an even number
c) eight   **d)** a number less than 7.

Compare your results with those of other students in your group.
Combine your results. Find for the whole group what % of all the throws gave

a) five   **b)** an even number   **c)** eight   **d)** a number less than 7.

Put the events a, b, c, d in order of how often each occurred, starting with the event that occurred **least** often.

There are six different possibilities when a dice is thrown: 1, 2, 3, 4, 5, 6.
Assuming the dice is **not biased**, the possibilities are all **equally likely**.
One of the six numbers is a 5. We say there is a **1 in 6 chance** of getting a 5.
Three of the numbers are even numbers so there is a **3 in 6 chance** of getting an even number.
There is no 8, so there is a **0 in 6 chance** of getting an 8. It is **impossible**.
All of the numbers are less than 7, so there is a **6 in 6 chance** of getting a number less than 7.
This event is **certain**.

2 **a)** How many possibilities are there when a coin is tossed?
   b) What is the chance of getting a head when you toss a coin?

3 A spinner is numbered 1 to 5 as shown.

   a) When it is spun, what is the chance of getting
      i) 4   **ii)** an even number   **iii)** an odd number?
   b) Which is more likely: an even number or an odd number?

4 A pack of cards is shuffled, then one is picked out at random.

   a) How many possibilities are there?
   b) What is the chance of getting
      i) an ace   **ii)** a diamond   **iii)** the ace of diamonds?

5 The letters of the alphabet are written on pieces of paper and put into a hat.
   A letter is taken out at random.

   a) How many possibilities are there?
   b) What is the chance of getting
      i) Z   **ii)** a vowel (a, e, i, o or u)
      iii) a consonant (i.e. a letter that is not a vowel)?

Use fractions, decimals and % to measure probability   HD2/L1.2

Probability is a measure of how likely something is to happen.
If an event is **impossible** we say the probability is **0**.
If an event is **certain** we say the probability is **1**.

Other events have probabilities between 0 and 1. The probabilities of such events can be written as fractions, decimals or percentages.
To find the fraction use:

> ▶ **Probability of an event** $= \dfrac{\text{Number of ways the event can happen}}{\text{Total number of possibilities}}$

To find the decimal, divide the numerator by the denominator.
To find the %, multiply the decimal by 100, (see page 130.)

Example

When a coin is tossed the probability of a head is $\frac{1}{2}$, **0.5** or **50%**.
You should get a head on about a half, i.e. 50% of the tosses.
Look back at your results from Activity 1 – how near were they to 50%?

> Head is 1 out of 2 possibilities

Example

A set of cards is numbered from 1 to 20. If you take a card at random:

a) the probability of getting 5 is
   1 in 20   or $\frac{1}{20}$ as a fraction   or   0.05 as a decimal   or   5% as a %

b) the probability of getting an odd number (i.e. 1, 3, 5, 7, 9, 11, 13, 15, 17, 19) is
   10 in 20   or $\frac{10}{20} = \frac{1}{2}$ as a fraction   or   0.5 as a decimal   or   50% as a %

c) the probability of getting a number less than 6 (i.e. 1, 2, 3, 4 or 5) is
   5 in 20   or $\frac{5}{20} = \frac{1}{4}$ as a fraction   or   0.25 as a decimal   or   25% as a %

d) the probability of getting 7 or more
   (i.e. 7, 8, 9, 10, 11, 12, 13, 14, 15, 16, 17, 18, 19 or 20) is
   14 in 20   or $\frac{14}{20} = \frac{7}{10}$ as a fraction   or   0.7 as a decimal   or   70% as a %

These probabilities can be shown and compared on a **probability line**:

least likely   P(5)   P(less than 6)   P(odd number)   P(7 or more)   most likely

$$0 \quad \frac{1}{20} \qquad \frac{1}{4} \qquad \frac{1}{2} \qquad \frac{7}{10} \qquad 1$$

Practice

1   A set of cards is numbered from 1 to 10. Suppose you take a card at random.

   a) Find the probability of each event as a fraction, decimal and %.
     i)   getting a 3   **ii)**   getting an odd number
     iii) getting less than 7   **iv)**   getting 8 or more
   b) Show the results on a probability line.

2   **a)** A dice is thrown. What is the probability of getting
     i) 5   **ii)** an even number   **iii)** 8   **iv)** a number less than 7?
     Give each answer as a fraction, a decimal and a %.
   b) Compare the answers with your results from Activity 3.

3   This spinner is numbered 1 to 5.

   a) When it is spun, what is the probability of getting
     i) 4   **ii)** an even number   **iii)** an odd number?
     Give each answer as a fraction, a decimal and a %.
   b) Show the results on a probability line.

4   A pack of cards is shuffled, then one is picked out at random.

   a) Find as fractions (in lowest terms) the probability of getting
     i)   a king   **ii)**   a club   **iii)** the king of clubs
     iv) a red card   **v)**   a red king   **iv)** a jack or queen.
   b) List the events in order of their probabilities, starting with the least likely.

5   Five 2p coins, two 10p coins and a £1 coin are put
   into a bag.
   A coin is taken out at random.

   a) Find as a fraction the probability that it is
     i)   2p   **ii)** 10p   **iii)** £1.
   b) Show the results on a probability line.

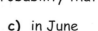

6   In a raffle the tickets are numbered from 1 to 1000.
   All the tickets ending in 0 or 5 win a prize. If you buy a ticket, what is the probability that
   you will get a prize? Give your answer as a decimal and a %.

7   A person says he was born in a leap year. What is the probability that he was born

   a) on Christmas Day   **b)** in January   **c)** in June
   d) in February   **e)** before May 1st?

In some situations the possibilities are not equally likely.
Look at this spinner.
There are 3 numbers but the probability of getting 1 is not $\frac{1}{3}$.
It is $\frac{1}{4}$ because the sector for 1 covers a quarter of the spinner.
If the spinner is spun 40 times, about 10 results should be 1s.

Sometimes you cannot use logic to find probabilities.
For example, suppose you toss a drawing pin. The possibilities for how it lands (point up or point down) are not equally likely. The only way of finding the probability is by doing an experiment like you did in Activity 2.

Data that has been collected can also be used to find probabilities.

Example

In one year, 304 635 boys and 289 999 girls were born in the UK.
The total number of babies was 594 634.

This suggests that   the probability that a baby is a boy $= \dfrac{304\ 635}{594\ 634}$

and   the probability that a baby is a girl $= \dfrac{289\ 999}{594\ 634}$

Use your calculator to write these fractions as %.
You should find that the probability of a boy is 51% and for a girl 49% (nearest %).
These are typical values – usually near 50% with slightly more boys than girls.

---

8 Look at the spinner shown above.

a) What is the probability of getting   **i)** 2   **ii)** 3?
b) Out of 40 spins, how many would you expect to be   **i)** 2   **ii)** 3?

9 **a)** If this spinner is spun, what is the probability of getting
   i) A   **ii)** B   **iii)** C?
   b) Out of 60 spins, how many would you expect to be
   i) A   **ii)** B   **iii)** C?

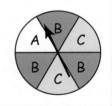

10 The table shows the number of sports accidents that needed hospital treatment during one year.
   a) Find the probability that a sports injury needing hospital treatment is from each category of sport. Give your answers as % to 1 dp.
   b) Interpret your answers to part **a)**.

Sport	No. of accidents
Ball sports	562 656
Combat sports	24 197
Wheel sports	38 757
Winter sports	23 410
Animal sports	22 625
Water sports	25 404
Other	43 020
Total	**740 069**

Identify possible outcomes of combined events

Two events are **independent** if the first has no effect on the second.

For example, when a couple have 2 children, the gender of the first child has no effect on the gender of the second.

Using B to mean boy and G to mean girl, all the possibilities can be shown in a table like this ————————————————————————→

or

in a tree diagram like this. ————————→

Both show that there are 4 possibilities:

BB   boy then another boy
BG   boy then a girl
GB   girl then a boy
GG   girl then another girl.

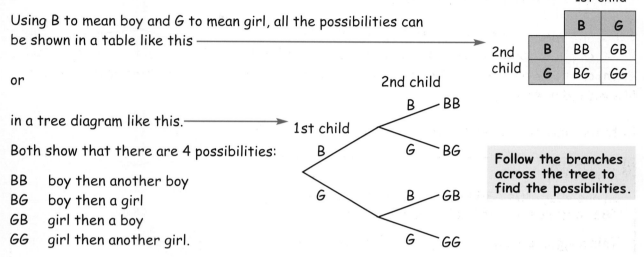

> Follow the branches across the tree to find the possibilities.

If the probability of a boy is about the same as a girl (see page 000), the 4 possibilities for 2 children are also approximately equally likely.

So about a quarter (1 out of 4) of all couples who have 2 children will have 2 boys, a quarter will have 2 girls and a half (2 out of 4) will have one of each.

Practice

1   The table shows all the possibilities when two dice are thrown. The centre of the table shows some of the total scores:
    $1+1=2$, $2+1=3$, $3+6=9$, $6+2=8$

    a) Copy and complete the table.
    b) How many totals are there in the centre of the table?
    c) Write down the probability of each possible total, giving your answers as fractions.
    d) Which total is most likely?

Score on 1st dice

	1	2	3	4	5	6
1	2	3				
2						8
3						
4						
5						
6			9			

Score on 2nd dice

2   Draw up another table like that in question 1. This time multiply the two scores together, instead of adding them. (Multiplying gives the **product** of the scores).
    What is the probability that the product is   **a)** odd   **b)** even?

3 a) Draw a table to show all the possibilities when 2 coins are tossed.

   b) Draw a tree diagram to show all the possibilities when 2 coins are tossed.

   c) What is the probability of getting: **i)** 2 heads   **ii)** the same on each coin?

4 A tree diagram showing the possible genders of 3 children has been started here:

Copy and complete it to show all the possible combinations of genders in a set of triplets.

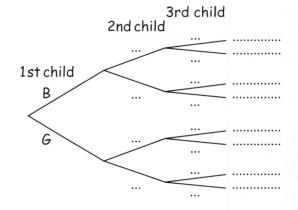

5 a) Draw a tree diagram to show all the possibilities when 3 coins are tossed.

   b) What is the probability of getting

      i) 3 tails   **ii)** 2 tails and 1 head (in any order)?

6 A gardener has bought some white, purple and yellow crocus bulbs, but he does not know which is which.

He plants 2 bulbs.

The tree diagram has been started to show all the possible combinations of colours he could get when his bulbs flower.

a) Copy and complete the diagram.

b) Write a list of all the possible combinations of colours.

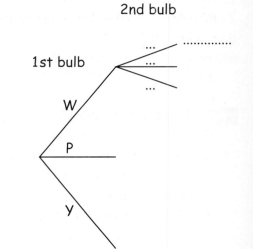

Activities

Use weather statistics to estimate the probability of different types of weather or temperatures or amounts of sunshine.

Find the insurance rates for different ages of car drivers, houses in different areas – link these to accident and crime rates.

Find data about accident rates from government websites and deduce which occupations or activities are the most likely to lead to accidents.

Answers

Number

1 Number Value

Numbers up to 1000 (p 1)

a Place value

1. a) 165   b) 53   c) 212
   d) 403   e) 990   f) 68
   g) 820   h) 7   i) 217
   j) 902

2. a) Two hundred and thirty-six;
   2 hundreds, 3 tens, 6 units
   b) One hundred and five; 1 hundred, 5 units
   c) Six hundred and seventeen;
   6 hundreds, 1 ten, 7 units
   d) Eighty-two; 8 tens, 2 units
   e) Seven hundred and fifty;
   7 hundreds, 5 tens
   f) Five hundred; 5 hundreds
   g) One hundred and twenty-three;
   1 hundred, 2 tens, 3 units
   h) Ninety; 9 tens
   i) Nine hundred and thirty-eight;
   9 hundreds, 3 tens, 8 units
   j) Three hundred and forty-four;
   3 hundreds, 4 tens, 4 units

3.

Planet	Number of days	Planet	Approx number of years
Earth	365	Pluto	248
Mercury	88	Jupiter	12
Mars	687	Neptune	165
Venus	225	Saturn	30
		Uranus	84

4. Mercury, Venus, Earth, Mars, Jupiter, Saturn, Uranus, Neptune, Pluto

b Count in 10s (p 3)

1. a) 41   91   121
   b) 461   501   531   571
   c) 403   443   483   513
2. a) 165   125   85
   b) 576   546   506   466
   c) 119   99   49   9

c Count in 100s (p 4)

1. a) 225   525   725   925
   b) 163   363   663   863
2. a) 782   582   282
   b) 807   607   307   7

d Odd and even numbers (p 4)

1. a)

$1 \times 2 =$	2	$6 \times 2 =$	12	$11 \times 2 =$	22	$16 \times 2 =$	32
$2 \times 2 =$	4	$7 \times 2 =$	14	$12 \times 2 =$	24	$17 \times 2 =$	34
$3 \times 2 =$	6	$8 \times 2 =$	16	$13 \times 2 =$	26	$18 \times 2 =$	36
$4 \times 2 =$	8	$9 \times 2 =$	18	$14 \times 2 =$	28	$19 \times 2 =$	38
$5 \times 2 =$	10	$10 \times 2 =$	20	$15 \times 2 =$	30	$20 \times 2 =$	40

   b) 0, 2, 4, 6 or 8

2. 8   80   180   280   172   754
   466   300   256   312   202

3. 3   209   77   99   403   127
   501   713   19   471   345

4. a) True. 32 and 180 are even.
   b) False. There cannot be as 435 is odd.
   c) True. 500 is even.
   d) Maybe. 1000 is even but each level may not necessarily have the same number of spaces.

Large numbers (p 5)

a Place value

1

		Thousands				
	M	H	T	U	H	T	U
a				2	0	0	0
b			3	2	0	0	0
c		1	6	5	2	0	0
d		1	0	9	8	7	0
e	4	2	0	0	0	0	0
f			9	0	7	5	0
g				8	0	2	5
h		1	1	9	0	0	0
i	6	2	9	9	0	0	0
j	9	0	0	0	3	0	6

2 **a)** Forty-five thousand
  b) Three hundred and seventy-five thousand
  c) Six million, seven hundred thousand
  d) Two hundred and five thousand
  e) Seventy thousand, seven hundred and fifty
  f) One million, two hundred thousand
  g) Five thousand and sixty-five
  h) Twenty thousand, three hundred and six
  i) Forty thousand, three hundred and
     fifty-two
  j) Nine million, six hundred and seventy
     thousand and eighty
  k) Five million, ninety thousand and four
     hundred
  l) Three million, five hundred and three
     thousand, two hundred and forty-one.

3 5 065, 20 306, 40 352, 45 000,
  70 750, 205 000, 375 000
  1 200 000, 3 503 241, 5 090 400,
  6 700 000, 9 670 080

4 **a) b)**

Year	Estimated population
1100	25 000
1300	100 000
1500	50 000
1600	200 000
1801	1 117 000
1851	2 685 000
1939	8 700 000
2000	7 640 000

  c) i) 1300 and 1500
         1939 and 2000
    ii) 1939

Greater than > and less than < (p 7)

1 **a)** $1 < 3$ **b)** $7 > 5$ **c)** $9 > 4$
  d) $0 < 1$
2 **a)** $2 < 8$ **b)** $6 > 1$ **c)** $18 > 13$
  d) $19 < 23$ **e)** $99 < 101$ **f)** $170 > 159$
3 **a)** $269 < 270$
  b) $15\,000 > 2500$
  c) $9\,900 > 7500$
  d) $50\,000 < 75\,000$
  e) $9 < 900$
  f) $10\,500 > 10\,499$
  g) $99\,900 < 100\,000$
  h) $4\,010\,000 > 4\,009\,999$

Positive and negative numbers in practical contexts (p 8)

1 **a)** $-5°C, -2°C, 0°C, 1°C, 4°C, 8°C$
  b) $-10°C, -8°C, -7°C, 6°C, 9°C, 10°C$
  c) $-18°C, -15°C, -10°C, 0°C, 12°C, 20°C$
2 **a)** $9°C, -1°C$
  b) $-16°C, -17°C, -14°C$
  c) $-18°C, -19°C, -17°C$
3 **a)** M Patel   **b)** J Robinson
4 Yes because the account will be £225
  overdrawn, £25 more than the agreed
  overdraft.

Compare numbers of any size (p 9)

1 a) 2 500 000   b) 2 560 000
   c) 1 700 000 000   d) 1 850 000 000
   e) 30 000 000   f) 300 000 000
   g) 1 300 000 000   h) 500 000 000
   i) 250 000

2 a) 2.5 million   b) 5.6 million
   c) 4.75 million   d) 3.8 billion
   e) 2.95 billion   f) 1.05 billion
   g) 20 million   h) 600 million
   i) 34.5 million   or 0.6 billion

3 £22 600 000,   £17 900 000
   £14 100 000,   £14 000 000

4 a) i)   Company B
    ii)   Company C
    iii)   Company B
   b) i)   Companies C, E and G
    ii)   Company E

2 Addition and Subtraction

Three-digit numbers

a Add in columns (p 11)

1 a) 379   b) 779   c) 496
   d) 489   e) 780   f) 672
   g) 394   h) 787   i) 500
   j) 318   k) 946   l) 305
   m) 400   n) 931   o) 621
   p) 610

2 a) 989   b) 472   c) 241

3 341 employees
4 440 photocopies
5 350 miles
6 482 boxes
7 £795
8 £326
9 215 tickets

b Add in your head (p 12)

1 a) 57   b) 57   c) 69
   d) 43   e) 72   f) 63
   g) 85   h) 98

2 a) 241   b) 181   c) 398
   d) 387   e) 208   f) 185
   g) 406   h) 246   i) 362
   j) 301   k) 568   l) 538
   m) 574   n) 371   o) 501
   p) 493

c Subtract in columns (p 14)

1 a) 211   b) 321   c) 200
   d) 515   e) 309   f) 227
   g) 70   h) 31   i) 153
   j) 199   k) 179   l) 67
   m) 245   n) 69   o) 299
   p) 501   q) 329   r) 299

2 a) 387   b) 97   c) 698

3 325 envelopes
4 £324
5 127 more men
6 £106
7 163 miles

d Subtract in your head (p 16)

1 a) 23   b) 16   c) 28
   d) 56   e) 19   f) 42
   g) 37   h) 34

2 a) 149   b) 199   c) 149
   d) 622   e) 401   f) 205
   g) 206   h) 199   i) 326
   j) 490   k) 157   l) 699
   m) 199   n) 299   o) 709
   p) 294

Add and subtract large numbers (p 16)

1 a) 52 359   b) 39 505
   c) 28 595   d) 160 499
   e) 3 740 000   f) 6 527 500
   g) 312 089   h) 212 475
   i) 1 525 500   j) 895 276
   k) 363 250   l) 296 350

2 23 868 miles
3 £47 762
4 1 332 000 people
5 1 734 miles
6 £1 186 400

7 a) £65 150   **b)** £934 850

8 a) 1 068 181   **b)** 250 235

Add and subtract numbers of any size (p 18)

1 a) 4.9°C   **b)** 4.7°C

c) 4.8°C   **d)** 0.7°C

2 a) 3.5 million   **b)** 2.6 million

c) £1 113 500 million   **d)** £6.5 billion

e) £2.25 billion   **f)** £2.41 billion

3 £2.19 million

4

Outlet	Total Profit (£ million)
A	4.7
B	−0.8
C	10.7
D	−4.4
Total	10.2

b) i) £0.4 million

ii) £0.8 million

iii) £1.2 million

iv) £5.5 million

v) £15.1 million

vi) £3.6 million

D **lost** £3.6 million more than B

3 Multiplication and Division

Recall multiplication facts (p 19)

1 a) 15   **b)** 80   **c)** 14   **d)** 16

e) 25   **f)** 18   **g)** 36   **h)** 42

i) 81   **j)** 32   **k)** 48   **l)** 63

m) 64   **n)** 28   **o)** 49   **p)** 54

2 a) i) 2, 4, 6, 8, 0

ii) 30, 50, 86, 162, 204, 318

b) i) 5, 0

ii) 65, 80, 100, 115, 125

c) They add up to 3, 6 and 9

d) They all add up to 9

As the digit in the tens column increases by 1 the digit in the units column decreases by 1

3 a) 60   **b)** 200   **c)** 360

d) 350   **e)** 270   **f)** 280

g) 540   **h)** 720   **i)** 640

j) 630   **k)** 480   **l)** 810

Multiplication methods (p 22)

1 a) 48   **b)** 93   **c)** 88   **d)** 126

e) 105   **f)** 172   **g)** 260   **h)** 450

i) 234   **j)** 448   **k)** 304   **l)** 534

m) 616   **n)** 441   **o)** 485   **p)** 837

2 60 rings

3 75 plates

4 180 minutes

5 £259

6 161 rooms

7 378 pages

8 425 miles

9 600 grams

Division

a Different ways (p 23)

1 a) 5   **b)** 5   **c)** 4   **d)** 7

e) 4   **f)** 5   **g)** 9   **h)** 7

i) 6 r 1   **j)** 4 r 2   **k)** 6 r 1   **l)** 5 r 3

m) 7 r 1   **n)** 6 r 3   **o)** 6 r 6   **p)** 8 r 3

2 £5 each

3 £8 per length

4 9p per pencil

5 8 tins

6 7 sweets (with 2 sweets left over)

7 6 cars (with 2 spare seats)

8 5 teams (with 4 players left over)

9 7 tables (with 2 spare seats)

10 2 trays left over (they get 6 each)

b Standard method (p 25)

1 a) 24   **b)** 33   **c)** 40

d) 12   **e)** 15   **f)** 23

g) 13   **h)** 19   **i)** 29

j) 29 r 1   **k)** 18 r 2   **l)** 12 r 2

m) 12 r 3   **n)** 17 r 2   **o)** 31 r 2

p) 14 r 5

2 18 doses

3 12 patients

4 £17

5 £25

6 14 metres

7 a) 12 trays   **b)** 3 plants

8   14 adults

9   2 pens

Multiply and divide whole numbers by 10 and 100

a Multiply by 10 and 100 in your head (p 26)

1   a) 130   b) 750   c) 1360

     d) 2020   e) 900   f) 1900

     g) 1200   h) 3700   i) 12 900

     j) 12 000   k) 30 300   l) 12 300

2   500 pence

3   200 ten pence coins

4   660 millimetres

5   1 500 centimetres

6   2 500 envelopes

7   £450

8   500 disks

9   £2 500

b Divide by 10 and 100 in your head (p 28)

1   a) 46   b) 460   c) 46   d) 460

     e) 53   f) 530   g) 53   h) 530

     i) 990   j) 75   k) 5 700   l) 38

2   £120

3   15p

4   72 centimetres

5   240 metres

6   2 750 boxes

7   350 boxes

8   176 calls

9   15 people

Use multiplication and division (p 28)

1   a) 28   b) 30   c) 10   d) 6

     e) 4   f) 63   g) 9   h) 6

     i) 8   j) 8   k) 9   l) 48

2   10 two pence coins

3   9 boxes

4   £9

5   £63

6   9 boxes

7   8 weeks

8   40 hours

9   £8 an hour

Recognise numerical relationships

a Multiples (p 29)

1   a) 12, 32, 40

     b) 21, 42, 70

     c) 12, 24

     d) 10, 30

2   a) 6, 12, 18, 24, 30, 36, 42, 48, 54, 60, 66,
         72, 78, 84, 90, 96

     b) 8, 16, 24, 32, 40, 48, 56, 64, 72, 80, 88, 96

     c) 9, 18, 27, 36, 45, 54, 63, 72, 81, 90, 99

b Square numbers (p 30)

1   1, 4, 9, 16, 25, 36, 49, 64, 81, 100
     (diagonal line from top left to bottom right)

2   9, 25, 49, 81, 100

c Use mental arithmetic to multiply multiples of 10 (p 30)

1   a) 90   b) 240   c) 140   d) 450

     e) 480   f) 270   g) 1400   h) 2000

     i) 4200   j) 3500   k) 3600   l) 7200

2   £100

3   800 words

4   £1200

5   300 people

6   2400 people

7   2700 kilograms

8   1500 people

9   3600 seconds

Multiply and divide large numbers

a Multiply large numbers (p 33)

1   a) 1025   b) 1920   c) 2236

     d) 2790   e) 2128   f) 1247

     g) 4368   h) 2508   i) 2520

     j) 3015   k) 2430   l) 3087

     m) 4305   n) 29 704   o) 12 825

     p) 27 360   q) 32 256   r) 12 978

     s) 67 968   t) 27 504

2   £720

3   1680 tins

4   £1134

5   1116 children

6   4080 seats

7 7000 miles

8 9125 cigarettes

9 31 025 days old

b Divide large numbers (p 34)

1 a) 985   b) 405   c) 881
   d) 3652   e) 4 210   f) 6 825
   g) 1813 r 4   h) 10 416 r 4
   i) 8375 r 2   j) 8158 r 2
   k) 5555 r 5   l) 20 056 r 1

2 250 people

3 £225

4 3221 tickets

5 4250 boxes

6 5200 samples

7 £22 500

8 £62 500

9 a) 42   b) 52   c) 45   d) 37
   e) 13   f) 25   g) 65   h) 136

10 a) £2040   b) £1250
    c) £2930   d) £3582

Efficient methods of calculating with numbers of any size

a Multiples, factors and prime numbers (p 36)

1 a) 98, 364, 720
   b) 165, 720, 945, 25 245
   c) 165, 243, 720, 945, 25 245
   d) 243, 720, 945, 25 245

2 a) 15   b) 12   c) 6   d) 7

3 a) 3, 6 and 12   b) 3 and 9

4 a) 5   b) 29

5 3

b Calculations with numbers of any size (p 37)

1 a) £300   b) £90   c) £36

2 42 000 statements

3 £150 000

4 128 000 people

5 £1 500 000

6 £300 000

7 £2 900 000

8 6.5 million

9 £375 000 or £0.375 million

10 £2.16 million

4 Rounding and Estimation

Approximation and estimation (numbers up to 1000)

a When to estimate (p 40)

1 a) Yes   b) No   c) Yes   d) No
   e) No   f) Yes   g) Yes   h) No
   i) Yes   j) No

b Round to the nearest 10 and 100 (p 41)

1 a) 40   b) 20   c) 20   d) 90
   e) 140   f) 220   g) 420   h) 990
   i) 410   j) 100   k) 700   l) 310
   m) 240   n) 180   o) 370   p) 710
   q) 370   r) 810   s) 900   t) 280

2 a) 200   b) 400   c) 600   d) 900
   e) 200   f) 400   g) 600   h) 900
   i) 400   j) 200   k) 800   l) 700
   m) 900   n) 1000   o) 200   p) 400
   q) 900   r) 800   s) 300   t) 100

c Use estimates to check calculations (p 43)

1 a) £70 + £30 = £100
      so answer is probably incorrect
   b) £160 − £70 = £90
      so answer is probably correct
   c) £70 + £60 = £130
      so answer is probably correct
   d) £90 ÷ £30 = 3
      so answer is probably incorrect
   e) £85 − £25 = £60 (or £90 − £30 = £60)
      so answer is probably correct
   f) 10 × £25 = £250
      so answer is probably correct
   g) £160 × 3 = £480
      so answer is probably incorrect
   h) £160 − £120 = £40
      so answer is probably incorrect

2 a) 889   b) 126

3 a) £338   b) £736   c) £858

Approximate and estimate with large numbers

a Round to the nearest 1000, 10 000, 100 000, 1 000 000 (p 45)

1 a) 5000   b) 7000
   c) 27 000   d) 31 000
   e) 256 000   f) 105 000
   g) 951 000   h) 1 366 000

2 a) 30 000   b) 50 000
   c) 150 000   d) 210 000
   e) 770 000   f) 230 000
   g) 680 000   h) 1 910 000

3 a) 500 000   b) 300 000
   c) 1 500 000   d) 4 600 000
   e) 1 700 000   f) 2 800 000
   g) 2 000 000   h) 12 800 000

4 a) 3 000 000   b) 3 000 000
   c) 7 000 000   d) 16 000 000
   e) 4 000 000   f) 2 000 000

5 a) 3 000 000 unemployed
   b) 7000 job losses
   c) 13 000 people attend charity event
       (or 12 800)
   d) £2 000 000 lottery win
   e) 4700 new jobs created (or 5000)
   f) 3 000 000 copies of record sold
   g) £21 000 000 profits for company
   h) 280 000 people to benefit
       (or 300 000)

b Use estimates to check calculations (p 46)

(Note there are alternative methods)

1 a) True
       500 000 – 200 000 = 300 000
   b) False
       100 000 × 2 doesn't equal 600 000
   c) True
       130 000 × 3 = 390 000
   d) False
       170 000 – 90 000 doesn't equal nearly
       200 000
   e) True
       620 000 + 35 000 = 655 000

   f) True
       500 000 + 150 000 = 650 000
   g) False
       167 000 + 20 000 = 187 000

2 a)

Income	Total £
2976 tickets @ £25 each *Check: Round 2976 to 3000 25 × 3 = 75 gives 75 000*	74 400
2204 tickets @ £12 each *Check: Round 2204 to 2000 12 × 2 = 24 gives 24 000*	26 448
1008 progs. @ £3 each *Check: 3 × 1 000 = 3 000*	3024
592 mugs @ £8 each *Check: Round 592 to 600 8 × 6 = 48 gives 4800*	4736
Total *Check:* $\frac{74+26}{100} + 3 + 5$ *= 108 thousand*	108 608

Expenditure	Total £
Hire of venue and insurance	17 750
Publicity and printing	4899
8 technicians @ £489 *Check: Round £489 to £500 8 × 500 = 40 × 100 = 4000*	3912
50 security staff @ £175 each *Check: Round £175 to £200 50 × 200 = 100 × 100 = 10 000*	8750
Performers	0
Total *Check* $\frac{18+5}{23} + 4 + 9$ *= 36 thousand*	35 311

   b) Income   108 608 –
       Expenditure   35 311
       Money Raised   £73 297
       Check 110 – 35 = 75 thousand

Use estimates to check calculations with numbers of any size (p 48)

1   Between 1935 and 1945

   $1\,585 - 912.33 = 672.67$ million

   $\qquad\qquad = 672\,670\,000$ increase

   check 1600 million – 900 million

   = 700 million

   Between 1945 and 1955

   $1\,585 - 1\,181.8 = 403.2$ million

   $\qquad\qquad = 403\,200\,000$ decrease

   check 1600 million – 1200 million

   = 400 million

   Between 1955 and 1965

   $1\,181.8 - 326.6 = 855.2$ million decrease

   $\qquad\qquad = 855\,200\,000$ decrease

   check 1200 million – 300 million

   = 900 million

   Between 1965 and 1975

   $326.6 - 116.3 = 210.3$ million

   $\qquad\qquad = 210\,300\,000$ decrease

   check 300 million – 100 million

   = 200 million

   Between 1975 and 1985

   $116.3 - 72 = 44.3$ million

   $\qquad\qquad = 44\,300\,000$ decrease

   Check 120 million – 70 million

   = 50 million

   Between 1985 and 1995

   $114.56 - 72 = 42.56$ million

   $\qquad\qquad = 42\,560\,000$ increase

   Check 110 million – 70 million

   = 40 million

2   a)   £21 498 081

   b)   £9 000 000 + 9 × £100 000

       + 700 × £2000

       + £30 000 × £70

       + £800 000 × £10

       = £21 400 000 (or alternatives)

5 Ratio and Proportion

Work with ratio and proportion

a Ratios (p 50)

1   a)   200 mℓ   b) 400 mℓ   c)   1000 mℓ = 1 ℓ

2   a)   1500 mℓ or 1.5 litres

   b)   3000 mℓ or 3 litres

   c)   No, $800 + 4\,800 = 5\,600$ mℓ

3

		Cement	Sand
Standard mortar		5 kg	25 kg
		10 kg	50 kg
		15 kg	75 kg
Strong mortar		3 kg	9 kg
		12 kg	36 kg
		20 kg	60 kg

b Direct proportion (p 51)

1   a)   i)   300 mℓ milk   4 tsp caster sugar

             900 g plain flour   4 tsp dried yeast

             300 mℓ plain yogurt 1 tsp salt

             2 eggs   2 tsp baking powder

                                4 tbls veg. oil

         ii)   75 mℓ milk   1 tsp caster sugar

             225 g plain flour   1 tsp dried yeast

             75 mℓ plain yogurt $\frac{1}{4}$ tsp salt

             1 small egg $\frac{1}{2}$ tsp baking powder

                                1 tbls veg. oil

   b)   50 mℓ milk, 150 g plain flour

       50 mℓ plain yogurt

2   a)   8 teaspoons   b)   2 teaspoons

   c)   1 teaspoon

3   a)   i)   500 mℓ (or 0.5 litres or $\frac{1}{2}$ litre)

       ii)   200 mℓ (or 0.2 litres or $\frac{1}{5}$ litre)

       iii)   100 mℓ (or 0.1 litres or $\frac{1}{10}$ litre)

   b)   i)   2 litres water : 5000 g or 5 kg plaster

       ii)   4 litres water : 10 000 g or 10 kg

         plaster

Calculate ratio and direct proportion

a Simplify ratios and find amounts (p 53)

1   a)   2 : 3   b)   1 : 5   c)   14 : 1

   d)   2 : 9   e)   3 : 1   f)   4 : 1 : 6

   g)   2 : 3 : 5   h)   33 : 18 : 10

2 a) i) $1:4$ ii) 400 mℓ

  b) i) $2:3$ ii) 600 mℓ

3 a) i) $50:450:500 = 1:9:10$

   ii)   720 mℓ moss, 800 mℓ leaf green

   iii) 200 mℓ white, 2000 mℓ (2 ℓ) leaf green

  b) i) $200:300:500 = 2:3:5$

   ii)   120 mℓ beige, 200 mℓ chocolate brown

   iii) 120 mℓ white, 300 mℓ chocolate brown

   iv)   300 mℓ white, 450 mℓ beige

4 a) $3:100$ b) $5:4$ c) $1:4$

  d) $13:2$ e) $1:50\,000$ f) $40:7$

  g) $1:2:9$ h) $4:2:2:3$

5 a) $50:4\,000 = 1:80$

  b) 3200 mℓ or 3.2 ℓ c) 30 mℓ

6 a) $1500\ g:400\ g:200\ g = 15:4:2$

  b) i)   150 g cereal, 40 g nuts

   ii)   160 g nuts, 80 g seeds

7 a) 500 m   b) 1 km

b Make a total amount (p 55)

1 a) 200 mℓ orange squash, 800 mℓ water

  b) 300 mℓ orange squash, 1200 mℓ water

2 a) 1 litre Tangerine, 1 litre White,

   3 litres Buttercup

  b) 200 mℓ Tangerine, 200 mℓ White,

   600 mℓ Buttercup

3 a) $12:5:3$

  b) i)   480 g cereal, 200 g fruit, 120 g nuts

   ii)   1080 g cereal, 450 g fruit, 270 g nuts

4 a) $15\,000:45\,000:150\,000$

   $1:3:10$

  b) 30 Afro Caribbean, 90 Asian and 300 white people

5 a) $4000:10\,000:16\,000 = 2:5:8$

  b) A £6000, B £15 000, C £24 000

  c) £75 000

  d) £187 500

  e) A £41 000, B £102 500, C £164 000

c Use ratios to compare prices (p 57)

1 a) Pack of 9   b) 600 mℓ bottle

  c) 350 g box   d) 100 envelopes

  e) 24 tins

2 a) 0.5 tonne @ £17.50 = £35 per tonne

   1 tonne @ £32.50 = £32.50 per tonne

   5 tonnes @ £120 = £24 per tonne

   25 kg @ £1.75 = £70 per tonne

   40 kg @ £2.50 = £62.50 per tonne

   5 kg @ £1.50 = £300 per tonne

  b) £7   c) 12p

6 Using Formulae

Evaluate expressions and make substitutions in formulae (p 58)

1 a) i)   Total cost =

     number of delegates $\times$ £15 + £75

   ii) $T = 15d + 75$

  b) i) £225   ii) £375   iii) £825

2 a) $C = 50w + 25$

  b) i)   125 mins (or 2 hrs 5 mins)

   ii)   150 mins (or $2\frac{1}{2}$ hours)

   iii)   65 mins (or 1 hour 5 mins)

3 a) $F = 0.8m + 2$

  b) i) £6   ii) £11.60   iii) £16

4 a) $P = 2.5a + 180$

  b) i) £190   ii) £205   iii) £217.50

5 a) i) £40   ii) £80   iii) £430

  b) £0.05 is the cost per extra card i.e. 5p

  c) The overall cost per card decreases

6 a) 19   b) 0   c) 20   d) 16

  e) 16   f) 6   g) 24   h) 22

  i) 17

7 a) 50 metres   b) 27 metres

8 a) $P = 6t + 5n$

  b) i) £63   ii) £115   iii) £300

9 a) £81 000   b) £ 114 000

  c) £195 000   d) £278 850

10 120 volts

11 a) 60 miles per hour

  b) 0.4 km per min

   (or 400 m per min or 24 km per hour)

12 a) $C = 10 + n(E + 18)$ or $C = n(E + 18) + 10$

  b) i) £79   ii) £135   iii) £223.75

13 a) 18 cm^2 b) 68 cm^2

  c) 10.5 cm^2 d) 285 cm^2

14 a) 100°C   b) 25°C

7 Mixed Operations and Calculator Practice

Solve problems (p 63)

1 576
2 £156
3 a) 786   b) 22
4 a) £468   b) £533
5 a) £895   b) £447.50
6 a) £153   b) £571
7 a) 270   b) 9
8 a) 5 × 5 litre tins and 1 × 2 litre tin
   b) 7 × 5 litre tins and 2 × 2 litre tins
   c) 25 × 5 litre tins, 1 × 2 litre tin and
       1 × 1 litre tin
9 a) 4 packs of 10
   b) 1 pack of 50 and 1 pack of 25
   c) 5 packs of 50 and 1 pack of 25
   d) 7 packs of 50 and 1 pack of 10
10 a) £11   b) £30
11 a) 3 packs of 2 (one pack is free) £6
   b) 4 packs of 2 (one pack is free) £9
   c) 1 pack of 10 £10
   d) 6 packs of 2 (2 packs are free) £12
12 a) £65   2 × £25 and 1 × £15
   b) £100   1 × £25 and 5 × £15
   c) £90   1 × £75 and 1 × £15
   d) £200   8 × £25
   e) £180   2 × £75 and 2 × £15
   f) £190   2 × £75, 1 × £25, 1 × £15

Calculate efficiently (p 66)

1 a) Part-time receptionist by £200 a year
   b) Warehouse assistant by £600 a year
2 a) i) £488   ii) £1 324   iii) £1 776
   b) £292
   c) £972
   d) i) 12 nights   ii) 6 nights

Calculate efficiently with numbers of any size (p 67)

1 55.6°C
2 £0.91 million

3 25th Feb £582.81 out
   26th Feb £817.11 out
   27th Feb £2778.86 in
   28th Feb £2097.68 out
4 1st quarter £20.05 in credit
   2nd quarter £18.65 in debit
   3rd quarter £16.75 in debit
   4th quarter £10.10 in credit

5 b)

Year	Profit £
1995	1 200 000
1996	700 000
1997	−300 000
1998	−550 000
1999	−100 000
2000	−1 000 000
2001	−500 000
2002	0
2003	500 000

   c) i) £2 200 000   ii) −£50 000

8 Fractions

Understand fractions (p 69)

a Fractions in words, numbers and sketches

1 a) $\frac{1}{3}$ b) $\frac{2}{5}$ c) $\frac{3}{8}$ d) $\frac{5}{12}$
2 a) one half   b) two thirds
   c) three quarters   d) three fifths
   e) five eighths   f) seven ninths
3 a) $\frac{1}{4}$, one quarter   b) $\frac{1}{5}$, one fifth
   c) $\frac{1}{9}$, one ninth   d) $\frac{5}{6}$, five sixths
   e) $\frac{2}{3}$, two thirds   f) $\frac{5}{8}$, five eighths
   g) $\frac{4}{7}$, four sevenths h) $\frac{7}{12}$, seven twelfths
   i) $\frac{4}{9}$, four ninths

b Shade fractions (p 70)

1 b, c
2 b, d

3 a)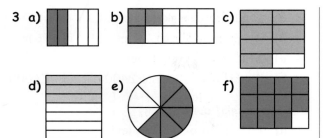
d) e) f)

or alternatives with the same number of sections shaded.

4 Fractions shown on students' own shapes

c Read about fractions (p 71)

1 half $\frac{1}{2}$, one third $\frac{1}{3}$

2 quarter $\frac{1}{4}$, three quarters $\frac{3}{4}$,
one and a half $1\frac{1}{2}$, half $\frac{1}{2}$

3 two thirds $\frac{2}{3}$, a third $\frac{1}{3}$

4 a third $\frac{1}{3}$, a quarter $\frac{1}{4}$, one and a half $1\frac{1}{2}$,
half $\frac{1}{2}$, one fifth $\frac{1}{5}$, three quarters $\frac{3}{4}$,
half $\frac{1}{2}$, three fifths $\frac{3}{5}$, a third $\frac{1}{3}$

Equivalent fractions (p 72)

a Use sketches

1 a) $\frac{1}{2} = \frac{2}{4} = \frac{3}{6}$ b) $\frac{1}{5} = \frac{2}{10}$
c) $\frac{3}{4} = \frac{6}{8} = \frac{9}{12}$ d) $\frac{3}{5} = \frac{12}{20}$

2 Students' own sketches

b Find the missing number (p 73)

1 4   2 8   3 3   4 6
5 10   6 8   7 12   8 25
9 1   10 1   11 2   12 7
13 3   14 5   15 3   16 6
17 a) 14, 21
   b) any 2 other fractions equal to $\frac{1}{7}$
18 a) 15, 45
   b) any 2 other fractions equal to $\frac{5}{7}$
19 a) any 3 other fractions equal to $\frac{3}{8}$
   b) any 3 other fractions equal to $\frac{2}{5}$
   c) any 3 other fractions equal to $\frac{4}{11}$
   d) any 3 other fractions equal to $\frac{7}{9}$
20 2, 4, 5, 7, 11, 15, 20, 100

c Find equivalent fractions in a list (p 74)

1 $\frac{2}{4}, \frac{3}{6}, \frac{6}{12}, \frac{5}{10}, \frac{4}{8}$
2 a) $\frac{6}{18}, \frac{4}{12}, \frac{5}{15}, \frac{2}{6}, \frac{3}{9}$ b) $\frac{6}{9}, \frac{8}{12}, \frac{4}{6}, \frac{12}{18}, \frac{10}{15}$

3 a) $\frac{2}{8}, \frac{5}{20}, \frac{3}{12}, \frac{4}{16}$ b) $\frac{12}{16}, \frac{9}{12}, \frac{15}{20}, \frac{6}{8}$

4 a) 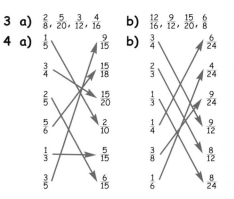   b)

d Write quantities as fractions (p 75)

1 a) $\frac{1}{2}$ cm   b) $\frac{2}{5}$ cm   c) $\frac{3}{5}$ cm
2 a) $\frac{1}{2}$ kg   b) $\frac{3}{4}$ kg   c) $\frac{1}{10}$ kg
   d) $\frac{1}{5}$ kg   e) $\frac{3}{5}$ kg
3 a) $\frac{1}{200}$ km   b) $\frac{1}{20}$ km   c) $\frac{1}{2}$ km
   d) $\frac{1}{10}$ km   e) $\frac{3}{20}$ km
4 a) $\frac{1}{50}\ell$ b) $\frac{1}{20}\ell$ c) $\frac{1}{5}\ell$
   d) $\frac{1}{2}\ell$ e) $\frac{2}{5}\ell$
5 a) $\frac{1}{5}$ m   b) $\frac{1}{2}$ m   c) $\frac{9}{10}$ m
   d) $\frac{4}{5}$ m   e) $\frac{1}{20}$ m   f) $\frac{1}{10}$ m
   g) $\frac{1}{5}$ m   h) $\frac{2}{5}$ m   i) $\frac{3}{5}$ m
   j) $\frac{1}{50}$ m

Compare fractions and mixed numbers

a Use fraction walls (p 76)

1 a) 2   b) 4   c) 8   d) 6
   e) 12   f) 6   g) 10   h) 14
2 a) $\frac{5}{16}, \frac{3}{8}, \frac{7}{16}$ b) $\frac{1}{2}, \frac{9}{16}, \frac{5}{8}$ c) $\frac{3}{4}, \frac{13}{16}, \frac{7}{8}$
3 a) 5, 10   b) 5   c) 2   d) 4
   e) 6   f) 10
4 $\frac{9}{10}, \frac{4}{5}, \frac{7}{10}, \frac{3}{5}, \frac{1}{2}, \frac{2}{5}, \frac{3}{10}, \frac{1}{5}, \frac{1}{10}$

b Compare fractions (p 77)

1 a) $\frac{1}{8}$ b) $\frac{1}{10}$ c) $\frac{1}{20}$ d) $\frac{1}{12}$
2 a) $\frac{1}{20}$ b) $\frac{1}{17}$ c) $\frac{1}{5}$ d) $\frac{1}{11}$
3 $\frac{1}{20}, \frac{1}{15}, \frac{1}{12}, \frac{1}{10}, \frac{1}{6}, \frac{1}{5}, \frac{1}{4}, \frac{1}{3}, \frac{1}{2}$
4 $\frac{1}{7}, \frac{1}{8}, \frac{1}{9}, \frac{1}{11}, \frac{1}{13}, \frac{1}{14}, \frac{1}{16}, \frac{1}{17}, \frac{1}{21}$
5 a) $\frac{3}{4}$ b) $\frac{1}{2}$ c) $\frac{2}{5}$ (with sketches)
6 a) $\frac{1}{2}$ b) $\frac{3}{5}$ c) $\frac{3}{4}$ (with sketches)
7 $\frac{3}{10}, \frac{2}{5}, \frac{3}{7}, \frac{1}{2}, \frac{3}{4}$

c Improper fractions and mixed numbers (p 78)

1 a) $1\frac{1}{2} = \frac{3}{2}$ b) $1\frac{4}{5} = \frac{9}{5}$
   c) $2\frac{3}{10} = \frac{23}{10}$ d) $3\frac{5}{6} = \frac{23}{6}$
   e) $1\frac{7}{9} = \frac{16}{9}$ f) $2\frac{3}{8} = \frac{19}{8}$

2 Mixed numbers and improper fractions on students' own shapes.

3 a) Mixed numbers and fractions on students' own shapes.

  b) $\frac{5}{8}, \frac{3}{4}, \frac{7}{8}, 1\frac{1}{4}, 1\frac{3}{8}, 1\frac{1}{2}, 2\frac{1}{8}$

d Find or Estimate fractions (p 79)

1 a) i) $\frac{1}{2}$ **ii)** $\frac{1}{2}$ **b) i)** $\frac{1}{3}$ **ii)** $\frac{2}{3}$
  c) i) $\frac{3}{4}$ **ii)** $\frac{1}{4}$

2 a) $\frac{4}{5}$ full   **b)** $\frac{3}{5}$ full   **c)** $\frac{2}{5}$ full

3 a) $\frac{1}{2}$ full   **b)** $\frac{2}{3}$ full   **c)** $\frac{3}{4}$ full

4 a) $\frac{3}{5}$ left   **b)** $\frac{1}{3}$ left   **c)** $\frac{1}{5}$ left

5 a) i) $\frac{1}{4}$ **ii)** $\frac{3}{4}$ **b) i)** $\frac{1}{3}$ **ii)** $\frac{2}{3}$
  c) i) $\frac{2}{3}$ **ii)** $\frac{1}{3}$ **d) i)** $\frac{5}{6}$ **ii)** $\frac{1}{6}$

Find a fraction of something

a By dividing when the numerator is 1 (p 81)

1 a) £28   **b)** 24 cm   **c)** £91
  d) £250   **e)** £21   **f)** £156
  g) 72 m   **h)** £286

2 12

3 a) £15   **b)** £30

4 a) 14   **b)** 56

5 15 litres

6 £85

7 a) 3500   **b)** 17 500

8 a) 125 g   **b)** 875 g

b Finding more than one part (p 82)

1 a) £630   **b)** £104   **c)** 30 m
  d) 150 g   **e)** 350 cm   **f)** £460
  g) £1800   **h)** 1460 kg

2 240

3 18

4 £33 750

5 31 050

6 165

7 £5750

8 360 000

c By combining unit fractions (p 83)

1 a) £1140   **b)** 42 kg   **c)** 324 m

2 a) Students' own sketches
  b) i) £480   **ii)** £120   **iii)** £600

3 a) Students' own sketches
  b) i) 64 m   **ii)** 32 m   **iii)** 96 m

4 a) Students' own sketches
  b) i) £3600   **ii)** £2400   **iii)** £6000

d Scale up and down (p 84)

1 a) 180 g potatoes, 300 g leeks,
      500 mℓ milk, 100 mℓ stock
  b) 360 g potatoes, 600 g leeks,
      1 ℓ or 1000 mℓ milk, 200 mℓ stock

2 a) $\frac{3}{4}$ **b)** 300 g nuts, 150 g breadcrumbs,
              180 g tomatoes, 3 onions

3 a) $\frac{4}{5}$ **b)** 240 g flour, 128 g sugar,
              112 g butter, 48 g ground almonds

4 a) 3 loaves, 600 g butter, 6 tomatoes,
      $1\frac{1}{2}$ cucumbers, 300 g pate, 225 g chicken,
      375 g cheese, $\frac{3}{4}$ lettuce
  b) 5 loaves, 1 kg or 1000 g butter,
      10 tomatoes, $2\frac{1}{2}$ cucumbers, 500 g pate,
      375 g chicken, 625 g cheese, $1\frac{1}{4}$ lettuce

Put fractions in order
(using a common denominator) (p 85)

1 a) $\frac{2}{3}$ **b)** $\frac{7}{9}$ **c)** $\frac{9}{10}$

2 a) $\frac{2}{5}, \frac{3}{5}, \frac{4}{5}$ **b)** $\frac{1}{7}, \frac{2}{7}, \frac{4}{7}, \frac{5}{7}$
  c) $\frac{1}{9}, \frac{2}{9}, \frac{4}{9}, \frac{5}{9}, \frac{8}{9}$

3 a) $\frac{1}{4}$ **b)** $\frac{3}{5}$ **c)** $\frac{3}{4}$ **d)** $\frac{4}{7}$

4 a) $\frac{3}{8}, \frac{1}{2}, \frac{5}{8}$ **b)** $\frac{1}{4}, \frac{3}{10}, \frac{2}{5}$
  c) $\frac{5}{16}, \frac{1}{2}, \frac{3}{4}, \frac{7}{8}$ **d)** $\frac{2}{3}, \frac{3}{4}, \frac{5}{6}, \frac{11}{12}$
  e) $\frac{3}{7}, \frac{1}{2}, \frac{5}{7}, \frac{3}{4}$ **f)** $\frac{1}{4}, \frac{1}{3}, \frac{3}{8}, \frac{5}{12}, \frac{1}{2}$

5 a) $\frac{4}{7}, \frac{1}{2}, \frac{2}{7}$ **b)** $\frac{5}{6}, \frac{2}{3}, \frac{5}{9}$
  c) $\frac{3}{4}, \frac{2}{3}, \frac{1}{2}, \frac{4}{9}$ **d)** $\frac{9}{10}, \frac{13}{15}, \frac{4}{5}, \frac{2}{3}$
  e) $\frac{5}{8}, \frac{7}{12}, \frac{5}{9}, \frac{4}{9}$ **f)** $\frac{13}{15}, \frac{11}{15}, \frac{7}{10}, \frac{2}{3}, \frac{3}{5}, \frac{2}{9}$

6 a) $\frac{3}{4}, 1\frac{1}{2}, 1\frac{3}{5}, 2\frac{1}{3}, 2\frac{2}{5}$
  b) $\frac{4}{7}, \frac{5}{8}, 1\frac{7}{12}, 1\frac{3}{4}, 1\frac{5}{6}$
  c) $\frac{4}{9}, \frac{5}{7}, 1\frac{3}{4}, 2\frac{3}{7}, 2\frac{1}{2}, 2\frac{2}{3}$
  d) $\frac{1}{4}, 1\frac{5}{8}, 1\frac{2}{3}, 1\frac{5}{6}, 1\frac{11}{12}, 2\frac{1}{8}$

Write one number as a fraction of another

a Simplest form (p 87)

1 $\frac{2}{5}$ **2** $\frac{3}{4}$ **3** $\frac{1}{3}$ **4** $\frac{2}{5}$ **5** $\frac{4}{5}$

6 $\frac{2}{3}$ **7** $\frac{1}{2}$ **8** $\frac{3}{4}$ **9** $\frac{1}{3}$ **10** $\frac{3}{4}$

11 $\frac{1}{5}$ **12** $\frac{3}{10}$ **13** $\frac{2}{3}$ **14** $\frac{3}{7}$ **15** $\frac{3}{5}$

b Write one quantity as a fraction of another
(p 88)

1 a) $\frac{1}{4}$ h   b) $\frac{1}{3}$ h   c) $\frac{4}{5}$ h

2 a) $\frac{1}{10}$ kg   b) $\frac{3}{4}$ kg   c) $\frac{2}{5}$ kg   d) $\frac{16}{25}$ kg

3 a) $\frac{3}{10}$ cl   b) $\frac{1}{2}$ cl   c) $\frac{1}{5}$ cl   d) $\frac{2}{5}$ cl   e) $\frac{3}{5}$ cl

4 a) $\frac{1}{20}$ kg   b) $\frac{1}{2}$ g   c) $\frac{1}{4}$ kg   d) $\frac{1}{4}$ g   e) $\frac{1}{5}$ kg

5 a) $\frac{1}{2}$ lb   b) $\frac{1}{4}$ lb   c) $\frac{3}{4}$ lb   d) $\frac{3}{8}$ lb

6 $\frac{2}{3}$ 7 $\frac{1}{5}$ 8 $\frac{3}{5}$ 9 $\frac{9}{16}$

10 a)

	Men	Women	Total
Car	240	300	540
Bus	120	270	390
Train	80	100	180
Cycle	15	10	25
Walk	25	40	65
Total	480	720	1200

   b) i) Men: Car $\frac{1}{2}$ Bus $\frac{1}{4}$ Train $\frac{1}{6}$
                Cycle $\frac{1}{32}$ Walk $\frac{5}{96}$
      ii) Women: Car $\frac{5}{12}$ Bus $\frac{3}{8}$ Train $\frac{5}{36}$
                 Cycle $\frac{5}{72}$ Walk $\frac{1}{18}$
   c) i) $\frac{2}{5}$ ii) $\frac{3}{5}$

c Estimate one quantity as a fraction of another **(p 90)**

1 a) $\frac{1}{4}$ b) $\frac{3}{4}$

2 a) i) $\frac{5}{6}$ ii) $\frac{4}{5}$
   b) both are 200, giving 1

3 a) i) $\frac{3}{4}$ ii) $\frac{2}{3}$ b) aii

4 a) i) $\frac{1}{10}$ ii) $\frac{1}{60}$ iii) $\frac{1}{30}$ iv) $\frac{7}{8}$
   b) i) $\frac{5}{8}$ ii) $\frac{3}{8}$

5 a) ii) $\frac{3}{4}$ b) $\frac{1}{4}$
   Note: Other answers are possible

6 a) 237 100 000
   b) i) $\frac{1}{6}$ ii) $\frac{1}{3}$ iii) $\frac{3}{8}$ iv) $\frac{1}{12}$

7 Paper $\frac{3}{10}$, Glass $\frac{1}{7}$, Compost $\frac{2}{7}$, Metal $\frac{1}{9}$
   Textiles $\frac{1}{70}$, Cans $\frac{1}{100}$, Other $\frac{1}{10}$

Add and subtract fractions

a Add and subtract fractions with the same denominator **(p 92)**

1 $\frac{4}{5}$ 2 $\frac{2}{5}$ 3 1   4 $\frac{2}{3}$

5 $\frac{5}{7}$ 6 $\frac{3}{7}$ 7 $\frac{1}{2}$ 8 $\frac{2}{3}$

9 $\frac{4}{5}$ 10 1   11 $\frac{2}{5}$ 12 $\frac{1}{2}$

13 a) $\frac{3}{5}$ b) $\frac{2}{5}$ 14 a) $\frac{3}{8}$ b) $\frac{1}{4}$

b Add and subtract fractions with different denominators **(p 93)**

1 $\frac{7}{10}$ 2 $\frac{1}{2}$ 3 $\frac{5}{6}$ 4 $\frac{1}{3}$

5 $\frac{11}{12}$ 6 $\frac{7}{20}$ 7 $\frac{1}{8}$ 8 $\frac{8}{9}$

9 $\frac{4}{15}$ 10 $\frac{19}{21}$ 11 $\frac{11}{15}$ 12 $\frac{3}{10}$

13 $\frac{3}{4}$ 14 $\frac{9}{40}$ 15 $\frac{29}{30}$ 16 $\frac{1}{18}$

17 $\frac{17}{36}$ 18 $\frac{3}{20}$ 19 0   20 $\frac{7}{8}$

21 a) $\frac{3}{4}$ b) $\frac{1}{4}$

c Improper fractions and mixed numbers **(p 94)**

1 $1\frac{4}{5}$ 2 $2\frac{3}{5}$ 3 $4\frac{1}{3}$ 4 $5\frac{2}{3}$

5 $3\frac{3}{4}$ 6 $4\frac{1}{2}$ 7 $6\frac{1}{2}$ 8 $1\frac{3}{7}$

9 $5\frac{1}{4}$ 10 $2\frac{5}{6}$ 11 $6\frac{1}{3}$ 12 $6\frac{3}{5}$

13 $2\frac{7}{8}$ 14 $3\frac{7}{10}$ 15 $4\frac{4}{9}$ 16 $1\frac{1}{3}$

17 $1\frac{1}{7}$ 18 $1\frac{5}{8}$ 19 $1\frac{1}{6}$ 20 $1\frac{1}{2}$

21 $1\frac{9}{28}$ 22 $1\frac{1}{5}$ 23 $2\frac{5}{24}$

d Add and subtract mixed numbers **(p 95)**

1 $\frac{3}{2}$ 2 $\frac{5}{2}$ 3 $\frac{7}{2}$ 4 $\frac{5}{3}$

5 $\frac{8}{3}$ 6 $\frac{11}{5}$ 7 $\frac{19}{5}$ 8 $\frac{13}{6}$

9 $\frac{11}{6}$ 10 $\frac{19}{8}$ 11 $\frac{17}{7}$ 12 $\frac{47}{8}$

13 $\frac{49}{10}$ 14 $\frac{31}{9}$ 15 $\frac{44}{7}$ 16 $2\frac{3}{4}$

17 $\frac{17}{20}$ 18 $5\frac{1}{3}$ 19 $1\frac{5}{12}$ 20 $8\frac{1}{8}$

21 $2\frac{5}{6}$ 22 $\frac{19}{20}$ 23 $6\frac{1}{10}$ 24 $3\frac{13}{15}$

25 $6\frac{1}{14}$ 26 $7\frac{1}{4}$ 27 $1\frac{1}{8}$

28 3 hours   29 $4\frac{1}{4}$ pounds

30 a) $15\frac{1}{2}$ hours   b) $1\frac{1}{4}$ hours
   c) $2\frac{3}{4}$ hours

9 Decimals

Understand decimals in context (up to 2 dp) **(p 98)**

1 a) 0.4 cm   b) 2.5 cm   c) 4.1 cm
   d) 5.6 cm   e) 7.8 cm   f) 10.3 cm
   g) 12.5 cm   h) 15.2 cm   i) 17.9 cm
   j) 20.6 cm   k) 21.4 cm   l) 23.7 cm

2 a) 2.5 cm, 2.4 cm, 2.1 cm, 1.9 cm, 1.8 cm
   b) 4.5 cm, 4.3 cm, 4.1 cm, 3.9 cm, 3.8 cm, 3.4 cm
   c) 11.1 cm, 10.7 cm, 10.6 cm, 10.5 cm, 9.9 cm, 9.6 cm

3 a) 100p   b) 218p   c) 109p
   d) 407p   e) 62p   f) 824p
   g) 570p   h) 904p   i) 1017p
   j) 1640p

4 a) £2.13 **b)** £4.02 **c)** £0.85
d) £3.50 **e)** £1.03 **f)** £6.00
g) £7.25 **h)** £9.37 **i)** £10.00
j) £24.09

5 a) £1.02   £1.19   £1.21   £1.37
  £1.46   £1.87   £2.07
b) £47.20   £56.78   £63.02
  £63.21   £66.18   £74.02
c) £10.07   £10.08   £10.70
  £11.01   £11.17   £11.91

6 a) 22 cm **b)** 107 cm **c)** 173 cm
d) 74 cm **e)** 133 cm **f)** 112 cm
g) 115 cm **h)** 67 cm **i)** 260 cm
j) 540 cm

7 a) 1.54 m **b)** 3.15 m **c)** 0.94 m
d) 1.2 m **e)** 7.62 m **f)** 4.02 m
g) 0.7 m **h)** 2.5 m **i)** 11.34 m
j) 22.3 m

8 a) 1.5 m   1.55 m   1.63 m   1.67 m
  1.72 m   1.74 m   1.8 m
b) 1.26 m   1.28 m   1.3 m   1.31 m
  1.32 m   1.39 m   1.4 m
c) 0.72 m   0.84 m   0.88 m   0.99 m
  1.01 m   1.02 m   1.03 m

9 a) i) 1.5 m **ii)** 7.5 m **iii)** 10.5 m
b) i) $2\frac{1}{2}$ m **ii)** $6\frac{1}{2}$ m **iii)** $15\frac{1}{2}$ m

Write and compare decimals up to 3 decimal places

a Place value (p 102)

1 a)

Hundreds 100s	Tens 10s	Units 1s	.	Tenths 10ths	Hundredths 100ths	Thousandths 1000ths
1	1	6	.	7	4	
	3	7	.	5	4	
	1	2	.	0	6	
		4	.	5	2	
5	3	6	.	0	9	
5	0	6	.	9	2	6
	6	7	.	3	5	4
1	2	7	.	0	6	3
1	0	7	.	4	0	1
2	3	1	.	0	7	9
6	1	9	.	1	0	2
4	2	3	.	0	7	3

b) i) $\frac{7}{10}$ **ii)** $\frac{4}{100}$
iii) 2 **iv)** $\frac{5}{10}$
v) 500 **vi)** $\frac{6}{1000}$
vii) $\frac{5}{100}$ **viii)** $\frac{3}{1000}$
ix) $\frac{4}{10}$ **x)** $\frac{9}{1000}$
xi) $600\frac{1}{10}$
xii) $20\frac{3}{1000}$

2

Hundreds 100s	Tens 10s	Units 1s	.	Tenths 10ths	Hundredths 100ths	Thousandths 1000ths
	5	7	.	3	2	
		6	.	9		
		1	2	.	4	1
1	0	0	.	3	5	
	9	6	.	0	7	
	1	2	.	5	0	6
4	9	7	.	6	4	3

3 a) $\frac{7}{10}$ **b)** $\frac{6}{100}$ **c)** $\frac{3}{1000}$ **d)** $\frac{4}{100}$
e) $3\frac{5}{100}$ **f)** $6\frac{4}{10}$ **g)** $15\frac{7}{1000}$ **h)** $8\frac{2}{100}$
i) $10\frac{6}{10}$ **j)** $240\frac{9}{1000}$

4 a) $\frac{1}{10} + \frac{7}{100}, \frac{17}{100}$ **b)** $\frac{4}{10} + \frac{9}{100}, \frac{49}{100}$
c) $\frac{3}{100} + \frac{1}{1000}, \frac{31}{1000}$ **d)** $\frac{3}{10} + \frac{5}{100} + \frac{7}{1000}, \frac{357}{1000}$
e) $6 + \frac{2}{10} + \frac{3}{100}, 6\frac{23}{100}$ **f)** $8 + \frac{4}{100} + \frac{3}{1000}, 8\frac{43}{1000}$
g) $42 + \frac{1}{10} + \frac{7}{1000}, 42\frac{107}{1000}$
h) $1 + \frac{2}{10} + \frac{4}{100} + \frac{1}{1000}, 1\frac{241}{1000}$
i) $502 + \frac{6}{10} + \frac{9}{100}, 502\frac{69}{100}$
j) $17 + \frac{6}{10} + \frac{5}{100} + \frac{3}{1000}, 17\frac{653}{1000}$

b Write decimals as common fractions (p 103)

1 $\frac{1}{2}$ **2** $\frac{1}{5}$ **3** $\frac{2}{5}$ **4** $\frac{3}{5}$ **5** $\frac{4}{5}$
6 $\frac{3}{20}$ **7** $\frac{7}{20}$ **8** $\frac{11}{20}$ **9** $\frac{1}{4}$ **10** $\frac{9}{20}$

c Put decimals in order of size (p 104)

1 a) 7.21   7.11   6.76   6.12   5.98
  5.03   5.02   4.68   4.32
b) 14.26   14.21   13.1   13.03
  12.97   12.5   12.43   12.07
c) 26.47   26.42   26.11   25.17
  25.06   21.8   21.5   21.43
d) 7.84   7.21   6.96   6.48   5.74
  4.06   3.5   3.21   3.19

2 a) 0.003   0.23   0.307   1.05
  1.075   1.11   1.761

b) 12.005   12.05   12.121   12.429
12.5   12.502

c) 19.006   19.16   19.375   20.095
21.101   21.35

d) 412.438 428.003   483.562 581.098
581.879 604.002

3 a) 2.032 kg   2.009 kg   1.762 kg   1.104 kg
1.045 kg

b) 1.707 kg   1.7 kg   1.077 kg   1.07 kg
1.007 kg

c) 0.405 kg   0.318 kg   0.201 kg   0.058 kg
0.041 kg

4 a) 11.099   11.909   12.009   12.037
12.056   12.201

b) 18.302   18.411   18.567   18.591
19.002   19.041

c) 25.021   25.072   25.503   25.601
26.001   26.057

Use a calculator to solve problems (p 105)

1 a) 14.05   **b)** £4.76   **c)** 2 m
d) 10.7   **e)** £3.71   **f)** £8.81
g) 4.5 m   **h)** 21.86   **i)** 15.09
j) £1.53 or £1.54   **k)** 1 kg   **l)** £28.60
m) 2.15   **n)** £0.78   **o)** 20
p) 6.75

2 £4.63   **3** £5.37   **4** £28
5 a) 5.25 m   **b)** 0.3 m
6 £18.54   **7** £8.76   **8** £4.26

Multiply and divide decimals by 10 and 100 (p 106)

1 a) 174   **b)** 563   **c)** 171.2
d) 117.43   **e)** 1 601   **f)** 11 220
2 a) 5.622   **b)** 6.304   **c)** 0.0144
d) 10.201   **e)** 0.5704   **f)** 1.06
3 a) 261.1   **b)** 0.577   **c)** 104
d) 1.21   **e)** 4 720   **f)** 5.6602
4 a) 300 mm   **b)** 370 cm   **c)** 1.45 m
d) 4.5 cm   **e)** 345p   **f)** £7.89
g) 66 cm   **h)** 0.65 litres   **i)** 1.567 kg
j) 1.8 cm   **k)** 600 m   **l)** 7.58 km

5 a) 7500 g   2.3 m   **b)** 0.5 m   750 g
230 cm   0.75 ℓ   1.2 ℓ   5 mℓ
2300 g   7.5 kg   0.75 kg   50 cm
75 cℓ   1.25 ℓ   1.2 cm   120 cℓ
125 cℓ   2.3 kg   0.5 cℓ   12 mm

Round decimal numbers and approximate (p 108)

1 a) 15   **b)** 13   **c)** 7   **d)** 4
e) 10   **f)** 6   **g)** 16   **h)** 12
i) 10   **j)** 12   **k)** 15   **l)** 1
m) 4   **n)** 6   **o)** 0   **p)** 27
q) 250   **r)** 100

2 £15   **3** 6 m   **4** £6   **5** 6 kg   **6** £14.50
7 a) 5.68   **b)** 16.59   **c)** 11.33
d) 21.90   **e)** 155.79   **f)** 16.22
g) 131.08   **h)** 6.75   **i)** 121.90
j) 1.89   **k)** 2.40   **l)** 16.71
m) 15.92   **n)** 13.56   **o)** 1.01
8 a) £1.27   **b)** 2.73 kg   **c)** £12.16
d) 17.42 m   **e)** 22.57 km   **f)** 14.73 g
g) 16.19 cm   **h)** £9.64   **i)** 0.47 ℓ
j) 15.10 km
9 a) £15   **b)** 14 kg   **c)** 5.11 litres
d) £31.57   **e)** £7.17   **f)** 6.60 m
10 a) 9.5   **b)** 12.4   **c)** 13.2
d) 6.7   **e)** 121.8   **f)** 5.7
g) 91.8   **h)** 151.9   **i)** 65.1
j) 73.6
11 a) 5.792   **b)** 16.938   **c)** 3.749
d) 0.974   **e)** 4.032   **f)** 16.770
g) 12.081   **h)** 27.901   **i)** 1.550
j) 17.700

Add and subtract decimals (p 110)

1 a) 9.1   **b)** 2.8   **c)** 23.36
d) 22.67   **e)** £7.77   **f)** £30.54
g) £127.16   **h)** 1.35 m   **i)** 163.16
j) 1.05   **k)** 127.57   **l)** 156.54
2 £136.86   **3** £882.81   **4** £6.51
5 £ 244.67   **6** £86.35   **7** £1927.61
8 150.25 m   **9** £415.41   **10** 309 m
11 a) Team A 91.13 seconds,
Team B 90.78 seconds
b) Team B by 0.35 seconds

12 a) 10.491   **b)** 6.315   **c)** 4.129

13 16.116 seconds

Multiply decimals (p 112)

1 a) 2.4   **b)** 0.02   **c)** 0.35

d) 0.12   **e)** 14.6   **f)** 59.1

g) 5.61   **h)** 14.85   **i)** 32.56

j) 5.14 (to 2 dp)   **k)** 10.52 (to 2 dp)

l) 1.24 (to 2 dp)   **m)** 37.89 (to 2 dp)

n) 8.02 (to 2 dp)   **o)** 66.25 (to 2 dp)

p) 13.05 (to 2 dp)

2 15 m   **3** 4.5 litres   **4** £223.13

5

Order No	Item description	Price of item	Quantity	Price
PHF/1357	A4 paper	£3.99	5	£19.95
PHF/1359	A3 paper	£4.75	3	£14.25
ZL/129	Box black pens	£0.85	8	£6.80
FL/376	White board pens	£1.02	6	£6.12
GH/76P	Chrome stapler	£4.50	3	£13.50
GH/76L	Staples	£0.49	12	£5.88
	Total cost of all items			£66.50

6 1238 m^2

7 a) 29.8   **b)** 1.6776   **c)** 22.3987

8 75 645 yen (nearest yen)

9 35.5 m^3 (to 1 dp)

10 10.1 m, 8.0 m^2

Divide decimals (p 114)

1 a) 12.3   **b)** 11.26   **c)** 15.98

d) 33.21   **e)** 15.32   **f)** 11.18

g) 141.02   **h)** 37.6425

2 a) 4   **b)** 3   **c)** 20   **d)** 2

e) 130   **f)** 34   **g)** 26.5   **h)** 360

i) 62.5   **j)** 48.57 (to 2 dp)

k) 1236   **l)** 36   **m)** 18.35 (to 2 dp)

n) 17   **o)** 960   **p)** 140

q) 5.23 (to 2 dp)   **r)** 15.19 (to 2 dp)

s) 3.11 (to 2 dp)   **t)** 47

3 1.2 mm per day   **4** £2.17, £2.17 and £2.16

5 50   **6** 6060

7 a) 1940   **b)** 31.5   **c)** 19.2   **d)** 113.6

8 £13   **9** £125

10 a) 32.02   **b)** 7.20   **c)** 13.76

d) 5.68   **e)** 41.17   **f)** 12.56

g) 12.45   **h)** 3.91   **i)** 21.62

11 a) £44.54   **b)** £29.69   **12** 9 rolls

10 Percentages

Understand percentages and find percentage increase and decrease

a Understand percentages (p 116)

1 black = 19%, orange = 21%,
grey = 17%, white = 43%

2 a) 34 squares red, 16 squares green
21 squares blue, 19 squares black

b) 10% are not coloured

3 a) $\frac{3}{100}$ **b)** $\frac{63}{100}$ **c)** $\frac{13}{100}$ **d)** $\frac{57}{100}$

e) $\frac{27}{100}$ **f)** $\frac{11}{100}$ **g)** $\frac{91}{100}$ **h)** $\frac{39}{100}$

4 a) 7%   **b)** 19%   **c)** 41%   **d)** 73%

e) 99%   **f)** 81%   **g)** 1%   **h)** 49%

5 a) 20%   **b)** 45%   **c)** 16%   **d)** 85%

6 a) 17p   **b)** 99p   **c)** 22p   **d)** 51p

b Percentage increase and decrease (p 117)

1 a) i) 25p   **ii)** 40p   **iii)** 35p

iv) 50p   **v)** 55p

b) i) 10p   **ii)** 16p   **iii)** 14p

iv) 20p   **v)** 22p

c) i) 15p   **ii)** 24p   **iii)** 21p

iv) 30p   **v)** 33p

2 Jan £9.20   Kate £7.40
Luke £8.68   Wes £7.76

3 a) 30p   **b)** 72p   **c)** £1.50

d) £3.42   **e)** £5.34

4 a) i) 20p   **ii)** 70p   **iii)** 60p

iv) 40p   **v)** 50p   **vi)** 80p

vii) 90p   **viii)** £1   **ix)** £1.70

x) £1.80

b) i) 16p   **ii)** 56p   **iii)** 48p

iv) 32p   **v)** 40p   **vi)** 64p

vii) 72p   **viii)** 80p   **ix)** £1.36

x) £1.44

c) i) 60p   **ii)** £2.10   **iii)** £1.80

iv) £1.20   **v)** £1.50   **vi)** £2.40

vii) £2.70   **viii)** £3   **ix)** £5.10

x) £5.40

d) i) 30p   ii) £1.05   iii) 90p
    iv) 60p   v) 75p   vi) £1.20
    vii) £1.35   viii) £1.50   ix) £2.55
    x) £2.70

5 a) £10   b) £3.90   c) £8
   d) £14   e) £9   f) £2
   g) £4.32   h) £15   i) £7.50

6 a) £72   b) £150   c) £452.16
   d) £3342.48

Find percentages of quantities and measurements (p 119)

1 a) 5   b) 6.3 km   c) 8.94 g
   d) 30p   e) £4.80   f) 26p

2 a) 12   b) £16.20   c) 2.4 km
   d) £1.50   e) 1.05 kg   f) 51p

3 a) 280   b) 18 m   c) 30 g
   d) 3.8 km   e) £14.40   f) £1.28

4 a) £80   b) 25 m   c) 48 km
   d) £7.50   e) 390 kg   f) 450 g

5 a) 125 g plain flour, 60 g butter
      45 g sugar, 140 g blackberries
      100 g redcurrants, 75 g strawberries
   b) 2 people

6 a) £45   b) 9 m   c) £240
   d) 5.4 cm   e) 6.2 kg   f) 32.5 m
   g) 42p   h) 80p   i) £2.37
   j) £10.50   k) 0.28 tonnes   l) 0.07 km

7 a) 24 g   b) 51 kg   c) 336 g
   d) 384 m   e) 10.8 kg   f) £64
   g) £114.80   h) £3.60   i) £44.24
   j) 72.8 m   k) 12.78 kg   l) 11.1 kg

8 a) 4 kg   b) £2.25   c) £3.12
   d) 21.8 m   e) 16.5 kg   f) 6.9 m
   g) £14.40   h) 5 m   i) 100 g
   j) £70   k) 72 litres   l) 33 kg
   m) 81.25 m   n) 85.5 m   o) 2688 kg
   p) £14 042

9 £19 485   10 £1505   11 £467.50

12 a) £15   b) 23.5 m   c) 3.2 m
   d) £6.20   e) 191.5 m   f) 4.75 cm
   g) £37.50   h) £6.85   i) 3.975 kg
   j) 24.75 m   k) 11.25 km   l) £1.65

13 a) £135   b) 72 m   c) 270°
   d) 390 m   e) 127.5 kg   f) £72.60
   g) £9.60   h) 93 cm   i) 3.6 m
   j) 13.86 kg   k) 15.6 g   l) £49.80

14 45 m   15 £60

16 75 tickets   17 45 seats

18 240 women   19 360 blue tiles

20 a) £5.99   b) 80.48 m   c) £32.98
   d) £217.47   e) 33.34 m   f) £ 13.99

21 £28.29   22 £10.73

23 £78.77   24 £33.75

Work out VAT (p 125)

1 a) £157.50   b) £420   c) £31.50
   d) £63   e) £17.15   f) £8.05
   g) £4.52   h) £1.68   i) £3.92
   j) £16.94   k) £21.14   l) £4.82
   m) £14.50   n) £8.73   o) £4.37
   p) £10.49   q) £1.39   r) £21

2 a) £171.50   b) £43.58   c) £10.48
   d) £12.16   e) £2.62   f) £10.50

Percentage increase and decrease (p 126)

1 a) i) £96   ii) £400   iii) £960
     iv) £1200   v) £840   vi) £713.60
   b) i) £90   ii) £375   iii) £900
     iv) £1125   v) £787.50   vi) £669

2 a) i) £858   ii) £132   iii) £88
     iv) £70.40   v) £1177   vi) £708.40
   b) i) £897   ii) £138   iii) £92
     iv) £73.60   v) £1230.50   vi) £740.60

3 £630   4 73.7m   5 £55.25

6 £19   7 a) 630   b) 270

8 72   9 £179.10

10 £780

11 i) £111.60   ii) £465   iii) £1116
   iv) £1395   v) £976.50   vi) £829.56

12 i) £842.40   ii) £129.60   iii) £86.40
   iv) £69.12   v) £1155.60   vi) £695.52

13 coffee maker £28.91   washer £351.33
     radio £13.98   camera £82.24

14 £360

Another way to increase or decrease by a percentage (p 128)

1 £8.24

2 chocolate bar 55p   tube sweets 33p
   packet sweets £1.32   box chocs £2.75

3 £39.20   4 £5200

Equivalent fractions, decimals and percentages

a Write percentages as decimals (p 128)

1 a) 0.25   b) 0.35   c) 0.4
   d) 0.3   e) 0.8   f) 0.05
   g) 0.1   h) 0.15   i) 0.04
   j) 0.08   k) 0.03   l) 0.09

2 a) 0.16   b) 0.32   c) 0.49
   d) 0.95   e) 0.64   f) 0.52
   g) 0.175   h) 0.625   i) 0.378
   j) 0.036   k) 0.025   l) 0.0125

b Write decimals as percentages (p 129)

1 a) 75%   b) 25%   c) 65%
   d) 60%   e) 6%   f) 10%
   g) 1%   h) 50%   i) 5%
   j) 90%   k) 9%   l) 99%

2 a) 29%   b) 57%   c) 43%
   d) 150%   e) 250%   f) 87.5%
   g) 32.5%   h) 6.5%   i) 0.5%
   j) 20.5%   k) 16.8%   l) 245%

c Write percentages as fractions (p 129)

1 a) $\frac{1}{10}$ b) $\frac{1}{5}$ c) $\frac{2}{5}$ d) $\frac{4}{5}$ e) $\frac{3}{10}$
   f) $\frac{9}{10}$ g) $\frac{1}{2}$ h) $\frac{1}{4}$ i) $\frac{1}{20}$ j) $\frac{3}{20}$
   k) $\frac{9}{20}$ l) $\frac{3}{100}$

2 a) $\frac{19}{100}$ b) $\frac{16}{25}$ c) $\frac{19}{20}$ d) $\frac{2}{25}$ e) $\frac{43}{50}$
   f) $\frac{18}{25}$

3 a) $\frac{3}{200}$ b) $\frac{1}{40}$ c) $\frac{8}{125}$ d) $\frac{1}{8}$ e) $\frac{17}{200}$
   f) $\frac{5}{8}$ g) $\frac{3}{8}$ h) $\frac{21}{200}$ i) $\frac{7}{80}$ j) $\frac{2}{3}$
   k) $\frac{16}{125}$ l) $\frac{3}{80}$

d Write fractions as decimals and percentages (p 130)

1 a) 0.1, 10%   b) 0.2, 20%
   c) 0.4, 40%   d) 0.8, 80%
   e) 0.3, 30%   f) 0.9, 90%

2

Fraction	Decimal	%
$\frac{1}{2}$	0.5	50%
$\frac{1}{4}$	0.25	25%
$\frac{3}{4}$	0.75	75%
$\frac{1}{10}$	0.1	10%
$\frac{1}{5}$	0.2	20%
$\frac{1}{3}$	0.33	$33\frac{1}{3}\%$

Fraction	Decimal	%
$\frac{2}{5}$	0.4	40%
$\frac{7}{10}$	0.7	70%
$\frac{7}{20}$	0.35	35%
$\frac{3}{5}$	0.6	60%
$\frac{9}{10}$	0.9	90%
$\frac{3}{20}$	0.15	15%

3 a) 0.45, 45%   b) 0.625, 62.5%
   c) 0.875, 87.5%   d) 0.675, 67.5%
   e) 0.28, 28%   f) 0.67, 66.67%

4 a) $\frac{3}{4}$, 0.76, 78%   b) 0.49, $\frac{1}{2}$, 51%
   c) 0.22, 24%, $\frac{1}{4}$ d) 19%, $\frac{1}{5}$, 0.21
   e) 50%, $\frac{5}{9}$, 0.58   f) 88%, $\frac{8}{9}$, 0.9
   g) 0.56, $\frac{7}{12}$, 59%   h) $\frac{7}{16}$, 45%, 0.49

Use a calculator to find percentages (p 132)

1 a) 14.3   b) £62.90   c) 4.92 m
   d) £426.40   e) 4.75 kg   f) 331.2 g
   g) 26.32   h) 5.06 cm   i) 2.24 litres
   j) 26.18 m   k) £483.84   l) 16.02
   m) 46.62 km   n) £6.75   o) 0.85
   p) 9 cm   q) £13.53   r) 8.84 m
   s) 1.75 m   t) £31.75

2 dress £42.29   stereo £205.61
   guitar £193.88   dinner service £105.74
   TV £293.74

3 A £181.30   B £186.75 Shop A is better buy

4 £19 665   5 £4485

6 See table at top of next page.

7 a) 4.5 inches × 3 inches
   b) 7.5 inches × 5 inches
   c) 7.98 inches × 5.32 inches
   d) 8.46 inches × 5.64 inches

Lender	Amount	Bayleys	Anchor	Rock Solid	Direct
APR		6.6	6.5	6.3	6.7
a)	£1000	£66	£65	£63	£67
b)	£2500	£165	£162.50	£157.50	£167.50
c)	£1750	£115.50	£113.75	£110.25	£117.25
d)	£3225	£212.85	£209.63	£203.18	£216.08
e)	£12 500	£825	£812.50	£787.50	£837.50
f)	£0.8 million	£52 800	£52 000	£50 400	£53 600

8 a) £32.76   b) 113.4 g   c) 690 m
   d) 34.02 cm   e) 31.68 km   f) 93.28 kg
   g) 65.55 m   h) 16.25 litres   i) £22.40
   j) £8.75
9 £96.24

Write one number as a percentage of another (p 134)

1 a) 60%   b) 40%   2 40%

3

Asst	1	2	3	4
Mark	18	56	52	66
out of	30	70	80	120
%	60%	80%	65%	55%

4 a) 50%   b) 33.33%   c) 5%
   d) 25%   e) 5%   f) 33%
5 8%   6 8%
7 a) £1045   b) 4.5%
8 60%   9 12.5%   10 28%
11 a) 32%   b) 14%   c) 57.33%
12 a) i) 66.67%   ii) 33.33%
13 46.30%
14 a) 28.55%   b) 6.98%
15 14.18%
16 a) 50%   b) 50%   c) 25%   d) 20%
17 a) i)   20% women   ii)   25% children
       iii) 55% men
18 a) £319.63
    b) i) 25%   ii) 10%   iii) 25%   iv) 40%

Measures, Shape and Space

1 Money

Add and subtract sums of money

a Line up the £s and pence (p 138)

1 a) £6.31   b) £16.80   c) £2.67
   d) £5.40   e) £4.35   f) £3.45
   g) £5.05   h) £2.60   i) £1.01
   j) £3.51   k) £25.56   l) £64.06
2 £8   3 £3.95   4 a) £3.09   b) £6.91

b Use a calculator to add and subtract money (p 139)

1 a) £2.05   b) £2.50   c) £2.98
   d) £3.02   e) £3.39   f) 97p
   g) £2.83   h) £4.45   i) 59p
   j) £6.25   k) £12.98   l) £12.52

Round to the nearest 10p or £

a Round to the nearest 10p (p 140)

1 a) 10p   b) 30p   c) 30p   d) 40p
   e) 90p   f) 60p   g) 30p   h) 60p
   i) 50p   j) 80p   k) 90p   l) 0p
2 a) £2.10   b) £4.40   c) £5.70
   d) £7.20   e) £6.90   f) £9.10
   g) £5.70   h) £4.20   i) £3.30
   j) £8.90   k) £18.00   l) £28.00
3 a) 40p + 30p + 40p = £1.10
   b) 30p + 30p + 50p = £1.10
   c) 40p + 30p + 50p = £1.20

b Round to the nearest £ (p 141)

1 a) £3   b) £3   c) £5   d) £5
   e) £7   f) £7   g) £8   h) £9
   i) £2   j) £1   k) £10   l) £20

2 a) £12   b) £34   c) £16   d) £27
e) £337   f) £9   g) £26   h) £24
i) £13   j) £229   k) £77   l) £76

3 a) i) £2 + £2 + £6 = £10
ii) £2 + £3 + £1 = £6
iii) £4 + £4 + £5 = £13
b) i) £10.16   ii) £6.53   iii) £13.09

Add, subtract, multiply and divide sums of money

a Understand place value of £s and pence (p 142)

1 a) £30   b) 3p   c) £3   d) 30p
e) £300

2 a) £90   b) 90p   c) £9   d) 9p
e) £900

3 a) £110   b) £25.20   c) £12.50
d) £30.05   e) £230.15   f) £413.25
g) £303.03   h) £325

4 £731.34, £732.61, £736.02, £741.12

5 a) ten pounds, fifty pence
b) five pounds, ninety-nine pence
c) twelve pounds, fifty pence
d) five hundred and five pounds
e) two pounds, fifteen pence
f) four hundred and ten pounds, four pence
g) forty-five pounds, forty-nine pence
h) two hundred and nine pounds, nine pence

6 £342.41   £342.14   £324.41   £324.14
£234.41   £234.14

b Add, subtract, multiply and divide money (p 143)

1 a) £19.43   b) £27.80   c) £89.94
d) £33.98   e) £13.01   f) £4.50
g) £5.16   h) £12.21   i) £31.25
j) £116.55   k) £2.10   l) 83p

2 a) £103.50   b) £132.10

3 £38.20   4 £17.98

Convert between currencies (p 144)

1 Mr Blank $1521 (US dollars)
Mrs Smith $1815 (Australian dollars)
Mr Hashan €858 (euro)
Miss Patten 14 088 rand
Ms Chang 379 300 yen
Mr Davies 11 538 rupees
Miss Bailey €125 125

2 Mr Wragg £416   Miss Yen £383
Mr Ennis £18   Ms Masters £70
Miss Dank £822   Mr Caine £1321
Ms Wright £29

3 £431

4 a) $416 (US dollars)   b) £236
c) £14

5 a) $2529   b) $331   c) £31

2 Time

Read and record dates (p 146)

1 a) 1st   b) February   c) 3rd
d) 4th   e) May   f) June
g) July   h) August
i) September   j) 10th
k) November   l) December

2 today's date – long/medium/short format

3 a) 2nd April 1979   b) 22/02/78

4 10/Mar/1876

5 25th July 1978

Read, measure and record time

a am and pm (p 148)

1 a) 7:00 am   b) 4:00 pm   c) 11:30 am
d) 5:00 pm   e) 1:00 am   f) 8:45 am

2 a) iii)   b) i)   c) ii)

3 any suitable suggestions

4 a) 12 hours   b) 13 hours   c) 17 hours
d) 9½ hours   e) 11 hours   f) 11½ hours

b Read and record time to the nearest 5 minutes (p 149)

1 a) 20 minutes past 2, 2:20
b) 40 minutes past 1, 1:40
c) 25 minutes past 11, 11:25
d) 50 minutes past 1, 1:50

2 a) 35 minutes past 10, 25 minutes to 11, 10:35

b) 40 minutes past 2, 20 minutes to 3, 2:40

c) 40 minutes past 12, 20 minutes to 1, 12:40

d) 45 minutes past 3, 15 minutes to 4, 3:45

e) 35 minutes past 2, 25 minutes to 3, 2:35

f) 55 minutes past 7, 5 minutes to 8, 7:55

g) 50 minutes past 11, 10 minutes to 12, 11:50

h) 55 minutes past 5, 5 minutes to 6, 5:55

Use the 12 and 24 hour clock

a The 12 and 24 hour clock (p 151)

1 a) 15:50   b) 07:00   c) 09:15

d) 22:26   e) 15:42   f) 13:30

g) 06:45   h) 00:05   i) 19:40

j) 18:59   k) 06:42   l) 20:25

2 a) 03:15   b) 16:45   c) 07:30

d) 08:50   e) 23:10   f) 12:00

g) 15:55   h) 07:45   i) 17:35

j) 14:50   k) 16:05   l) 11:10

3 a) 16:06   b) 15:15   c) 08:11

d) 09:45   e) 18:50   f) 23:35

g) 10:55   h) 12:12   i) 21:20

j) 18:30

4 a) 11:30 pm   b) 6:45 am   c) 7:12 am

d) 4:45 pm   e) 12:10 pm   f) 1:10 am

g) 12:16 pm   h) 2:10 pm   i) 12 am

j) 6:05 am   k) 1:46 pm   l) 9:15 am

5 a) 15:52, 8 minutes to 4 in the afternoon, 3:52 pm

b) 03:46, 14 minutes to 4 in the morning, 3:46 am

c) 17:05, 5 minutes past 5 in the afternoon, 5:05 pm

d) 23:54, 6 minutes to midnight, 11:54 pm

e) 19:09, 9 minutes past 7 in the evening, 7:09 pm

f) 16:32, 28 minutes to 5 in the afternoon, 4:32 pm

b Use timetables (p 153)

1 a) i) 0628   ii) 0703

b) 0702

c) i) 0620   ii) 0633

d) 0640

e) 0707

f) i) 0637   ii) 0648

2 a) 8:45 am   b) 12:20 pm

c) i) 2:10 pm   ii) 3 pm

d) 8:53 am   e) 12:45 pm

f) i) 9:15 am   ii) 12:30 pm   iii) 12:55 pm

g) 2:03 pm

Units of time (p 154)

1 a) 30   b) 3   c) 30   d) 200

e) 15   f) 1000   g) 6   h) 104

i) 14   j) 26

2 a) i) 30   ii) 30   iii) 29

b) i) 62   ii) 61

3 a) minutes   b) seconds

c) days   d) days or weeks

e) hours   f) weeks or months

g) years or centuries

4 a) 210   b) 3   c) 270   d) 5

e) 36   f) $2\frac{1}{2}$ g) 49   h) 5

i) 450   j) 5   k) 3000   l) 10

5 2   6 £1250   7 4 weeks

8 150 seconds   9 105 min   10 13 weeks

11 a) £78   b) £312

Calculate time

a Add and subtract time in hours, minutes and seconds (p 156)

1 a) 5 hours 20 minutes

b) 8 minutes 57 seconds

c) 3 minutes 35 seconds

d) 6 minutes 15 seconds

e) 9 hours 45 minutes

f) 4 hours 5 minutes

2 a) 2 hours 20 minutes

b) 1 hour 40 minutes

c) 1 minute 20 seconds

d) 52 seconds

e) 3 hours 35 minutes

f) 1 minute 21 seconds

3 a) 11 minutes

b) 7 minutes 15 seconds

4 55 minutes

b Find the difference between times by adding on (p 156)

1 a) 2 hours 41 min   b) 2 hours 42 min
   c) 2 hours 45 min   d) 1 hour 33 min
   e) 3 hours 48 min   f) 3 hours 50 min
   g) 4 hours 15 min   h) 8 hours 36 min
   i) 3 hours 41 min   j) 5 hours 50 min
   k) 9 hours 45 min   l) 21 hours 45 min

2 a) 3 hours 30 min   b) 6 hours 15 min
   c) 5 hours 30 min   d) 4 hours 15 min
   e) 5 hours 30 min   f) 7 hours 45 min

3 a) 5 hours 21 min   b) 4 hours 18 min
   c) 4 hours 6 min   d) 4 hours 12 min
   e) 4 hours 35 min   f) 2 hours 13 min
   g) 2 hours 32 min   h) 2 hours 24 min
   i) 3 hours 25 min   j) 3 hours 9 min
   k) 4 hours 14 min   l) 2 hours 12 min

c Find the difference between times by subtracting (p 158)

1 a) 2 hours 27 min   b) 2 hours 29 min
   c) 1 hour 13 min   d) 1 hour 33 min
   e) 7 hours 26 min   f) 6 hours 11 min
   g) 1 hour 49 min   h) 3 hours 45 min
   i) 1 hour 27 min   j) 4 hours 17 min
   k) 1 hour 40 min   l) 10 hours 29 min

2 a) i)   3 hours 48 minutes
       ii)   3 hours 43 minutes
       iii) 2 hours 38 minutes
       iv)   4 hours 7 minutes
   b) 5 minutes

Use timers (p 159)

1 analogue and digital clocks (as in question) showing:
   a) 10:30 pm   b) 6 am
   c) 11:15 pm   d) 8:30 am

2 a) start cooking 17:30   b) start cooking 15:15
       cooking time   1:30   cooking time   2:15
   c) start cooking 18:35   d) start cooking 17:15
       cooking time   1:40   cooking time   1:45

3 a) 06:30 to 09:00 and 17:00 to 23:00
   b) 07:00 to 09:00 and 19:00 to 24:00 (00:00)

4 dials showing times given in the question

5 a) 1 minute, 16 seconds and 47 hundredths of a second, 1 min 16.47 s
   b) 1 minute, 21 seconds and 5 hundredths of a second, 1 min 21.05 s
   c) 1 minute, 16 seconds and 59 hundredths of a second, 1 min 16.59 s
   d) 1 minute, 22 seconds and 2 tenths of a second, 1 min 22.20 s
   e) 1 minute, 17 seconds and 8 hundredths of a second, 1 min 17.08 s
   f) 1 minute, 22 seconds and 4 tenths of a second, 1 min 22.40 s

6 a) 2.21 s   b) 0.56 s   c) 2.15 s
   d) 10.68 s   e) 13.52 s   f) 25.02 s

7 02:16.43, 02:34.05, 02:44.51, 02:49.30, 03:00.24, 03:01.09

   17.62 s,   10.46 s,   4.79 s,   10.94 s,   0.85 s

3 Length

Understand distance: kilometres and miles (p 162)

1 a) A, D   b) B, C
2 appropriate answers
3 a) 50 miles   b) 2 km   c) $\frac{1}{2}$ mile
   d) 1 mile   e) 10 miles   f) 1 km
   g) 80 miles (a and g could be interchanged)

Find the distance

a Use distances marked on a map (p 163)

1 a) 8 miles   b) 8 miles   c) 8 miles
   d) 17 miles   e) 16 miles   f) 18 miles
   g) 11 miles   h) 15 miles
2 23 miles   3 26 miles

b Use a mile/kilometre chart (p 164)

1 a) 261 miles   b) 284 miles   c) 95 miles
   d) 239 miles   e) 84 miles   f) 416 miles
2 a) 98 km   b) 106 miles   c) 45 miles
   d) 82 km   e) 48 miles   f) 11 miles
   g) 72 km   h) 255 km

Measure length in metric units

a Measure in millimetres and centimetres (p 166)

1 b) i) 3 cm   ii) 31 mm
   c) i) 5 cm   ii) 48 mm
   d) i) 7 cm   ii) 66 mm
   e) i) 7 cm   ii) 74 mm
   f) i) 9 cm   ii) 93 mm
   g) i) 11 cm   ii) 106 mm
   h) i) 11 cm   ii) 113 mm

2 a) 2 cm   b) 30 mm   c) 5 cm
   d) 70 mm   e) 6 cm   f) 80 mm
   g) 4 cm   h) 90 mm   i) 12 cm

3 a) 1.5 cm   b) 12 mm   c) 2.6 cm
   d) 13 mm   e) 1.4 cm   f) 21 mm
   g) 8.4 cm   h) 39 mm   i) 12.5 cm

4 a) 32 mm, 3 cm 2 mm, 3.2 cm
   b) 89 mm, 8 cm 9 mm, 8.9 cm
   c) 31 mm, 3 cm 1 mm, 3.1 cm
   d) 63 mm, 6 cm 3 mm, 6.3 cm
   e) 103 mm, 10 cm 3 mm, 10.3 cm
   f) 76 mm, 7 cm 6 mm, 7.6 cm
   g) 21 mm, 2 cm 1 mm, 2.1 cm
   h) 52 mm, 5 cm 2 mm, 5.2 cm

5 e b f d h a c g

6 a) 74 mm, 7 cm 4 mm, 7.4 cm
   b) 46 mm, 4 cm 6 mm, 4.6 cm
   c) 68 mm, 6 cm 8 mm, 6.8 cm

7 a) 26 mm, 2 cm 6 mm, 2.6 cm
   b) 52 mm, 5 cm 2 mm, 5.2 cm
   c) 33 mm, 3 cm 3 mm, 3.3 cm
   d) 44 mm, 4 cm 4 mm, 4.4 cm
   e) 49 mm, 4 cm 9 mm, 4.9 cm
   f) 43 mm, 4 cm 3 mm, 4.3 cm
   g) 28 mm, 2 cm 8 mm, 2.8 cm

b Measure in metres, centimetres and millimetres (p 170)

1 c) 99 cm, 990 mm   d) 102 cm, 1020 mm
   e) 104 cm, 1040 mm   f) 107 cm, 1070 mm
   g) 110 cm, 1100 mm   h) 112 cm, 1120 mm

2 c) 0.99 m   d) 1.02 m   e) 1.04 m
   f) 1.07 m   g) 1.1 m   h) 1.12 m

3 c) i) 361 cm   ii) 3.61 m
   d) i) 370 cm   ii) 3.7 m
   e) i) 361 cm   ii) 3.61 m
   f) i) 363 cm   ii) 3.63 m
   g) i) 369 cm   ii) 3.69 m
   h) i) 367 cm   ii) 3.67 m

4 c) 360.7 cm, 3607 mm, 3 m 607 mm, 3.607 m
   d) 370.3 cm, 3703 mm, 3 m 703 mm, 3.703 m
   e) 361.3 cm, 3613 mm, 3 m 613 mm, 3.613 m
   f) 363.1 cm, 3631 mm, 3 m 631 mm, 3.631 m
   g) 369.3 cm, 3693 mm, 3 m 693 mm, 3.693 m
   h) 366.6 cm, 3666 mm, 3 m 666 mm, 3.666 m

Estimate lengths between marked divisions (p 171)

1 a) A i) 10 cm   ii) 10.3 cm
    B i) 7 cm   ii) 6.7 cm
    C i) 4 cm   ii) 4.3 cm
    D i) 13 cm   ii) 12.6 cm
    E i) 9 cm   ii) 8.8 cm
    F i) 2 cm   ii) 2.3 cm
    G i) 10 cm   ii) 9.5 cm
   b) as a) ii)

Use appropriate units for measuring (p 172)

1 a) 1 m   b) 40 km   c) 2 m
   d) 3 cm   e) 30 cm   f) 14 cm
   g) 11 cm   h) 3 mm   i) 1 mm
(Alternative answers possible for some parts.)

Be accurate or round up (p 172)

1 a) accurate   b) round up   c) accurate
   d) round up   e) accurate

Convert between metric lengths (p 173)

1 a) 23 mm   b) 43 mm
   c) 43 500 mm   d) 4500 mm
   e) 12 450 mm   f) 2 000 000 mm

2 a) 1300 cm   b) 4000 cm
   c) 960 cm   d) 1370 cm
   e) 6.5 cm   f) 250 000 cm

3 a) 4 m   b) 5000 m   c) 24 m
   d) 5840 m   e) 740 m   f) 3.534 m
   g) 5.3 m   h) 0.68 m   i) 0.96 m
   j) 13 750 m   k) 659 m   l) 50 m

4 a) 7 km   b) 9.4 km   c) 4.5 km
   d) 95 km   e) 2.5 km

5 a) 4000 m   b) 500 cm   c) 450 mm
   d) 5 km   e) 25 cm   f) 3.6 m
   g) 2.75 m   h) 0.275 km   i) 3600 m
   j) 270 cm   k) 122 mm   l) 7.563 km

6 6 mm, 2.6 cm, 200 mm, 0.5 m, 650 mm, 150 cm, 2 m

7 2.5 m   8 10 km

9 a) 60 cm   b) 0.6 m

10 a) 75 cm   b) 750 mm

11 a) 50 cm   b) 25 cm   c) 500 mm
   d) 250 mm   e) $\frac{2}{5}$ m   f) $\frac{3}{10}$ m

Calculate with metric lengths

a Metres and centimetres (p 175)

1 a) 5.3 m   b) 3.3 m   c) 4.5 m
   d) 4.25 m   e) 10.65 m   f) 3.64 m
   g) 2.25 m   h) 2.75 m   i) 3.8 m

2 a) $7\frac{1}{2}$ m   b) $2\frac{1}{4}$ m   c) $3\frac{3}{4}$ m   d) $4\frac{3}{4}$ m
   e) $4\frac{1}{4}$ m   f) $1\frac{1}{4}$ m   g) $11\frac{1}{2}$ m   h) $2\frac{1}{2}$ m

b Metres and millimetres (p 176)

1 a) 2.675 m   b) 3.025 m   c) 2.115 m
   d) 2.25 m   e) 7.7 m   f) 2.034 m

c Mixed calculations (p 176)

1 a) 2.625 m   b) 5.47 m   c) 3.045 m

2 3.43 m   3 5.45 m   4 2.9 m

5 a) 22.2 m   b) 13.8 m

6 a) $1\frac{1}{4}$ m
   b) i) $5\frac{9}{10}$ m or 5.9 m   ii) $1\frac{3}{5}$ m or 1.6 m

Use a scale on a plan or map (p 177)

1

Room	Length on plan	Actual length	Width on plan	Actual width
Bedroom	3 cm	3 × 2 = 6 m	2 cm	2 × 2 = 4 m
Kitchen	2.5 cm	2.5 × 2 = 5 m	1.5 cm	1.5 × 2 = 3 m
Living room	4 cm	4 × 2 = 8 m	3 cm	3 × 2 = 6 m
Bathroom	1.5 cm	1.5 × 2 = 3 m	1 cm	1 × 2 = 2 m
Cupboard	1 cm	1 × 2 = 2 m	0.5 cm	0.5 × 2 = 1 m

2

	Measurements on the plan				Actual measurements			
	House length	House width	Plot length	Plot width	House length	House width	Plot length	Plot width
House A	11 mm	6 mm	25 mm	16 mm	11 m	6 m	25 m	16 m
House B	10 mm	9 mm	35 mm	16 mm	10 m	9 m	35 m	16 m
House C	13 mm	10 mm	28 mm	16 mm	13 m	10 m	28 m	16 m
House D	17 mm	6 mm	31 mm	16 mm	17 m	6 m	31 m	16 m

3 a) A 57 mm   B 73 mm   C 32 mm   D 51 mm
   b) A 5.7 m   B 7.3 m   C 3.2 m   D 5.1 m

		Measurement on drawing in mm	Actual measurement
i)	The length of the house.	70 mm	7 m
ii)	The width of the downstairs window.	22 mm	2.2 m
iii)	The width of the smaller upstairs window.	22 mm	2.2 m
iv)	The width of the larger upstairs window.	28 mm	2.8 m
v)	The height of the downstairs window.	19 mm	1.9 m
vi)	The height of the upstairs windows.	16 mm	1.6 m
viii)	The width of the front porch.	28 mm	2.8 m

4 a) i) approx 15 km   ii) approx 10 km
     iii) approx 30 km   iv) approx 13 km
   b) i) approx 19 km   ii) approx 17 km
     iii) approx 28 km   iv) approx 35 km

5

	Length on map	Actual distance
Tutor's home to A	7.6 cm	3.8 km
Tutor's home to B	5.4 cm	2.7 km
Tutor's home to C	2.6 cm	1.3 km
Tutor's home to D	3.8 cm	1.9 km

(Allow ±0.2 km)

Use ratios on scale drawings (p 180)

1 a) 50 m   b) 30 m   c) 25 m
   d) 20 m   e) 10 m   f) 6 m
   g) 16 m   h) 11.5 m

2 a)

Room		on plan	actual distance
Lounge	Length	30 mm	6 m
	Width	25 mm	5 m
Kitchen	Length	18 mm	3.6 m
	Width	14 mm	2.8 m
Bathroom	Length	15 mm	3 m
	Width	12 mm	2.4 m
Bedroom	Length	24 mm	4.8 m
	Width	16 mm	3.2 m

b) 2 m

3 a) A 41 mm × 19 mm   B 38 mm × 19 mm

   C 31 mm × 16 mm   D 47 mm × 16 mm

b) A 8.2 m × 3.8 m   B 7.6 m × 3.8 m

   C 6.2 m × 3.2 m   D 9.4 m × 3.2 m

4 a) 6.6 m   **b)** 3.3 m   **c)** 3 m

   d) 2.4 m   **e)** 4.05 m   **f)** 2.7 m

   g) 11.4 m   **h)** 10.8 m

5

Distance		On map	Actual
a)	The Minster – Hospital	2.4 cm	0.6 cm
b)	The Minster – Cemetry	5.6 cm	1.4 cm
c)	Snow Close Farm – Hospital	5.6 cm	1.4 cm
d)	College – The Minster	4 cm	1 km
e)	Snow Close Farm – The Minster	6 cm	1.5 cm
f)	Schools – Hospital	3.6 cm	0.9 km
g)	Studley – The Minster	5 cm	2.25 km

6 a) 1 : 100   **b)** 1 : 50

   c) 1 : 20   **d)** 1 : 2000

   e) 1 : 50 000   **f)** 1 : 250 000

   g) 1 : 160   **h)** 1 : 125 000

   i) 1 : 1000   **j)** 1 : 200 000

   k) 1 : 5   **l)** 1 : 2500

7 Lines of length:

   a) i) 6 cm   **ii)** 13 cm

   b) i) 3.2 cm   **ii)** 4.8 cm

   c) i) 13 cm   **ii)** 8.7 cm

   d) i) 7 cm   **ii)** 4.3 cm

   e) i) 4.5 cm   **ii)** 3.6 cm

   f) i) 4.2 cm   **ii)** 9 cm

   g) i) 7 cm   **ii)** 11.4 cm

8 Scale drawing should have the dimensions shown below:

Measure lengths in imperial units (p 183)

1 a) $1\frac{1}{8}''$ **b)** $1\frac{13}{16}''$ **c)** $1\frac{3}{16}''$

   d) $1\frac{1}{3}''$ **e)** $\frac{3}{4}''$ **f)** $1\frac{5}{8}''$

   g) $1\frac{3}{8}''$ **h)** $1\frac{9}{16}''$ **i)** $\frac{11}{16}''$

   j) $1\frac{15}{16}''$ **k)** $1\frac{5}{8}''$ **l)** $\frac{3}{4}''$

Convert imperial lengths (p 184)

1 a) 180 in   **b)** 72 in   **c)** 336 in

   d) 192 in   **e)** 72 in   **f)** 432 in

   g) 113 in   **h)** 54 in

2 a) 6 ft   **b)** 240 ft   **c)** $2\frac{1}{2}$ ft

   d) 12 ft   **e)** 15 ft   **f)** 5 ft

   g) 4 ft   **h)** $2\frac{1}{3}$ ft

3 a) 2 yd   **b)** 5 yd

   c) 7040 yd   **d)** 4 yd

4 a) 3 miles   **b)** 9 miles

   c) 10 miles   **d)** 6 miles

5 a) 45 ft   **b)** 15 yd

6 Jan 4 ft 10 inches   Imran 5 ft 5 inches

   Carl 6 ft 1 inch

Convert between metric and imperial lengths

a Approximate metric/imperial conversions (p 185)

1

inches	centimetres
2 in	5 cm
6 in	15 cm
8 in	20 cm
3 in	7.5 cm
7 in	17.5 cm
10 in	25 cm
32 in	80 cm
18 in	45 cm
40 in	100 cm

yards/feet	centimetres	metres
2 ft	60 cm	0.6 m
$2\frac{1}{2}$ ft	75 cm	0.75 m
1 yd or 3 ft	90 cm	0.9 m
$3\frac{1}{2}$ ft or 1 yd $\frac{1}{2}$ ft	105 cm	1.05 m
$4\frac{1}{2}$ ft	135 cm	1.35 m
5 ft or 1 yd 2 ft	150 cm	1.5 m
7 ft or 2 yd 1 ft	210 cm	2.1 m
2 yd 2 ft	240 cm	2.4 m
3 yd	270 cm	2.7 m

2 a) i) 50 miles **ii)** 130 miles
   iii) 18.75 miles
b) i) 96 km **ii)** 384 km
   iii) 48 km

3

		miles	km
a)	Paris to Boulogne	159	254
b)	Brussels to Calais	135	216
c)	Berlin to Cherbourg	847	1355
d)	Brussels to Dieppe	194	310
e)	Paris to Dunkerque	174	278
f)	Frankfurt to Amsterdam	283	453
g)	Munich to Boulogne	590	944
h)	Turin to Ostend	604	967
i)	Zurich to Calais	476	762
j)	Warsaw to Dieppe	1047	1675

b More accurate conversions (p 187)
1 a) 10.16 cm **b)** 22.86 cm **c)** 26.67 cm
  d) 30.48 cm **e)** 45.72 cm
2 a) 9.14 m **b)** 5.48 m **c)** 4.11 m
  d) 2.13 m **e)** 4.57 m
3 a) 5.91 in **b)** 17.72 in **c)** 9.76 in
  d) 98.43 in **e)** 118.11 in
4 a) 29.8 miles **b)** 9.9 miles **c)** 24.8 miles
  d) 18.6 miles **e)** 14.6 miles
5 a) 24.2 km **b)** 40.3 km **c)** 67.6 km
  d) 48.3 km **e)** 15.3 km
6 a) 1030 km **b)** 1755 km
7 99 miles   **8** 75 mph and 62 mph

4 Weight

Measure weight in metric units

a Know metric units of weight (p 188)
1 a) g **b)** kg **c)** g
  d) g **e)** kg **f)** mg

b Weigh on balance scales (p 189)
1 any weights which match the given amounts
2 any weights that add to 1 kg.
3 any weights which match the given amounts
4 a) 7 kg **b)** 4 kg
  c) 2 kg **d)** 8 kg
  e) 4 kg 200 g **f)** 7 kg 300 g
  g) 2 kg 600 g **h)** 2 kg 870 g
  i) 5 kg 80 g **j)** 5 kg 389 g
  k) 5 kg 20 g **l)** 1 kg 5 g
5 a) 4000 g **b)** 2000 g **c)** 3000 g
  d) 1000 g **e)** 1500 g **f)** 1250 g
  g) 2500 g **h)** 3750 g
6 a) 500 g **b)** 700 g **c)** 530 g
  d) 220 g **e)** 750 g **f)** 30 g
  g) 160 g **h)** 420 g **i)** 640 g
  j) 750 g or $\frac{3}{4}$ kg **k)** 500 g or $\frac{1}{2}$ kg
  l) 250 g or $\frac{1}{4}$ kg

c Measure in grams and kilograms (p 190)
1 a) 2 **b)** 500 g
  c) i) 500 g **ii)** 2 kg 500 g **iii)** 4 kg
    iv) 5 kg 500 g **v)** 7 kg 500 g **vi)** 9 kg
2 a) 6 kg **b)** 10 **c)** 100 g
  d) i) 700 g **ii)** 2 kg 300 g
    iii) 3 kg 400 g **iv)** 4 kg 400 g
    v) 5 kg 200 g
  e) i) 0.7 kg **ii)** 2.3 kg
    iii) 3.4 kg **iv)** 4.4 kg
3 a) 500 g
  b) i) 50 g **ii)** 150 g
    iii) 300 g **iv)** 450 g
4 iii) 4 kg **iv)** 5 kg **v)** 7 kg **vi)** 9 kg
5 a) i) 1 kg 200 g **ii)** 2 kg 700 g
    iii) 3 kg 800 g **iv)** 5 kg 200 g
    v) 6 kg 800 g

b) i)   1.2 kg   ii)   2.7 kg
    iii) 3.8 kg   iv)   5.2 kg
    v)   6.8 kg

6 a) 50 g   b) 10 g
  c) i)   120 g   ii)   270 g
  iii) 490 g   iv)   640 g
  v) 830 g   vi)   940 g

7 a) A 6 kg   B 12.5 kg   C 18 kg
     D 27 kg   E 34.5 kg   F 42.5 kg
  b) i)   6.5 kg   ii)   9 kg   iii)   8 kg

8 a) 1 kg   b) 200 g
  c) A 2 kg 600 g   B 5 kg 200 g
     C 9 kg   D 12 kg 400 g
     E 16 kg 600 g   F 20 kg 800 g
  d) i)   2 kg 600 g   ii)   3 kg 400 g
     iii) 4 kg 200 g

Estimate weights between marked divisions (p 192)

(Allow any equivalent weights and some leeway)

1 a) A 250 g   B 650 g   C 975 g
     D 1525 g   E 1950 g   F 2350 g
  b) i)   400 g   ii)   550 g   iii)   400 g
     iv) 2100 g   v)   975 g   vi)   875 g
  c) A 1 kg   B 600 g   C 275 g
  d) D 975 g   E 550 g   F 150 g
  e) 2300 g

Choose units and instruments (p 193)

1 a) 410 g   b) 25 g   c) 5 kg
  d) 125 g   e) 1 kg 500 g   f) 50 g
  g) 250 g   h) 500 g   i) 1 kg
  (Allow reasonable alternatives)

2 a) kg   b) g   c) 10 g   d) 100 g   e) 10 g

3 a) P A   Q B   R A   S B   b) Q, S, R, P
  c) B there are extra divisions allowing you to
      weigh more accurately

Convert between metric weights (p 194)

1 a) 4 kg   b) 6.5 kg   c) 5.485 kg
  d) 34.5 kg   e) 0.8 kg   f) 0.25 kg
  g) 300 kg   h) 0.75 kg   i) 4000 kg
  j) 3 540 kg   k) 500 kg   l) 250 kg

2 a) 7000 g   b) 4500 g   c) 8268 g
  d) 16 400 g   e) 3 050 g   f) 300 g
  g) 60 g   h) 1025 g   i) 2 g
  j) 7.5 g   k) 0.5 g   l) 1000 g

3 a) 44 000 mg   b) 30 500 mg
  c) 3300 mg   d) 830 mg
  e) 12 300 mg   f) 70 mg
  g) 50 000 mg   h) 3 750 000 mg

4 a) 503 tonnes   b) 42 tonnes
  c) 4.5 tonnes   d) 0.589 tonnes

5 a) 3000 kg   b) 500 mg
  c) 1 500 g   d) 500 kg
  e) 7000 kg   f) 250 mg
  g) 0.75 tonnes   h) 5 tonnes
  i) 10 000 g

6 a) 0.4 kg 450 g   4 000 000 mg
      0.4 tonnes   450 kg
  b) 25 600 mg   0.25 kg   330 g   0.45 kg   ½ kg

Calculate using metric weights

a Kilograms and grams (p 196)

1 a) 5.7 kg   b) 3.075 kg   c) 3.15 kg
  d) 2.25 kg   e) 3.77 kg   f) 2.27 kg
  g) 4.7 kg   h) 1.6 kg   i) 3.94 kg
  j) 1.625 kg   k) 1.65 kg   l) 4.044 kg
  m) 2.345 kg   n) 0.996 kg or 996 g

2 a) 3.25 kg   b) 1.75 kg   c) 6.025 kg

3 6.05 kg   4 285 g   5 1.8 kg   6 960 g

7 850 g   8 a) 650 g   b) 3.25 kg

b Mixed calculations (p 197)

1 14.5 kg   2 10   3 3.61 kg
4 2.64 kg   5 2.1 kg   6 350 g
7 15   8 15 g   9 50
10 50

c Kilograms and tonnes (p 197)

1 16 days   2 400
3 a) 48 tonnes
  b) i)   locomotive
      ii)   52 tonnes more than the cars
  c) 300 tonnes   d) 448 tonnes

Convert imperial weights (p 198)

1 a) 32 oz   b) 70 oz   c) 100 oz
  d) 192 oz   e) 72 oz   f) 55 oz
  g) 4 oz   h) 8 oz   i) 12 oz
  j) 40 oz

2 a) 1 lb   b) 6 lb   c) 3 lb
  d) 8 lb   e) 5 lb   f) 28 lb
  g) 56 lb   h) 35 lb   i) 4480 lb
  j) 3360 lb

3 a) 3 lb 8 oz   b) 5 lb 2 oz
  c) 2 lb 6 oz   d) 4 lb 9 oz
  e) 2 lb 12 oz f) 1 lb 4 oz
  g) 3 lb 7 oz   h) 5 lb 1 oz

Calculate using imperial weight (p 199)

1 13 st 1 lb   2 8 st 3 lb
3 a) 68 lb   b) 4 st 12 lb
4 a) 149 lb   b) 10 st 9 lb
5 149 lb or 10 st 9 lb
6 a) see chart below
  b) 20 lb or 1 st 6 lb
  c) 1 st 2 lb or 16 lb

Week 1	Week 2	Week 3	Week 4	Week 5	Week 6
4 lb	4 lb	4 lb	3 lb	3 lb	2 lb
12 st 11 lb	12 st 7 lb	12 st 3 lb	12 st	11 st 11 lb	11 st 9 lb
179 lb	175 lb	171 lb	168 lb	165 lb	163 lb

Convert between metric and imperial weights

a Approximate metric/imperial conversions (p 200)

1 a) 100 g   b) more
2 a) 15 oz   b) 10 oz   c) 22 oz
  d) 11 oz   e) 19 oz   f) 29 oz
3 a) 350 g   b) 25 g   c) 125 g
  d) 200 g   e) 100 g   f) 90 g
  g) 65 g   h) 190 g

b More accurate conversions (p 201)

1 a) 8.8 lb   b) 10 kg   c) 19.8 lb
  d) 5.45 kg
2 a) 112 g   b) 5 oz   c) 420 g
  d) 2.5 oz

5 Capacity

Measure capacity and volume

a Know metric measures (p 203)

1 a) 2   b) 5   c) 10
2 a) 1000 mℓ b) 500 mℓ   c) 250 mℓ
  d) 750 mℓ   e) 1500 mℓ
3 a) 3 ℓ   b) 5 ℓ   c) 9 ℓ
  d) 12 ℓ   e) 4½ ℓ

b Measure in litres and millilitres (p 203)

1 a) i) 200 mℓ   ii) 600 mℓ
    iii) 1000 mℓ iv) 1200 mℓ
    v) 1600 mℓ
  b) i) 0.2 litres ii) 0.6 litres
    iii) 1 litre   iv) 1.2 litres
2 a) 1 litre   b) 100 mℓ   c) 50 mℓ
  d) i) 100 mℓ   ii) 250 mℓ
    iii) 500 mℓ iv) 750 mℓ
    v) 950 mℓ
  e) 500 mℓ
3 a) 200 mℓ   b) 5   c) 20 mℓ
  d) 10 mℓ
  e) i) 30 mℓ   ii) 60 mℓ
    iii) 110 mℓ iv) 130 mℓ
    v) 170 mℓ

Estimate between marked divisions (p 204)

1 ii) 275 mℓ   iii) 225 mℓ   iv) 175 mℓ
  v) 145 mℓ   vi) 60 mℓ
2 a) 200 mℓ
  b) i) 30 mℓ   ii) 60 mℓ   iii) 90 mℓ
    iv) 140 mℓ   v) 190 mℓ

Choose units and instruments (p 205)

1 a) litres   b) mℓ   c) mℓ
  d) litres   e) litres   f) mℓ
2 a) C b) C c) B d) A e) A
3 a) B   b) B   c) B   d) A
  e) A   f) A   g) B   h) A
4 a) 100 mℓ   b) 100 mℓ   c) mℓ
  d) 10 mℓ   e) litre
  f) litre or 100 mℓ   g) mℓ

Convert between millilitres, litres and centilitres (p 207)

1 a) 5000 mℓ   b) 2600 mℓ   c) 12 500 mℓ
   d) 3625 mℓ   e) 682 mℓ   f) 1850 mℓ
   g) 5063 mℓ   h) 750 mℓ   i) 83 mℓ
   j) 40 mℓ

2 a) 6 ℓ   b) 3.5 ℓ   c) 11 ℓ
   d) 1.1 ℓ   e) 65.4 ℓ   f) 0.33 ℓ
   g) 0.25 ℓ   h) 0.425 ℓ   i) 7.3 ℓ
   j) 5.32 ℓ

3 a) 3400 mℓ   b) 6250 mℓ
   c) 3630 mℓ   d) 8760 mℓ

4 a) i)   1 ℓ 200 mℓ   ii) 1.2 ℓ
   b) i)   3 ℓ 830 mℓ   ii) 3.83 ℓ
   c) i)   4 ℓ 935 mℓ   ii) 4.935 ℓ
   d) i)   5 ℓ 769 mℓ   ii) 5.769 ℓ
   e) i)   15 ℓ 800 mℓ   ii) 15.8 ℓ
   f) i)   5 ℓ 98 mℓ   ii) 5.098 ℓ

5 a) & g)   b) & k)   c) & l)
   d) & h)   e) & j)   f) & i)

6 C A D B

7 a) 3 ℓ   b) 2.5 ℓ   c) 30.5 ℓ
   d) 7.4 ℓ   e) 0.5 ℓ   f) 0.33 ℓ
   g) 0.75 ℓ   h) 32.1 ℓ

8 a) 3 cℓ   b) 50 cℓ   c) 25 cℓ
   d) 8.5 cℓ   e) 350 cℓ   f) 175 cℓ
   g) 50 cℓ   h) 46 cℓ

Calculate using metric units of capacity

a Litres and millilitres (p 209)

1 a) 3.7 ℓ   b) 3.425 ℓ   c) 9.075 ℓ
   d) 4.53 ℓ   e) 2.08 ℓ   f) 6.75 ℓ
   g) 205 mℓ   h) 5.96 ℓ   i) 2.66 ℓ
   j) 4.375 ℓ

2 6.5 ℓ   3 1.62 ℓ

4 a) 6.83 ℓ   b) 1.08 ℓ
   c) 4.57 ℓ   d) 8.99 ℓ

5 a) 500 mℓ   b) 400 mℓ   c) 400 mℓ
   d) 160 mℓ

6 a) 4.67 ℓ   b) 730 mℓ or 0.73 ℓ
   c) B and D   d) 800 mℓ   e) 5 ℓ

b Mixed calculations (p 209 or 210)

1 a) 20 mℓ   b) 7   2 20

3 4.8 ℓ   4 a) 9.6 ℓ   b) 7
5 9   6 a) 1.8 ℓ   b) 75 mℓ
7 4.25 ℓ   8 6 ℓ

9 a) 150 mℓ orange, 200 mℓ lemonade,
       75 mℓ rum, 50 mℓ tequila
   b) 475 mℓ

10 Depends on number in group

Measure with metric and imperial units

Activity (p 211)

1 a) less   b) more

Convert imperial units of capacity (p 212)

1 a) 3 pints   b) 2 pints
   c) 3.5 pints   d) 7.5 pints
   e) 32 pints   f) 12 pints
   g) 4 pints   h) 2 pints

2 a) 3 gallons   b) $\frac{1}{4}$ gallon
   c) 7.5 gallons   d) 17.5 gallons

3 a) 40 fl oz   b) 2 fl oz
   c) 10 fl oz   d) 5 fl oz

Calculate using imperial units of volume (p 212)

1 a) 20 fl oz lemonade   10 fl oz orange
       5 fl oz apple $2\frac{1}{2}$ fl oz lemon
       2 fl oz tequila
   b) $39\frac{1}{2}$ fl oz

2 $\frac{3}{4}$ gal   3 a) 40   b) £14.96

4 6 gallons

5 a) i)   80 pints   ii) 560 pints
       iii) 29 200 pints
   b) i)   10 gallons   ii) 70 gallons
       iii) 3650 gallons

Convert between metric and imperial measures

a Approximate metric/imperial conversions (p 213)

1 a) a litre   b) 1 pint
2 a) $3\frac{1}{2}$ pt   b) 2 ℓ   c) 4 fl oz
   d) 10 gal   e) 18 ℓ   f) 240 mℓ

3 $\approx \frac{2}{3}$ litre   4 a) 10 ℓ   b) 6 fl oz

b More accurate conversions (p 214)

1 a) 1.14 ℓ   b) 5 pt   c) 4.56 ℓ
   d) 7.02 pt (to 2 dp)

2 a) 22.75 ℓ   b) 110 gal (nearest gal)
   c) 40.95 ℓ   d) 7.91 gal (to 2 dp)

3 a) 4.4 gallons   b) 54.5 litres (to 1 dp)

4 85.2 mℓ

5 a) 364 litres
   b) 3.85 gal   c) 21 weeks

Use conversion scales and tables (p 214)

1 a) i)   16 km   ii)   5 miles
    iii)   13 km   iv)   7.5 miles
   b) i)   68 km   ii)   42 or 43 miles
   c) i)   59.2 km   ii)   37 miles

2

Length in inches	1	2	$3\frac{1}{8}$	$3\frac{1}{2}$	$3\frac{7}{8}$	$4\frac{1}{2}$	$4\frac{3}{4}$	$5\frac{1}{4}$	$5\frac{3}{8}$	$5\frac{5}{8}$
Length 1cm	2.5	5.1	8	8.9	10	11.5	12.1	13.3	13.7	14.3

3 a)   57 kg, 9 st   b)   66 kg, 10 st 6 lb
   c)   73 kg, 11 st 7 lb   d)   86 kg, 13 st 7 lb
   e)   94 kg, 14 st 11 lb   f)   300 mℓ, 10.6 fl oz
   g)   225 mℓ, 8 fl oz   h)   370 mℓ, 13 fl oz
   i)   510 mℓ, 18 fl oz

4 a) 3.107 miles   b) 96.56 km
   c) 77.25 km   d) 11.18 miles

6 Temperature

Measure temperature (p 216)

1 a) 40°C   b) 35°C
   c) i)   35.5°C   ii)   36.6°C   iii)   36.9°C
   iv) 37.2°C   v)   37.6°C   vi)   38°C

2 a) 50°C   b) 0°C
   c) i)   12°C   ii)   23°C   iii)   26°C
   iv)   35°C   v)   44°C

3 a) 50°C   b) 0°C   b) 2°C
   d) i)   3°C   ii)   16°C   iii)   27°C
   iv)   36°C   v)   44°C

4 a) 9°C   b) 7°C   c) 8°C
   d) 16°C   e) 24°C   f) 27°C

5 a) 9°C   b) 18°C   c) 7°C

6 a) 54°C   b) 11°C   c) 6 000°C
   d) 20°C   e) 0°C   f) 28°C

Temperatures below freezing point (p 217)

1 a) 50°C   b) −20°C

c) i)   22°C   ii)   13°C   iii)   8°C
   iv)   2°C   v)   −2°C   vi)   −6°C
   vii) −12°C   viii) −17°C
d) i)   22°C   ii)   −17°C

2 a

3 a)   21°C   12°C   2°C   −2°C   −12°C   −21°C
   b)   23°C   14°C   4°C   0°C   −2°C   −4°C
   c)   7°C   5°C   3°C   1°C   −2°C   −7°C

4 a) 9°C   b) 14°C   c) 14°C
   d) 16°C   e) 22°C   f) 41°C
   g) 5°C   h) 17°C

5 a) 23°C   b) 26°C   c) 21°C
   d) 18°C   e) 26°C   f) 19°C
   g) 9°C   h) 14°C

6 a) i) 6°C   ii) −5°C
   b)   days 4, 5, 6, 7, 8   c)   11°C

7

Sitting room	21°C	10°C	15°C	24°C
Dining room	20°C	9°C	14°C	23°C
Kitchen	16°C	5°C	10°C	19°C
Bedroom 1	19°C	8°C	13°C	22°C
Bedroom 2	16°C	5°C	10°C	19°C
Bedroom 3	13°C	2°C	7°C	16°C

Celsius and Fahrenheit (p 220)

1 a) i)   200°C   ii) 180°C   iii) 110°C
   b) i)   400°F   ii) 350°F   iii) 225°F

2 a) 350°F   b) 400°F
   c)   dials showing
     i) 180°C (meat), 350°F (meat)
     ii) 200°C (poultry), 400°F (poultry)

Use scales to convert temperatures (p 220)

1 32°F

2 a) 86°F   b) 113°F   c) 73°F
   d) 14°F   e) 5°F   f) 21°F

3 a) 27°C   b) 10°C   c) 6°C
   d) −8°C   e) 41°C   f) −20°C

Use formulae to convert temperatures (p 221)

1 a) 68°F   b)   86°F   c) 41°F
   d) 59°F   e)   50°F   f) 77°F
   g) 53.6°F   h)   57.2°F

2 a) 11°C   **b)** 19°C   **c)** 34°C

   d) 9°C   **e)** 27°C   **f)** 13°C

   g) 15°C

7 Perimeter, Area and Volume

Perimeter (p 222)

1 a) 11.8 cm   **b)** 14.8 cm   **c)** 15.5 cm

   d) 13.4 cm   **e)** 16.7 cm

2 a) 21 m   **b)** 21 m   **c)** 218 m   **d)** 18.8 m

3 5 m   **4** 3.8 m

5

Length	Width	Perimeter
6 cm	2 cm	16 cm
10 mm	6 mm	32 mm
20 cm	6.2 cm	52.4 cm
4.5 m	3 m	15 m
20 mm	15 mm	70 mm
2.7 m	2.25 m	9.9 m

6 Any dimensions which fit the given perimeters.

7 1300 m   **8** 320 cm   **9** 7.8 m

Area

a Measuring in square units (p 225)

1 a) 5 cm^2 **b)** 7 cm^2 **c)** 8 cm^2

2 Any 4 shapes with an area of 12 cm^2.

b Area of a rectangle (p 225)

1 a) 15 m^2 **b)** 26 m^2 **c)** 400 mm^2

   d) 15 cm^2 **e)** 1700 mm^2

   f) 9750 cm^2 or 0.975 m^2

2 Any dimensions which match the given areas.

3 a) 54 m^2 **b)** 1080 g

4 a) £43.96   **b)** 4.32 m^2

Circles

a Circumference (p 227)

1 a) 10p diameter = 2.4 cm   £1 = 2.2 cm

   b) 10p circumference = 7.5 cm   £1 = 6.9 cm

2 a) 31.4 cm **b)** 44.0 cm   **c)** 4.7 m

   d) 5.0 m   **e)** 141.3 m or 141.4 m **f)** 94.2 m

3

Radius	Diameter	Circumference
2 cm	4 cm	12.6 cm
15 mm	30 mm	94.2 mm
3 m	6 m	18.8 m
1.2 m	2.4 m	7.5 m
2.5 cm	5.0 cm	15.7 cm
12.0 mm	24.0 mm	75.4 mm

4 151 cm

5 251 cm

b Area of a circle (p 228)

1 a) 3.1 m^2 **b)** 28.3 cm^2

   c) 78.5 cm^2 **d)** 15.2 m^2

2 a) 153.9 cm^2 **b)** 12.6 m^2

   c) 201.0 mm^2 or 201.1 mm^2

   d) 452.2 mm^2 or 452.4 mm^2

   e) 706.5 cm^2 or 706.9 cm^2

   f) 6.2 m^2

3 a) 50.2 cm^2 or 50.3 cm^2

   b) 314 mm^2 or 314.2 mm^2 **c)** 95.0 cm^2

   d) 4.9 m^2 **e)** 153.9 mm^2

   f) 5024 cm^2 or 5026.5 cm^2

4 4420 cm^2

5 a) 31 cm

   b) 754.4 cm^2 or 754.8 cm^2

   c) 176.6 cm^2 or 176.7 cm^2

   d) 578 cm^2

Areas of composite shapes (p 229)

1 a) 21 m^2 **b)** 13 m^2 **c)** 21 m^2

   d) 18.32 m^2 **e)** 25.8 m^2

2 a) i) 5.76 m^2 **ii)** 10.32 m^2

     iii) 1.13 m^2 **iv)** 24.55 m^2

   b) 210 g   **c)** 1.23 kg or 1230 g

3 a) 10.8 m^2

   b) area of walls = 29.04 m^2 area of door and

     window = 3.4 m^2

     walls less door and window = 25.64 m^2

   c) No (3 litres are needed).

Use formulae to find areas (p 231)

1 a) 6 cm^2　　b) 10.8 m^2　　c) 94.5 cm^2

2 1.05 m^2　　　3 4800 cm^2 or 0.48 m^2

4 180 cm^2　　　5 2.2 m^2　　6 4.7 m^2

Volume of a cuboid (p 232)

1 a) 6 cm^3　　b) 4 cm^3　　c) 18 cm^3

　d) 30 cm^3

2 a) 36 m^3　　b) 8000 mm^3

　c) 32.4 cm^3　d) 28.8 cm^3

3

Length	Width	Height	Volume
2 cm	4 cm	5 cm	40 cm^3
3 m	3.4 m	3.5 m	35.7 m^3
4 mm	2.5 mm	6 mm	60 mm^3
9 cm	6.2 cm	8 cm	446.4 cm^3

4 0.5 m^3　　　　5 4000 cm^3

6 Any dimensions which make a volume of 1 litre

7 $112\,500 \text{ cm}^3$　　8 $15\,625 \text{ mm}^3$

9 a) 100 cm　　b) $10\,000 \text{ cm}^2$

　c) $1\,000\,000 \text{ cm}^3$

10 1st 0.384 m^3　2nd 0.224 m^3　3rd 0.14 m^3

　b) 0.748 m^3

11

Length	Width	Height	Volume
4 m	2 m	3 m	24 m^3
3 cm	2 cm	8 cm	48 cm^3
2 m	3 m	9 m	54 m^3
4 cm	4 cm	4 cm	64 cm^3

Volume of a cylinder (p 234)

1 a) 56.5 cm^3　　b) 19.6 m^3

　c) 2.4 m^3　　　d) 17.0 m^3

　e) 6.8 cm^3

2 a) 9.0 m^3

　b) 1017.4 cm^3 or 1017.9 cm^3

　c) 62.2 m^3　　　d) 45.2 m^3

　e) 282.6 cm^3 or 282.7 cm^3

　f) 0.4 m^3

3 a) 3.77 m^3　　b) 7.85 cm^3

　c) 2.71 cm^3　　d) 0.92 m^3

　e) 0.11 m^3　　　f) 0.57 m^3

4 0.34 m^3

Use formulae to find volumes (p 235)

1 1200 cm^3

2 a) $75\,000 \text{ cm}^3$　　b) 2 bags

3 a) 60 cm^3　　　b) 416

4 27 litres

8 Shape

Angles (p 237)

1 a) 1　　　　b) 2　　　　c) 3

　d) 2　　　　e) 4　　　　f) 4

2 Any 10 objects with right angles

3 a) i) $90°$　　ii) $180°$　　iii) $270°$

　b) $360°$

Parallel lines (p 238)

1 B D

2 Any examples of parallel lines

2-D shapes (p 239)

1

	Number of angles that are:		
	Right angles	Smaller	Larger
Square	4		
Rectangle	4		
Regular Hexagon			6
Regular Octagon			8
Regular Pentagon			5
Parallelogram		2	2
Rhombus		2	2
Trapezium		2	2

2

	4 sides equal	4 right angles	Opposite sides equal	Opposite angles equal	No parallel lines	1 pair of parallel lines	2 pairs of parallel lines
Square	✔	✔	✔	✔			✔
Rectangle		✔	✔	✔			✔
Parallelogram			✔	✔			✔
Rhombus	✔		✔	✔			✔
Trapezium						✔	

Line symmetry (p 240)

1. a) 1   b) 2   c) 1
   d) 1   e) 1   f) 2
   g) 1   h) 0   i) 1
   j) 0   k) 2   l) 1

2. a) parallelogram
   b) none
   c) rectangle, rhombus
   d) square, regular hexagon

3.

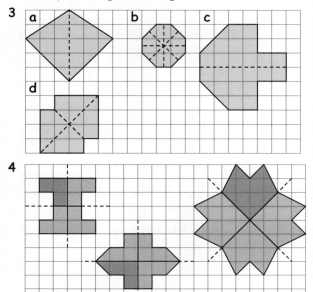

4.

5. students' diagrams

Tessellations (p 241)

1. a) 8   b) 8   c) 28   d) 8
2. a) hexagon, triangle
   b) pentagon, 4 sided polygon
   (also called a quadrilateral)

3-D shapes (p 242)

1.

	Shape of faces	No. of faces	No. of edges	No. of vertices
Cube	Squares	6	12	8
Cuboid	Rectangles	6	12	8
Cylinder	Circles and curved rectangles	3	2	0
Square-based pyramid	Square and triangles	5	8	5
Triangular prism	Triangles and rectangles	5	9	6

Solve problems involving 2-D and 3-D shapes (p 244)

1. a) 88 cm   b) 22 cm
2. a) length 1.6 m   b) height 1.15 m
3. a) 45 tiles   b) 180 tiles
4. a) i) 24 tiles   ii) 112 tiles   b) 136 tiles
5. 360   6 168
7. a) i) 295 cm   ii) 310 cm   iii) 350 cm
   b) 4-man   c) 10 cm   d) 4-man   e) 9

Handling Data

1 Extracting and Interpreting Information

Information from lists, tables, diagrams, pictograms and bar charts

a Find information from lists (p 246)

1. a) alphabetically   b) easy to find items
   c) 791455   d) 787652
   e) Doctor's
2. a) by date   b) Dinner date
   c) 20th April   d) 17th March
   e) Between dinner date and wedding anniversary

3. a) at random   b) 4
   c) none   d) semi-skimmed
4. a) alphabetically   b) by date
   c) by date   d) alphabetically
   e) alphabetically in categories

b Find information from tables (p 249)

1. a) 11   b) 7   c) 11   d) 17
   e) Do-It-Yourself (19 students)
2. a) £11.00   b) £11.99   c) video
   d) Horror   e) £3.01
3. a) i) £190   ii) £399
   b) i) Ford Focus   ii) 14 days
   c) Fiat Punto   d) £190
   e) Vauxhall Tigra   f) £105

4 a) 791/755   **b)** 11:10   **c)** 06:30
d) Gatwick-Pula   **e)** Saturday
5 a) Title & headings
b) Redrawn table with suitable title and headings
c) £1286   **d)** £500
e) i) Altea or Hotel Esplendia   **ii)** FB
iii) 7 nights
f) £105
6 a) £78.60   **b)** £225.50

c Find information from diagrams (p 252)

1 a) Go straight on at the roundabout.
The college is on the left.
b) Turn left at the roundabout.
The college is on the left.
c) Go straight on until the roundabout.
Turn right and the college is on the left.
d) Turn right at the first junction, follow the road past the school and round the left-hand bend. The college is on the right.
e) Turn left at the Town Hall then right at the roundabout. The college is on the left.
f) Turn left at the traffic lights then right at the roundabout. The college is on the left.
2 (Accept suitable alternative routes).
a) Turn right from the college, then left at the roundabout. The post office is on the left.
b) Turn left out of the school. Turn right at the 1st T-junction and left at the 2nd T-junction. The petrol station is on the right.
c) Turn left out of the gym. Turn left at the 1st T-junction and right at the 2nd T-junction and right at the 3rd T-junction. The fish and chip shop is on the right.
d) Turn right out of the cinema. Turn left at the 1st T-junction, right at the 2nd T-junction and right at the 3rd T-junction, then first left. The supermarket is on the left.
e), f) There is more than one good answer

d Find information from pictograms (p 253)

1 a) 450
b) i) Music Box   **ii)** George's Records
c) 150   **d)** 2300
2 a) i) carpet   **ii)** decorating
b) i) curtains £80 bed linen £70   **ii)** £465
carpet £155   furniture £104
decorating £56   (allow ± £5)

e Find information from bar charts (p 254)

1 a)

Type of drink	Number of workers
Tea	25
Decaff tea	12
Coffee	30
Decaff coffee	13
Water	7
Fruit juice	15

b) 13   **c)** 8   **d)** 25   **e)** 102
2 a) i) 38   **ii)** 65   **iii)** 39   **iv)** 21
b) i) Soaps   **ii)** Music
c) 17   **d)** 300
3 a) i) Germany   **ii)** Ireland
b) UK 60 million, Spain 40 million
Netherlands 16 million, Ireland 4 million
Germany 83 million, Belgium 10 million
c) i) 23 million   **ii)** 44 million
d) 64 million
4 a)

Student	Height (m)
Jane	1.5
Debbie	1.6
David	1.9
Nasma	1.7
Tyla	1.8
Rae	1.7
Gary	1.8

b) Jane   **c)** David
d) Rae   **e)** Gary

5 a)   Title, vertical axis label (gridlines)

b)   Cheese   c)   Baked Beans

d)

Filling	No. bought
Baked Beans	16
Cheese	37
Chicken tikka	28
Coleslaw	19
Tuna	18

e)   118   f)   19

6 a)   Chart B

b)   i), ii) Students' own estimates

(exact values given below)

Year	Chart A	Chart B
1	51	51
2	59	59
3	62	62
4	63	63
5	68	68

iii) Chart B

7 a)   Catering, Electrical installation

b)   i)   5   ii)   2   iii) 10

c)   i)   26   ii)   35   iii) 34

d)   i)   92   ii)   110

8 a)   i)   Pete   ii)   £460

b)   i)   Adrian   ii)   £310

c)   Ahmed £450, Jim £360, Sam £420

d)   i)   Sam   ii)   £300

e)   i)   Adrian & Jim   ii)   £210

f)   i)   Adrian £100, Ahmed £180, Jim £150,
         Pete £220, Sam £120

ii)   Pete, Ahmed, Jim, Sam, Adrian

9   Any 3 examples of each type of data

10

Magazine	a nearest million	b nearest 100 000
What's On TV?	4 million	4 400 000
TV Times	3 million	2 900 000
TV & Satellite	1 million	1 000 000
TV Quick	2 million	2 000 000
TV Choice	1 million	1 100 000
Radio Times	3 million	3 400 000

11 a)   Maths   b)   Media

c)   Allow ±2% on A & U, ±4% on others

Subject	A	B	C	D	E	U
Computing	8%	15%	22%	24%	20%	11%
Law	15%	19%	21%	20%	15%	10%
Maths	37%	19%	15%	11%	8%	10%
Media	12%	25%	32%	21%	8%	2%

Information from pie charts and line graphs

a Find information from pie charts (p 261)

1 a)   work   b)   1.5 hours

c)   24 hours – total time in a day

2 a)   i) drive   ii) cycle

b)   i) $\frac{1}{4}$ ii) $\frac{1}{10}$ iii) $\frac{1}{5}$ iv) $\frac{2}{5}$ v) $\frac{1}{20}$

c)   walk 40, drive 160, bus 100,
     train 80, cycle 20

3 a)   A $\frac{1}{8}$ B $\frac{1}{4}$ C $\frac{1}{2}$ D $\frac{1}{8}$

b)   A 6   B 12   C 24   D 6

4 a)   i) T   ii) F   iii) T   iv) T

b)   Terraced, Flats, Semi-detached,
     Detached & Bungalows (approx equal)

5 a)

Flat mate	Angle	Amount to pay
Bev	120°	120 × £0.50 = £60
Mary	40°	40 × £0.50 = £20
Jan	100°	100 × £0.50 = £50
Oliver	20°	20 × £0.50 = £10
Matt	80°	80 × £0.50 = £40
	Total	£180

6 a)   Paint   b) more   c) true

d)   Wallpaper £1755, Paint £2340
     Decorating equipment £945,
     Plants £1440, Gardening tools £1260,
     Other £360 (Allow ±£22.50)

7 a)   1.5 workers

b)   360 factory workers, 48 sales workers,
     42 managers

c)   540

8 a) i), ii), iv), vi)

b) i) 96°   **ii)** 2.5 people

iii) & c) i)

	Fri	Sat
Men	240	250
Women	420	370
Children	240	580
Total	**900**	**1200**

c) ii) as **a) i)**

b Find information from line graphs (p 266)

(allow approximate answers)

1 a) i) 1 hour   **ii)** 0.5°C

b) every 2 hours

c) i) 5.5°C   **ii)** 14:00

d) i) – 3.5°C   **ii)** 04:00

e) i) 08:00   **ii)** 00:20, 18:40

(±10 min)

f) i) 04:00 to 14:00

ii) 00:00 to 04:00 and 14:00 to 24:00

g) 06:00 to 10:00

2 a) 5 mm

b) i) November   **ii)** 150 mm

c) i) September   **ii)** 35 mm

d) 76 mm ± 5 mm   **e)** 1072 mm ± 20 mm

3 a) i) Graph B

ii)

Year	Profits (£000s)
1	2130
2	2420
3	2390
4	2510
5	2680

(allow ±10)

b) Axis does not start at zero.

4 a) i) 10 gallons ≈ 45 litres

ii) 5 gallons ≈ 23 litres

iii) 18 gallons ≈ 82 litres

iv) 7.5 gallons ≈ 34 litres

b) i) 40 litres ≈ 9 gallons

ii) 72 litres ≈ 16 gallons

iii) 24 litres ≈ 5.5 gallons

iv) 67 litres ≈ 14.5 gallons

c) 68 litres   **d)** 18 gallons

5 a) i) 2°C   **ii)** 5°F

b) i) 20°C ≈ 68°F   **ii)** 48°C ≈ 118°F

iii) 75°C ≈ 167°F   **iv)** 27°C ≈ 81°F

v) – 10°C ≈ 14°F   **vi)** – 7°C ≈ 19°F

c) i) 50°F ≈ 10°C   **ii)** 140°F ≈ 60°C

iii) 75°F ≈ 24°C   **iv)** 205°F ≈ 96°C

v) 184°F ≈ 84°C   **vi)** 28°F ≈ –2°C

d) freezes at 32°F, boils at 212°F

6 a) i) April   **ii)** May

b) i) December

ii) January & December

c) i) 0.5 hour (or 30 minutes) per day

ii) 2 hours per day

d) i) 3.4 hours (or 3 hours 24 minutes) per day

ii) 2.7 hours (or 2 hours 42 minutes) per day

e) More sunshine in England than in Scotland. Least sunshine in winter, but more in spring than in summer.

7 a) i) December   **ii)** April & August

iii) January

b) i) August   **ii)** December   **iii)** August

c) 5.7 million tonnes of oil equivalent

d) i) 21.4 million tonnes of oil equivalent

ii) 14.5 million tonnes of oil equivalent

e) More in winter than summer – many people use natural gas for heating.

2 Collecting and Illustrating Data

Record information using a tally chart (p 272)

1 a) Cat 19, Rabbit 5, Bird 7, Fish 6, Reptile 2, Other 11, None 13

b) Cat

c) Any type of pet not in the table, e.g. hamster

2 a)

Number of pets	Tally	Frequency
0	⊮⊮ ⊮⊮ III	13
1	⊮⊮ ⊮⊮ ⊮⊮ ⊮⊮ ⊮⊮ I	26
2	⊮⊮ IIII	9
3	⊮⊮ II	7
4	II	2
5	I	1
6	II	2

b) i) 13   ii) 7   iii) 5

c) 60

3 a)

Grade	Tally	Frequency
Distinction	卌 II	7
Merit	卌 卌 IIII	14
Pass	卌 卌 卌 IIII	19
Fail	卌 卌	10

b) 50   c) i) $\frac{7}{50}$ ii) $\frac{2}{25}$ d) 20%

4 a)

No. of Books	Tally	Frequency
1	卌 卌 卌 卌 卌 卌 I	31
2	卌 卌 卌 I	16
3	卌 卌 IIII	14
4	卌 卌 I	11
5	卌 III	8
6	IIII	4

b) 1   c) 84   d) 14% (nearest %)

Illustrate data using a pictogram or bar chart

a Using a pictogram (p 274)

1 Sunshine at a seaside resort in a week in August

Monday	☀ ☀ ☀
Tuesday	☀ ☀
Wednesday	☀ ◖
Thursday	☀ ☀ ◖
Friday	☀ ☀ ☀ ☀
Saturday	☀ ☀ ☀ ☀ ☀
Sunday	☀ ☀ ☀ ☀ ◖

Key: ☀ = 2 hours   ◖ = 1 hour

2 Number of houses sold by estate agent

January	🏠🏠🏠
February	🏠🏠🏠
March	🏠🏠🏠🏠🏠
April	🏠🏠🏠🏠🏠
May	🏠🏠🏠🏠🏠🏠
June	🏠🏠🏠🏠🏠🏠

Key: 🏠 = 10 houses

3 Students' own design of pictogram

b Using a bar chart (p 275)

1 a) Allow other scales

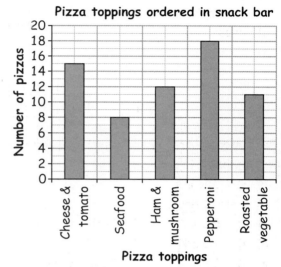

Pizza toppings ordered in snack bar

b) i) pepperoni   ii) seafood

2 a) Allow other scales

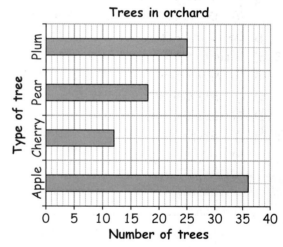

Trees in orchard

b) i) apple   ii) 7

3 a) Students' own bar charts

b) France

c) i) 48   ii) 9

4 a) Students' own bar charts

b) Adventure   c) Musical

d) Adventure, Children's, Horror, Thriller, Comedy, Sci-fi, Musical

5 a) Students' own bar charts

b) Most houses he supplies get 1 paper. As the number of papers increases, the number of houses decreases.

6 a) Students' own bar charts

b) i) Sun   **ii)** Guardian

c) Sun, Mirror, Mail, Telegraph, Express, Times, Star, Guardian

7 a) allow other scales

Life expectancy

b) i) UK   **ii)** Angola

c) i) Life expectancy is longer for females than males in all countries.

ii) Russia

d) The UK closely followed by the USA have the best life expectancy for both men and women.

Life expectancy is also reasonably good in China and Brazil.

Life expectancy in Russia is reasonably good for women but poorer for men.

Life expectancy for men is slightly better in India than Russia, but about 10 years less for women.

Life expectancy is poor for both men and women in Afghanistan being just over half that in the UK.

Angola has the worst life expectancy of all, being less than half that in the UK for both men and women.

8 a)

Industry	Number of employees (thousands)		
	Male	Female	Total
Hotels & restaurants	3288	3575	6863
Transport & communication	1319	489	1808
Finance & business	3053	2659	5712
Education & health	2204	4890	7094
Other	861	923	1784

b) Allow other scales.

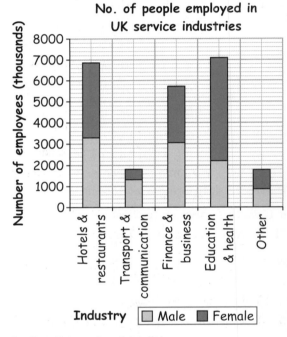

No. of people employed in UK service industries

c) i) Education & health

ii) Hotels & restaurants

iii) Education & health

Illustrate data using a pie chart (p 279)

1 a) Grades achieved by students on a course

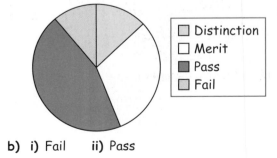

b) i) Fail   **ii)** Pass

2 a) 24   **b)** 15°

c)

Lunch	No. of students	Angle
Sandwich	6	$6 \times 15 = 90°$
Pasta	5	$5 \times 15 = 75°$
Baked potato	8	$8 \times 15 = 120°$
Salad	4	$4 \times 15 = 60°$
Pizza	1	$1 \times 15 = 15°$
Total	24	360°

d) Students' choice of lunch

☐ Sandwich
☐ Pasta
☐ Baked potato
☐ Salad
☐ Pizza

3 a) Angles: 0 cars 94°, 1 car 165°,
              2 cars 79°, 3 or more cars 22°

Car ownership by households in the UK

☐ No car
☐ 1 car
☐ 2 cars
☐ 3 or more cars

b) 1   **c)** more than $\frac{1}{4}$

4 a) Angles: W Europe 130°, E Europe 22°,
              Asia 114°, N America 75°,
              Other 19°

Production of cars

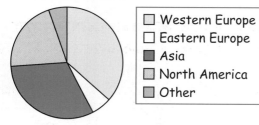

☐ Western Europe
☐ Eastern Europe
☐ Asia
☐ North America
☐ Other

b) Western Europe

5 a) Angles: Post 56°, News & mags 110°,
              Radio 16°, TV 128°, Trans &
              outdoor 23°, Other 27°

Spending on advertising

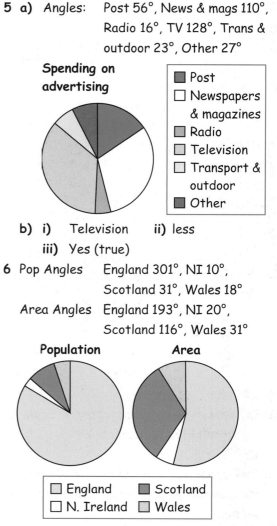

☐ Post
☐ Newspapers & magazines
☐ Radio
☐ Television
☐ Transport & outdoor
☐ Other

b) i) Television   **ii)** less
   iii) Yes (true)

6 Pop Angles   England 301°, NI 10°,
              Scotland 31°, Wales 18°

Area Angles   England 193°, NI 20°,
              Scotland 116°, Wales 31°

Population   **Area**

☐ England   ☐ Scotland
☐ N. Ireland   ☐ Wales

England has over $\frac{3}{4}$ of the population but just over $\frac{1}{2}$ of the land area. Scotland has over $\frac{1}{4}$ of the land area but a much smaller proportion of the population. Wales and Northern Ireland also have a greater proportion of the land area than their population would suggest. This means that the population density in England is greater than in any of the other countries. Scotland is more sparsely populated than the other countries.
(or other valid comments)

Draw graphs

a Draw a line graph (p 281)

1 a)

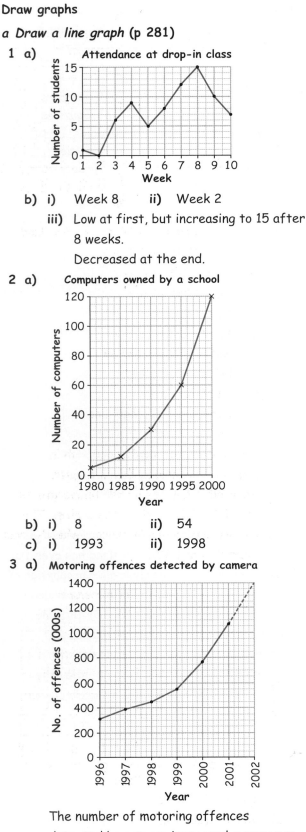

Attendance at drop-in class

b) i)   Week 8   ii)   Week 2

iii) Low at first, but increasing to 15 after
8 weeks.
Decreased at the end.

2 a)

Computers owned by a school

b) i)   8   ii)   54

c) i)   1993   ii)   1998

3 a)

Motoring offences detected by camera

The number of motoring offences
detected by camera increased every year
between 1996 and 2001.

b) If the trend continues the number
detected in 2002 would be nearly
1 400 000.

4 a)

Noise level in factory

b) 9:45 am, 12:15 pm, 1:35 pm, 3:15 pm

c) 6 hours 50 minutes (allow ±10 min)

d) Starts low at 8 am (before most of work
begins), builds to peak of almost 90 dB at
11 am (peak time for morning work), then
falls to 74 dB at 1 pm (lunchtime – less
work going on) before rising again to about
84 dB between 2 pm and 3 pm (peak period
for afternoon work).
Finally falls to 54 dB at 5 pm (most of work
finished for day).

5 a) i)

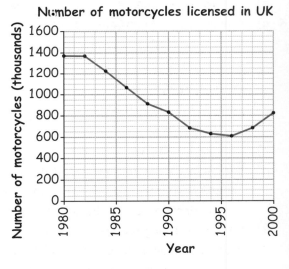

Number of motorcycles licensed in UK

ii)

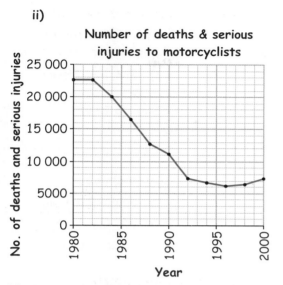

Number of deaths & serious injuries to motorcyclists

b) Decrease in the number of motorcycles and accidents to motorcyclists between 1980 and 1996 followed by an increase in both. Graphs have very similar shapes.

6 a)

Clothing Sales

b) i) London Dec, Manchester Dec

  ii) London Feb, Manchester Feb

  iii) London – Jan, Nov, Dec

       Manchester – Dec

c) i) Jan   **ii)** Jul

d) Both sold a lot in January (sales) and in December (before Christmas). Both sold less in February (after the sales), but then sales rose during the spring with London reaching a peak in June and Manchester in July. Sales at both shops dipped slightly in August. From September onwards the sales in London increased, whereas in Manchester sales didn't rise significantly until after October.

7 a)

Average monthly temperatures

b) i) E&W 16.5°C August,

    Scot 14°C August

    NI 15°C August

  ii) E&W 5.3°C January,

    Scot 3.5°C December

    NI 4.9°C December

  iii) E&W Jan, Dec

    Scot Jan, Feb, Mar, Dec

    NI Feb, Dec

c) All low in winter months and high in summer, reaching a peak in August. Generally E&W has higher temperatures than NI, with Scotland the coolest. The only exception was in January when NI was warmer than E&W.

8 a)

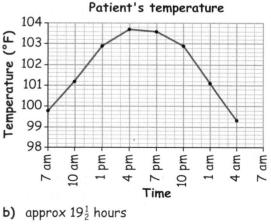

Patient's temperature

b) approx $19\frac{1}{2}$ hours

c) 5:20 am (approx)

b Draw and use conversion graphs **(p 285)**

1 **a)** Horizontal 0.2 inches, Vertical 0.5 cm

   c) **i)** 6 in = 15.2 cm

   ii) 9 in = 22.9 cm

   iii) 2.6 in = 6.6 cm

   iv) 4.3 in = 10.9 cm

   v) 10 cm = 3.9 in

   vi) 25 cm = 9.8 in

   vii) 18 cm = 7.1 in

   viii) 12.5 cm = 4.9 in

   Allow ±0.5 cm and ±0.2 in

2 **a)**

Conversion graph for kilograms and pounds

   b) Copy and complete the following:

   i) 15 kg = 33 lb   **ii)** 9 kg = 19.8 lb

   iii) 12.5 kg = 27.5 lb   **iv)** 30 lb = 13.6 kg

   v) 14 lb = 6.4 kg   **vi)** 38.5 lb = 17.5 kg

   Allow ±1 lb and ±0.5 kg

3 Averages and Range

Find the mean (p 287)

1 **a)** 1.8   **b)** 6   **c)** 6.6

   d) 4.25   **e)** 0.375 kg   **f)** £40

2 **a)** Andy 45, Imran 37, Mark 24, Stuart 28.75, Tim 39.75

   b) **i)** Andy   **ii)** Mark

3 **a)** £7   **b)** No – nobody gets £7 per hour

4 **a)** 303   **b)** 189.6

5 **a)** Jen £6.40, Kim £5.60, Ben £7.50, Nasma £6.40, Mike £5.20, Wes £5.80

   b) £6.15   **c)** Jen, Ben, Nasma

(*Using a pictogram data*): (p 274)

1 6.4 hours per day (1 dp)

2 45 houses (nearest whole number)

(*Using a bar chart data*): (p 275)

1 12.8 pizzas (1 dp)   2 22.8 trees (1 dp)

3 39.5 properties   4 190 films

6 3 669 000 readers (nearest thousand)

(*Draw a line graph data*): (p 281)

1 7.3 students   3 590 000 offences

4 72.8 dB

5 Number of motorcycles per year:
   928 thousand (nearest thousand)
   Number of motorcycle accidents per year:
   12 700 (nearest hundred)

6 London £256 000 (nearest £thousand)
   Manchester £202 000 (nearest £thousand)

Level 2 (p 290)

6 **a)** 20   **b)** 0.9 errors per page

7 **a)** 2.85 children per family   **b)** 10

8 **a)** 1.2 trains per day   **b)** 24%

9 **a)** 3   **b)** 18.1 years (1 dp)

10 **a)** **i)** 2 goals per match

   ii) 1.1 goals per match (1 dp)

   b) at home

Find the mode and median (p 292)

1 'best' average underlined (matter of opinion)
   mean given to 1 dp when not exact

   a) mode = 1, median = 1, mean = 1.6 (pints)

   b) modes = 16, 17, median = 16.5, mean = 16.2

   c) mode = 18 years, median = 19 years,
   mean = 21.1 years

   d) mode = 28 minutes, median = 29 minutes,
   mean = 29.6 minutes

   e) no mode, median = 1.2 m, mean = 1.21 m

(Find the mean data): **(p 287-288)**

1 **a)** mode = 2, median = 2

  b) no mode, median = 5

  c) no mode, median = 6 years

  d) modes = 4, 5, median = 4.5

  e) modes = 0.36 kg, 0.41 kg, median = 0.375 kg

  f) mode £10, median £10

2 No modes as all the scores are different.
Medians: Andy 32.5, Imran 43, Mark 24,
Stuart 29, Tim 39
The mean uses **all** the scores.

(p 293)

2 **a)** **i)** 4 years   **ii)** 3 years   **iii)** 3.05 years

  b) Median

3 **a)** **i)** 14   **ii)** 13   **iii)** 12.95

  b) Mode

(Find the mean data): **(p 288-291)**

Most appropriate averages given in brackets

 3 mode, median both £5 per hour
   (mode , median)

 6 mode = 0 errors, median = 1 error (median)

 7 mode = 2 children, median = 2.5 children (mode)

 8 mode = 1 train, median = 1 train (mode , median)

 9 mode = 17 years, median = 18 years
   (mode, median)

10 home   mode = 1 goal, median = 1.5 goals
            (mode)

    away   mode = 1 goal, median = 1 goal
            (mode , median)

(p 294)

4 **a)** **i)** 1 attempt   **ii)** 2 attempts

  b) **i)** 2 attempts   **ii)** 2 attempts

  c) **i)** 1.85 attempts **ii)** 2.1 attempts

  d) men – lower mean and mode

(Using a bar chart data): **(p 276)**

5 mean = 1.7 (1 dp), mode = 1, median = 1
mode and median – possible number of
newspapers

Find the range **(p 295)**

1 **a)** Apricots 18p, Grapefruit 12p, Peaches 33p,
Pineapple 9p

  b) **i)** Pineapple   **ii)** Peaches

2 **a)**

Alex	mean = 43.3	range = 83
Cilla	mean = 44.5	range = 49
Kath	mean = 57	range = 75
Paul	mean = 76.9	range = 115
Rhona	mean = 66.5	range = 147
Paul	mean = 59.1	range = 88

  b) Paul, highest mean

  c) Cilla, lowest range

(Find the mean data): **(p 287-288)**

1 **a)** 4 students   **b)** 12 calls

  c) 11 years   **d)** 8 letters

  e) 0.09 kg   **f)** £240

2 Andy 109 runs, Imran 68 runs, Mark 26 runs,
Stuart 23 runs, Tim 27 runs

3 £10 per hour

4 198 tickets

5 £2.30

(Find the mode and median data): **(p 292)**

1 **a)** 6 pints   **b)** 6 students

  c) 16 years   **d)** 11 minutes

  e) 0.09 m

(p 296)

3 **a)** 77.9 minutes (1 dp)   **b)** 120 minutes

4 **a)** 5 visits   **b)** 3 visits

5 **a)** **i)** 7 years   **ii)** 5 years

  b) **i)** 10 years   **ii)** 11 years

  c) The boys' ages are more spread out than
the girls' ages. On average the girls are
older.

(Find the mean data): **(p 290-291)**

 6 4 errors   7 5 children

 8 4 late trains   9 6 years

10 Home 6 goals, Away 4 goals

(Find the mode and median data): **(p 293-294)**

2 3 years   3 12

4 Men 4 attempts, Women 4 attempts

6 a) i) 3 points   **ii)** 5 points

    iii) 5.1 points (1 dp)   **iv)** 6 points

b) i) 3 points   **ii)** 3 points

    iii) 3.8 points (1 dp)   **iv)** 5 points

c) On average the women were awarded fewer points and the points awarded to women were less variable.

4 Probability

Show some events are more likely than others (p 298)

1 a), e) depend on students

    b) unlikely   **c)** impossible   **d)** certain

2 a) 2   **b)** 1 in 2

3 a) i) 1 in 5   **ii)** 2 in 5   **iii)** 3 in 5

    b) odd number

4 a) 52

    b) i) 4 in 52 (or 1 in 13)

       ii) 13 in 52 (or 1 in 4)   **iii)** 1 in 52

5 a) 26

    b) i) 1 in 26   **ii)** 5 in 26   **iii)** 21 in 26

Use fractions, decimals and % to measure probability (p 301)

1 a) i) $\frac{1}{10}$, 0.1, 10%   **ii)** $\frac{1}{2}$, 0.5, 50%

    iii) $\frac{3}{5}$, 0.6, 60%   **iv)** $\frac{3}{10}$, 0.3, 30%

b)

P(3)   P(odd number)

P(8 or more)   P(less than 7)

0    $\frac{1}{10}$ $\frac{3}{10}$ $\frac{1}{2}$ $\frac{3}{5}$ 1

2 a) i) $\frac{1}{6}$, 0.17 (2 dp), 16.7% (1 dp)

    ii) $\frac{1}{2}$, 0.5, 50%   **iii)** 0, 0, 0%

    iv) 1, 1, 100%

3 a) i) $\frac{1}{5}$, 0.2, 20%   **ii)** $\frac{2}{5}$, 0.4, 40%

    iii) $\frac{3}{5}$, 0.6, 60%

b)

P(even number)

P(4)   P(odd number)

0    $\frac{1}{5}$ $\frac{2}{5}$ $\frac{3}{5}$ 1

4 a) i) $\frac{1}{13}$ **ii)** $\frac{1}{4}$ **iii)** $\frac{1}{52}$ **iv)** $\frac{1}{2}$ **v)** $\frac{1}{26}$ **vi)** $\frac{2}{13}$

    b) the king of clubs, a red king, a king, a jack or queen, a club, a red card

5 a) i) $\frac{5}{8}$ **ii)** $\frac{1}{4}$ **iii)** $\frac{1}{8}$

b)

P(£1)   P(10p)   P(2p)

0    $\frac{1}{8}$ $\frac{1}{4}$ $\frac{5}{8}$ 1

6 0.2, 20%

7 a) $\frac{1}{366}$ **b)** $\frac{31}{366}$ **c)** $\frac{5}{61}$ **d)** $\frac{29}{366}$ **e)** $\frac{121}{366}$

8 a) i) $\frac{1}{4}$ **ii)** $\frac{1}{2}$

    b) i) 10   **ii)** 20

9 a) i) $\frac{1}{6}$ **ii)** $\frac{1}{2}$ **iii)** $\frac{1}{3}$

    b) i) 10   **ii)** 30   **iii)** 20

10 a) Ball sports 76.0%, Combat sports 3.3%, Wheel sports 5.2%, Winter sports 3.2%, Animal sports 3.1%, Water sports 3.4%, Other 5.8%

    b) Far more hospital treatments are for injuries from ball sports than from any other type of sport.

Identify possible outcomes of combined events (p 303)

1 a)

Score on 1st dice

	1	2	3	4	5	6
1	2	3	4	5	6	7
2	3	4	5	6	7	8
3	4	5	6	7	8	9
4	5	6	7	8	9	10
5	6	7	8	9	10	11
6	7	8	9	10	11	12

Score on 2nd dice

b) 36

c) $P(2) = \frac{1}{36}$, $P(3) = \frac{1}{18}$, $P(4) = \frac{1}{12}$, $P(5) = \frac{1}{9}$, $P(6) = \frac{5}{36}$, $P(7) = \frac{1}{6}$, $P(8) = \frac{5}{36}$, $P(9) = \frac{1}{9}$, $P(10) = \frac{1}{12}$, $P(11) = \frac{1}{18}$, $P(12) = \frac{1}{36}$

d) 7

2

Score on 1st dice

	1	2	3	4	5	6
1	1	2	3	4	5	6
2	2	4	6	8	10	12
3	3	6	9	12	15	18
4	4	8	12	16	20	24
5	5	10	15	20	25	30
6	6	12	18	24	30	36

Score on 2nd dice

a) $\frac{1}{4}$ b) $\frac{3}{4}$

3 a)

1st coin

		H	**T**
2nd coin	**H**	HH	TH
	T	HT	TT

b)

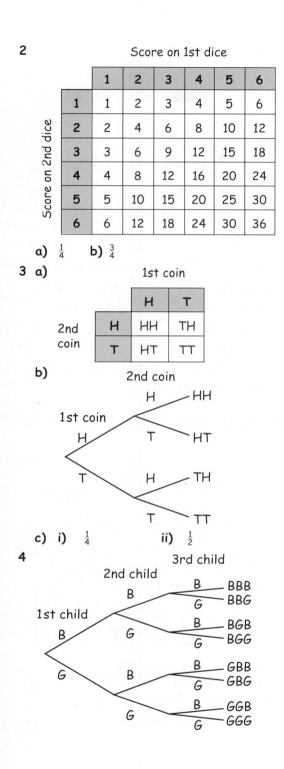

2nd coin

1st coin

c) i) $\frac{1}{4}$ ii) $\frac{1}{2}$

4

3rd child

2nd child

1st child

5 a)

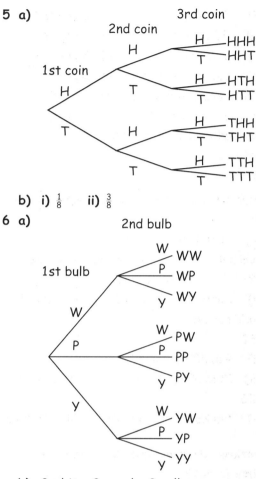

3rd coin

2nd coin

1st coin

b) i) $\frac{1}{8}$ ii) $\frac{3}{8}$

6 a)

2nd bulb

1st bulb

b) 2 white, 2 purple, 2 yellow,
1 white and 1 purple, 1 white and 1 yellow,
1 purple and 1 yellow

Index